The ONE YEAR® family DEVOTIONS

TYNDALE HOUSE PUBLISHERS, INC.
CAROL STREAM, ILLINOIS

Visit Tyndale's exciting Web site at www.tyndale.com

The One Year Family Devotions, Volume 1

Revised and updated in 2000.

Stories written by V. Louise Cunningham, Jorlyn A. Grasser, Jan L. Hansen, Nancy G. Hill, Ruth I. Jay, Dean Kelley, Sherry L. Kuyt, Agnes G. Livezey, Deborah S. Marett, Hazel W. Marett, Sara L. Nelson, Raelene E. Phillips, Linda A. Piepenbrink, Victoria L. Reinhardt, Phyllis Robinson, Deana L. Rogers, Catherine Runyon, Charlie VanderMeer, Geri Walcott, Linda M. Weddle, Barbara J. Westberg, and Carolyn E. Yost. Authors' initials appear at the end of each story. All stories are taken from issues of *Keys for Kids*, published bimonthly by the Children's Bible Hour, Box 1, Grand Rapids, MI 49501.

Library of Congress Catalog Card Number 88-71950

ISBN-13: 978-0-8423-2541-7, softcover
ISBN-10: 0-8423-2541-7, softcover

Printed in the United States of America

14 13 12 11
24 23 22 21

The One Year
FAMILY DEVOTIONS

CONTENTS

INTRODUCTION 9

JANUARY

1 A Guide for the Trip
2 Back to the Beginning
3 More Than Forgiveness
4 See No Evil
5 Fox and Geese
6 How Many Bibles?
7 The Strange Bird
8 Don't Wait Too Long!
9 Take the Garbage Out
10 Well-Protected
11 A Very Important Letter
12 Noisy Kids! (Part 1)
13 Noisy Kids! (Part 2)
14 I'll Do It
15 Here's My Gift
16 Are You a PK?
17 Is That Me?
18 Cat in the Window
19 Garbage In—Garbage Out
20 I Wish I Could
21 Dangerous Games
22 Baby's First Steps
23 Telltale Mirror
24 Something Special
25 Snowflakes and People
26 Take off the Labels
27 The Finished Job
28 I'll Do the Dishes
29 What Do You Hear?
30 Work and Pray
31 Jonathan's Ministry

FEBRUARY

1 It Ought to Hurt
2 Wonderfully Made
3 Higher Ways
4 Beware of the Foe
5 Second Choice
6 Taxes! Taxes!
7 On Thin Ice
8 Glowing Coals
9 The Missing Sweater
10 How Dumb Are You?
11 Guard Duty
12 An Old Piece of Wood
13 Bend Your Knees
14 A Special Love
15 Poisoned Minds
16 A Cage or a Castle?
17 Old and Honorable
18 What We Have
19 Give Them a Chance!
20 An Important Seal
21 God's Training School
22 The Mighty Egg
23 Growing Up (Part 1)
24 Growing Up (Part 2)
25 A Man of Principle
26 Pretty Package
27 Free As the Air
28 The Homecoming
29 The Hitchhiker

MARCH

1 Watch Your Manners
2 Sunday Morning
3 Temporary Permanent
4 Horn-a-thon
5 Meat, Milk, and Michael
6 The Birth Certificate
7 Please Pass the Peas
8 Really Empty
9 A Bad Start
10 Does It Taste Good?
11 Double Exposure (Part 1)
12 Double Exposure (Part 2)
13 Trash or Treasure?
14 Seedless Oranges
15 Too Many People?
16 Better Late Than Never
17 God Gives the Increase
18 Cloudy Skies
19 Sent but Not Delivered
20 A Strong Hand
21 God's Mouthpiece
22 Just Carrots?
23 Getting Even
24 Here Comes the Sun (Part 1)
25 Here Comes the Sun (Part 2)

26 Here Comes the Sun (Part 3)
27 Something Beautiful
28 Watching like a Hawk
29 Two Kinds of Sin
30 Don't Be a Chicken
31 Follow the Leader

APRIL

1 April Birthday!
2 Danger: Mosquitoes!
3 Substitute Teacher
4 A Messed-up Messenger
5 Healing the Hurt (Part 1)
6 Healing the Hurt (Part 2)
7 No Letter Today
8 Company's Coming
9 Too Much Salt
10 Sidetracked
11 Where the Fish Are
12 The Wrong Shoes
13 It's Time to Move
14 God's Patchwork Quilt
15 Dig Deep
16 Love
17 Joy
18 Peace
19 Patience
20 Kindness
21 Goodness
22 Faithfulness
23 Gentleness
24 Self-Control
25 Instant Everything
26 The Hibernating Christian
27 It Happened to Me
28 The Doctor Knows Best
29 Erasing Sin
30 A Special Down Payment

MAY

1 The Band Trip
2 Don't Gulp It Down
3 No Trespassing
4 Ticket Trouble
5 No Stains
6 The Warning
7 By Myself, Daddy
8 Lisa's Demonstration
9 Keep on Asking
10 Imperfect Parents
11 Mothering
12 For Stepmother (Part 1)
13 For Stepmother (Part 2)
14 A Gift for Mother
15 Malnourished Christians
16 The Race of Life (Part 1)
17 The Race of Life (Part 2)
18 Cause for Fear
19 Should I Tell?
20 Bad Bowling
21 Just like Toothpaste
22 Mary's Disciple
23 Needed: Small Lights
24 Behind Prison Bars
25 Tools and Talents
26 Cathy's Creation
27 We Remember (Part 1)
28 We Remember (Part 2)
29 Iron Shoes
30 Decisions! Decisions!
31 Ugly but Beautiful

JUNE

1 The Open Umbrella
2 The Snapping Turtle
3 Pass the Potatoes
4 Owe No One
5 Daily Benefits
6 An Unjoyful Sound
7 Smile, God Loves You
8 The Counselor Hunt
9 Darkness or Light
10 Doing Your Best
11 Two Buckets
12 Caught in a Trap
13 To Rain or Not to Rain
14 A Letter for You
15 Smelly Presents
16 A Funny Kind of Love
17 A Better Person
18 Do I Have To?
19 How Can You Tell?
20 No Doubt about It
21 Don't Fence Me In
22 The Right Tools
23 Just a Mite
24 A Noisy Witness
25 Ready or Not
26 Balloons for All (Part 1)
27 Balloons for All (Part 2)
28 Do It Yourself
29 An Exciting Letter
30 A Small Light

INTRODUCTION

You have in your hands a year's worth of delightful stories, all of them adapted from *Keys for Kids,* a bimonthly publication of the Children's Bible Hour. For years the Children's Bible Hour has made this devotional magazine available free of charge to any family requesting a copy. Their fine ministry to parents and children has been much appreciated over the years, and Tyndale House is proud to present in one volume this one year collection of the many stories made available through *Keys for Kids.*

Each day's story provides a contemporary illustration of the day's Scripture reading. Following each story is a "How About You?" section that asks children to apply the story to their own lives. And following this is a memory verse, usually taken from the Scripture reading. Many of these memory verses are taken from the New Living Translation of the Bible, but in many cases another version has been used for the sake of clarity. Each devotion ends with a "key," a two- to five-word summary of the day's lesson.

The stories here are geared toward families with children ages 8 to 14. Children can enjoy reading these stories by themselves, but we hope that you will use them in a daily devotional time that involves the whole family. Like the many stories in the Bible that teach valuable lessons about life, the stories here are made to speak not only to children but also to adults. They are simple, direct, and concrete, and, like Jesus' parables, they speak to all of us in terms we can easily understand. And like all good stories, they are made for sharing, so look upon them as the basis for family sharing and growth.

1 January

A GUIDE FOR THE TRIP

FROM THE BIBLE:

Your word is a lamp for my feet
and a light for my path.
I've promised it once, and I'll
promise again:
I will obey your wonderful
laws.
I have suffered much, O Lord;
restore my life again, just as
you promised.
Lord, accept my grateful thanks
and teach me your laws.
My life constantly hangs in the
balance,
but I will not stop obeying
your law.
The wicked have set their traps
for me along your path,
but I will not turn from your
commandments.
Your decrees are my treasure;
they are truly my heart's
delight.
I am determined to keep your
principles,
even forever, to the very end.

PSALM 119:105-112

The Bible—life's guidebook

AUSTIN HATED family devotions, but his parents thought they were important. "The Bible is about now, tomorrow, and forever," Mom said. "From the past we learn not to make the same mistakes others made."

Dad nodded. "We also learn that Jesus, God's Son, lived on earth without making one mistake."

Austin thought the Bible was boring. "It's all about people who lived thousands of years ago," he said. "Things are different now."

When Dad announced that he was going to Australia on business and his family could go along, Austin was excited. One day he brought home a book and maps from his schoolteacher. "Mr. Tucker's been to Australia," Austin said. "He told me all about it. Lots of things are different there, so he loaned me a guidebook. It tells you things to do and what not to do and how to have a good trip."

"That's great, Austin," Dad told him, "but won't it bore you to read this?"

"It won't bore me," replied Austin. "It helped Mr. Tucker; it'll help me learn how to get along in that country, too."

Dad nodded. "A guidebook is a good idea," he agreed, "but since you never seemed interested in reading the guidebook for your most important journey, I'm a little surprised that you're interested in this one."

Austin stared at Dad. "What journey?" he asked. "What guidebook?"

"Your journey through life," answered Dad. "The Bible is the guidebook, and God—the author—is the best guide for that journey."

Austin had never thought of it that way. "You're right, Dad," Austin agreed.

HOW ABOUT YOU? Are you trying to journey through life without a guide? The Bible is filled with instruction and help for you. It has all you need to know to make a good trip through life. *A.G.L.*

TO MEMORIZE: Your word is a lamp for my feet and a light for my path. *Psalm 119:105*

2 January

BACK TO THE BEGINNING

FROM THE BIBLE:

So if you are standing before the altar in the Temple, offering a sacrifice to God, and you suddenly remember that someone has something against you, leave your sacrifice there beside the altar. Go and be reconciled to that person. Then come and offer your sacrifice to God.

MATTHEW 5:23-24

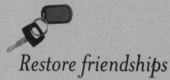

Restore friendships

"I CAN'T do it!" Diana cried out.

"What can't you do?" Dad said.

"I can't get these figures to balance," sniffed Diana. "Tomorrow, when I turn in our club treasurer's report, everyone will think I'm dumb. And Janet will be happy!"

Dad looked at Diana's report. "I thought she was your best friend. Why would she be happy if you made a mistake?"

Diana hesitated. "Well, we both wanted to be treasurer. When I got elected, she still tried to tell me how to do the job. I told her I'd do things my own way. Since then we haven't been speaking," Diana said sadly.

"I'm sorry to hear that, and I know God must be, too," said Dad. "Say, Diana, go back to the beginning and add up your figures one by one."

Diana tried it, and it worked. "I found my mistake, Dad!" she exclaimed.

"It usually helps to go back to the beginning," Dad said. "In fact, why don't you go back to the beginning of your quarrel with Janet, too?"

"What do you mean?" asked Diana.

"Both of you wanted your own way in the beginning. That was selfish," Dad explained. "How about apologizing to Janet for wanting your own way? Listen to what she has to say. I'm sure she has some good ideas."

Diana sighed. "OK, Dad. I'll go back to the beginning and tell Janet I was wrong. I want us to be friends again."

HOW ABOUT YOU? Have you had a disagreement with someone? Are you sure it was all that person's fault? Ask God to show you what you might have done wrong. Confess your sin to God; then go to the other person and apologize. A restored friendship will make you both happy. Don't carry a grudge. *J.L.H.*

TO MEMORIZE: Now it is time to forgive him and comfort him. Otherwise he may become so discouraged that he won't be able to recover.
2 Corinthians 2:7

MORE THAN FORGIVENESS

FROM THE BIBLE:

And the Lord said to Moses, "Suppose some of the people sin against the Lord by falsely telling their neighbor that an item entrusted to their safekeeping has been lost or stolen. Or suppose they have been dishonest with regard to a security deposit, or they have taken something by theft or extortion. Or suppose they find a lost item and lie about it, or they deny something while under oath, or they commit any other similar sin. If they have sinned in any of these ways and are guilty, they must give back whatever they have taken by theft or extortion, whether a security deposit, or property entrusted to them, or a lost object that they claimed as their own, or anything gained by swearing falsely. When they realize their guilt, they must restore the principal amount plus a penalty of 20 percent to the person they have harmed. They must then bring a guilt offering to the priest, who will present it before the Lord. This offering must be a ram with no physical defects or the animal's equivalent value in silver."

LEVITICUS 6:1-6

ANDY LIKED PRAYING with his mother at bedtime. One night, after his usual prayers, he remembered something else. "Oh, forgive me, Lord, for running into Mrs. Evans's fence this afternoon and breaking her rosebush. I guess I shouldn't have been cutting across her lawn. Amen."

"Andy," his mother said gently, "you didn't mention anything to me about Mrs. Evans's fence. What happened?"

Andy frowned. "Do I have to tell you? God has forgiven me, hasn't he? I asked him to forgive me."

"Certainly God has forgiven you," Mom assured him. "But I might be able to help you make amends if you share what happened."

"Make amends?" Andy was puzzled.

"God's Word tells us that if our sin hurts someone else, then we must do our best to make amends—to make things right," explained Mom. "God forgives the sin if we're truly sorry and confess it, but it's up to us to do whatever we can to straighten out the situation. Perhaps you need to go and see Mrs. Evans and apologize."

Andy was quiet for a few moments. "I need to apologize—and ask if I can pay for the damage," he said.

"That's an excellent idea," Mom said. "When you ask God's forgiveness, your actions should show that you are truly sorry."

HOW ABOUT YOU? Have you done something wrong to someone? In Old Testament times, sacrifices had to be offered in such a case, and the situation had to be corrected. Since Jesus made the supreme sacrifice for all our sins, we no longer have to offer such sacrifices. But we do need to make amends—even if it's embarrassing or inconvenient. God cannot accept our service and devotion if we refuse to correct our mistakes. *C.R.*

TO MEMORIZE: They must then make restitution for whatever holy things they have defiled by paying for the loss. *Leviticus 5:16*

Make amends

4 January

SEE NO EVIL

FROM THE BIBLE:

Stop loving this evil world and all that it offers you, for when you love the world, you show that you do not have the love of the Father in you. For the world offers only the lust for physical pleasure, the lust for everything we see, and pride in our possessions. These are not from the Father. They are from this evil world. And this world is fading away, along with everything it craves. But if you do the will of God, you will live forever.

1 JOHN 2:15-17

See no evil

HOLLY TURNED ON the television as soon as she awoke each day. After school, she watched it almost nonstop until bedtime. She didn't think TV harmed her in any way, and she didn't really care what she watched. Unfortunately, her parents didn't pay much attention to what she watched either. Many programs were bad!

She watched a couple shows that were immoral in words and actions. The actors wore indecent clothing and were often drinking alcohol. On Tuesday night, Holly watched a comedy program that included a lot of swearing. When talk shows came on, Holly laughed at the dirty jokes.

At Sunday school one week, Holly's little sister sang, "Oh, be careful, little eyes, what you see . . . for the Father up above is looking down in love, so be careful, little eyes, what you see!" Then the teacher told the children they should never look at anything that they wouldn't want Jesus to look at with them.

That week Holly didn't enjoy television much. On one afternoon soap opera, an unmarried woman was trying to steal another woman's husband. Holly knew God wouldn't like to look at that. On Tuesday evening the comedy program was only half over when Holly turned off the set because the actors were using swear words. Holly felt ashamed because she realized that when she was hurt or upset, she often said dirty words under her breath. *It's because I hear them all the time on TV,* she thought to herself. *Those programs aren't good for me. From now on I'm going to be more careful about what I let my eyes see!*

HOW ABOUT YOU? Are you careful about what you let your eyes see on the television? You should choose programs that are clean and wholesome. And many times it is a good idea to turn the set off. *R.E.P.*

TO MEMORIZE: I will refuse to look at anything vile and vulgar. *Psalm 101:3*

5 January

FOX AND GEESE

FROM THE BIBLE:

If you think you are standing strong, be careful, for you, too, may fall into the same sin. But remember that the temptations that come into your life are no different from what others experience. And God is faithful. He will keep the temptation from becoming so strong that you can't stand up against it. When you are tempted, he will show you a way out so that you will not give in to it.

1 CORINTHIANS 10:12-13

Escape from sin

AMY AND KYLE had invited their friends to play fox and geese. The children shuffled their feet into the snow to make a giant wheel-shaped design with eight spokes.

"Remember, the center is the safe zone," Kyle instructed. "But you must use the escape spokes to get there. If the fox catches you, you're it."

Bryan volunteered to be the first fox. The children romped in the snow until Amy and Kyle were called in for lunch. "You seemed to be having fun out there," observed Mom. "But every time I looked out, Bryan was it," she said.

Kyle laughed. "That was Bryan's own fault. He always tried to get as close to the fox as possible before he'd run. Then he'd get caught."

"And he never used the escape routes until it was too late," Amy added.

"You know, we sometimes ignore the escape routes in life, too," Mom said. "When we face temptations, we can run to Jesus for safety. But if we get too close to sin, we'll get caught by it."

"Like the time I sat with the older kids at the basketball game even though I knew they were troublemakers?" Amy said.

"That's right," agreed Mom. "You could have escaped by sitting with Christian friends."

"And the time I listened to those bad jokes instead of walking away," Kyle said.

"Yes," Mom said with a smile. "If we read God's Word, pray, and follow his commands, we'll understand the way to escape sin."

HOW ABOUT YOU? Do you run away from sin before you get involved? You should. Ask Jesus for help. He will show you the way to escape. *J.L.H.*

TO MEMORIZE: God is faithful. He will keep the temptation from becoming so strong that you can't stand up against it. When you are tempted, he will show you a way out so that you will not give in to it. *1 Corinthians 10:13*

6 *January*

HOW MANY BIBLES?

FROM THE BIBLE:

The law of the Lord is perfect,
reviving the soul.
The decrees of the Lord are trustworthy,
making wise the simple.
The commandments of the Lord are right,
bringing joy to the heart.
The commands of the Lord are clear,
giving insight to life.
Reverence for the Lord is pure,
lasting forever.
The laws of the Lord are true;
each one is fair.
They are more desirable than gold,
even the finest gold.
They are sweeter than honey,
even honey dripping from the comb.
They are a warning to those who hear them;
there is great reward for those who obey them.

PSALM 19:7-11

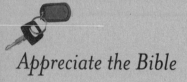

Appreciate the Bible

"I'VE GOT the New Testament they gave us in Christian school, and the Kids' Application Bible Mom and Dad gave each of us when we turned eight," Tim called from his room to Tina's.

"Did you count the one you got for memorizing all those verses in vacation Bible school?" Tina yelled back.

"Why are you two shouting?" their father called from the foot of the stairs.

Tina ran to the top of the steps. "Daddy, the man who spoke to our Bible club today told us to go count the number of Bibles we have," she explained. "He said there are people in communist countries who would give six months' wages to get a part of the Scriptures in their own language. Tim owns four Bibles of his own, and I've found three so far."

Later, the kids counted their parents' Bibles, too. They discovered a total of 18 Bibles in their home. "Tina thinks we have more than most people because Dad's a preacher," said Tim.

"Probably," Mom said, "but I'm sure most Christians in this country have several."

"It's hard for us to realize that some Christians don't have the freedom to read God's Word," said Dad. "And there are some countries where people don't have a Bible because it's never been translated into their language."

The children hadn't thought of that. That night the family thanked God for their freedoms and for the availability of God's Word. They prayed for Christians living in countries where God's Word is not honored. They also prayed that the Bible would be available soon to every nation.

HOW ABOUT YOU? Do you take your Bible for granted? Never forget to be thankful for the Bible. Pray for those who are not blessed with Bibles as you are. *R.E.P.*

TO MEMORIZE: Humbly accept the message God has planted in your hearts, for it is strong enough to save your souls. *James 1:21*

7 January

THE STRANGE BIRD

FROM THE BIBLE:

King Nebuchadnezzar of Babylon came to Jerusalem and besieged it with his armies. . . . Then [Nebuchadnezzar] ordered Ashpenaz, who was in charge of the palace officials, to bring to the palace some of the young men of Judah's royal family and other noble families, who had been brought to Babylon as captives. "Select only strong, healthy, and good-looking young men," he said. "Make sure they are well versed in every branch of learning, are gifted with knowledge and good sense, and have the poise needed to serve in the royal palace. Teach these young men the language and literature of the Babylonians." The king assigned them a daily ration of the best food and wine from his own kitchens. . . . Some of them would be made his advisers in the royal court.

Daniel, Hananiah, Mishael, and Azariah were four of the young men chosen, all from the tribe of Judah. . . . But Daniel made up his mind not to defile himself by eating the food and wine given to them by the king. He asked the chief official for permission to eat other things instead.

DANIEL 1:1, 3-6, 8

"HEY, MOM, we worked on our bird badge in Boy Scouts today," said Ryan. "Did you know that a mockingbird has been known to change its tune 87 times in seven minutes? What a strange bird!"

"That's amazing!" said Mom.

The next day Mom overheard one of Ryan's teammates talking to him after his basketball game. "Hey, Ryan, I stole a pack of my dad's cigarettes," said Jim. "Wanna meet me in the back of the school for a quick smoke?"

"Sounds like fun," said Ryan, "but I can't. I have to go some place."

As Ryan turned, he bumped into Tom, a boy from his Sunday school class. "Hey, Ryan," said Tom, "did you know that Jim stole a pack of cigarettes?"

"I know," interrupted Ryan. "And they call that fun?"

On the way home in the car, Mom asked, "How's my 'strange bird' doing tonight? You know—my mockingbird?" Then Mom explained. "I'm really pleased that you didn't agree to meet Jim tonight, but I did hear a 'little bird' change his tune pretty quickly this afternoon. 'Sounds like fun,' you said one minute, and the next minute you said, 'They call that fun?' "

"Oh, that," replied Ryan sheepishly. He knew he should have told Jim right out why he wouldn't smoke with him. When they reached home, Ryan went to the telephone. "I'm gonna call Jim and tell him the real reason I wouldn't join him," he said.

HOW ABOUT YOU? Do you change your tune like a mockingbird, depending on what other "birds" you are near? It's difficult to take a stand for what you really believe to be right when your friends don't agree, but with God's help, it is possible. Daniel did it. You can, too! *P.R.*

TO MEMORIZE: Daniel made up his mind not to defile himself by eating the food and wine given to them by the king. *Daniel 1:8*

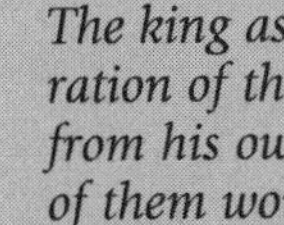

Always stand for right

8 January

DON'T WAIT TOO LONG!

FROM THE BIBLE:

The Holy Spirit says,
"Today you must listen to his voice.
Don't harden your hearts against him
as Israel did when they rebelled,
when they tested God's patience in the wilderness.
There your ancestors tried my patience,
even though they saw my miracles for forty years.
So I was angry with them, and I said,
'Their hearts always turn away from me.
They refuse to do what I tell them.' " . . .

Be careful then, dear brothers and sisters. Make sure that your own hearts are not evil and unbelieving, turning you away from the living God. You must warn each other every day, as long as it is called "today," so that none of you will be deceived by sin and hardened against God.

HEBREWS 3:7-10, 12-13

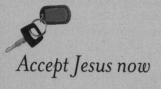

Accept Jesus now

ONE SUNDAY MORNING at church a visitor named Peter Black shared his testimony of what the Lord was doing in his life.

Jeremy could hardly believe his ears. This man had been a criminal—in and out of prison for 20 years! Now he was a Christian telling other people about Jesus. *How exciting!* thought Jeremy. *I wish I had a testimony like that!*

After church Jeremy's parents invited Mr. Black to their home for dinner. As they sat at the table, the guest smiled at Jeremy and said, "Your mother tells me you're a Christian, too."

"That's right," said Jeremy. "But I was only five when I asked Jesus into my heart. I don't have an exciting story to tell like you do."

A sad look came over Mr. Black's face. "Son, I have spent nearly half my life in jail," he said. "Because of my prison record, I have a hard time finding a job. I've been married and divorced twice and have three children who hardly even know me. My health is poor because of all the drinking and drugs I used to do. I'm glad I finally accepted the Lord, but that didn't undo the terrible consequences of the sins in my life. Be thankful you came to know him early!"

I do thank you, Lord, Jeremy prayed silently. *Thank you for saving me as a little boy—so that I can serve you my whole life!*

HOW ABOUT YOU? Did you accept Christ as your Savior at a young age? If so, thank him now, and determine to live your whole life in his service. If you've put off accepting the Lord, don't wait any longer. Accept him today. If you wait, your sins may leave scars that you will carry with you all your life. *S.L.K.*

TO MEMORIZE: God is ready to help you right now. Today is the day of salvation. *2 Corinthians 6:2*

TAKE THE GARBAGE OUT

FROM THE BIBLE:

Come and listen, all you who fear God,
and I will tell you what he did for me.
For I cried out to him for help,
praising him as I spoke.
If I had not confessed the sin in my heart,
my Lord would not have listened.
But God did listen!
He paid attention to my prayer.
Praise God, who did not ignore my prayer
and did not withdraw his unfailing love from me.

PSALM 66:16-20

Leave sin, then pray

"IS DAD HOME yet?" Jason asked eagerly. "Mr. Williams wants to hire me to sweep and clean the hardware store after school each day. If it's OK with Dad, the job is mine!"

Mom smiled. "Dad will be home soon, but you'd better take the garbage out. He told you to do it this morning."

"OK," said Jason as he went to his room. When Dad came in, Jason hurried to meet him. "Dad," he said, "guess what?"

"First, take the garbage out," said Dad as he hung up his coat.

Jason tried again. "I have a chance to get a job."

"I see the garbage is still there," Dad replied.

"I'll get it in a minute. But can't we talk?" whined Jason.

"We can as soon as you take the garbage out," Dad replied firmly.

Jason sighed, then quickly took out the garbage. "I'm sorry I didn't do it sooner," he said. Dad smiled as Jason told him about his job opportunity.

During family devotions that night, Dad asked Jason to read Psalm 66. When he finished reading, Jason grinned. "I know what it means when it says God won't hear us if we have sin in our hearts. Dad, you wouldn't listen to me until I took out the garbage. And God won't listen to us until we get rid of the garbage of sin in our lives."

"You're right, Son," Dad said with a grin. "That's important for us to learn."

HOW ABOUT YOU? Does God seem far away from you? Do you feel like nobody is listening when you pray? Maybe God is saying, "Take out the garbage, and then I'll listen." Are you clinging to cheating? Swearing? Dishonesty? Disobedience? Whatever it is, get rid of it. You cannot expect God to answer your prayers when you deliberately sin. *H.W.M.*

TO MEMORIZE: If I had not confessed the sin in my heart, my Lord would not have listened. *Psalm 66:18*

10 January

WELL-PROTECTED

FROM THE BIBLE:

He will shield you with his
wings.
He will shelter you with his
feathers.
His faithful promises are your
armor and protection. . . .
If you make the Lord your
refuge,
if you make the Most High
your shelter,
no evil will conquer you;
no plague will come near your
dwelling.

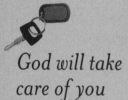

PSALM 91:4, 9-10

God will take care of you

"OOOH! I don't feel good," moaned Shelly as she came to the breakfast table. "Can't I just stay home today?" She sat down and clutched her stomach.

"If you really don't feel well, you should stay home," said Mom.

Later that morning Shelly put on one of her mother's aprons to help make cookies. Shelly squealed as one of the eggs broke and slid down her apron and onto the floor. "Oh, no! It's a good thing I have a big apron on."

"It certainly is!" agreed Mom, as she helped clean up the mess. Looking at Shelly thoughtfully, she said, "The stomachache seems to have disappeared." As Shelly nodded, Mom continued. "Do you think you really were sick, honey, or were you just nervous about going to a new school?"

"Oh, Mom," exclaimed Shelly, "I wish we had never moved! I feel so strange in this school, and I don't know anybody."

"It will get better," Mom assured her. "You know, it's a good thing you had the protection of that apron as we made cookies. But are you aware that you also have protection as you go to school?" Shelly looked surprised as Mom continued, "You're a Christian, a child of God, and he is your protection. God will take care of you, even in a new school and among many new faces. Remember, he is with you always."

Shelly nodded slowly. "Ann and Barb were friendly yesterday. I guess I'll go this afternoon and take them a cookie," she decided. "It shouldn't be so bad if I just remember I'm well protected."

HOW ABOUT YOU? What are you afraid of? A new school? A difficult class? A school bully? The dark? If you're a Christian, God is your protection in whatever situation you face. Trust him. *H.W.M.*

TO MEMORIZE: The Lord is my light and my salvation—so why should I be afraid? *Psalm 27:1*

11 January

A VERY IMPORTANT LETTER

FROM THE BIBLE:

Every time I think of you, I give thanks to my God. I always pray for you, and I make my requests with a heart full of joy because you have been my partners in spreading the Good News about Christ from the time you first heard it until now. And I am sure that God, who began the good work within you, will continue his work until it is finally finished on that day when Christ Jesus comes back again.

It is right that I should feel as I do about all of you, for you have a very special place in my heart. We have shared together the blessings of God, both when I was in prison and when I was out, defending the truth and telling others the Good News.

PHILIPPIANS 1:3-7

Write to missionaries

"WHATCHA DOIN'?" asked Josh, as his sister pondered what to write next.

"I'm writing a letter to Mr. Sandborn," Jamie said. "He's the missionary who came and spoke at our church last fall."

"He probably doesn't even remember you," said Josh.

"I know," replied Jamie, "but I thought he might like to get a letter since he works all alone in that village."

Some days later, in a small, run-down hut, a missionary sighed in the sweltering heat and sat down at the table. He was tired and discouraged, because the work was progressing so slowly. What was this long envelope addressed in a child's unfamiliar handwriting?

He unfolded the letter. "Dear Mr. Sandborn," it said, "I just wanted to tell you we're all thinking of you and praying for you. I liked it when you came to our church last fall. I remember the things you told us about having faith in God. I will try to have more faith. Because of you, I think I would like to be a missionary someday. Thank you for your help. Love, Jamie."

Mr. Sandborn sat for a few moments, and then he breathed a prayer of thanks for the encouragement of that simple letter. *Perhaps this is God's way of letting me know he intends to use my ministry here,* he thought. *Maybe I need more faith, too.*

He smiled as he looked out the window at the village children playing in the sand. Then he took out a piece of paper. He had to write a thank-you letter to a very important person.

HOW ABOUT YOU? Have you thought about ways you could encourage the missionaries you know? Even a child can write a simple letter to a missionary. You may never know just how much it means to someone far away. Why not write one this week?
S.L.K.

TO MEMORIZE: Good news from far away is like cold water to the thirsty. *Proverbs 25:25*

12 January

NOISY KIDS!
(PART 1)

FROM THE BIBLE:

As you enter the house of God, keep your ears open and your mouth shut! Don't be a fool who doesn't realize that mindless offerings to God are evil. And don't make rash promises to God, for he is in heaven, and you are only here on earth. So let your words be few.

Just as being too busy gives you nightmares, being a fool makes you a blabbermouth.

So when you make a promise to God, don't delay in following through, for God takes no pleasure in fools. Keep all the promises you make to him. It is better to say nothing than to promise something that you don't follow through on. In such cases, your mouth is making you sin. And don't defend yourself by telling the Temple messenger that the promise you made was a mistake. That would make God angry, and he might wipe out everything you have achieved.

Dreaming all the time instead of working is foolishness. And there is ruin in a flood of empty words. Fear God instead.

ECCLESIASTES 5:1-7

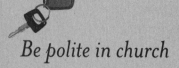

Be polite in church

"I HEARD some sad news at the church board meeting last night," Mr. Lansing told his son, Eric.

Eric looked up. "What was it, Dad?"

"It involves the Peterson family who moved into the yellow house on Elm Street," Dad told him. "Last Sunday they attended our church, and on Monday night Pastor Helms visited them." That didn't sound sad to Eric. That sounded happy! Dad continued, "They said they liked Pastor Helms's message, at least what they heard of it. The sad part is that three boys were sitting behind them, talking and laughing during the entire service. The Petersons said they were going to look for another church."

"That's too bad," Eric said. Then he remembered that some new people had been sitting in front of him and his friends at church! *He* was one of those who had been talking!

"Son, we've told you before that it's not only important to listen for what you can get out of a message, but it is just plain bad manners to disturb those around you! For the next month you will sit with Mom and me. If you do sit with your friends again after that, you will sit somewhere in front of Mom and me, not behind us."

Eric nodded numbly. "Yes, Dad." He knew what else he'd have to do. He'd have to go to the Petersons' house and apologize to them for making so much noise. He'd also invite them to come to church again.

HOW ABOUT YOU? Do you listen quietly during church? There have been many occasions when people haven't come back to a church because of disruptions such as whispering during the service. Sit still. Be polite to those who are around you. Welcome new people instead of being rude to them! *L.M.W.*

TO MEMORIZE: Guard your steps when you go to the house of God. Go near to listen. *Ecclesiastes 5:1* (NIV)

13 January

NOISY KIDS!
(PART 2)

FROM THE BIBLE:

Teach me, O Lord,
to follow every one of your principles.
Give me understanding and I will obey your law;
I will put it into practice with all my heart.
Make me walk along the path of your commands,
for that is where my happiness is found.
Give me an eagerness for your decrees;
do not inflict me with love for money!
Turn my eyes from worthless things,
and give me life through your word.
Reassure me of your promise,
which is for those who honor you.
Help me abandon my shameful ways;
your laws are all I want in life.
I long to obey your commandments!
Renew my life with your goodness.

PSALM 119:33-40

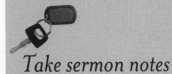

Take sermon notes

ERIC FELT GOOD. Even though it had been hard to do, he had gone and apologized to the Petersons. And he'd asked them to visit the church once again. They agreed, and as they walked in the door the next Sunday, they even gave Eric a friendly "Hi."

Before the service started, Eric's dad handed him a notebook and a pen. "I want you to write down ten truths that the pastor gives in his message today," Dad instructed him.

Eric didn't think he'd be able to understand the pastor's message, but he nodded and took the notebook. He listened attentively, and before long he was actually enjoying the sermon! By the end of the service, Eric had written down 12 important thoughts—two more than his dad had told him to write! He realized that he hadn't been able to understand before because he hadn't even tried to listen!

After church Eric showed the pastor his notes. "I'm going to do this every week, Pastor Helms," he said. "I'll suggest to the other kids that they try it, too!" Eric felt good. Not only had the Petersons come back to church, but he had learned a good way to listen to the pastor's sermons and to understand them.

HOW ABOUT YOU? Do you take notes on your pastor's sermons? Even if you just write down the Scripture he uses, or the main topic, it will help you to remember what he says. If he uses a word you don't understand, write that down on a piece of paper and ask him to explain it after church. You could also ask your dad and mom to discuss the message with you. They can help you understand, too. *L.M.W.*

TO MEMORIZE: Work hard so God can approve you. Be a good worker, one who does not need to be ashamed and who correctly explains the word of truth. *2 Timothy 2:15*

14 January

I'LL DO IT

FROM THE BIBLE:

"But what do you think about this? A man with two sons told the older boy, 'Son, go out and work in the vineyard today.' The son answered, 'No, I won't go,' but later he changed his mind and went anyway. Then the father told the other son, 'You go,' and he said, 'Yes, sir, I will.' But he didn't go. Which of the two was obeying his father?"

They replied, "The first, of course."

Then Jesus explained his meaning: "I assure you, corrupt tax collectors and prostitutes will get into the Kingdom of God before you do. For John the Baptist came and showed you the way to life, and you didn't believe him, while tax collectors and prostitutes did. And even when you saw this happening, you refused to turn from your sins and believe him."

MATTHEW 21:28-32

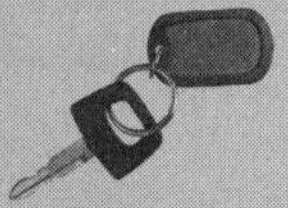

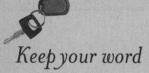

Keep your word

WHEN MRS. BROWN asked Paul to distribute invitations to the after-school Bible club in her home, he agreed readily. "I'd like these passed out today," explained Mrs. Brown. "The club starts the day after tomorrow."

"No problem," said Paul.

At home, Paul told his mom about the invitations. Then he laid them on an end table and went out to play. After supper he did his homework and worked on his model car. The next day, Mom found them.

After school that day, Paul burst into the house. "That Rick!" he exploded angrily to his mom. "He told me he'd return a book to the library for me, and he didn't do it! Now I have to pay a fine. He should . . ." His voice trailed off when he saw the invitations in his mother's hand. "Oh no," he murmured. "I forgot."

"Paul, I'm disappointed that you didn't do the job you said you'd do," said Mom. "Your experience with Rick is a good lesson on the importance of doing what you promise. If you can't or don't want to help, say so right away. Don't say you'll do something, causing someone to depend on you, and then fail him or her. When you do that, you're failing God, too."

Paul took the invitations from her hand. "I know it's late, but I'll still run around the neighborhood with these right now," said Paul. "I'm sorry, and I'll apologize to Mrs. Brown, too."

HOW ABOUT YOU? Are you faithful to do whatever you said you'd do? It's easy to make quick promises but not so easy to carry them out. Make sure you follow through on promises made to others. God always keeps his promises, and he wants us to be like him. *C.E.Y.*

TO MEMORIZE: Dear friend, you are doing a good work for God when you take care of the traveling teachers who are passing through. *3 John 1:5*

15 January

HERE'S MY GIFT

FROM THE BIBLE:

"And Solomon, my son, get to know the God of your ancestors. Worship and serve him with your whole heart and with a willing mind. For the Lord sees every heart and understands and knows every plan and thought. If you seek him, you will find him. But if you forsake him, he will reject you forever. So take this seriously. The Lord has chosen you to build a temple as his sanctuary. Be strong, and do the work." . . .

Then David continued, "Be strong and courageous, and do the work. Don't be afraid or discouraged by the size of the task, for the Lord God, my God, is with you. He will not fail you or forsake you. He will see to it that all the work related to the Temple of the Lord is finished correctly."

1 CHRONICLES 28:9, 20

Serve God cheerfully

CHRISTA ENJOYED playing the piano, but she hated practicing. When Kent asked her to accompany his trumpet solo at Bible club, she reluctantly agreed. Yet she was either too busy or unwilling to give up her free time to practice with him. Finally they practiced just before the program.

During the next few months, Christa was often invited to play for various groups. She usually agreed to play but seemed unenthusiastic. She grumbled about how busy it made her.

"Is it really so bad?" Mom asked.

Christa scowled. "You always tell me I should use my gift of music for the Lord, but now that I'm using it, you're still not satisfied."

That evening Christa asked her older brother, Bill, for help with her math assignment.

"I'm busy," Bill replied.

"But I have a test tomorrow, and you explain it so well," pleaded Christa.

"Call one of your friends to help you," Bill said.

"I'm sure you can take a little time to help your sister," suggested Mom.

"Oh, all right," Bill growled. "I'll be in my room when you need me."

"Oh, Mother!" said Christa. "When he's grouchy, I don't even want his help. Why can't he be pleasant about it?"

"Are you always pleasant when people ask you to do something?" asked Mom gently.

Christa blushed as she remembered how reluctant she'd been to play for someone that afternoon. "I guess playing the piano unwillingly isn't really using my gift for the Lord at all, is it?" she admitted. "I'm going to do it more cheerfully from now on!"

HOW ABOUT YOU? Are you grumpy when you are asked to serve in some way? Solomon was told to serve God with his "whole heart and with a willing mind." That's good advice! You should be happy to serve the Lord who has done so much for you. *H.W.M.*

TO MEMORIZE: Worship the Lord with gladness. Come before him, singing with joy. *Psalm 100:2*

16 January

ARE YOU A PK?

FROM THE BIBLE:

How we praise God, the Father of our Lord Jesus Christ, who has blessed us with every spiritual blessing in the heavenly realms because we belong to Christ. Long ago, even before he made the world, God loved us and chose us in Christ to be holy and without fault in his eyes. His unchanging plan has always been to adopt us into his own family by bringing us to himself through Jesus Christ. And this gave him great pleasure.

So we praise God for the wonderful kindness he has poured out on us because we belong to his dearly loved Son. He is so rich in kindness that he purchased our freedom through the blood of his Son, and our sins are forgiven. He has showered his kindness on us, along with all wisdom and understanding.

EPHESIANS 1:3-8

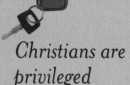

Christians are privileged

PETER HEADED for church. The guys there were talking and laughing, but when he approached, they got quiet. "What's up?" Peter asked.

"Nothin', since you got here," Buck said. "We gotta be careful what we say or do around a PK—a preacher's kid—right, guys?" The boys nodded and laughed.

That evening Peter complained to his dad. "I'm tired of being teased just because you're a pastor," he said. "I wish you had some other job."

The following weekend, Peter wiped out on his snowboard and broke his leg. His parents prayed with him at the hospital. Others stopped by to visit and pray with him, too. Soon his bedside table was filled with cards and toys. "You sure get a lot of attention," said his hospital roommate, Kyle.

"I guess it's because my dad's a preacher," Peter said, "and a lot of people know me."

"You're lucky to have a dad who prays for you," replied Kyle. "All my dad does is yell at me. You're a privileged kid, Peter."

On his way home from the hospital that day, Peter said, "I've always complained that *PK* meant 'preacher's kid.' But now I see that it means 'privileged kid,' too. I have special privileges that I've taken for granted."

HOW ABOUT YOU? Are you a PK—a privileged kid? You are if you're a Christian. Maybe you feel left out when you see some of the things other kids do. Maybe you don't like being a Christian when kids make fun of you. Don't fret, and don't envy the world's pleasures. You are richly blessed! Your sins are forgiven, you're on your way to heaven, your heavenly Father cares for you, and he answers prayer. He's all you need. *J.L.H.*

TO MEMORIZE: You are a chosen people. You are a kingdom of priests, God's holy nation, his very own possession. This is so you can show others the goodness of God. *1 Peter 2:9*

17 January

IS THAT ME?

FROM THE BIBLE:

Dear brothers and sisters, when I was with you I couldn't talk to you as I would to mature Christians. I had to talk as though you belonged to this world or as though you were infants in the Christian life. I had to feed you with milk and not with solid food, because you couldn't handle anything stronger. And you still aren't ready, for you are still controlled by your own sinful desires. You are jealous of one another and quarrel with each other. Doesn't that prove you are controlled by your own desires? You are acting like people who don't belong to the Lord. When one of you says, "I am a follower of Paul," and another says, "I prefer Apollos," aren't you acting like those who are not Christians?

Who is Apollos, and who is Paul, that we should be the cause of such quarrels? Why, we're only servants. Through us God caused you to believe. Each of us did the work the Lord gave us.

1 CORINTHIANS 3:1-5

"I DIDN'T understand the pastor's message," said Keith. "He said the people in the church at Corinth were babies. Weren't there any adults?"

"This might help you understand," Mom said. She put a cassette tape in the player and turned it on.

Keith heard some giggles, and then Dad started talking: "Welcome to the Browns. It's September 16, and Keith is three years old. He's going to tell us what he did in Sunday school today."

Keith heard more giggles and then, "I builded with blocks, and I sanged loud, and my teacher telled a story."

"Is that really me talking?" Keith laughed as the babyish voice went on to recite the ABCs. "I sound so little!"

"You *were* little, Keith," agreed Mom. "It would be silly if you talked that way now, wouldn't it?"

"Yeah, I've grown up a lot since then."

"Well," Mom said, "many of the people in Corinth had been Christians for a long time, but they still were acting like babies, spiritually. They had come to believe in Christ as Savior, but instead of studying the Scriptures, they were arguing over whether Paul or Apollos was the better preacher."

"Oh, I see," Keith said thoughtfully. "I want to grow spiritually just like I've grown physically. I'd hate to sound like a baby Christian all my life."

HOW ABOUT YOU? Have you been a Christian very long? Have you been growing spiritually or do you still act like a baby in the Lord? You should know more about the Bible this year than you did last year. Spiritual growth comes by talking to God, reading your Bible, and serving the Lord. Make sure these things are part of your life. *L.M.W.*

TO MEMORIZE: You must crave pure spiritual milk so that you can grow into the fullness of your salvation. Cry out for this nourishment as a baby cries for milk. *1 Peter 2:2*

Grow spiritually

18 January

CAT IN THE WINDOW

FROM THE BIBLE:

Don't worry about anything; instead, pray about everything. Tell God what you need, and thank him for all he has done. If you do this, you will experience God's peace, which is far more wonderful than the human mind can understand. His peace will guard your hearts and minds as you live in Christ Jesus. . . . Not that I was ever in need, for I have learned how to get along happily whether I have much or little. I know how to live on almost nothing or with everything. I have learned the secret of living in every situation, whether it is with a full stomach or empty, with plenty or little. For I can do everything with the help of Christ who gives me the strength I need.
PHILIPPIANS 4:6-7, 11-13

Be content with Christ

DANAE AND BRET were sitting on the couch, looking at a new catalog. Their mom was working on a quilt. "Mom," Danae whined, pointing to a picture, "I still want an outfit like this one. Wouldn't my friends be impressed!"

"I want a talking robot," said Bret, turning the page. "This one's voice activated and not all that expensive! Couldn't you buy it for me?"

Just then, Molly, their cat, meowed from the windowsill.

"Look at Molly!" Danae laughed. "She's watching those birds out in the front yard again."

"That dumb cat," said Bret. "By now she ought to know she can't get those birds through the window."

Mom looked at Molly. The cat's tail twitched with excitement as she stared intently at the birds she couldn't reach. "Molly is silly," she agreed. "Almost as silly as two children I know."

"Us?" asked Bret. "What do you mean?"

"Molly is making herself miserable by longing for something she can't have," explained Mom. "You and Danae have the same problem. You both know we can't afford to buy anything new right now because of Dad's job situation. Yet you persist in thinking about the things you can't have instead of enjoying what you do have. You're at least as silly as Molly."

The children were silent for a moment. Then Bret put the catalog down. "We're sorry, Mom," he said. "Come on, Danae. Let's go play that new game we got for Christmas."

HOW ABOUT YOU? Are there things you would like, but you know you can't have them right now? Don't allow your mind to dwell on those things. God wants you to realize that he is enough to make you happy. Also, he sees the dangers and problems that would come if you always got your way. Be content with what he gives you. *S.L.K.*

TO MEMORIZE: Stay away from the love of money; be satisfied with what you have. *Hebrews 13:5*

GARBAGE IN—GARBAGE OUT

FROM THE BIBLE:

So Jesus said again, "I assure you, unless you eat the flesh of the Son of Man and drink his blood, you cannot have eternal life within you. But those who eat my flesh and drink my blood have eternal life, and I will raise them at the last day. For my flesh is the true food, and my blood is the true drink. All who eat my flesh and drink my blood remain in me, and I in them. I live by the power of the living Father who sent me; in the same way, those who partake of me will live because of me. I am the true bread from heaven. Anyone who eats this bread will live forever and not die as your ancestors did, even though they ate the manna."

JOHN 6:53-58

Feed your mind good things

ONE EVENING, while helping Mom do the dishes, Beth dropped a glass and broke it. Just then a swear word slipped out.

Mom looked at her in shock. "Why, Beth! What has gotten into you?"

"I don't know!" Beth cried. "I am a Christian, but lately I can't seem to control what I think and say."

"Sounds to me like you're being programmed wrongly," suggested Mom.

"What do you mean?" asked Beth.

"Well, do you remember when you first used a computer at school? I believe you were taught the concept of 'garbage in—garbage out.' "

"Sure," Beth answered. "If we put wrong information—'garbage'—into the computer, all we can get out of it is garbage."

Mom nodded. "It's the same with your mind," she explained. "What you program into it is what eventually comes out of it through your speech. If you read the wrong kind of books and magazines, watch movies or TV programs with bad language or immoral ideas, and run around with kids who swear, that's the 'program' going into your mind."

"Oh," said Beth thoughtfully. "So I have to replace the garbage in my mind with good stuff—like good programs and good Christian friends."

"That's the idea," Mom said, smiling, "and also through Bible reading and prayer. Then you won't have a problem with what comes out of your mouth."

HOW ABOUT YOU? Do you ever find yourself saying bad words when you really don't want to? Today's memory verse may sound strange to you, but it has a lesson for you. You "partake" of Jesus by programming your mind with him—through reading and meditating on the Bible through prayer. Then he will help you to live the way he wants you to. *R.E.P.*

TO MEMORIZE: I live by the power of the living Father who sent me; in the same way, those who partake of me will live because of me. *John 6:57*

20 January

I WISH I COULD

FROM THE BIBLE:

"Here comes that dreamer!" they exclaimed. "Come on, let's kill him and throw him into a deep pit. We can tell our father that a wild animal has eaten him. Then we'll see what becomes of all his dreams!"

But Reuben came to Joseph's rescue. "Let's not kill him," he said. "Why should we shed his blood? Let's just throw him alive into this pit here. That way he will die without our having to touch him." Reuben was secretly planning to help Joseph escape, and then he would bring him back to his father.

So when Joseph arrived, they pulled off his beautiful robe and threw him into the pit. . . . They noticed a caravan of camels in the distance coming toward them. It was a group of Ishmaelite traders taking spices, balm, and myrrh from Gilead to Egypt.

Judah said to the others, "What can we gain by killing our brother? That would just give us a guilty conscience. Let's sell Joseph to those Ishmaelite traders. Let's not be responsible for his death; after all, he is our brother!" And his brothers agreed.

GENESIS 37:19-27

Don't envy another's talent

JODY PUT her hands over her ears so that she wouldn't hear her friend, Laura, play the piano solo. After church everyone would talk about Laura's wonderful playing, and Jody didn't want to hear that, either. She was envious; she wished she could play well enough to play in church.

That week, the all-school track meet was held at Jody's school. All the classes were competing against one another in running events. Jody confidently waited on the sidelines. She had been chosen to run the cross-country race. She had always been the fastest runner in her class.

"You running the last event?" Jody turned to see Laura standing next to her.

"Probably," Jody said, looking away.

"I wish I could run as fast as you do," said Laura. "I can't even beat a turtle."

Jody looked at Laura in surprise. "That's funny," she laughed. "I always wished I could play the piano as well as you do, and you were wishing you could run as fast as I can."

"I guess we've both been pretty silly," Laura said with a grin. "Hope you win your race."

Later that afternoon, Jody told her mother about her conversation with Laura. Mom smiled. "It's a waste of time to wish we could do something someone else is doing. Our job is to use the abilities God gave us the best way we know how."

HOW ABOUT YOU? Have you ever wished you could write, play an instrument, or draw as well as someone else could? Have you ever disliked someone because of his or her abilities? Today's Scripture gives an example of the terrible sin that resulted from envy. Remember, God made each person unique and gave each one different abilities. Don't be envious of someone else's talent. Instead, be happy with the talent you have. *L.M.W.*

TO MEMORIZE: Love is patient and kind. Love is not jealous or boastful or proud. *1 Corinthians 13:4*

21 January

DANGEROUS GAMES

FROM THE BIBLE:

You adulterers! Don't you realize that friendship with this world makes you an enemy of God? I say it again, that if your aim is to enjoy this world, you can't be a friend of God. What do you think the Scriptures mean when they say that the Holy Spirit, whom God has placed within us, jealously longs for us to be faithful? He gives us more and more strength to stand against such evil desires. As the Scriptures say,

"God sets himself against the proud,
but he shows favor to the humble."

So humble yourselves before God. Resist the Devil, and he will flee from you. Draw close to God, and God will draw close to you. Wash your hands, you sinners; purify your hearts, you hypocrites. Let there be tears for the wrong things you have done. Let there be sorrow and deep grief. Let there be sadness instead of laughter, and gloom instead of joy. When you bow down before the Lord and admit your dependence on him, he will lift you up and give you honor.

JAMES 4:4-10

Run from temptation

AS CARRIE AND DAD drove along, they saw some children dashing back and forth across the busy street. "It looks like those kids are trying to get as close to the cars as they can without getting hit!" exclaimed Carrie.

Dad shook his head. "What a dangerous game!" A little farther along, Dad pointed to a liquor store. "That store reminds me of a dangerous game I used to play," he said. "I was a lot like those children playing in the street."

"What do you mean?" Carrie asked.

"Drinking can be as dangerous as an oncoming car," said Dad. "When I was younger, I would go into bars with my unsaved friends, but I'd drink pop. I was trying to get as close as possible to the things in the world, even though I was a Christian. Can you see why that was dangerous?"

Carrie nodded. "You might have been persuaded to drink alcohol, and that could have led to more drinking. You could even have gotten addicted to it."

"That's right," agreed Dad. "When I finally gave my life completely to Christ, I had to learn some new rules. My question no longer is, How close to the world can I get? My question now is, How close to *Christ* can I get while I live in this sinful, old world?"

HOW ABOUT YOU? Do you think it might be fun to do things you've been told are wrong? Do you feel it's all right to be in places where un-Christlike activities are going on, as long as you don't join in? Sometimes it seems that people in the world—and Christians, too—are having a wonderful time, but they don't realize how close they are to disaster. Stay as far away from temptation as you can. *C.R.*

TO MEMORIZE: If your aim is to enjoy this world, you can't be a friend of God. *James 4:4*

22 *January*

BABY'S FIRST STEPS

FROM THE BIBLE:

We may know that these things make no difference, but we cannot just go ahead and do them to please ourselves. We must be considerate of the doubts and fears of those who think these things are wrong. We should please others. If we do what helps them, we will build them up in the Lord. For even Christ didn't please himself. As the Scriptures say, "Those who insult you are also insulting me." Such things were written in the Scriptures long ago to teach us. They give us hope and encouragement as we wait patiently for God's promises.

May God, who gives this patience and encouragement, help you live in complete harmony with each other—each with the attitude of Christ Jesus toward the other. Then all of you can join together with one voice, giving praise and glory to God, the Father of our Lord Jesus Christ.

So accept each other just as Christ has accepted you; then God will be glorified.

ROMANS 15:1-7

New Christians need help

"I'M GIVING UP on Janet," said Ellen as she tossed her schoolbooks on the table.

"Why?" asked Mom.

"Because she's driving me crazy! One day she acts like a Christian, and the next she lies or cheats or swears. I was glad when she became a Christian a month ago, but now I think she's hopeless."

"Don't give up on her," said Mom. "You need to pray for Janet and help her understand how to live for the Lord."

After supper, Ellen was playing with her baby brother. "Mom, look at Davy!" Ellen exclaimed. "He wants to walk!" Sure enough, when Ellen stood Davy on his feet, he took a tottering step toward her. "He took his first step by himself!" exclaimed Ellen. "I'm going to teach him to take one more."

Mother smiled as she heard Ellen encourage and help the baby to walk. "Come to Ellen, Davy," coaxed the girl. Over and over Ellen put Davy back on his feet; he never took more than two steps before he'd tumble to the floor.

"Better give up," advised Mother. "He'll never be able to walk. He just keeps falling down."

Ellen looked up in surprise. "Give up?" she asked as she picked up the baby. "He just needs more help."

Mother chuckled. "You're exactly right, Ellen. Davy does need your help. And so does Janet. She's a 'baby' Christian. She's going to need lots of help in learning to walk spiritually—to live as a Christian should live."

HOW ABOUT YOU? Do you know a Christian whose spiritual walk is not as good as you think it should be? Perhaps he is a baby Christian who is learning the first steps of Christian living. He needs your prayers and your encouragement, just as you need the help of older Christians. *G.W.*

TO MEMORIZE: We who are strong ought to bear with the failings of the weak. *Romans 15:1* (NIV)

TELLTALE MIRROR

FROM THE BIBLE:

And remember, it is a message to obey, not just to listen to. If you don't obey, you are only fooling yourself. For if you just listen and don't obey, it is like looking at your face in a mirror but doing nothing to improve your appearance. You see yourself, walk away, and forget what you look like. But if you keep looking steadily into God's perfect law—the law that sets you free—and if you do what it says and don't forget what you heard, then God will bless you for doing it.

JAMES 1:22-25

God's Word reveals sin

"I DIDN'T TELL your Sunday school teacher anything about you," Mother answered calmly.

Dad slipped the car into gear. "And I know I didn't."

"Then how did Miss Gauger know that I . . ." Jason stopped. Even his folks didn't know about some things Miss Gauger had talked about. She had looked at him and read in the Bible about some of his secret sins. "I . . . ," Jason began again. Then he changed the subject. "Look at Marcie's face."

"What's wrong with my face?" Marcie licked her lips.

Mother smiled and handed the little girl a mirror from her purse. "What have you been eating?"

"We had chocolate cake in Sunday school," Marcie said.

Later, as they gathered around the table for lunch, Jason laughed. "Marcie, you didn't wash your face."

"I forgot," she said as she hurried to wash it.

Jason laughed. "She saw herself in the mirror, but she still forgot."

"Have you ever seen yourself in the 'mirror' of the Word of God, Jason?" Dad asked.

Jason gulped. "Yes, but I never thought of the Bible as a mirror before."

"It's like a mirror," replied Dad. "It shows us our sin."

"But it doesn't do much good to see our faults if we don't correct them," added Mother.

"My face is clean now," Marcie said, returning to the table.

"Let's make sure our hearts are clean, too," Dad said. "When the Lord shows you you've sinned, ask him to forgive you and wash you clean."

HOW ABOUT YOU? When you look in the mirror of God's Word, do you like what you see? If you see sin in your life, don't forget it or try to hide it. Instead, confess it to God and ask him to forgive you. He wants to cleanse you and help you live as you should. *B.J.W.*

TO MEMORIZE: Wash me clean from my guilt. Purify me from my sin. *Psalm 51:2*

24 January

SOMETHING SPECIAL

FROM THE BIBLE:

And the Holy Spirit helps us in our distress. For we don't even know what we should pray for, nor how we should pray. But the Holy Spirit prays for us with groanings that cannot be expressed in words. And the Father who knows all hearts knows what the Spirit is saying, for the Spirit pleads for us believers in harmony with God's own will. And we know that God causes everything to work together for the good of those who love God and are called according to his purpose for them. For God knew his people in advance, and he chose them to become like his Son, so that his Son would be the firstborn, with many brothers and sisters. And having chosen them, he called them to come to him. And he gave them right standing with himself, and he promised them his glory.

What can we say about such wonderful things as these? If God is for us, who can ever be against us?

ROMANS 8:26-31

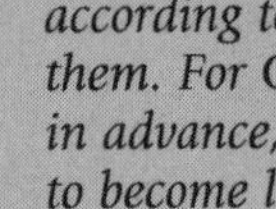

All things work together for good

JON WATCHED his grandmother mix shortening and sugar. "I'm making your favorite cake, Jon—chocolate." As Jon smiled faintly, Grandma added, "Is anything wrong?"

Jon snorted. "Everything's wrong! Dad's getting transferred, so I have to leave all my friends. And the doctor says I have to wear a brace on my injured leg for a year. How can I ever make new friends wearing a metal monster? If God loved me, he wouldn't let all this happen to me." Jon slammed his fist on the table.

"Here, have a taste." Grandma handed him the cocoa.

"Yuck!" Jon drew back.

"Then how about this?" Grandma dipped a spoon into the shortening and sugar mixture.

Jon frowned. "No way am I going to taste that!"

"Then how about some flour, or baking soda, or this egg?"

Jon grinned. "Aw, Grandma, you're teasing me."

Grandma smiled. "You know, the Bible says all things work together for good in the life of a Christian. It doesn't say all things are good. Cocoa or a raw egg isn't good alone, but when I mix all the ingredients together . . ."

"Mmmm, mmmm, good!" Jon said.

"So in life," Grandma continued as she mixed flour into the batter, "when God gets through mixing a Christian's experiences together—the bitter, the sweet, the happy, the sad—life comes out good. Moving and wearing a brace are bitter experiences for you now, but trust God, Jon. He'll add some 'sugar' and some 'flavoring' and in the end it will be good. Even better than my cake."

HOW ABOUT YOU? Have you had to swallow some bitter experiences lately? Be patient. All the ingredients are not in yet, but God is making something special out of you. *B.J.W.*

TO MEMORIZE: We know that God causes everything to work together for the good of those who love God and are called according to his purpose for them. *Romans 8:28*

27 January

THE FINISHED JOB

FROM THE BIBLE:

I have fought a good fight, I have finished the race, and I have remained faithful. And now the prize awaits me—the crown of righteousness that the Lord, the righteous Judge, will give me on that great day of his return. And the prize is not just for me but for all who eagerly look forward to his glorious return.

2 TIMOTHY 4:7-8

Finish what you start

"STAND STILL, Staci, while I measure this hem," said Mother.

"Will my dress be finished by tomorrow night so I can wear it to Lydia's piano recital?"

Mother nodded. "Probably. Are you finished with your science project?"

"No," Staci said. "I decided not to enter the science fair."

"But you spent hours on your project!"

Staci shrugged. "I know. But I'm tired of it."

"Just like you got tired of the pillow you were making Grandma for her birthday?" Mother asked.

"Yeah, but she liked the scarf I bought her." Staci slipped the dress over her head and handed it to her mother.

After school the next day, Staci skipped down the hall to the sewing room. She stopped in the doorway. "Mother," she wailed, "my dress isn't done!"

Mother shrugged. "I know. I got tired of it."

"Got tired of it!" cried Staci. "But, Mother, it's almost done now. Aren't you going to finish it?"

"I guess it would be foolish for me not to finish your dress, wouldn't it?" asked Mother quietly. "Just like it was foolish for you to stop working on your science project and your grandmother's pillow."

"Ooohhh," Staci moaned.

"Only when a job is finished does it bring satisfaction," said Mother. "I don't believe the Lord is satisfied, either, when we leave a job half done. He requires faithfulness even in small things."

"Mother, if you'll finish my dress, I'll finish my science project."

Mother smiled. "It's a deal."

HOW ABOUT YOU? How many unfinished projects do you have? Start today to discipline yourself to complete what you start. Jesus finished the task he came to earth to do. The apostle Paul finished his assignment. Before the Lord will trust you with a big job, he has to know you can finish little ones. *B.J.W.*

TO MEMORIZE: I have fought a good fight, I have finished the race, and I have remained faithful.
2 Timothy 4:7

28 January

I'LL DO THE DISHES

FROM THE BIBLE:

For the power of the life-giving Spirit has freed you through Christ Jesus from the power of sin that leads to death. The law of Moses could not save us, because of our sinful nature. But God put into effect a different plan to save us. He sent his own Son in a human body like ours, except that ours are sinful. God destroyed sin's control over us by giving his Son as a sacrifice for our sins. He did this so that the requirement of the law would be fully accomplished for us who no longer follow our sinful nature but instead follow the Spirit.

Those who are dominated by the sinful nature think about sinful things, but those who are controlled by the Holy Spirit think about things that please the Spirit. If your sinful nature controls your mind, there is death. But if the Holy Spirit controls your mind, there is life and peace. For the sinful nature is always hostile to God. It never did obey God's laws, and it never will.

ROMANS 8:2-7

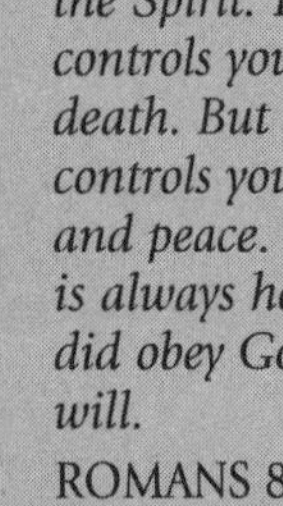

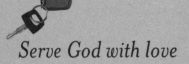

Serve God with love

"MY SUNDAY SCHOOL teacher said something I still can't figure out," Jan announced to her mom one evening.

"Oh? What did he say?" asked Mom.

"He said the only way to be really happy as a Christian is to always do what God wants us to do, instead of doing what we want. But how can we be happy if we're always doing things we don't want to do? That would make me miserable, not happy!"

"In a way, you're right," agreed Mother. "If the Christian life were just a matter of forcing ourselves to do unpleasant things, it wouldn't be very enjoyable. But I think you're overlooking something."

"What's that?" asked Jan.

Mother smiled. "Remember how you reacted when I asked you to wash the dishes tonight?"

"I complained," Jan admitted sheepishly.

"Yes," Mom said, with a chuckle. "But last night, when I wasn't feeling well, you cleaned the whole kitchen just to surprise me."

Jan grinned. "I did it to be nice, not because I had to."

"In other words, you did it out of love," explained Mother. "And that's the real secret of a happy Christian life. If we try to serve God in our own strength and out of a sense of duty, we'll never be truly happy. But when we serve the Lord out of love and gratitude, he gives us joy and contentment. That's what makes the difference!"

HOW ABOUT YOU? Do you ever serve God grudgingly, just because you feel you have to? When you don't feel like doing the things you should, admit it to God and ask for the Spirit's help. Then do what he wants you to do out of love for him. That way you'll truly be a happy Christian! *S.L.K.*

TO MEMORIZE: Now we can obey God's laws if we follow after the Holy Spirit and no longer obey the old evil nature within us. *Romans 8:4* (TLB)

29 January

WHAT DO YOU HEAR?

FROM THE BIBLE:

Let the godly sing with joy to the Lord,
for it is fitting to praise him.
Praise the Lord with melodies on the lyre;
make music for him on the ten-stringed harp.
Sing new songs of praise to him;
play skillfully on the harp and sing with joy.
For the word of the Lord holds true,
and everything he does is worthy of our trust.
PSALM 33:1-4

Music influences you

"MATTHEW, turn off that music."

"Aw, Mom, everybody listens to rock music," protested Matthew. "Besides, it doesn't hurt me."

"But it does!" said Mom. "Both the words and the music get into your mind and influence you whether you realize it or not."

Matthew sighed. "Is Dad home yet?" he asked.

"Not yet," Mom replied. "Since he was made manager of Burger Stop, he's had extra responsibilities. Shall we surprise him for dinner?"

Matthew brightened. "Yeah! Let's go!"

Matthew's father saw them come in. "I'll be with you in a minute," he said.

As they sat down, Matthew heard his dad singing a tune under his breath as he walked away. "Come to Big Al's, bring all your pals. Our burgers are the best, in the east and the west."

Matthew laughed. "Dad, you're advertising for the competition!"

Dad turned and grinned sheepishly. "I heard it on the radio while I was driving to work this morning, and it got into my head. I'd better be more careful about what I listen to."

On the way home, Matthew was thoughtful. "If hearing that song could make Dad advertise for the wrong restaurant without even knowing it, maybe the songs I hear influence me more than I thought they did, too. I'm going to be more careful about what I hear."

HOW ABOUT YOU? What kind of music do you listen to? Do the words please God? Advertisers know that words set to music stay with you even longer than spoken words. Would you invite Jesus to listen with you? If you're a Christian he is with you. Be sure that both the words and the sound of the music please him, and that they don't hurt your testimony. *H.W.M.*

TO MEMORIZE: Be sure to pay attention to what you hear. The more you do this, the more you will understand. *Mark 4:24*

30 January

WORK AND PRAY

FROM THE BIBLE:

But when Sanballat and Tobiah and the Arabs, Ammonites, and Ashdodites heard that the work was going ahead and that the gaps in the wall were being repaired, they became furious. They all made plans to come and fight against Jerusalem and to bring about confusion there. But we prayed to our God and guarded the city day and night to protect ourselves.
NEHEMIAH 4:7-9

Work and pray

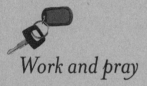

"SHOULDN'T YOU be studying your spelling?" asked Mom.

"I'll do it as soon as this program's over," said Lynn.

But when the TV show ended, Amy called. Lynn chatted on the phone until bedtime. *No time to study now,* she thought sleepily. *I'll just have to ask the Lord to help me.*

As she took the test the next day, she asked God to help her do well. But she got a D! "Doesn't the Bible say that if we lack wisdom we should ask God for it?" she asked Mom that evening.

Just then the phone rang. "That was Amy," Lynn said as she returned. "Is it okay if I go to town with her? And may I have some money to buy a lock for my locker? Lots of kids are getting things ripped off at school."

"That's a shame," said Mom. "But I have an idea. Why don't you pray about it? Ask the Lord to protect your things."

"Mother!" exclaimed Lynn. "It's good to pray about it, but it only makes sense to put a lock on, too."

"Wouldn't that be true regarding your spelling test, too?" asked Mom. "You didn't study. Yet you expected God to help you remember things you never learned."

Lynn looked ashamed. "I guess I knew better. After this I'll study hard. Then I know God will help me, too."

HOW ABOUT YOU? Do you pray about your schoolwork? About friends who need to know the Lord? Prayer is very important, but it is only part of the battle. You also need to study. You need to witness. When the walls of Jerusalem were being built, God's people prayed *and* put guards in place to watch for enemy attacks. Jesus told his disciples to watch and pray. We, too, must pray, and we must also work. *H.W.M.*

TO MEMORIZE: Keep alert and pray. Otherwise temptation will overpower you. *Matthew 26:41*

31 January

JONATHAN'S MINISTRY

FROM THE BIBLE:

But Jesus called them together and said, "You know that in this world kings are tyrants, and officials lord it over the people beneath them. But among you it should be quite different. Whoever wants to be a leader among you must be your servant, and whoever wants to be first must become your slave. For even I, the Son of Man, came here not to be served but to serve others, and to give my life as a ransom for many."
MATTHEW 20:25-28

You can be a minister

"WE HAD a birthday party for Pastor Wilson today," announced Jonathan on the way home from Sunday school. "It would be fun to be a minister. That's what I'm going to be when I grow up."

"I don't know how much fun it would be, but I'm sure it's rewarding," Dad said.

"Could we stop by Grannie Nelson's and check on her?" asked Mom.

"Do we have to?" groaned Jonathan. "I'm hungry, and you know how she talks and talks."

"She's lonely," replied Mom. "She needs someone to minister to her."

"Minister to her?" Jonathan echoed. "If she needs a preacher, tell Pastor Wilson."

"I didn't say she needs a preacher," Mom said. "Grannie Nelson needs a 'minister.' We can't all be preachers, but we can all be ministers—even you, Jonathan!"

"I will be one when I grow up if I don't starve to death first," Jonathan complained.

"You can minister to Grannie Nelson now," Mom insisted. "A minister is simply a servant."

"Pastor Wilson isn't a servant!" said Jonathan.

"Yes, he is," Dad corrected. "He is God's servant."

"To be a minister, you must be willing to serve others," added Mom.

"Remember how young Samuel ministered to the Lord?" Dad asked as they parked in Grannie Nelson's driveway. "He ministered to the Lord by serving Eli. He lit the lamp in the tabernacle, swept the floors, and ran errands."

"Well, then," said Jonathan, "I guess I'd better start now. Maybe Grannie Nelson needs her kitchen swept."

HOW ABOUT YOU? Did you know that all Christians are to be ministers? As a servant of Jesus Christ, your job is to serve others. Look around you. Find one person today whom you can serve. You'll be surprised how much fun it is! And remember, as you serve people, you are actually ministering to the Lord. *B.J.W.*

TO MEMORIZE: Whoever wants to be a leader among you must be your servant. *Matthew 20:26*

1 February

IT OUGHT TO HURT

FROM THE BIBLE:

Have mercy on me, O God,
because of your unfailing love.
Because of your great compassion,
blot out the stain of my sins.
Wash me clean from my guilt.
Purify me from my sin.
For I recognize my shameful deeds—
they haunt me day and night.
Against you, and you alone, have I sinned;
I have done what is evil in your sight.
You will be proved right in what you say,
and your judgment against me is just.
For I was born a sinner—
yes, from the moment my mother conceived me.
But you desire honesty from the heart,
so you can teach me to be wise in my inmost being.
Purify me from my sins, and I will be clean;
wash me, and I will be whiter than snow. . . .
Create in me a clean heart, O God.
Renew a right spirit within me.
Do not banish me from your presence,
and don't take your Holy Spirit from me.
Restore to me again the joy of your salvation,
and make me willing to obey you.

PSALM 51:1-7, 10-12

Don't get used to sin

JACK AND WENDY were hungry for candy. "Hey, let's sneak some candy from the cupboard," said Wendy. "Mom will never know."

"Doesn't that make you feel guilty?" Jack asked.

"Nah," said Wendy. "At first I felt guilty, but it doesn't bother me anymore."

When Jack saw his sister eating a chocolate bar, he couldn't resist. The two finished their candy and went outside to build a snow fort.

After a while their feet were cold, but they wanted to finish the snow fort. When Mom called them inside, she was shocked to see how wet and cold their feet were. "Why didn't you come inside when your feet got cold?" she scolded.

"We wanted to finish our fort," said Wendy. "Besides, they didn't feel so cold after a while!"

Mom looked grim. "That sensation of cold was meant to warn you so that you wouldn't get frostbite. The most dangerous time is not when your feet feel cold, but when you stop feeling it." She rubbed their feet gently. "It reminds me of sin. We're in danger if our conscience stops bothering us when we do something wrong."

When Mom left the room, the children looked at each other, remembering the candy they'd eaten.

"Now that my feet are getting warmed up, they hurt," said Jack. "And my conscience hurts too."

"Mine, too," agreed Wendy. "And it's going to hurt more when we tell Mother about the candy we took. But I'm sure we'll feel better afterward!"

HOW ABOUT YOU? Are there habits or activities in your life that made you feel guilty in the past but not anymore? You may have changed, but God's standards of right and wrong haven't. Confess your sin, and be willing to follow the "pricking" of your conscience and of the Holy Spirit. Don't let yourself become "numb" to sin! *S.L.K.*

TO MEMORIZE: Create in me a clean heart, O God. Renew a right spirit within me. *Psalm 51:10*

2 February

WONDERFULLY MADE

FROM THE BIBLE:

Then God said, "Let us make people in our image, to be like ourselves. They will be masters over all life—the fish in the sea, the birds in the sky, and all the livestock, wild animals, and small animals."

So God created people in his own image;
God patterned them after himself;
male and female he created them.

God blessed them and told them, "Multiply and fill the earth and subdue it. Be masters over the fish and birds and all the animals."

GENESIS 1:26-28

Never mock God's plan

PETER OPENED a book his friend, Dave, had given him. "Oh no! This has embarrassing pictures of people in it!"

Dad put the book on a high shelf. "I think we should all have a talk."

That evening Dave came over to see Peter's new pups. Outside, the boys and Peter's dad talked about the billions of stars and how God knows each one by name. "But man is the greatest of all creation," Dad said. "The human spine is a series of 33 rings with 150 joints, so I can bend my back in any direction, yet I'm capable of supporting five hundred pounds."

"And don't forget the heart," said Peter. "It's no larger than a fist, yet I've heard it pumps blood at the rate of four thousand gallons a day."

"We didn't even mention the brain, or lungs, or our wonderful fingers," Dad added, "but it's clear that this great handiwork of God is nothing to laugh about."

Dave was surprised. "What do you mean, 'laugh about'?"

Dad explained, "When God made the world, he planned for a man and a woman to marry, love each other, and have a family. But there are people who make jokes, pictures, books, or movies that mock God's plan for us. To have anything but pure thoughts about our bodies is evil and sinful in God's sight. Now what do you think we should do with the book you gave Peter?"

"Just burn it," said Dave. "You know, it kind of scares me that I made fun of God's work. I'll ask him to forgive me."

HOW ABOUT YOU? Are you ever tempted to laugh at embarrassing pictures of the people God created? He doesn't want only your heart. He also wants your body to be used in his service. *A.G.L.*

TO MEMORIZE: Thank you for making me so wonderfully complex! Your workmanship is marvelous—and how well I know it. *Psalm 139:14*

3 February

HIGHER WAYS

FROM THE BIBLE:

"My thoughts are completely different from yours," says the Lord. "And my ways are far beyond anything you could imagine. For just as the heavens are higher than the earth, so are my ways higher than your ways and my thoughts higher than your thoughts.

"The rain and snow come down from the heavens and stay on the ground to water the earth. They cause the grain to grow, producing seed for the farmer and bread for the hungry. It is the same with my word. I send it out, and it always produces fruit. It will accomplish all I want it to, and it will prosper everywhere I send it. You will live in joy and peace. The mountains and hills will burst into song, and the trees of the field will clap their hands! Where once there were thorns, cypress trees will grow. Where briers grew, myrtles will sprout up. This miracle will bring great honor to the Lord's name; it will be an everlasting sign of his power and love.

ISAIAH 55:8-13

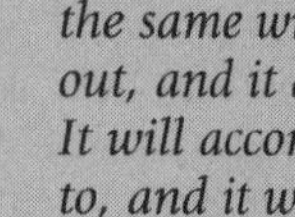

Trust God's higher ways

A CHILLY WIND whipped through the cemetery. Joel tried to listen as the minister read from the Bible. *I wonder if Grandpa went to heaven,* he thought for the hundredth time. On the way home, Joel asked his parents.

"We're not sure, Son," said Dad. "Grandpa never showed any interest when I talked to him about God."

"But Grandpa died on his knees beside his bed," Mom added gently. "The day before that, I spent some special time praying that he would receive Jesus as his Savior from sin. It's possible Grandpa did that just before he died."

Joel sighed. "I wish we knew for sure."

"I do too, Son, but it's out of our hands now," Dad said. "Many times we explained to Grandpa how to be saved, and for years we prayed he would understand and accept God's gift. We were kind to him, always hoping he would see the difference Jesus made in our lives and would want to know him too."

"God promises that his Word will accomplish what he sends it to do," added Mom. "His ways are higher than ours, and he does all things right."

At home Joel went to his room and picked up the baseball mitt Grandpa had given him. *Dear Lord,* he prayed, *thank you that Grandpa knew the way to be saved. Thank you that you do everything right.*

HOW ABOUT YOU? It always hurts when a loved one dies, but it's especially painful when you don't know if the person went to heaven. If you're in that position, try not to fret. Rest in the knowledge that God's ways are right. Pray for those who are still alive but unsaved. Be kind and loving, and make sure they know the way to heaven. *C.E.Y.*

TO MEMORIZE: Just as the heavens are higher than the earth, so are my ways higher than your ways and my thoughts higher than your thoughts.
Isaiah 55:9

4 February

BEWARE OF THE FOE

FROM THE BIBLE:

Dear friends, do not believe everyone who claims to speak by the Spirit. You must test them to see if the spirit they have comes from God. For there are many false prophets in the world. This is the way to find out if they have the Spirit of God: If a prophet acknowledges that Jesus Christ became a human being, that person has the Spirit of God. If a prophet does not acknowledge Jesus, that person is not from God. Such a person has the spirit of the Antichrist. You have heard that he is going to come into the world, and he is already here.

But you belong to God, my dear children. You have already won your fight with these false prophets, because the Spirit who lives in you is greater than the spirit who lives in the world.

1 JOHN 4:1-4

Beware of false teaching

SANDY AND DAD were watching the news. Then a commercial came on. "Look, Dad," Sandy said. "Could we order some of that jewelry for Mom's birthday? She'd love it! They're selling those diamonds and rubies and pearls so cheap—and it says they're genuine, too."

"There's another word on the screen too," Dad said, pointing to it. "It's spelled *f-a-u-x,* and it's pronounced 'foe.' "

"That's probably a fancy name for the jewelry," Sandy suggested. "I'll look it up."

After she found the word in the dictionary, Sandy exclaimed, "Wow, it means false! Genuine false gems!"

"A lot of people will spend their money on that jewelry, and then some jeweler will tell them it's not real," Dad said. He got up and went to answer the doorbell.

"Who was that, Dad?" Sandy asked after her father shut the front door.

"Some people wanting to leave some literature and tell me about their religion," Dad answered. "But I already know what those people believe, and it's false teaching. It fools a lot of people, though."

"How come?" asked Sandy.

"Remember how easy it was to believe the gems in that commercial were real—until you looked up the word *faux?*" Dad said. "Well, those people make their message sound good, too. They even quote Bible verses, although incorrectly. We need to know the Bible well so we can be on guard against false teaching."

HOW ABOUT YOU? Are you aware that false teachers may try to get you to believe as they do? Study the Bible to know what is really true. Notice that today's memory verse talks about people who searched the Scriptures daily. You do that too. Don't let false teaching fool you. *S.L.N.*

TO MEMORIZE: The people of Berea . . . searched the Scriptures day after day to check up on Paul and Silas, to see if they were really teaching the truth. *Acts 17:11*

5 February

SECOND CHOICE

FROM THE BIBLE:

And do not forget the things I have done throughout history. For I am God—I alone! I am God, and there is no one else like me. Only I can tell you what is going to happen even before it happens. Everything I plan will come to pass, for I do whatever I wish. I will call a swift bird of prey from the east—a leader from a distant land who will come and do my bidding. I have said I would do it, and I will.

ISAIAH 46:9-11

Let God choose

THE SNYDER FAMILY was expecting a new baby. "I'm going to pray for a little brother," said seven-year-old Steve.

"Tell God how you feel, but then leave it to him whether to send us a girl or a boy," his parents said. "Meanwhile, we need to look for a bigger house to rent."

Finally they found just the one they wanted. The rent was a little too high, but they decided they could manage it. Dad called the landlord, only to learn that the house had just been rented. They were forced to take their second choice. "Didn't you pray that God would let us have the first house?" Steve asked.

"Not exactly," Mom answered. "We prayed God would give us his choice."

Their new home needed repair, but the landlord let them do the work for part of the rent. Then, the landlord suggested they apply the rent toward buying the house. So the Snyders were soon homeowners!

"I'm getting my bedroom ready for my brother and me," Steve said proudly.

"Don't be so sure you'll have a brother," his sister told him. "I'd rather have a girl."

The big day came. The new baby arrived, and it was a girl! Although Steve was disappointed, he did enjoy holding the baby in the hospital. "Steve, how do you feel now about your baby sister?" Dad asked.

"She is kinda cute," Steve said with a grin. "God chose her for us, so she must be the best choice!"

"I'm sure she is," Mom said, smiling.

HOW ABOUT YOU? Is your second (or even third or fourth) choice sometimes God's choice for you? As today's Scripture says, God knows the end from the beginning. He knows what's best for you. *B.J.W.*

TO MEMORIZE: Only I can tell you what is going to happen even before it happens. Everything I plan will come to pass, for I do whatever I wish. *Isaiah 46:10*

TAXES! TAXES!

FROM THE BIBLE:

On their arrival in Capernaum, the tax collectors for the Temple tax came to Peter and asked him, "Doesn't your teacher pay the Temple tax?"

"Of course he does," Peter replied. Then he went into the house to talk to Jesus about it.

But before he had a chance to speak, Jesus asked him, "What do you think, Peter? Do kings tax their own people or the foreigners they have conquered?"

"They tax the foreigners," Peter replied.

"Well, then," Jesus said, "the citizens are free! However, we don't want to offend them, so go down to the lake and throw in a line. Open the mouth of the first fish you catch, and you will find a coin. Take the coin and pay the tax for both of us."

MATTHEW 17:24-27

Pay taxes cheerfully

GINGER was at the store, buying five stickers with her allowance. "That will be fifty cents for the stickers, plus sales tax," the cashier said.

"Oh no!" groaned Ginger. "I forgot about the sales tax! I guess I can only buy four stickers today."

At home again, Ginger showed her stickers to her mother. "Mom, why do we have to pay taxes?"

"Taxes are used to pay for many things," answered Mother. "They're used to keep our roads repaired and to pay for teachers, policemen, firemen, and government workers. People have paid taxes for a long time—even in Bible times."

"They did?" Ginger was surprised.

"Yes," said Mother. "There were taxes on the sale of animals, land, slaves, and produce, as well as taxes to support the temple. During the time Jesus lived, the Jews hated the tax collectors because they took more money than they should and kept some for themselves. But Jesus can change anyone, and he called one of those tax collectors to be one of his disciples."

"Really? Which one?" asked Ginger.

"Matthew," said Mother. "Later Matthew wrote one of the gospels. Because he had kept careful records as a tax collector, it helped him to record many things Jesus taught. He even recorded a time when Jesus paid taxes."

"Oh, I remember!" Ginger exclaimed. "Jesus sent Peter to find money in the mouth of a fish. It was used to pay taxes for himself and Peter." She paused and grinned. "Well, if Jesus paid taxes, I guess I can too!"

HOW ABOUT YOU? Sometimes taxes may seem unfair or too high. But try to remember that they are needed for many things. When the burden is unfair, we can work toward lowering taxes. Nevertheless, God says we are to pay them. *V.L.C.*

TO MEMORIZE: Pay your taxes. . . . For government workers need to be paid so they can keep on doing the work God intended them to do. *Romans 13:6*

7 February

ON THIN ICE

FROM THE BIBLE:

Do not do as the wicked do or follow the path of evildoers. Avoid their haunts. Turn away and go somewhere else, for evil people cannot sleep until they have done their evil deed for the day. They cannot rest unless they have caused someone to stumble. They eat wickedness and drink violence!

The way of the righteous is like the first gleam of dawn, which shines ever brighter until the full light of day. But the way of the wicked is like complete darkness. Those who follow it have no idea what they are stumbling over.

Pay attention, my child, to what I say. Listen carefully. Don't lose sight of my words. Let them penetrate deep within your heart, for they bring life and radiant health to anyone who discovers their meaning.

Above all else, guard your heart, for it affects everything you do.

PROVERBS 4:14-23

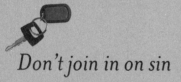

Don't join in on sin

"WHY CAN'T I GO? It seems like a fair exchange," Connie told her mother. "Karen is willing to come to church tomorrow if I go with her this afternoon."

Mother shook her head. "She wants you to go to a horror movie, right? I don't think that's the way to win your friend to the Lord."

"But, Mother!" protested Connie. "It will get Karen to come to church."

"No, Connie," Mother said firmly.

Connie was angry, but later Mother permitted her to go ice-skating with some friends at Horn's Lake. When she returned home, she was bursting with excitement. "Mom, you know Jack Wolter? He zipped right past the danger sign toward the middle of the lake. But the ice didn't hold him. One leg went right through into the freezing water. I screamed for help, and some men on duty rescued him!"

"Oh, good!" said Mother. "But why didn't you rescue him yourself? You took that lifesaving swim class last summer."

Connie looked at her mother in disbelief. "Are you kidding? The men used boards and ropes to crawl out and reach Jack. If I had skated out there, it would have broken more ice and made things worse!"

"I'm glad you realized that," Mother said. "Now think about this—you don't rescue someone in sin by joining him or her. If you do, you might both get trapped in sin."

Connie nodded, thinking of Karen. She would have to find some other way to help her.

HOW ABOUT YOU? In order to win a friend to Jesus, are you sometimes tempted to go somewhere or do something you know is wrong? If you yield to that temptation, you're just fooling yourself—you're not winning your friend. The way to win others to Jesus is through living a pure life before them. Pray for them. *H.W.M.*

TO MEMORIZE: Do not participate in the sins of others. Keep yourself pure. *1 Timothy 5:22*

GLOWING COALS

FROM THE BIBLE:

And so, dear friends, we can boldly enter heaven's Most Holy Place because of the blood of Jesus. This is the new, life-giving way that Christ has opened up for us through the sacred curtain, by means of his death for us.

And since we have a great High Priest who rules over God's people, let us go right into the presence of God, with true hearts fully trusting him. For our evil consciences have been sprinkled with Christ's blood to make us clean, and our bodies have been washed with pure water.

Without wavering, let us hold tightly to the hope we say we have, for God can be trusted to keep his promise. Think of ways to encourage one another to outbursts of love and good deeds. And let us not neglect our meeting together, as some people do, but encourage and warn each other, especially now that the day of his coming back again is drawing near.

HEBREWS 10:19-25

"MOM, CAN I go skiing with Jan next Sunday?" asked Amy. "Jan told me her family worships God by feeling his presence in nature."

"That sounds good," Mom said, "but I wonder how much you'd even think about God if you were skiing instead of attending church. Dad and I don't think it's right to skip church in favor of skiing."

That evening Dad added a log to the fire in the fireplace. Suddenly, with a loud crack, a small ember flew out onto the hearth. Amy jumped and then laughed as she watched it glow for a few seconds before it faded and turned black.

"That startled me," said Amy, grinning. "It sure didn't burn long after it got separated from the rest of the logs, did it?"

"No, it didn't," said Mom. "Amy, does Jan still go to Bible club and junior choir?"

"Not for the last few weeks," answered Amy.

"Any of the church youth activities?"

Amy shook her head.

"You know, the ember that fell from the fireplace illustrates what can happen to God's children when they no longer meet with God's people," Mom said. "That ember was giving light and warmth with the others, but all by itself it soon grew cold. When God's people worship and pray together, they're like glowing coals. They strengthen each other. But all alone, they often grow cold."

Amy nodded her head. "I'll see if I can get Jan to come back to Bible club," she decided. "It will be a step in the right direction."

HOW ABOUT YOU? Do you worship regularly with God's people? God knows you need the encouragement and warmth of their fellowship. And together you can do great things for him. *H.W.M.*

TO MEMORIZE: Let us not neglect our meeting together, as some people do, but encourage and warn each other, especially now that the day of his coming back again is drawing near. *Hebrews 10:25*

Attend church regularly

9 February

THE MISSING SWEATER

FROM THE BIBLE:

Always judge your neighbors fairly, neither favoring the poor nor showing deference to the rich.

Do not spread slanderous gossip among your people.

Do not try to get ahead at the cost of your neighbor's life, for I am the Lord.

Do not nurse hatred in your heart for any of your relatives.

Confront your neighbors directly so you will not be held guilty for their crimes.

Never seek revenge or bear a grudge against anyone, but love your neighbor as yourself. I am the Lord.

LEVITICUS 19:15-18

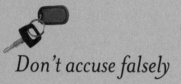

Don't accuse falsely

"MOM, I CAN'T find my lavender sweater," wailed Caitlin. "The last time I wore it was Sunday."

"Maybe you left it at church," Mom suggested. "Call and ask if anyone turned it in." But the sweater wasn't there.

"We'll keep looking for it," Mom said.

Caitlin searched in vain for her sweater. She wanted to wear it to a Sunday school party at Melissa's house on Friday evening, but now she'd have to wear something else. Arriving at the party, Caitlin stared in amazement at Marci, one of the girls in her class. Drawing Melissa close, she whispered, "Marci's wearing my lavender sweater! She must have picked it up at Sunday school."

"Are you sure?" Melissa whispered back.

"Of course," Caitlin hissed. "She couldn't afford a sweater like that!"

When some girls told Marci they liked her sweater, she said, "My mother bought it at a garage sale."

"I'll bet," muttered Caitlin. She was angry and told several girls that Marci had stolen her sweater. The party wasn't much fun for her after that.

When Caitlin reached home, her grandmother met her at the door. Caitlin gave her a big hug as Mother said, "You'll be glad to see what Grandma brought you." Mother handed Caitlin her lavender sweater.

"But . . . where did you find this?" Caitlin stammered.

"You left it at my house last Sunday," Grandma told her.

Tears welled up in Caitlin's eyes. "I've made a terrible mistake," she sighed. "I'll tell you about it after I make some phone calls."

HOW ABOUT YOU? Have you ever falsely accused someone? Did you apologize? Next time you're tempted to accuse someone, wait! God says Christians should be slow to speak. He knows that hasty conclusions are often wrong. Hurting others with false accusations is a poor testimony. If you have done that, be sure to apologize. *B.J.W.*

TO MEMORIZE: Be quick to listen, slow to speak, and slow to get angry. *James 1:19*

HOW DUMB ARE YOU?

FROM THE BIBLE:

You must remain faithful to the things you have been taught. You know they are true, for you know you can trust those who taught you. You have been taught the holy Scriptures from childhood, and they have given you the wisdom to receive the salvation that comes by trusting in Christ Jesus. All Scripture is inspired by God and is useful to teach us what is true and to make us realize what is wrong in our lives. It straightens us out and teaches us to do what is right. It is God's way of preparing us in every way, fully equipped for every good thing God wants us to do.

2 TIMOTHY 3:14-17

Start the day with God

BEVERLY wished she could skip family devotions on busy days like today. She was already running late and had to wait until after devotions to eat breakfast. "How come we have to do this every single day?" she asked when Dad finally ended his prayer.

Ignoring her question, Dad held the cereal box toward her, then pulled it back. "Oh, maybe you don't want breakfast," he said.

"Of course I want breakfast!" Beverly exclaimed.

"Well, you won't be eating lunch today, will you?" her father asked.

Beverly looked at him in surprise. "Why wouldn't I? I always take a sack lunch to school."

"What about supper?" Dad asked.

Beverly was getting irritated. "Dad, I always eat supper."

He nodded. "You always have, but I wondered if you were thinking of giving up eating on busy days."

Beverly looked first at her mom and then at Dad. "Give up eating?" she repeated. "I'm not that dumb!" Suddenly she stopped. "Oh," she added slowly, "you're trying to tell me that it would be just as dumb to quit having my spiritual food, right?"

"Right," agreed Dad with a smile. "Reading the Bible every day is like eating good meals every day. I think it's good to start the day with God's Word—just like it's important to have a good breakfast."

Beverly flashed a big grin as she poured cereal in her bowl. "I'll eat to that!" she said.

HOW ABOUT YOU? You wouldn't be dumb enough to go very long without food for your body, would you? Are you dumb enough to go without food for your soul? It's important to feed upon God's Word each and every day. *R.I.J.*

TO MEMORIZE: All Scripture is inspired by God and is useful to teach us what is true and to make us realize what is wrong in our lives. It straightens us out and teaches us to do what is right. *2 Timothy 3:16*

11 February

GUARD DUTY

FROM THE BIBLE:

You can enter God's Kingdom only through the narrow gate. The highway to hell is broad, and its gate is wide for the many who choose the easy way. But the gateway to life is small, and the road is narrow, and only a few ever find it. . . .

Not all people who sound religious are really godly. They may refer to me as "Lord," but they still won't enter the Kingdom of Heaven. The decisive issue is whether they obey my Father in heaven. On judgment day many will tell me, "Lord, Lord, we prophesied in your name and cast out demons in your name and performed many miracles in your name." But I will reply, "I never knew you. Go away; the things you did were unauthorized."

MATTHEW 7:13-14, 21-23

Good works won't save you

JULIANNE AND BRETT were taking a box lunch to their father, who worked as a gate guard at a local factory. He greeted them as they approached the gate. "Sorry, but you can't get through here without a badge," he said sternly.

Julianne giggled. "Daddy, you know it's us. We brought your lunch."

Dad smiled. "I'll be off for lunch in five minutes. Wait here."

At lunchtime, they sat under a tree. "Dad, does everyone need to have a badge to get inside the factory?" Julianne asked as she munched on one of Dad's potato chips.

"Yes," said Dad. "The badge shows they belong here."

"But what if you know the person?" asked Brett.

"It makes no difference," Dad said. "He still needs a badge."

"How come?" asked Julianne. "It doesn't seem fair."

"Oh, it is," Dad replied. "The company will issue a free badge to all those who have business inside the factory. It's for their own protection, and the company's, too. It keeps outsiders from hindering our production or from getting hurt by wandering into the wrong place."

"I guess if you really want to be inside, you'll get a badge," Brett said.

"Right," Dad replied. "Sometimes people try to sneak in, but that doesn't work." Closing his lunch box, he added, "That reminds me of the way some people try to get into heaven, too. They will try to sneak in by doing good works, or they'll claim God knows them. But accepting Jesus is the only way to heaven." Just then the factory whistle blew. "I must get back to work," Dad said. "See you at supper."

HOW ABOUT YOU? Do you want to go to heaven? You can't get there by your own good works. You must accept Jesus as your personal Savior. Do it today. Tomorrow may be too late! *J.L.H.*

TO MEMORIZE: People are declared righteous because of their faith, not because of their work. *Romans 4:5*

12 February

AN OLD PIECE OF WOOD

FROM THE BIBLE:

The Lord gave another message to Jeremiah. He said, "Go down to the shop where clay pots and jars are made. I will speak to you while you are there." So I did as he told me and found the potter working at his wheel. But the jar he was making did not turn out as he had hoped, so the potter squashed the jar into a lump of clay and started again.

Then the Lord gave me this message: "O Israel, can I not do to you as this potter has done to his clay? As the clay is in the potter's hand, so are you in my hand."

JEREMIAH 18:1-6

Become a new creation

JASON WAS HELPING his dad pile firewood in the backyard when their neighbor, Mr. Stevens, walked by.

"Looks like you got some walnut here," said Mr. Stevens as he picked up a piece that Jason's dad had trimmed from a tree in the woods. "May I borrow this for a week?"

"Sure," said Dad. Jason wondered why Mr. Stevens would want to borrow the chunk of wood. His dad was puzzled too.

A week later, Mr. Stevens stopped by and returned the piece of walnut firewood, except now it was a beautifully whittled duck! "Wow!" Jason said. "Look what you did with just an old piece of wood!"

"We'll put this on our fireplace mantel instead of in the fire," Jason's dad said. "Thank you, Mr. Stevens."

The older man smiled. "Come over sometime and see my collection of ducks," he said. "I enjoy carving them. When I see the old piece of wood change into something beautiful, I like to think of what the Lord did for me. I was an unworthy sinner, living a life of pride and selfishness, yet the Lord made me a new creation in him!"

"I never thought of it like that," Jason said. "From now on, every time I look at the duck made out of firewood, I'll think of how the Lord made the old sinful me into a new creature, too!"

HOW ABOUT YOU? Have you ever thought that the Lord couldn't love you because you're "so bad"? He tells you in his Word that he loved the whole world so much that he gave his life. He does love you, and if you accept him as your personal Savior, he will change you into a new creation! *L.M.W.*

TO MEMORIZE: You have clothed yourselves with a brand-new nature that is continually being renewed as you learn more and more about Christ, who created this new nature within you. *Colossians 3:10*

13 February

BEND YOUR KNEES

FROM THE BIBLE:

Listen to my prayer, O God.
Do not ignore my cry for help!
Please listen and answer me,
for I am overwhelmed by my troubles.

PSALM 55:1-2

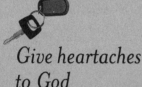

Give heartaches to God

RICKY SAT slumped on the porch as Uncle Bob and his mother unloaded furniture. His dad had filed for divorce. Now he and his mother were moving to a smaller, cheaper place. Ricky had cried and begged, but nothing had changed—except him. He felt bitter. He didn't even try to pray anymore. But he did feel terribly lonely. He not only missed his father; he missed his heavenly Father, too.

Mother smiled as she and Uncle Bob came up the stairs. *How can she be smiling?* Ricky thought angrily. *Maybe she asked Dad to leave.*

"Please help us lift this dresser," Mother called.

Ricky grumbled as he stooped over to lift his end. "No, Ricky!" Uncle Bob shouted. "You'll hurt your back that way. Lift your load with your knees, not your back."

Mother sighed. "That's what I've been doing, Bob."

"Good," said Uncle Bob. "You don't need a backache on top of your heartache."

"I'm not talking about lifting furniture," said Mother. "I'm talking about my heavy heart. I've been lifting it to God on my knees in prayer. I've found it's not the load that can hurt you, it's how you carry it. I don't want to get bitter. I want to keep trusting God."

"How about you, Ricky?" asked Uncle Bob. "How have you been carrying your heartache? You need to lift that load with your knees, too. Let your heavenly Father help you carry it."

Ricky smiled. "I will, Uncle Bob." Then he bent his knees and lifted his end of the dresser.

HOW ABOUT YOU? Are you carrying a heavy load? Does it seem you have more than your share of troubles? Don't try to carry them alone. Get on your knees and lift your load to the Lord in prayer. He'll help you carry it. *B.J.W.*

TO MEMORIZE: Give all your worries and cares to God, for he cares about what happens to you.
1 Peter 5:7

14 February

A SPECIAL LOVE

FROM THE BIBLE:

Dear friends, let us continue to love one another, for love comes from God. Anyone who loves is born of God and knows God. But anyone who does not love does not know God—for God is love.

God showed how much he loved us by sending his only Son into the world so that we might have eternal life through him. This is real love. It is not that we loved God, but that he loved us and sent his Son as a sacrifice to take away our sins.

1 JOHN 4:7-10

God loves you

"I DON'T SEE what's so special about Jesus dying to save people," Bobby said bluntly.

"You don't?" his mother said in amazement.

"No," he said. "Lots of soldiers have died so we can be free."

"True," agreed Mother, "and that's special, isn't it?"

"Sure," said Bobby, "but if I could die to save ten people from hell, I think I'd do it. Jesus saved thousands of people when he died. Wouldn't anyone be willing to die to save as many people as Jesus did?"

His mother thought for a minute, then answered, "Bobby, would you die for a thousand grasshoppers?"

Bobby grinned. "You kiddin'?"

"I'm serious," said Mother. "Don't you suppose we look like grasshoppers in the sight of the Lord?"

Bobby frowned. Somehow he had always pictured God as just another man, not as a great big God looming over him.

"But there's one important difference between how you see a grasshopper and how God sees you," Mother continued. "You may not care about the grasshopper, but God *loves* you! The Bible tells us that while we were still sinners, Christ died for us. His love makes all the difference in the world."

Bobby smiled.

His mother hugged him. "Bobby, if you had been the only person in the world, Jesus would have died just for you. In fact, he did die for you—for you, personally."

HOW ABOUT YOU? Jesus died for you, too. What love! All the love we talk about on Valentine's Day is nothing compared to the love of Jesus. Do you appreciate what he did for you on the cross? Have you received his gift of salvation? If not, why don't you invite him now to be your Savior and to take control of your life. Then thank him for loving you. *B.J.W.*

TO MEMORIZE: God showed his great love for us by sending Christ to die for us while we were still sinners. *Romans 5:8*

15 February

POISONED MINDS

FROM THE BIBLE:

My dear brothers and sisters, how can you claim that you have faith in our glorious Lord Jesus Christ if you favor some people more than others?

For instance, suppose someone comes into your meeting dressed in fancy clothes and expensive jewelry, and another comes in who is poor and dressed in shabby clothes. If you give special attention and a good seat to the rich person, but you say to the poor one, "You can stand over there, or else sit on the floor"—well, doesn't this discrimination show that you are guided by wrong motives? . . .

But if you pay special attention to the rich, you are committing a sin, for you are guilty of breaking that law.

And the person who keeps all of the laws except one is as guilty as the person who has broken all of God's laws.

JAMES 2:1-4, 9-10

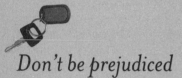

Don't be prejudiced

TOMMY WAS the new boy at school. He was a Native American Indian, and most of the children in his grade had never seen an Indian. His mother greeted him as he arrived home one day. "How was school?" she asked.

"Awful!" answered Tommy. "The kids think Indians wear war paint and feathers and say, 'Ugh! How! Me Big Chief Tommy Hawk.' "

"Oh, Tommy. Has someone been teasing you?"

Tommy nodded, almost in tears.

"I know what it's like," Mother said. "I'm an Indian too. But I'm proud of my heritage. The fact is, anywhere you live, you will meet people with prejudices."

"What are prejudices?" asked Tommy.

"Prejudices are opinions people form before the facts are known. They include a dislike of people who are different," Mother said. "Tell me about the other kids in your class."

"They're mostly just regular kids," answered Tommy. "Marsha's different, though. Every day a chauffeur in a big black Cadillac brings her to school and picks her up. She's a snob!"

"Tommy!" exclaimed Mother.

"Well, she is," Tommy insisted. "She goes around with her nose in the air."

"Tommy," scolded Mother, "you don't even know Marsha, but you're judging her like others judged you.

"There are more kinds of prejudices than just racial prejudices," Mother continued. "Some people are prejudiced against other religions, or against the rich, the poor, or the disabled. All prejudices are wrong. That's what the Bible is talking about when it says we shouldn't show partiality."

HOW ABOUT YOU? Do you tease or avoid someone of a different race, someone who attends a different church, or someone who is different in other ways? This is not pleasing to God. Ask him to forgive you, and determine to treat those "different" people just as you would want to be treated yourself. *B.J.W.*

TO MEMORIZE: If you pay special attention to the rich, you are committing a sin. *James 2:9*

A CAGE OR A CASTLE?

FROM THE BIBLE:

Keep on asking, and you will be given what you ask for. Keep on looking, and you will find. Keep on knocking, and the door will be opened. For everyone who asks, receives. Everyone who seeks, finds. And the door is opened to everyone who knocks. You parents—if your children ask for a loaf of bread, do you give them a stone instead? Or if they ask for a fish, do you give them a snake? Of course not! If you sinful people know how to give good gifts to your children, how much more will your heavenly Father give good gifts to those who ask him.

MATTHEW 7:7-11

Find happiness in God's will

BRYAN CUT doors and windows in an old refrigerator carton, put an old throw rug in it, and climbed inside. Mother soon heard little Joey crying from Bryan's room. "Mommy, Bryan won't let me come in his castle!"

"He keeps jumping around inside," complained Bryan. "He'll wreck it." Mother set Joey in his high chair and gave him some toys.

Later, Mother again heard Joey crying. She was surprised to see him inside the big box, crying as he peered out the window. "Bryan won't let me out of the cage!" he sobbed.

"Bryan!" scolded Mother. "Take that chair away from the door and let Joey out."

Bryan sheepishly moved the chair, and his little brother scrambled out quickly.

"He kept trying to get in, so I thought if I made him stay in there awhile, he'd get tired of it," said Bryan. "I turned it into a cage, but it's still the same box."

Mother looked thoughtfully at the castle-turned-cage. "You know, that cage reminds me of how some people feel about obeying God. They think they won't ever be happy because they won't get to do what they want to do. But people who really know the Lord consider his will to be the happiest castle on earth. They want to obey him, because they love him. It all depends on how you look at it!"

HOW ABOUT YOU? Do you go to church, read the Bible, and sing in the choir out of duty or habit? Or do you really enjoy serving the Lord and doing his will? The place that he wants you to serve him may seem like a "cage" or a "castle," depending on how you look at it. God knows what's best for you. Be happy where he puts you. *S.L.K.*

TO MEMORIZE: Whatever is good and perfect comes to us from God above. *James 1:17*

17 February

OLD AND HONORABLE

FROM THE BIBLE:

Never speak harshly to an older man, but appeal to him respectfully as though he were your own father. Talk to the younger men as you would to your own brothers. Treat the older women as you would your mother, and treat the younger women with all purity as your own sisters.

The church should care for any widow who has no one else to care for her. But if she has children or grandchildren, their first responsibility is to show godliness at home and repay their parents by taking care of them. This is something that pleases God very much.

1 TIMOTHY 5:1-4

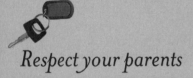

Respect your parents

"I JUST READ the strangest story," Anne told her mom. "It's about a man and his wife. The man's father lived with them. He was old and sick, and his hands shook. The couple got tired of seeing him knock over their good dishes, so they made him eat from a wooden bowl and sit in the corner. But when the old man still spilled food, they made him eat out of a feeding trough for animals!"

"That is strange—and cruel," said Mom.

"Here's the strangest part of the story," Anne continued. "The couple had a son, and one day they saw him whittling, hollowing out a log. The father asked what he was doing, and the boy said, 'I'm making a trough so it will be ready when you're old and come to live with me.' " Anne paused. "Mom, do you think that's a true story?"

"Probably not," answered her mother, "but there are many people who don't respect or care for their parents."

Anne nodded. "Connie's grandmother lives with them and isn't allowed to come out of her room when they have company. Connie says it's because she's had a stroke and talks funny."

"That's sad," said Mother with a sigh. "God's Word instructs children to honor their parents, no matter how old they are. If you start showing them respect and honor when you're young, it will become a habit. Then it will be natural for you to show them love and care when they get old."

HOW ABOUT YOU? Do you honor your parents and show respect to your grandparents? Do you treat all old people the way you'll want to be treated when you grow old? God commands you to respect and honor your parents all your life. Start now, and it will be easier to do when you're older. *C.R.*

TO MEMORIZE: Love each other with genuine affection, and take delight in honoring each other. *Romans 12:10*

18 February

WHAT WE HAVE

FROM THE BIBLE:

True religion with contentment is great wealth. After all, we didn't bring anything with us when we came into the world, and we certainly cannot carry anything with us when we die. So if we have enough food and clothing, let us be content. But people who long to be rich fall into temptation and are trapped by many foolish and harmful desires that plunge them into ruin and destruction. For the love of money is at the root of all kinds of evil. And some people, craving money, have wandered from the faith and pierced themselves with many sorrows.

But you, Timothy, belong to God; so run from all these evil things, and follow what is right and good. Pursue a godly life, along with faith, love, perseverance, and gentleness. Fight the good fight for what we believe. Hold tightly to the eternal life that God has given you, which you have confessed so well before many witnesses.

1 TIMOTHY 6:6-12

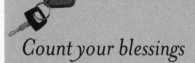

Count your blessings

JARED SIGHED as he unlocked the door and went inside. He shut the door and locked it. "Tim's lucky. His mom is home baking cookies, but I have to peel potatoes and put dumb old meat loaf in the oven," he said. The apartment seemed less empty when he talked out loud. "I wish I had a pet."

Jared grumbled as he peeled potatoes. Soon his mother came home. "Hi, honey, how was school?"

"OK," he said.

"Thanks for putting the meat loaf in the oven. It sure smells good." She looked at him closely. "Is something wrong?"

He hesitated, but soon he was telling her his troubles, especially that he hated coming home to an empty house.

"You know I have to work," Mom said. "I'd rather be home, or at least work from home, but right now that's not possible. And I wish you could have a pet, but the landlord won't allow that."

Her shoulders slumped, but then she sat up. "Jared, you have something very important that many of your friends don't have—you have Jesus," she reminded him. "Why don't we make a list of the things we have. I'll start." Mom picked up a pen and paper. "We have a place to live."

"And clothes," Jared added.

Mom wrote it down. "You can go to school, and I have a job," she said. "What else?"

"Friends."

"We have a church where we can worship God."

Jared sniffed the air and grinned. "We have meat loaf. Let's eat!"

HOW ABOUT YOU? Do your friends have something you wish you had? Instead of dwelling on it, make a list of what you have. Learn to be content in your circumstances and even give thanks for them. As you do, you'll find they don't seem quite so bad anymore. *V.L.C.*

TO MEMORIZE: No matter what happens, always be thankful, for this is God's will for you who belong to Christ Jesus. *1 Thessalonians 5:18*

19 February

GIVE THEM A CHANCE!

FROM THE BIBLE:

Every time I think of you, I give thanks to my God. I always pray for you, and I make my requests with a heart full of joy because you have been my partners in spreading the Good News about Christ from the time you first heard it until now. And I am sure that God, who began the good work within you, will continue his work until it is finally finished on that day when Christ Jesus comes back again. . . .

I pray that your love for each other will overflow more and more, and that you will keep on growing in your knowledge and understanding. For I want you to understand what really matters, so that you may live pure and blameless lives until Christ returns. May you always be filled with the fruit of your salvation—those good things that are produced in your life by Jesus Christ—for this will bring much glory and praise to God.

PHILIPPIANS 1:3-6, 9-11

Help Christians grow

RUDY SLOUCHED in a chair. "Hey, Mom, remember I told you that my friend, Pete, accepted Christ last month?"

"Of course I remember," said Mother.

"Well, I saw Pete smoking in the school parking lot today," Rudy said. "I figured he would quit smoking now that he's a Christian. I even heard him use a swear word. Some Christian he turned out to be!"

Mother looked thoughtful. "That's too bad, Rudy," she began. Just then, they heard a faint cry coming from down the hall. "Your sister's awake," said Mother. "Would you go tell her she can get up from her nap?"

Rudy looked puzzled. "But Jennifer's only six months old," he argued. "You know that babies can't walk until they're about a year old. Give her a chance to grow up!"

"The same chance you're giving Pete, you mean?" asked his mother. Rudy looked confused, so after she had gone to get Jennifer, Mother explained. "Babies can't do everything as soon as they're born; they need time to grow. It's the same way with new Christians. As they go to church, read the Bible and pray, and spend time with other Christians, God helps them grow spiritually. But we have to be patient. It takes time!"

"I see," said Rudy. "I'll try being more of a friend to Pete, and I'll pray that God will help him grow—and me, too!"

HOW ABOUT YOU? You may be tempted to criticize when you see a new Christian falling into sin. But he or she needs help and encouragement, not criticism. Perhaps you can share some Bible verses that deal with the problem. Then pray for that person and wait for God to help him or her grow. *S.L.K.*

TO MEMORIZE: God, who began the good work within you, will continue his work until it is finally finished on that day when Christ Jesus comes back again. *Philippians 1:6*

20 February

AN IMPORTANT SEAL

FROM THE BIBLE:

God's truth stands firm like a foundation stone with this inscription: "The Lord knows those who are his," and "Those who claim they belong to the Lord must turn away from all wickedness."

In a wealthy home some utensils are made of gold and silver, and some are made of wood and clay. The expensive utensils are used for special occasions, and the cheap ones are for everyday use. If you keep yourself pure, you will be a utensil God can use for his purpose. Your life will be clean, and you will be ready for the Master to use you for every good work.

Run from anything that stimulates youthful lust. Follow anything that makes you want to do right. Pursue faith and love and peace, and enjoy the companionship of those who call on the Lord with pure hearts.

2 TIMOTHY 2:19-22

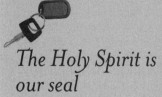

JASON WATCHED his father stamp several envelopes with an embosser. "What are you doing, Dad?" he asked.

"This is our company's seal, Jason. It displays our trademark and our motto," Dad explained. "The raised marks make it impossible for anyone to erase it."

"What's your company motto?" asked Jason.

" 'Old-fashioned service with new-fashioned materials,' " said Dad proudly.

"Do all companies have seals?" Jason asked.

"Some do," said Dad. "So do the fifty states. Our Wisconsin seal says, 'Forward.' Our country has a seal too. It's a Latin phrase that means, 'Out of many, one.' "

"Hey, that's neat," Jason said.

"There's another important seal, Jason," said Dad. "Take your Bible and look up 2 Timothy 2:19."

Jason quickly turned to the verse and read, "Nevertheless the solid foundation of God stands, having this seal: 'The Lord knows those who are His.' "

"You see, Jason, when we became Christians we were sealed with the Holy Spirit," said Dad. "*Our* motto could be 'The Lord knows those who are his.' "

Jason nodded. "It's kinda like your company's seal, Dad," he decided. "It can't be erased. And when people see the seal on a letter, they know it's from your business. When we're sealed with the Holy Spirit, people should be able to see that we belong to the Lord!"

HOW ABOUT YOU? Have you ever seen a seal with a motto or a picture representing a country or a business? If you're a Christian, you were sealed with the Holy Spirit when you believed in Christ alone to save you. You belong to the Lord, and nothing can change that. But, remember, others should be able to see by your life that you have his seal upon you.
L.M.W.

TO MEMORIZE: Having believed, you were marked in him with a seal, the promised Holy Spirit.
Ephesians 1:13 (NIV)

The Holy Spirit is our seal

21 February

GOD'S TRAINING SCHOOL

FROM THE BIBLE:

In everything you do, stay away from complaining and arguing, so that no one can speak a word of blame against you. You are to live clean, innocent lives as children of God in a dark world full of crooked and perverse people. Let your lives shine brightly before them. Hold tightly to the word of life, so that when Christ returns, I will be proud that I did not lose the race and that my work was not useless. But even if my life is to be poured out like a drink offering to complete the sacrifice of your faithful service (that is, if I am to die for you), I will rejoice, and I want to share my joy with all of you. And you should be happy about this and rejoice with me.

PHILIPPIANS 2:14-18

Be patient

"HI, MOM, hi Gram." Shelly put her books down.

"Hello, Shelly," said Mom. "I was fixing some coffee for Gram and me. Would you like some juice?"

"Sure," answered Shelly.

"Why are we all dressed up?" asked Grandma.

"We're having dinner with the Hoyles," Mom replied.

"The Hoyles are so nice. I remember when we spent a week with them at the lake. It was so pretty. . . ." Grandma's voice trailed off. Shelly slammed down her glass. She must have heard that story a hundred times! Mom shot a warning look at Shelly. Shelly opened one of her books.

"Why are we all dressed up?" Grandma asked again, and again Mom answered patiently. "The Hoyles are such nice people," said Grandma. Shelly picked up her book and juice and left the room.

"Mom, how can you be so patient?" Shelly asked later.

"I remind myself that Grandma is sick with Alzheimer's disease and she doesn't remember," Mom said. "It's like a short circuit in the brain. She can't help it."

Shelly frowned. "But how come she has to live here? My friends laugh at her."

"I know it isn't easy sometimes," Mom said, "but we love Grandma, and this is what is best for her."

Grandma came to the bedroom door and smiled. "Why are we all dressed up?" she asked.

Shelly sighed, then grinned. "We're having dinner with the Hoyles, Gram."

"They're such nice people. I remember the time we were together at the lake," Grandma said cheerfully.

"Tell me about it, Grandma," said Shelly.

HOW ABOUT YOU? Do you need extra understanding or patience with a friend or family member? Ask the Lord to help you develop that patience. As you honor him by showing love and kindness now, you will also be preparing for whatever ministry the Lord has for you as an adult. *V.L.C.*

TO MEMORIZE: By standing firm, you will win your souls. *Luke 21:19*

22 February

THE MIGHTY EGG

FROM THE BIBLE:

If someone says, "I love God," but hates another Christian, that person is a liar; for if we don't love people we can see, how can we love God, whom we have not seen? And God himself has commanded that we must love not only him but our Christian brothers and sisters, too.

1 JOHN 4:20-21

Love, don't criticize

"OH, GOOD! I love scrambled eggs!" Julie said as she and John came to the breakfast table. After thanking God for the food, they began to eat.

"I'm looking forward to hearing our new pastor's sermon today," said Dad.

"I'm sure Mrs.Grady won't like it," mumbled John. "She's always complaining that the sermon is too long or not as good as our old pastor's."

"People sure like to criticize others, don't they?"

"I'm afraid they do, and that's a shame," Mother said, "especially among Christians. As members of Christ's body, we should love one another. We get enough criticism from the world without picking on each other!"

Dad took a raw egg out of the refrigerator. "This discussion reminds me of something I read about eggs," he said and held it up. "An eggshell is strong enough so that the hen can sit on it without breaking it. The rounded shape protects the chick if the egg is struck from the outside. But do you know how the small, helpless chick is able to hatch?"

"It pecks its way out," said John.

"Right," said Dad. "Although the shell resists pressure well from the outside, it cracks easily when pecked from within. In the same way, a church can resist outside pressure and persecution as long as Christians unite together in love. But when they start picking on one another, their fellowship is easily destroyed."

Julie smiled. "I'll remember that the next time I'm tempted to criticize someone—especially another Christian," she said.

HOW ABOUT YOU? Are you in the habit of criticizing your pastor, your Sunday school teacher, or others in your church family? You should be especially careful about criticizing Christians. Satan himself is called "the accuser of our brethren" in Revelation 12:10. Don't do his work for him. Remember "the mighty egg"! *S.L.K.*

TO MEMORIZE: [Jesus said,] "Your love for one another will prove to the world that you are my disciples." *John 13:35*

23 February

GROWING UP
(PART 1)

FROM THE BIBLE:

You made all the delicate, inner parts of my body
and knit me together in my mother's womb.
Thank you for making me so wonderfully complex!
Your workmanship is marvelous—and how well I know it.
You watched me as I was being formed in utter seclusion,
as I was woven together in the dark of the womb.
You saw me before I was born.
Every day of my life was recorded in your book.
Every moment was laid out
before a single day had passed.

PSALM 139:13-16

Love the disabled

MADELINE AND ERIC were so happy to have a new baby brother. Madeline especially liked to help Mother take care of little Luke. But one day when the children came home from school, they found Dad in deep thought and Mother wiping her eyes. "Mother! What's wrong?" Madeline asked. "You took Luke to the doctor today, didn't you? Is there something wrong with him?"

"Yes, Madeline, there is," answered Mother. "Luke isn't growing normally. He's not doing the things he should be doing at his age. The doctor calls it being developmentally disabled or mentally slow."

Eric and Madeline were stunned! Their baby brother was slow mentally? How could God allow such a thing to happen? "But, why, Mother?" they asked. "Why?"

Dad answered. "We don't know why. We only know that God has a reason—a good reason—and that he's in control. Someday, perhaps in heaven, we'll know why. But in the meantime we'll just go on loving him and caring for him."

Madeline burst into tears. "Not normal!" she exclaimed. "Luke's not normal!"

Dad spoke again. "This is hard to accept," he said, "but God is never unfair. Luke needs us more, so we'll love him more. In giving him love and happiness, we'll gain love and happiness too."

HOW ABOUT YOU? Do you know any disabled people? For reasons known only to himself, God made some people with special challenges—physical and/or mental disabilities. Make an effort to smile at them and talk to them. Never stare at them, make fun of them, or say unkind things about them. There are many wonderful, lovable human beings with special problems, and they have much to offer. Remember, God made them. He loves them, and you can love them too. *A.G.L.*

TO MEMORIZE: Who makes people so they can speak or not speak, hear or not hear, see or not see? Is it not I, the Lord? *Exodus 4:11*

AFTER MADELINE and Eric learned that their baby brother would never be able to do some of the things most children do, their attitudes toward him changed. Eric played with Luke more and encouraged him to learn new things. But Madeline gave him less attention. She only helped take care of him when she had to.

"Madeline," said Mother one day, "you used to love to take Luke for a ride in the park. Why don't you do that anymore?"

Madeline blushed. "It just isn't the same as before," she stammered. "Luke's not like other babies. Taking care of him isn't fun anymore."

"Luke is the same sweet baby he always was," Mother told her. "But *you* have changed! You're not the same sweet, happy girl that you were."

"But, Mother," objected Madeline, "you can't blame me for being disappointed!"

"We were all disappointed," Mother replied, "but we didn't all grow bitter. You were saved several years ago. If you were growing spiritually, as you should be, you would be concerned about Luke instead of yourself. You wouldn't be ashamed. Madeline, you are disabled too! You're a spiritually disabled child."

"Oh, Mother," Madeline said, her eyes glistening with tears. "I never thought of myself that way! Please forgive me. Here—give Luke to me. I'll love him and help take care of him. Oh, Luke, you are sweet!"

Mother smiled. "And so are you, dear—now! You are growing again."

HOW ABOUT YOU? Are you growing spiritually? Are you learning to be more cheerful and to be kinder to your brothers and sisters? Are you being more helpful around the house? Growing physically and mentally are important, but we often forget that growing spiritually is even more important. Learn from God's Word what he wants of you. Ask him to help you grow. *A.G.L.*

TO MEMORIZE: Grow in the special favor and knowledge of our Lord and Savior Jesus Christ. *2 Peter 3:18*

GROWING UP
(PART 2)

FROM THE BIBLE:

So get rid of all malicious behavior and deceit. Don't just pretend to be good! Be done with hypocrisy and jealousy and backstabbing. You must crave pure spiritual milk so that you can grow into the fullness of your salvation. Cry out for this nourishment as a baby cries for milk, now that you have had a taste of the Lord's kindness.

Come to Christ, who is the living cornerstone of God's temple. He was rejected by the people, but he is precious to God who chose him.

And now God is building you, as living stones, into his spiritual temple. What's more, you are God's holy priests, who offer the spiritual sacrifices that please him because of Jesus Christ.

1 PETER 2:1-5

Grow spiritually

25 February

A MAN OF PRINCIPLE

FROM THE BIBLE:

Happy are people of integrity,
who follow the law of the Lord.
Happy are those who obey his decrees
and search for him with all their hearts.
They do not compromise with evil,
and they walk only in his paths.
You have charged us
to keep your commandments carefully.
Oh, that my actions would consistently
reflect your principles!
Then I will not be disgraced
when I compare my life with your commands.
When I learn your righteous laws,
I will thank you by living as I should!

PSALM 119:1-7

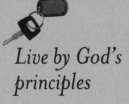

Live by God's principles

"HEY, STEVE! How many raffle tickets do you want?" asked Jon after school.

"None. I don't believe in raffle tickets."

"If you don't sell tickets, you won't be doing your share to earn money for our class trip," Jon scolded. "Let me know tomorrow how many you'll take."

Steve sighed. Should he give in and sell the tickets? Other kids in his class were Christians, and it didn't seem to bother them. But he agreed with Dad's argument that buying raffle tickets was like buying lottery tickets; it was gambling.

That evening, Steve and his dad watched a film on the life of Eric Liddell. Eric, a Scotsman, had been expected to win a gold medal in the 100-meter race during the 1924 Olympics. He refused to run, however, when he learned the race would be held on Sunday. He felt it was important to honor God by keeping the Lord's Day special for him. Later he was able to compete in the 400-meter race and win a gold medal.

After seeing the film, Steve knew what to do. "I'll earn money for our class trip by mowing lawns instead of selling raffle tickets," he told his dad.

Dad nodded. "I'm proud of you, Son," he said. "Although others ran in that Olympic race and won gold medals, Eric is the one who is most remembered today. And he's remembered not for running a race but for being a man of principle!"

HOW ABOUT YOU? Are you having trouble making decisions? Don't let anyone talk you into listening to certain types of music, watching questionable TV shows, or doing anything that goes against the Bible. Learn to live how God wants you to live. Be a person of principles—God's principles—and stick to them. *J.L.H.*

TO MEMORIZE: If you obey the commands of the Lord your God and walk in his ways, the Lord will establish you as his holy people. *Deuteronomy 28:9*

PRETTY PACKAGE

FROM THE BIBLE:

Stop judging others, and you will not be judged. For others will treat you as you treat them. Whatever measure you use in judging others, it will be used to measure how you are judged. And why worry about a speck in your friend's eye when you have a log in your own? How can you think of saying, "Let me help you get rid of that speck in your eye," when you can't see past the log in your own eye? Hypocrite! First get rid of the log from your own eye; then perhaps you will see well enough to deal with the speck in your friend's eye. . . .

Do for others what you would like them to do for you. This is a summary of all that is taught in the law and the prophets.

MATTHEW 7:1-5, 12

Don't judge by appearance only

WHEN LIANA came into the kitchen one morning, her family surprised her with shouts of "Happy birthday!"

"We thought we'd let you open presents now," said Mother, pointing to the gifts beside Liana's plate.

Eagerly, Liana reached for a package with a teddy bear on top. Inside, she found a cute little notepad and pen from her brother. "Thanks, Bro," she said. Next, she opened a package wrapped in rainbow colors. It was from her sister, and it contained a new coloring book and markers. "Oh, good!" she exclaimed. "Half of my old markers are dried up." Finally, she reached for a plain white envelope and pulled out a small certificate. Her eyes widened. "I'm going to get a kitty?" The certificate read, "Good for one small kitten. Love, Mom and Dad."

"You and Mom can pick it up after school," said Dad, smiling.

"Oh, thank you!" she said.

As they went to get the kitten after school, Liana told her mother about a new girl in her class. "She looks kind of sloppy. She could use some new clothes. And her hair is a straggly mess."

"Be careful, Liana. People notice how others look, but the Lord sees the heart," Mother reminded her. "You can't tell what's in the package by the wrappings, you know." As they pulled up in front of the pet store, Liana agreed. She remembered the contents of the plain white envelope.

HOW ABOUT YOU? Do you make quick judgments when you meet new kids? Do you decide whether you like them by what they wear rather than by what they are? That's not God's way. He judges others—and you—by what he sees inside. Don't judge people just by the way they look. Ask the Lord to help you love them as he does. *H.W.M.*

TO MEMORIZE: People judge by outward appearance, but the Lord looks at a person's thoughts and intentions. *1 Samuel 16:7*

27 February

FREE AS THE AIR

FROM THE BIBLE:

When people work, their wages are not a gift. Workers earn what they receive. But people are declared righteous because of their faith, not because of their work.

King David spoke of this, describing the happiness of an undeserving sinner who is declared to be righteous:

"Oh, what joy for those whose
disobedience is forgiven,
whose sins are put out of sight.
Yes, what joy for those
whose sin is no longer counted
against them by the Lord."

ROMANS 4:4-8

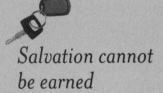

Salvation cannot be earned

"I DON'T UNDERSTAND Sherri," Rachel told her mother. "First she gave me a cute eraser to pay me back for helping her with her math. Then she gave me a Tootsie Roll to pay me back for a cookie I gave her. She always thinks she has to pay me back."

Mom shook her head.

"She even thinks she has to pay God for everything he gives," Rachel continued. "She wonders how anybody could accept the idea that people go to heaven by believing in Jesus. She said she's earning her way by being baptized and joining the church and by living a good life."

"Oh, that is serious!" exclaimed Mother. "Let's pray that she'll see how foolish that is."

A couple days later, Rachel and Sherri conducted an experiment in science class. By combining several chemicals, they made a gas that smelled like rotten eggs! "Air! Give me air!" gasped Sherri as she rushed to the window. Rachel, too, gulped cold air. Suddenly Rachel got an idea. "Hold your breath, Sherri," she said, "until you pay for the air!"

"What?!"

"You said you wouldn't take something for nothing, remember?" Rachel reminded her. "Yet every day, you breathe the air for free. If you can accept God's gift of air, why is it so hard to accept his gift of salvation?"

Sherri nodded slowly. "Maybe I better think that over again."

HOW ABOUT YOU? The air that God gives us is a wonderful gift, isn't it? It would be foolish to think we could ever pay for it. Salvation is an even more wonderful gift. You can never earn it. All you can earn is death—being separated from God forever. Will you choose to refuse God's gift of salvation, or will you accept it and receive eternal life? *H.W.M.*

TO MEMORIZE: For the wages of sin is death, but the free gift of God is eternal life through Christ Jesus our Lord. *Romans 6:23*

THE HOMECOMING

FROM THE BIBLE:

For we know that when this earthly tent we live in is taken down—when we die and leave these bodies—we will have a home in heaven, an eternal body made for us by God himself and not by human hands. . . .

So we are always confident, even though we know that as long as we live in these bodies we are not at home with the Lord. That is why we live by believing and not by seeing. Yes, we are fully confident, and we would rather be away from these bodies, for then we will be at home with the Lord.

2 CORINTHIANS 5:1, 6-8

Heaven is the Christian's "home"

LINDA WAS SAD. She and her family had just returned from her grandmother's funeral. An older sister, Brooke, lived far away. Brooke had a baby only three days old, so she wasn't able to come to the funeral. "Now Grandma will never get to see Brooke's baby," Linda cried.

Her parents comforted her. "Try to understand that God knows best," they told her. "You need to trust him."

One night Linda went to a slumber party. The fun was just beginning when Linda's father telephoned to say she'd have to come home—he had a surprise for her. Linda protested, but Dad was firm and came to pick her up. Arriving at home, she unhappily opened the door to the house and heard a familiar voice call, "Surprise!" It was Brooke and her husband, Bob, with baby Jane!

"Oh, let me see the baby!" Linda exclaimed. "Isn't she cute!"

What a happy time they had visiting and admiring the baby. "But I still wish Grandma could have seen Jane," said Linda.

"We all do," answered Dad. "But having Brooke's family come home reminds me of the homecoming that is taking place in heaven because Grandma 'came home.' It's been eight years since she has seen Granddad. And then there was her brother, who was killed in the war, and other relatives and friends who went to heaven before she did."

Linda was thoughtful. "You mean God called her home to heaven just as you called me home tonight?"

"That's right," Dad said with a smile. "Just think how happy she is in heaven right now."

Linda was beginning to understand. "God does know best, doesn't he?"

HOW ABOUT YOU? Has someone you love gone to heaven? When it hurts, remember how happy he or she is. God knows what is best for you, too. Trust him. *B.J.W.*

TO MEMORIZE: For to me, living is for Christ, and dying is even better. *Philippians 1:21*

29 February

THE HITCHHIKER

FROM THE BIBLE:

But I don't need to write to you about the Christian love that should be shown among God's people. For God himself has taught you to love one another. Indeed, your love is already strong toward all the Christians in all of Macedonia. Even so, dear friends, we beg you to love them more and more. This should be your ambition: to live a quiet life, minding your own business and working with your hands, just as we commanded you before. As a result, people who are not Christians will respect the way you live, and you will not need to depend on others to meet your financial needs.

1 THESSALONIANS 4:9-12

Do your share

"OH, NO!" exclaimed Mother. "Look where they stacked the firewood! I told them to put it on the patio."

"Looks like you get to move the firewood, Justin," said Dad as they pulled into the driveway.

"Why do I get all the dirty jobs around here?" demanded Justin.

"I have to work on the car, Mother has to cook dinner, and I hardly think Jennifer can move all that wood."

"Can, too!" argued four-year-old Jennifer. Later, as Justin loaded a red wagon with wood, Jennifer announced, "I'm gonna help you."

"Great," said Justin unenthusiastically as he began to pull a load. "Wow! This is heavy!"

Jennifer got behind the wagon and started pushing. "See, Justin, I can help."

"Yeah," agreed Justin reluctantly. "That does help." For several loads they worked together. Then Justin noticed that the loads were heavier. "Either I'm getting tired or the wood is gaining weight," he complained.

Dad looked up from his work. "No wonder it's heavier," he laughed. "You have a hitchhiker!" When Justin turned around, he saw Jennifer sitting on top of the wood.

"You get off right now, Jennifer!" ordered Justin.

"Now you can understand how much easier things are when everyone in the family does his fair share," said Dad as he helped Jennifer get down safely. "When someone sits down on the job, it's harder for everyone else. Jennifer is small, but when she pushed, your job was easier. When she hitchhiked, it made your job harder."

"Sure did," agreed Jason. "Now, little hitchhiker, start pushing again!"

HOW ABOUT YOU? Do you grumble and complain about doing your share of the work? Perhaps you do have more responsibility than your little brother or sister. That's because you're able to pull a heavier load. Be a good worker, not a hitchhiker. *B.J.W.*

TO MEMORIZE: This should be your ambition: to live a quiet life, minding your own business and working with your hands. *1 Thessalonians 4:11*

1 March

WATCH YOUR MANNERS

FROM THE BIBLE:

I will sing of your love and
justice.
I will praise you, Lord, with
songs.
I will be careful to live a
blameless life—
when will you come to my
aid?
I will lead a life of integrity
in my own home.
I will refuse to look at
anything vile and vulgar.
I hate all crooked dealings;
I will have nothing to do with
them.
I will reject perverse ideas
and stay away from every evil.
I will not tolerate people who
slander their neighbors.
I will not endure conceit and
pride.
I will keep a protective eye on the
godly,
so they may dwell with me in
safety.
Only those who are above
reproach
will be allowed to serve me.

PSALM 101:1-6

"EXCUSE ME." Dave reached across his sister's plate to get the salt.

"Next time you do that," scolded Alicia, "I'll pour salt on your head."

"Children!" exclaimed Mother. "Watch your manners! Dave, if you want something, please ask to have it passed."

As Alicia started to leave the table, Dad stopped her. "Alicia, you should first ask to be excused."

"Tell you what, kids—let's make a game to help you," Mother suggested. "Each time you use good manners, you get a check mark beside your name. Each time you use bad manners—like reaching in front of someone or interrupting when someone else is talking—we'll erase a check mark. At the end of each week, the winner gets a special treat."

The plan worked well. At the end of the first week, Dave was only a few points behind Alicia.

"Hey, this is fun," said Dave after receiving a check mark the next week. "I'm getting gooder and gooder at remem—"

"Better and better, not gooder and gooder," Alicia interrupted sarcastically.

"Oops!" Mother erased a mark behind Alicia's name. "You forgot the rule—don't interrupt."

The next day Dave was invited to stay overnight at his friend Bill's house. Bill's mother called the next day to say how well Dave behaved at their house.

That evening, Mom placed a check next to Dave's name. And when Alicia politely asked Dad to pass the milk, Mom placed a check next to Alicia's name. "I'm very proud of you, kids," she said.

HOW ABOUT YOU? Do you usually use your worst manners on your own family? Practicing good manners is important, and the place to begin is at home. Be thoughtful and courteous. Ask the Lord to help you overcome the weaknesses in your manners. *C.V.M.*

TO MEMORIZE: I will be careful to live a blameless life . . . I will lead a life of integrity in my own home. *Psalm 101:2*

Practice good manners

2 March

SUNDAY MORNING

FROM THE BIBLE:

Give to the Lord the glory he deserves!
Bring your offering and come to worship him.
Worship the Lord in all his holy splendor.
Let all the earth tremble before him.
Tell all the nations that the Lord is king.
The world is firmly established and cannot be shaken.
He will judge all peoples fairly.
Let the heavens be glad, and let the earth rejoice!
Let the sea and everything in it shout his praise!
Let the fields and their crops burst forth with joy!
Let the trees of the forest rustle with praise
before the Lord!
For the Lord is coming!
He is coming to judge the earth.
He will judge the world with righteousness
and all the nations with his truth.

PSALM 96:8-13

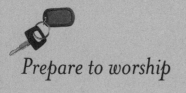

Prepare to worship

THE RUSH to get ready each Sunday morning at the Langs' house was getting out of hand. "Has anyone seen my blue socks and my Sunday school book?" yelled Steve. "I still have to learn this week's verse."

Leah rolled over in bed. "Morning already?" she said with a yawn. "It seems like I just got home from baby-sitting a little while ago." She got up and staggered down the hall. "Morning," she murmured as Mother emerged from the laundry room with Steve's blue socks. "Where's the iron, Mom? I have to press my dress."

Somehow, the Langs made it to church almost on time. They enjoyed the morning, although Leah had trouble keeping her eyes open during the sermon. On the way home, Dad spoke up. "I'm embarrassed about being late for Sunday school so often," he said. "Our Sunday mornings seem more and more disorganized, and they don't prepare our hearts for worship. Any suggestions?"

"We should get our clothes ready on Saturday," said Mother. "I'm at fault for allowing that problem."

"I should do my Sunday school lesson earlier in the week," admitted Steve.

"I feel badly about being so tired," said Leah. "I'm going to let people know I can only baby-sit until ten o'clock on Saturdays."

"And I'll start Sunday morning by playing Christian music on the stereo," said Dad. "That may help to prepare our minds to really worship the Lord."

HOW ABOUT YOU? What was it like at your house last Sunday morning? Were you prepared to worship God and learn from him when you walked into church? Why not follow the suggestions given in the story? Have your clothes ready on Saturday, learn your memory verse early, and get a good night's sleep. Then you'll be alert to learn from God's Word. *D.L.R.*

TO MEMORIZE: Enter his gates with thanksgiving; go into his courts with praise. Give thanks to him and bless his name. *Psalm 100:4*

TEMPORARY PERMANENT

TIM POURED a glass of milk to drink with the snack his mother had left for him. She was at the beauty salon getting a permanent. Tim was usually hungry after school, but today the food was as tasteless as sawdust. He sighed as he thought about his troubles. First, he'd lost his science assignment, and his teacher said he would have to do it over. His best friend had ignored him all day, and Tim didn't know why. Finally, Tim felt clueless about the afternoon math lesson, but he was too discouraged to ask for help.

"Why the unhappy face?" asked Mother, coming in the door.

"Everything went wrong today," mumbled Tim. As his mother sat down, he noticed her hair. "Your hair looks nice, Mom. Will it always stay this way now?"

Mother laughed. "I wish it would, but after a while it will start to lose its curl," she said.

"Well, why is it called a 'permanent' then?" asked Tim.

Mother smiled. "I think it's misnamed," she replied. "Many things we call 'permanent' don't last forever. But there's something that does—God's love. It's really permanent. His love goes on and on. Even when things go wrong and it seems he's forgotten us, he really hasn't. His love is still there."

Tim smiled. "That's nice to remember after the kind of day I've had," he said. "Thanks, Mom. When I look at your temporary permanent, I'll remember that God's love is really permanent."

HOW ABOUT YOU? When things go wrong, especially one thing after another, it's easy to get discouraged and forget God's love. But God doesn't forget you. His love is there, whether you're feeling it or not. It's an everlasting love. *C.E.Y.*

TO MEMORIZE: Long ago the Lord said to Israel: "I have loved you, my people, with an everlasting love. With unfailing love I have drawn you to myself." *Jeremiah 31:3*

FROM THE BIBLE:

O God, we meditate on your
unfailing love
as we worship in your Temple.
As your name deserves, O God,
you will be praised to the ends
of the earth.
Your strong right hand is
filled with victory.
Let the people on Mount Zion
rejoice.
Let the towns of Judah be
glad,
for your judgments are just.
Go, inspect the city of Jerusalem.
Walk around and count the
many towers.
Take note of the fortified walls,
and tour all the citadels,
that you may describe them
to future generations.
For that is what God is like.
He is our God forever and
ever,
and he will be our guide until
we die.

PSALM 48:9-14

God's love is permanent

4 March

HORN-A-THON

FROM THE BIBLE:

Take care! Don't do your good deeds publicly, to be admired, because then you will lose the reward from your Father in heaven. When you give a gift to someone in need, don't shout about it as the hypocrites do—blowing trumpets in the synagogues and streets to call attention to their acts of charity! I assure you, they have received all the reward they will ever get. But when you give to someone, don't tell your left hand what your right hand is doing. Give your gifts in secret, and your Father, who knows all secrets, will reward you.

And now about prayer. When you pray, don't be like the hypocrites who love to pray publicly on street corners and in the synagogues where everyone can see them. I assure you, that is all the reward they will ever get. But when you pray, go away by yourself, shut the door behind you, and pray to your Father secretly. Then your Father, who knows all secrets, will reward you.

MATTHEW 6:1-6

Give and serve unselfishly

"MOM, WILL YOU sponsor me for our school's jump-a-thon?" Jane waved a piece of paper. "Each of us kids will spend time jumping rope to raise money for starving people in Africa. People sign this list to donate a certain amount of money for every minute we jump."

Mom looked at the paper. "This is being held on the same day as the church prayer walk," she said. "I'm afraid you won't be able to go, honey. But it is a good cause, so I'll give a donation anyway."

"But, Mom!" Jane pouted. "The school is giving prizes to the kids who jump the longest, and the TV cameras will be there."

"I thought this was to benefit the starving people in Africa," said Mom. "It sounds like you're more interested in the attention and the prizes." Jane blushed, and her mom sighed. "Maybe this should be called a horn-a-thon instead of a jump-a-thon."

"What?" said Jane. "No one will be blowing horns!"

"They might be," replied Mom. "Jesus told us we should give to others quietly and without drawing unnecessary attention to ourselves. In Bible days, the Pharisees had someone blow a trumpet as they were on their way to do a good deed. In God's eyes, their giving had no eternal value because it was done out of pride instead of love."

"I see what you mean," Jane admitted. "I guess I have been kind of selfish. Instead of the jump-a-thon, I'll try to earn money by baby-sitting."

"That's the right attitude!" Mother said, smiling.

HOW ABOUT YOU? Do you give and serve the way God wants you to—simply, generously, without expecting reward? Don't seek recognition from others for every good thing you do. Obey God with the right attitude, and he'll reward you. *S.L.K.*

TO MEMORIZE: Take care! Don't do your good deeds publicly, to be admired, because then you will lose the reward from your Father in heaven. *Matthew 6:1*

5 March

MEAT, MILK, AND MICHAEL

FROM THE BIBLE

You have been Christians a long time now, and you ought to be teaching others. Instead, you need someone to teach you again the basic things a beginner must learn about the Scriptures. You are like babies who drink only milk and cannot eat solid food. And a person who is living on milk isn't very far along in the Christian life and doesn't know much about doing what is right. Solid food is for those who are mature, who have trained themselves to recognize the difference between right and wrong and then do what is right.
HEBREWS 5:12-14

Study God's Word

"AMANDA, HAVE YOU studied your Sunday school lesson and memorized your Bible verse?" asked her mom as she put one-year-old Michael in his high chair.

"No, Mom. The lesson seemed too hard. And the memory verse is thirty-six words long. I can't learn that!" answered nine-year-old Amanda.

As Mom tied Michael's bib, the telephone rang. "Amanda, will you feed Michael while I answer the phone?" Mom asked.

"OK, baby brother," Amanda said, "open your mouth. Oh, Michael, don't drool it down your chin!" Suddenly he banged his fist right into the bowl of baby food. Amanda was so startled she screamed. That made Michael cry, and he rubbed his grubby little fist in his eyes. When Mom returned, Amanda was trying to clean up the floor. "Oh, Mom, this is gross!" she said. "Can't I just give him a bottle?"

"Babies do need milk," answered Mom, grabbing a fresh dishcloth. "But as they grow older, they also need solid food to grow strong."

After dinner, Mom again suggested that Amanda study her Sunday school lesson. "But I told you," whined Amanda, "it's too hard!"

Mom then reminded Amanda of the day she had committed her life to Jesus Christ. "After three years as a Christian, you should be growing and wanting to learn deeper things about God. Just as Michael is learning to eat solid food, you ought to be eating the 'meaty' part of the Bible," she explained.

Amanda listened thoughtfully. "OK, Mom," she said finally. "I'll study my lesson and memorize that verse. I don't want to be a baby Christian forever!"

HOW ABOUT YOU? If you have been a Christian for any length of time, have you grown spiritually? You need to eat the 'meat' as well as drink the 'milk' of God's Word. *R.E.P.*

TO MEMORIZE: Solid food is for those who are mature, who have trained themselves to recognize the difference between right and wrong. *Hebrews 5:14*

6 March

THE BIRTH CERTIFICATE

FROM THE BIBLE:

Salvation that comes from trusting Christ—which is the message we preach—is already within easy reach. In fact, the Scriptures say, "The message is close at hand; it is on your lips and in your heart."

For if you confess with your mouth that Jesus is Lord and believe in your heart that God raised him from the dead, you will be saved. For it is by believing in your heart that you are made right with God, and it is by confessing with your mouth that you are saved. As the Scriptures tell us, "Anyone who believes in him will not be disappointed." Jew and Gentile are the same in this respect. They all have the same Lord, who generously gives his riches to all who ask for them. For "Anyone who calls on the name of the Lord will be saved."

ROMANS 10:8-13

You can know you're saved

"DAD . . . I know I've asked Jesus to forgive my sins and take over my life, but how can I really know I'm saved?"

Nathan's dad was delighted to talk about this with his son. "Who are your parents?" he asked.

"That's obvious!" said Nathan. "You and Mom are."

"How do you know?" Dad continued.

"Well, you've always been my parents." Dad opened a desk drawer and took out a piece of paper. "Hey, that's my birth certificate!" exclaimed Nathan. "It says right on it when I was born. That's proof!"

"Well, Nathan, God's Word is as good as this birth certificate—even better," Dad assured him. "You don't have to doubt anything in God's Word. He says if you believe in Jesus as your Savior and Lord, you're his child. When you trusted Jesus to save you from sin, we noted it in your Bible. Let's look."

Nathan opened his Bible and read from the inside cover page: "Nathan accepted the Lord Jesus Christ into his heart on April 10, 1999."

"Let's add a Bible verse," suggested Dad. After discussing it, Nathan copied Romans 10:13 into the front cover of his Bible. "Now," said Dad, "think of this Scripture as another kind of birth certificate—proof of your new birth in the Lord Jesus Christ."

"Thanks, Dad," Nathan said. "I know I'm saved because God says so."

HOW ABOUT YOU? Do you ever wonder if you're really saved? Make sure you've accepted Jesus as your personal Savior. Then pick a verse (such as John 1:12, John 3:16, Acts 16:31, Romans 10:9, or Romans 10:13) that tells you that you now belong to him. Whenever Satan causes you to doubt it, point to that verse. If you have truly done what it says, you are saved. *D.K.*

TO MEMORIZE: Anyone who calls on the name of the Lord will be saved. *Romans 10:13*

PLEASE PASS THE PEAS

FROM THE BIBLE:

I have become a servant of everyone so that I can bring them to Christ. When I am with the Jews, I become one of them so that I can bring them to Christ. When I am with those who follow the Jewish laws, I do the same, even though I am not subject to the law, so that I can bring them to Christ. When I am with the Gentiles who do not have the Jewish law, I fit in with them as much as I can. In this way, I gain their confidence and bring them to Christ. But I do not discard the law of God; I obey the law of Christ.

When I am with those who are oppressed, I share their oppression so that I might bring them to Christ. Yes, I try to find common ground with everyone so that I might bring them to Christ. I do all this to spread the Good News, and in doing so I enjoy its blessings.

1 CORINTHIANS 9:19-23

Learn about missionaries

"I KNOW YOU don't care for peas, Josh, but I want you to take a few," said Dad. Joshua reluctantly dropped a few peas on his plate.

"Pretend you're a missionary, like in the book I'm reading," suggested Sarah. "The natives have invited you to dinner. They offer you food you've never seen before. If you want them to accept you, you have to eat their food or you'll hurt their feelings."

"You mean they don't have peas in some countries? I'll go there!" Joshua said, grinning. "In the meantime, I'll pretend these peas are bugs!"

As Sarah made a face, Joshua turned to Mom. "Some night, let's all pretend we're in a different country. That would be fun!"

"Good idea," agreed Mom. "Let's pick a country where our church has a missionary. How about Japan? We could sit on the floor and eat with chopsticks."

"Or how about Italy?" said Sarah. "We could have pizza."

"I have an international cookbook," Mom said. "Sarah and I can do the cooking."

"I can decorate some place mats," offered Joshua. "I'll draw a map and pictures showing the country's products and plants on them."

Dad smiled. "I'll find out what kind of work the missionary does—whether it's starting churches, working in hospitals, or translating the Bible," he said. "Let's have our first missionary dinner next Saturday."

"Good," agreed Mom. "Now Joshua, since you're still in the United States, you need to finish your peas."

HOW ABOUT YOU? Could your family plan a "missions night"? If preparing a whole foreign dinner seems too difficult, perhaps Mom could prepare one special dish or dessert. In any case, find out where the missionaries from your church live and learn something about their countries. Doing this will help you to pray intelligently for them. *V.L.C.*

TO MEMORIZE: I try to find common ground with everyone so that I might bring them to Christ.
1 Corinthians 9:22

8 March

REALLY EMPTY

FROM THE BIBLE:

Once you were dead, doomed forever because of your many sins. . . . But God is so rich in mercy, and he loved us so very much, that even while we were dead because of our sins, he gave us life when he raised Christ from the dead. (It is only by God's special favor that you have been saved!) For he raised us from the dead along with Christ, and we are seated with him in the heavenly realms—all because we are one with Christ Jesus. And so God can always point to us as examples of the incredible wealth of his favor and kindness toward us, as shown in all he has done for us through Christ Jesus.

God saved you by his special favor when you believed. And you can't take credit for this; it is a gift from God. Salvation is not a reward for the good things we have done, so none of us can boast about it. For we are God's masterpiece. He has created us anew in Christ Jesus, so that we can do the good things he planned for us long ago.

EPHESIANS 2:1, 4-10

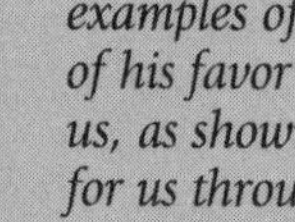

Works don't save

"MOM," KRISTEN ASKED, "can I make some lemonade?"

"I doubt it," teased her brother, Trevor. "It takes far more talent than you possess."

"Oh, hush," said Kristen. "May I make some, Mother?"

"You can, and you may," said Mother.

Kristen went to the cupboard and took out a packet of powdered lemonade. After measuring sugar into a pitcher, she picked up the lemonade packet. She was going to tear it open, but held it up and inspected it instead. Then she took out a different packet and compared the two, feeling them and shaking them.

"I was right," declared Trevor. "She can't make lemonade. She's all confused."

Kristen ignored him. "Mother, I don't think this packet has a thing in it. It feels empty."

Mother checked the packet. "You're right, Kristen. It is empty, but don't tear it open. I think I'll use it as an object lesson for my Sunday school class."

"An object lesson?" asked Kristen. "Of what?"

"It reminds me of people who pretend to be Christians," replied Mother. "Like this packet, they look fine on the outside—they're faithful in church and generous—so others are often fooled by them."

"Just like you were fooled by this packet when you bought it," said Trevor.

Mother nodded. "But God isn't fooled by anyone. He sees their hearts, and he knows they're really empty."

HOW ABOUT YOU? Are you putting on a good front and fooling people? Remember, you're not fooling God. All the nice things you do cannot save you. You need to trust in Jesus as your personal Savior, and then you will be a Christian. God wants to make you the "real thing." *H.W.M.*

TO MEMORIZE: For it is by grace you have been saved, through faith—and this not from yourselves, it is the gift of God—not by works, so that no one can boast. *Ephesians 2:8-9* (NIV)

9 March

A BAD START

FROM THE BIBLE:

Always be full of joy in the Lord. I say it again—rejoice! Let everyone see that you are considerate in all you do. Remember, the Lord is coming soon.

Don't worry about anything; instead, pray about everything. Tell God what you need, and thank him for all he has done. If you do this, you will experience God's peace, which is far more wonderful than the human mind can understand. His peace will guard your hearts and minds as you live in Christ Jesus.

And now, dear brothers and sisters, let me say one more thing as I close this letter. Fix your thoughts on what is true and honorable and right. Think about things that are pure and lovely and admirable. Think about things that are excellent and worthy of praise. Keep putting into practice all you learned from me and heard from me and saw me doing, and the God of peace will be with you.

PHILIPPIANS 4:4-9

Don't be a grumbler!

"MIKE, GET UP! Time to get ready for school," called Mother. Mike pulled the covers over his head and kept dreaming about being the pilot of a 747. It would be exciting to travel around the world. "Mike," Mother called again. "I want you to get up now. Do you hear me?"

"Yes." Mike's voice was muffled by the pillow over his head.

"Mike, I said now!"

Mike sighed as he stumbled out of bed.

"It's raining," Mike moaned as he entered the kitchen a little later. "Why can't the sun ever shine?" He eyed the breakfast table. "Oh, yuck!" he said with a frown. "Oatmeal! I can't stand oatmeal!"

Just then his sister, Abbie, came to the table. She was chattering excitedly about the field trip her class would be taking that day. "We never go on field trips. I hate school," complained Mike.

"Mike," asked Mother, "would you please give thanks before we eat?"

"Dear heavenly Father," prayed Mike, "thank you for the beautiful day you have given us, and thank you for the food. In Jesus' name, Amen."

"Mike, I think something is very wrong," said Mother as she passed the oatmeal.

"What do you mean?"

"You thanked the Lord for the beautiful day, but all you've done so far is grumble," she told him.

Mike sighed. Yes, he had been grumbling since he got out of bed—and that was only a half hour ago!

"I'm sorry, Lord," he whispered. "Help me to get a new start on this day!"

HOW ABOUT YOU? Do you grumble when Mom calls you in the morning? Do you complain about the food? Sometimes boys and girls get in the habit of grumbling about everything. The Bible tells you to rejoice. Be a joyful Christian, not a grumbling Christian. *L.M.W.*

TO MEMORIZE: This is the day the Lord has made. We will rejoice and be glad in it. *Psalm 118:24*

10 March

DOES IT TASTE GOOD?

FROM THE BIBLE:

Oh, how I love your law!
I think about it all day long.
Your commands make me wiser
than my enemies,
for your commands are my
constant guide.
Yes, I have more insight than my
teachers,
for I am always thinking of
your decrees.
I am even wiser than my elders,
for I have kept your
commandments.
I have refused to walk on any
path of evil,
that I may remain obedient to
your word.
I haven't turned away from your
laws,
for you have taught me well.
How sweet are your words to my
taste;
they are sweeter than honey.
Your commandments give me
understanding;
no wonder I hate every false
way of life.

PSALM 119:97-104

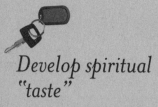

Develop spiritual "taste"

AARON POKED at his pie. "Nothin' tastes good today," he said to his grandfather. "I wish my tongue would quit feeling so funny." Aaron had been to the dentist, and one side of his mouth had been numbed so it wouldn't hurt when the dentist drilled his teeth.

Grandpa chuckled. "Give it time," he advised. "When the dentist numbed your mouth, it numbed the taste buds on your tongue, too. Why don't you save the pie till later?" Aaron nodded and got up. "Aaron," said Grandpa, reaching for his Bible, "would you like to read with me?"

Aaron shrugged. "I'm goin' out to play with the guys," he answered.

"Spiritual taste buds numbed, too?" asked Grandpa.

Aaron stopped. "Huh?"

"I remember when you first asked Jesus to be your Savior," answered Grandpa. "You were really excited about it. You wanted to know what God expected of you as a Christian and what promises he gives to his children. You used to sit with me, and we'd read together from God's Word. We'd have some 'spiritual food' together—remember?"

Aaron nodded. He had enjoyed those times. But so many other things demanded his attention lately. Maybe Grandpa was right. Maybe his spiritual taste buds were numbed.

Grandpa smiled as Aaron sat beside him. "Good," he said. "The numbness in your mouth will go away by itself. But we have to work at getting over spiritual numbness. A good way to start is to get back into God's Word."

HOW ABOUT YOU? Are you less interested in the Bible than you once were? Have your spiritual taste buds been numbed by such things as TV programs, personal hobbies, friends, or homework? Make up your mind to get rid of spiritual numbness. Pray. Read your Bible. Say with the psalmist, "Oh, how I love Your law!" *H.W.M.*

TO MEMORIZE: How sweet are your words to my taste; they are sweeter than honey. *Psalm 119:103*

11 March

DOUBLE EXPOSURE
(PART 1)

FROM THE BIBLE:

Do not do as the wicked do or follow the path of evildoers. Avoid their haunts. Turn away and go somewhere else, for evil people cannot sleep until they have done their evil deed for the day. They cannot rest unless they have caused someone to stumble. They eat wickedness and drink violence!

The way of the righteous is like the first gleam of dawn, which shines ever brighter until the full light of day. But the way of the wicked is like complete darkness. Those who follow it have no idea what they are stumbling over.

PROVERBS 4:14-19

Avoid exposure to sin

JEFF WAS ANNOYED. His folks wouldn't let him go to Andy's party Friday night because Andy's parents were out of town. "Why do my parents have to be so old-fashioned?" Jeff muttered. "Even Ryan gets to go."

The next day, Ryan came over. "Chris Borelli is in the hospital," he said. "They think he may have spinal meningitis—and we sat next to him on the bus yesterday! Mom says if he has it, we'll probably have to get shots!"

"Oh no!" groaned Jeff. "How come?"

"Because it's contagious, and we've been exposed," Ryan said.

"I sure hope Chris is going to be all right," said Jeff. "Hey, how was the party last night?"

"Just be glad you didn't go!" said Ryan. "Andy's older brother was doing drugs with some friends. I didn't like the loud music and the way they were acting, so I left—just before the police came!"

When Jeff's mother walked in, they told her. "That's why I didn't want you to go, Jeff. I didn't want you to be exposed to sin."

"But we're exposed to sin every day, everywhere!" said Jeff.

"That's true," agreed Mother. "But there's more danger some places than others."

Ryan nodded. "We were in more danger sitting next to Chris on the bus than we would have been somewhere else," he said. "And I was in more danger at the party than you were at home. Wow! Two close calls for me in one day—double exposure!"

HOW ABOUT YOU? Do the places you go, the friends you choose, and the TV programs you watch expose you to sin? Do they encourage you to drink alcohol, smoke, cheat, swear, or disobey? If so, you are in great danger. You need to avoid these kinds of influences or you may fall into sin. *B.J.W.*

TO MEMORIZE: Whoever walks with the wise will become wise; whoever walks with fools will suffer harm. *Proverbs 13:20*

12 March

DOUBLE EXPOSURE
(PART 2)

FROM THE BIBLE:

Happy are people of integrity,
who follow the law of the Lord.
Happy are those who obey his decrees
and search for him with all their hearts.
They do not compromise with evil,
and they walk only in his paths.
You have charged us
to keep your commandments carefully.
Oh, that my actions would consistently
reflect your principles!
Then I will not be disgraced
when I compare my life with your commands.
When I learn your righteous laws,
I will thank you by living as I should!
I will obey your principles.
Please don't give up on me!
PSALM 119:1-8

Be exposed to good

JEFF AND RYAN went out to the garage to work on Jeff's bike. Soon Jeff's mother joined them. "Good news, boys," she told them. "Chris's mother just called to say that Chris has a viral infection. He'll be in the hospital for a couple days, but he doesn't have meningitis."

"Whoopee!" yelled the boys. "Old Chris is going to be OK! And we don't have to get shots!" As they started working on the bike again, Ryan said seriously, "I was just thinking about my double exposure. It's too bad we can't take shots to prevent sin."

Jeff's mother smiled. "There are no shots for that," she agreed. "There is something we can do, though. We can keep our resistance up. You know that we keep up our physical resistance to disease by eating a balanced diet and getting proper rest and exercise. How do you suppose we keep up our spiritual resistance to sin?"

The boys thought about it. "I guess going to church would help," offered Ryan.

Jeff nodded. "Yeah, and praying and reading the Bible."

"Good," approved Mother. "And don't forget the importance of good Christian friends, good books, and good music. Expose yourself to these things, and you will be less likely to fall into sin."

HOW ABOUT YOU? Do you regularly attend church and Sunday school where the Bible is clearly taught? Do you read the Bible and give thanks to God every day? Do you listen to music that honors God? Do the books you read draw you closer to him? Do you seek the companionship of Christian friends? All these things will help build up your resistance to sin. *B.J.W.*

TO MEMORIZE: I want you to see clearly what is right and to stay innocent of any wrong. *Romans 16:19*

13 March

TRASH OR TREASURE?

FROM THE BIBLE:

Listen to me, dear brothers and sisters. Hasn't God chosen the poor in this world to be rich in faith? Aren't they the ones who will inherit the Kingdom he promised to those who love him? And yet, you insult the poor man! Isn't it the rich who oppress you and drag you into court? Aren't they the ones who slander Jesus Christ, whose noble name you bear?

Yes indeed, it is good when you truly obey our Lord's royal command found in the Scriptures: "Love your neighbor as yourself." But if you pay special attention to the rich, you are committing a sin, for you are guilty of breaking that law.
JAMES 2:5-9

Everyone is valuable

CASSIE WAS DIGGING for treasure in the old trash pile behind her uncle and aunt's barn. When she found an old fruit jar with "1898" stamped on the bottom, Cassie showed it to Aunt Elise. "I saw one like it in the antique store for thirty dollars," she told her.

Aunt Elise smiled. "You found it, and you may keep it." Cassie squealed with pleasure. Then Aunt Elise asked, "Do you remember Rebecca, who lives next door? She's coming over this afternoon."

"Oh, no!" groaned Cassie. "She's trashy and dumb. She's not my type at all. She's not even a Christian."

"I'm surprised to hear you say that," said Aunt Elise. "Tell you what. Go clean that old fruit jar and then bring it back to me." When Cassie returned, Aunt Elise examined the jar.

"It's pretty, now that it's cleaned up," she said. "Strange, isn't it, that until today, no one realized its value? In a way, Rebecca is like this jar."

"She is?"

"Yes," said Aunt Elise. "And so are you. One day you lay in the trash pile of sin, too, but God recognized your value. He picked you up, washed you, and gave you a new shine. Rebecca is still lost, but she is very valuable! So valuable that Jesus died for her."

Cassie looked ashamed. "I'm glad she's coming over, Aunt Elise. I'll pray God uses me to help her come to him so she can get a new shine, too."

HOW ABOUT YOU? Is there someone you think is too "trashy" to play with? What does it really matter if his clothes are wrinkled or torn or if he doesn't always use correct English? God looks beneath all that and sees a precious soul. Perhaps by being a friend to that person, God will allow you to uncover the treasure of that soul. *B.J.W.*

TO MEMORIZE: Don't be afraid; you are worth more than many sparrows. *Luke 12:7* (NIV)

14 March

SEEDLESS ORANGES

FROM THE BIBLE:

A farmer went out to plant some seed. As he scattered it . . . some seed fell on a footpath, where it was stepped on, and the birds came and ate it. Other seed fell on shallow soil with underlying rock. This seed began to grow, but soon it withered and died for lack of moisture. Other seed fell among thorns that shot up and choked out the tender blades. Still other seed fell on fertile soil. This seed grew and produced a crop one hundred times as much as had been planted. . . .

The seed is God's message. The seed that fell on the hard path represents those who hear the message, but then the Devil comes and steals it away and prevents them from believing and being saved. The rocky soil represents those who hear the message with joy. But like young plants in such soil, their roots don't go very deep. They believe for a while, but they wilt when the hot winds of testing blow. The thorny ground represents those who hear and accept the message, but all too quickly the message is crowded out by the cares and riches and pleasures of this life. And so they never grow into maturity. But the good soil represents honest, good-hearted people who hear God's message, cling to it, and steadily produce a huge harvest.

LUKE 8:5-8, 11-15

Plant the "seed" of the gospel

"THE PASTOR talked about witnessing at school, but I can't witness there," said Scott as he poured potting soil into a clay pot for his school project.

"Oh?" Mother asked.

"None of the Christians I know witness at school. It's just not a good place to talk about the Lord," said Scott as he brushed dirt off his hands. "People make fun of you if you try." He changed the subject. "Can we go to the store now and get the oranges for my project?"

"Sure," replied Mother.

After they arrived at the grocery store, Scott and his mother looked for oranges with seeds in them. "All I can find are seedless oranges," said Scott. "How's a guy supposed to grow an orange tree without seeds?"

"That would be a trick!" Mom laughed. "You know," she added, "I wonder if the Lord might be feeling as sad as you."

"Because all the oranges are seedless?" Scott asked.

"No," Mother said. "Because your school has only seedless Christians."

"Seedless Christians?" said Scott. "I don't get it."

"You said none of the Christians witness at school," said Mother. "None of them plant the seeds of the gospel. You have the seeds of God's Word, but you refuse to scatter them. You're no more help to the unsaved than if you weren't Christians."

Scott felt ashamed. "You've got a point, Mom," he said. "I'm going to try witnessing to my friends, even if others laugh at me."

HOW ABOUT YOU? Do you scatter the "seed" of the Word of God? Do you tell the kids at school and in your neighborhood about Jesus? God doesn't promise that it will be easy, but he does promise that it will eventually bring results. Let him spread the gospel through you. He will bless you as you witness. *S.L.N.*

TO MEMORIZE: They weep as they go to plant their seed, but they sing as they return with the harvest. *Psalm 126:6*

15 March

TOO MANY PEOPLE?

FROM THE BIBLE:

Children are a gift from the
Lord;
they are a reward from him.
Children born to a young man
are like sharp arrows in a
warrior's hands.
How happy is the man whose
quiver is full of them!
He will not be put to shame
when he confronts his
accusers at the city gates.

PSALM 127:3-5

Babies are a blessing

ONE MORNING Paul awoke and found his mother reading her Bible at the kitchen table. His six brothers and sisters were still sleeping. "Mom, do you ever wish you didn't have all us kids?" he asked.

"Of course not!" Mother said. "What made you ask that?"

"Well," replied Paul, "my social studies teacher said that if every couple had only one child, all our problems would be solved."

Mother looked thoughtful. "I doubt Mr. Rader is a Christian," she said. "The Bible speaks of children as a 'gift' and a 'reward.' "

Paul was confused. "But if you and Dad didn't have all of us, you'd have more money."

Mother smiled. "Do you think we'd trade any of you precious children for a new couch, a car, or a few more hours of free time?"

"I guess not," replied Paul.

"God created this world to provide for the needs of *all* people," said Mother. "If there doesn't seem to be enough to go around, it's because of our own selfishness. Even today many people are starving, while others have far more than they need."

"That's true," agreed Paul.

"Remember when little Christopher was born?" his mother asked. "We all had to 'tighten our belts' to pay the hospital bill."

"But nobody minded," Paul said. "We love Christopher."

"And that's what the world needs—not more things, but more love," said Mother. "We need the love that only comes by knowing Christ as Savior."

HOW ABOUT YOU? Are you worried that there are too many people in the world? Do you think of babies as a problem or a blessing? God is still in control, and he has a plan for every human being. He knows them before they're even born—and he sent his own Son to save them. Let's thank God for the blessing of babies! *S.L.K.*

TO MEMORIZE: Children are a gift from the Lord; they are a reward from him. *Psalm 127:3*

16 *March*

BETTER LATE THAN NEVER

FROM THE BIBLE:

Or don't you know that your body is the temple of the Holy Spirit, who lives in you and was given to you by God? You do not belong to yourself, for God bought you with a high price. So you must honor God with your body.

1 CORINTHIANS 6:19-20

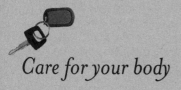

Care for your body

STEVE HAD a sore in his mouth. *Maybe I should tell Mom,* he decided. When Mom saw the sore, she made a doctor's appointment.

"Do you use smokeless tobacco?" the doctor asked.

"Well, yeah," admitted Steve. For about a year he and two of his sixth-grade friends had been buying tobacco from a little store where the cashier never asked questions. The boys met behind the school to chew. Then they'd suck on mints to avoid smelling like tobacco.

"This sore is caused from tobacco around the gumline," the doctor told Steve. "Tobacco sometimes changes the cells, causing cancer."

Steve turned white. "You mean I . . . I have cancer?"

"You could have the beginning of it," the doctor replied. "I've seen more cases of this since kids began chewing tobacco. Your sore is very small, so I can get it out with some surgery."

A week after his mouth surgery, Steve returned to the doctor's office. "If you don't use tobacco from now on, you may not have any more problems," the doctor said. "But I want you back for occasional checkups."

On the way home Steve saw a billboard that showed a strong, handsome man taking some smokeless tobacco. "Give yourself some pleasure," read the billboard.

"They shouldn't advertise something that can hurt people!" exploded Steve.

"As Christians, we have to be careful not to let such advertisements influence us," said Mom. "We need to avoid anything harmful to the body God gave us."

"Too bad I learned the hard way," said Steve, "but better late than never."

WHAT ABOUT YOU? Are you fooled by advertisers who make harmful products sound exciting and glamorous? God wants you to stay away from things that harm your body. Don't do anything that could destroy God's wonderful workmanship. *C.E.Y.*

TO MEMORIZE: For God bought you with a high price. So you must honor God with your body.
1 Corinthians 6:20

GOD GIVES THE INCREASE

FROM THE BIBLE:

Who is Apollos, and who is Paul, that we should be the cause of such quarrels? Why, we're only servants. Through us God caused you to believe. Each of us did the work the Lord gave us. My job was to plant the seed in your hearts, and Apollos watered it, but it was God, not we, who made it grow. The ones who do the planting or watering aren't important, but God is important because he is the one who makes the seed grow. The one who plants and the one who waters work as a team with the same purpose. Yet they will be rewarded individually, according to their own hard work. We work together as partners who belong to God. You are God's field, God's building—not ours.

Because of God's special favor to me, I have laid the foundation like an expert builder. Now others are building on it. But whoever is building on this foundation must be very careful. For no one can lay any other foundation than the one we already have—Jesus Christ.

1 CORINTHIANS 3:5-11

DARIA WALKED in and slammed the door. "My, my," her father said. "Did you mean to slam the door that way?"

"I meant it," Daria yelled. "I'm mad!"

"Want to talk about it?" Dad asked.

"You'll think I'm awful," she said angrily. "It's about Rhonda Kelly."

"She's the girl you've been witnessing to, isn't she?"

Daria nodded. "She just became a Christian."

"That's wonderful!" exclaimed Dad.

"Yeah, but I've been witnessing to her for so long, and I didn't even get to lead her to Jesus!"

"Who did?" Dad asked.

"Mrs. Noll did, but I'm the one who prayed and talked to her," Daria said. "I even gave her a Bible for her birthday."

Dad smiled slightly. "That may be the very reason Rhonda was ready to accept Christ."

"But why wouldn't God let me be the one to finally lead her to the Lord?" she asked.

Dad picked up a Bible and turned the pages of the New Testament. "That's the way it often works," he said. "Here in 1 Corinthians Paul said, 'I have planted, Apollos watered, but God gave the increase.' It looks like God allowed you to plant and Mrs. Noll to water. And at just the right time, God did the saving."

Daria thought about what her father had said. It really didn't matter who led Rhonda to Christ. The important thing was that she was now a Christian. And maybe it was because Daria had faithfully witnessed for all those months.

HOW ABOUT YOU? Are you happy when someone accepts Jesus as Savior, even if others don't give you the credit for your part? Remember, though it is up to you to "plant and water"—to faithfully witness—only God can give the increase. Only he can save. Your part is to be faithful. *R.I.J.*

TO MEMORIZE: We work together as partners who belong to God. *1 Corinthians 3:9*

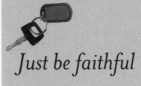

Just be faithful

18 March

CLOUDY SKIES

FROM THE BIBLE:

O Lord, you have examined my heart
and know everything about me.
You know when I sit down or stand up.
You know my every thought when far away.
You chart the path ahead of me
and tell me where to stop and rest.
Every moment you know where I am.
You know what I am going to say
even before I say it, Lord.
You both precede and follow me.
You place your hand of blessing on my head.
Such knowledge is too wonderful for me,
too great for me to know!

PSALM 139:1-6

Accept what God sends

SCOTT STARED out the plane window at the thick clouds. Why had God allowed his older brother to be in that accident? He enjoyed visiting Mark in college, but now he and his parents would be visiting him in the hospital.

When the flight attendant brought lunch, Scott wasn't hungry. "I keep thinking about Mark," he told his parents.

Dad sighed. "We feel the same way, Scott. But remember, God cares about his children. He knows what he's doing in our lives."

Scott nodded, but he wasn't sure he agreed. Picking up his fork, he began to eat. When he finished, he turned with a sigh to the window again. "Look!" he exclaimed. "I can see everything!" Pressing his nose to the glass, he stared down at the colorful fields and the cars and trucks that looked like tiny toys. "Look at that little train! Ohhh, I wish I had a camera!" Scott's face had brightened.

Mom leaned over. "You know, that scenery was there below the clouds the whole time," she said. "You just couldn't see it."

"That's true," replied Scott.

"Think of Mark's accident in the same way," said Dad. "To us, the whole situation is cloudy; we can't see anything good in it."

"And you're saying that God can?" asked Scott.

"Right," Dad replied. "If we've accepted Jesus as Savior through faith, then we need to also live by faith. We should accept what he brings into our life."

HOW ABOUT YOU? Have things happened in your life that make you think nothing is going to turn out right? Don't let the hard things of life control your attitude. Remember that God knows what he's doing. His plan is always good, even though you can't see it. If you trust him, you'll soon have the right attitude. *G.W.*

TO MEMORIZE: He knows the way that I take; when he has tested me, I will come forth as gold. *Job 23:10*

19 March

SENT, BUT NOT DELIVERED

FROM THE BIBLE:

"Anyone who calls on the name of the Lord will be saved."

But how can they call on him to save them unless they believe in him? And how can they believe in him if they have never heard about him? And how can they hear about him unless someone tells them? And how will anyone go and tell them without being sent? That is what the Scriptures mean when they say, "How beautiful are the feet of those who bring good news!"
ROMANS 10:13-15

Deliver God's message

SADLY, THE COWEN family said good-bye to Aniceta. They were taking a three-month break from their work as missionaries in Mexico. Aniceta had helped them translate the New Testament into her language.

One day Joey suggested they send Aniceta a letter. "Then she'll know we're praying for her."

"Good idea, Joey," agreed Dad. "Mail isn't delivered in the mountains where she lives, but her son, Isauro, lives in town. We could send the letter to him, and he could deliver it to his mother."

As soon as the family returned to Mexico, they visited Aniceta. She was thrilled. "You are back. Praise the Lord. You gone so long. I hear nothing."

"Didn't you get our letter?" Joey asked.

"No letter," Aniceta replied.

The family was puzzled. Later they visited Isauro in town. He remembered receiving the letter, but had forgotten to deliver it.

"Isauro failed us, Dad," said Joey on the way home. "He didn't deliver the letter, so Aniceta thought we had forgotten her."

"Yes, Isauro neglected his job," Dad answered. "But we often act the same way."

"We do?" Joey asked.

"God has written the Bible to let people know he hasn't forgotten them. God expects those of us who love him to deliver that message to people who haven't heard. But often we fail to do this," explained Dad. "Many people are still waiting to hear that God loves them."

Joey understood. "I'll help all I can, Dad. I'll start by telling Isauro about Jesus again."

HOW ABOUT YOU? Have you received God's message and accepted his Son as your Savior? If so, how long has it been since you told someone else about it? Don't be guilty of failing to deliver God's message to the world. He needs ambassadors who will carry his Word to the world. Can he count on you? *J.L.H.*

TO MEMORIZE: How beautiful are the feet of those who bring good news! *Romans 10:15* (NIV)

20 March

A STRONG HAND

FROM THE BIBLE:

[Jesus said,] "My sheep recognize my voice; I know them, and they follow me. I give them eternal life, and they will never perish. No one will snatch them away from me, for my Father has given them to me, and he is more powerful than anyone else. So no one can take them from me. The Father and I are one."
JOHN 10:27-30

God keeps you

"WANT THIS quarter, Terri? You can have it if you can get it." Terri hesitated, knowing how her big brother loved to tease. Slowly she walked toward him. When she was close, she lunged for his hand. But just as quickly, Tony's fist closed over the quarter.

Terri laughed as she tried to open Tony's fist, but the quarter was secure.

Finally Mom intervened. "That's enough, you two," she said. "Tony, you shouldn't always be teasing your sister."

"Teasing her?" Tony slapped his forehead in mock dismay. "I'm just giving her an object lesson like any good brother should do."

"What object lesson?" asked Terri.

"Well, I heard you learning your Sunday school memory verse—the one about nobody being able to pluck us out of the Father's hand," explained Tony. "So I just gave you a demonstration of what a safe place a hand can be."

"That's not bad," commented Mom. "You couldn't force Tony's hand open, although there are some people who could. But nobody—not even Satan—is strong enough to open God's hand. God is much stronger than anybody or anything." She smiled at Tony. "Good job, Son."

"Thanks, Mom." Tony grinned at his sister. "And just to show you what a good guy I am, you can keep this quarter!"

HOW ABOUT YOU? Aren't you glad that, as a Christian, God holds you securely in his hand? You may get discouraged at times, but God loves you and holds you. You are his. You must—and should—feel sad when you disobey, lie, or sin in any way. But God still loves you and holds you. You're still his. As you ask his forgiveness for what you have done, thank him for loving you and keeping you safely in his hand.
H.W.M.

TO MEMORIZE: My Father, who has given them to me, is greater than all; so no one can snatch them out of my Father's hand. *John 10:29* (NIV)

21 March

GOD'S MOUTHPIECE

FROM THE BIBLE:

But Moses pleaded with the Lord, "O Lord, I'm just not a good speaker. I never have been, and I'm not now, even after you have spoken to me. I'm clumsy with words."

"Who makes mouths?" the Lord asked him. "Who makes people so they can speak or not speak, hear or not hear, see or not see? Is it not I, the Lord? Now go, and do as I have told you. I will help you speak well, and I will tell you what to say."

EXODUS 4:10-12

Be God's mouthpiece

IT WAS YOUTH night, and the young people were in charge of the entire evening church service. They used their talents to sing, play instruments, work in the nursery, put on a skit, usher, collect the offering, and even preach.

Afterwards, Mr. Mendoza approached Marie. "You did a fine job on your ventriloquism," he said. "The skit had a good message, too. I'm in charge of a special program we're planning where I work. Would you do a skit there?"

Marie was so pleased with Mr. Mendoza's comments that she readily agreed. But later she changed her mind. "I forgot that Mr. Mendoza works at that center for children who have been in trouble with the law," she told her mother. "I can't give a talk there."

"Why not?" asked Mother. "Those children need to hear the gospel, too."

"But they're tough kids," Marie said. "They'll laugh at me. I can't do it!"

To Marie's surprise, Mother agreed. "You're right. They're too tough!" she said. "Just send your dummy with Mr. Mendoza. Let the dummy share the Good News."

"Mother," Marie said, "you know the dummy can't talk without me! I put the words in his mouth. He can't do anything without me."

Mother smiled. "That's how God works, too," she said. "You are God's mouthpiece. Without him your words will be meaningless. But he'll give you his power and the words to say if you ask him."

"OK, I'll ask God for help," Marie agreed. "Without him I can do nothing."

HOW ABOUT YOU? Do you speak up for Jesus whenever you get a chance? Are you using your talents to serve him? If you try to do things in your own strength, you'll fail. Ask Jesus for help. He will give you strength. *J.L.H.*

TO MEMORIZE: I will give you the right words and such wisdom that none of your opponents will be able to reply! *Luke 21:15*

22 March

JUST CARROTS?

FROM THE BIBLE:

There is a time for everything,
a season for every activity
under heaven.
A time to be born and a time to
die.
A time to plant and a time to
harvest.
A time to kill and a time to heal.
A time to tear down and a
time to rebuild.
A time to cry and a time to
laugh.
A time to grieve and a time to
dance.
A time to scatter stones and a
time to gather stones.
A time to embrace and a time
to turn away.
A time to search and a time to
lose.
A time to keep and a time to
throw away.
A time to tear and a time to
mend.
A time to be quiet and a time
to speak up.
A time to love and a time to
hate.
A time for war and a time for
peace.

ECCLESIASTES 3:1-8

Become a well-balanced person

JOEL CAME in with a mystery novel under his arm. "Hi, Joel, how did the spelling test go?" Dad asked.

"It went OK," Joel replied. He felt guilty because he'd been up late reading his novel, not studying.

All week Joel read so late into the night that he could hardly get up for school. He neglected his friends, his chores, and his Sunday school lesson.

On Sunday, his father noticed Joel carrying a mystery book into church. "I hope you don't plan to read your book in church."

Joel fidgeted. "Could I read between services?" Dad shook his head.

That noon, Mom set a big bowl of carrots on the table. Then she sat down with the family. "Is that it?" Joel asked in disbelief. "Where's the rest of the food?"

"The rest?" asked Mother. "Carrots are good for you. I thought you liked them."

"They're OK, but not that many of 'em," said Joel. "Where's all the other stuff we need for a balanced diet?"

"Did I hear the word *balance?*" Dad said. "Joel, that word not only applies to food, but also to your whole life. People get off balance by doing too much of one thing and neglecting other things. Reading is good, but don't neglect your family, friends, schoolwork, or the Lord to do it."

Joel blushed. "I guess I'll try harder to have a 'balanced life.' "

"Yes," said Mom, pulling a pan out of the oven. "You can start by having a good meal!"

HOW ABOUT YOU? Do you spend too much time doing one thing? You should take care of your body by getting proper food, sleep, and exercise. Take care of your mind by studying, reading good books, and listening in church and Sunday school. Spend time with people and also with the Lord. *S.L.N.*

TO MEMORIZE: And Jesus grew in wisdom and stature, and in favor with God and men. *Luke 2:52* (NIV)

GETTING EVEN

FROM THE BIBLE:

Never pay back evil for evil to anyone. Do things in such a way that everyone can see you are honorable. Do your part to live in peace with everyone, as much as possible.

Dear friends, never avenge yourselves. Leave that to God. For it is written,

"I will take vengeance;
I will repay those who deserve it,"
says the Lord.

Instead, do what the Scriptures say:

"If your enemies are hungry, feed them.
If they are thirsty, give them something to drink,
and they will be ashamed of what they have done to you."

Don't let evil get the best of you, but conquer evil by doing good.

ROMANS 12:17-21

Overcome evil with good

"ERIC THREW dirt in my face," Justin sobbed as Mother washed the dirt from his eyes. Finally, the last speck was out. "I'll get even with Eric if it's the last thing I do," Justin threatened.

Mother frowned. "Your friend was wrong, but getting even is also wrong and won't accomplish anything."

"It'll teach him not to throw dirt in people's eyes," Justin argued.

At bedtime when Dad read Romans 12:17-21, Justin scowled. "Does that mean I'm supposed to be good to Eric to make him ashamed of the way he treated me? Is that how I get even?"

Mother shook her head. "You're not supposed to get even. The nineteenth verse says, 'Do not avenge yourselves . . . "Vengeance is Mine; I will repay," says the Lord.' "

"How's the Lord going to repay Eric for what he did?" Justin wanted to know. "I hope he gets him really good!"

"Maybe he knows Eric has already suffered enough," Dad replied. "He's probably one really scared fellow, wondering how badly you were hurt."

"But the Bible says to heap coals of fire on our enemy's head," Justin pointed out. "Isn't that getting even?"

"That was written before people had matches. If their fire went out, they had to borrow live coals from a neighbor, and they carried them in a pot on their heads," Dad explained. "So this verse is telling you to help your enemy. Don't get revenge. Overcome his evil with your good."

"That sounds hard," Justin grumbled.

"Not nearly as hard as it would be to keep fighting with him," Mother said.

Justin grinned. "I guess I would prefer to have Eric for a friend rather than an enemy."

HOW ABOUT YOU? Has someone mistreated you? Are you planning to get even? Ask God to give you a forgiving spirit. Start overcoming evil with good. *B.J.W.*

TO MEMORIZE: Do not be overcome by evil, but overcome evil with good. *Romans 12:21* (NIV)

24 March

HERE COMES THE SUN
(PART 1)

FROM THE BIBLE:

And the Lord replied to Moses, "I will indeed do what you have asked, for you have found favor with me, and you are my friend."

Then Moses had one more request. "Please let me see your glorious presence," he said.

The Lord replied, "I will make all my goodness pass before you, and I will call out my name, 'the Lord,' to you. I will show kindness to anyone I choose, and I will show mercy to anyone I choose. But you may not look directly at my face, for no one may see me and live." The Lord continued, "Stand here on this rock beside me. As my glorious presence passes by, I will put you in the cleft of the rock and cover you with my hand until I have passed. Then I will remove my hand, and you will see me from behind. But my face will not be seen."

EXODUS 33:17-23

You can't "see" God

AS PAUL HELPED Grandpa in the garden one cloudy spring day, he brought up something puzzling. "How can God be three different persons and still be only one?" said Paul. "My Sunday school teacher says God is a Trinity—that there's the Father, the Son, and Holy Spirit, but they're all one."

"That is hard to understand," Grandpa agreed, "but it's in the Bible." He handed Paul a package of radish seeds. "Want to plant these?"

"Sure," said Paul, looking up into the sky. "But I wish the sun would come out." As Paul began to sow the tiny seeds, Grandpa smiled. "You just mentioned the sun up in the sky, and it's a good illustration of the Trinity."

"It is?" Paul asked.

"Yes, it illustrates God the Father," Grandpa said. "Tell me, has anyone ever seen the sun?"

"Sure," said Paul.

"Wrong!" said Grandpa. "No one has seen the great ball of fire we call the sun without going blind. It's impossible to look directly at the sun. What we see is light from the sun."

"And that's like God the Father?"

"Exactly," said Grandpa. "The Bible says no one has seen God the Father. He is so great and glorious that human beings cannot look at him. But we know him through the Bible and through nature."

Paul thought about Grandpa's explanation. "OK. But what about the Son and the Spirit?"

"I'll get to those," replied Grandpa. "First, let's water the area we've planted."

HOW ABOUT YOU? Do you have trouble believing in God because you can't see him? You can't see the sun either, but you certainly don't doubt that it exists. Even though you can't understand everything about God, you can believe what the Bible teaches about him. *G.W.*

TO MEMORIZE: No one has ever seen God. But his only Son, who is himself God, is near to the Father's heart; he has told us about him. *John 1:18*

25 March

HERE COMES THE SUN
(PART 2)

FROM THE BIBLE:

In the beginning the Word already existed. He was with God, and he was God. He was in the beginning with God. He created everything there is. Nothing exists that he didn't make. Life itself was in him, and this life gives light to everyone. The light shines through the darkness, and the darkness can never extinguish it.

God sent John the Baptist to tell everyone about the light so that everyone might believe because of his testimony. John himself was not the light; he was only a witness to the light. The one who is the true light, who gives light to everyone, was going to come into the world.

But although the world was made through him, the world didn't recognize him when he came. Even in his own land and among his own people, he was not accepted. But to all who believed him and accepted him, he gave the right to become children of God.

JOHN 1:1-12

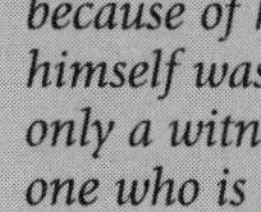

Jesus is God

AS PAUL PULLED the hose over to the garden, the clouds parted to let the sun shine through. "Look Grandpa!" he exclaimed. "Here comes the sun!"

Grandpa looked serious as he glanced around the garden. "Do you mean that big ball in space is coming down here?" he asked.

"Oh, Grandpa," laughed Paul, "you know what I mean. We can see the sunlight!"

Grandpa chuckled. "Right," he agreed, "and your own words can help explain the Trinity."

"What do you mean?" Paul asked.

Grandpa sat under a tree and Paul joined him. "Remember what we said about not being able to see God?" he asked.

"Sure," said Paul. "Just as we don't actually see the sun, we don't see God the Father."

"Right," said Grandpa. "Yet Jesus—God the Son—came down to earth from the Father. Men did see him, so we can learn about the Trinity by getting to know Jesus, the light of the world."

"I think I see what you mean," said Paul.

"We say 'the sun' whether we're talking about the actual ball of fire or the light that comes from it. They're essentially the same thing," continued Grandpa. "God the Father and God the Son are also one. We call both 'God,' for both are God."

"That takes care of one being two and two being one," said Paul. "But what about God the Holy Spirit?"

Grandpa stood up. "Let's water this garden," he said, "and we'll talk about it while we work."

HOW ABOUT YOU? Do you think of Jesus as a baby in a manger? As a good man? As a good friend? He's all of that, but also much more. He is God! All the great and wonderful things you know about God are also true of Jesus. As you learn about Jesus in the Bible, you will be learning about God. *G.W.*

TO MEMORIZE: I and the Father are one. *John 10:30* (NIV)

26 March

HERE COMES THE SUN
(PART 3)

FROM THE BIBLE:

Oh, there is so much more I want to tell you, but you can't bear it now. When the Spirit of truth comes, he will guide you into all truth. He will not be presenting his own ideas; he will be telling you what he has heard. He will tell you about the future.
JOHN 16:12-13

The Holy Spirit is God

"TAKE THE HOSE to the end of the garden," suggested Grandpa. "Start watering there."

Paul followed instructions and began to gently spray the ground with water. "This will help the seeds sprout," he said.

"You bet," agreed Grandpa as he raked some dirt. "Remember the garden we planted last year?"

"Sure do!" exclaimed Paul. "We had the best radishes, carrots, and beans in the neighborhood. It was fun to watch them grow."

"Besides water, what made them grow?" asked Grandpa.

"The sun, I guess," replied Paul.

"Actually, the chemical power of the sun helps plants grow," said Grandpa. "That power is very distinct from the actual sun and from the sunlight, yet it is one with them. When we speak of it, we say 'the sun,' for it is the sun."

"Wow! That's a little hard to understand," said Paul, "but are you about to say that the Holy Spirit is like the chemical power of the sun?"

"Yes!" said Grandpa, chuckling. "The Holy Spirit is one with God the Father and God the Son. He is God the Holy Spirit. He quietly works in our hearts. The Holy Spirit gives Christians the power they need to live for God. And he makes the unsaved person realize he needs to accept Jesus."

Paul grinned at his grandfather. "You should have been a preacher, Grandpa," he said. "Thanks for helping me understand the Bible."

HOW ABOUT YOU? Do you know much about the third person of the Trinity, the Holy Spirit? If you're a Christian, he lives in you and helps you understand spiritual truths. Listen to him and obey. If you're not a Christian, the Holy Spirit is telling you that accepting Jesus as Savior is the most important decision you'll ever make. Listen to him and trust in Christ. *G.W.*

TO MEMORIZE: God has given us his Spirit as proof that we live in him and he in us. *1 John 4:13*

SOMETHING BEAUTIFUL

FROM THE BIBLE:

Now we know only a little, and even the gift of prophecy reveals little! But when the end comes, these special gifts will all disappear.

It's like this: When I was a child, I spoke and thought and reasoned as a child does. But when I grew up, I put away childish things. Now we see things imperfectly as in a poor mirror, but then we will see everything with perfect clarity. All that I know now is partial and incomplete, but then I will know everything completely, just as God knows me now.

There are three things that will endure—faith, hope, and love—and the greatest of these is love.

1 CORINTHIANS 13:9-13

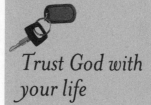

Trust God with your life

NOTHING GOOD happened anymore! First, Zachary's best friend moved away. Then his faithful old dog died. His thoughts were gloomy as he passed the church on his way to school.

"Morning, Zac," said Mr. Barry, the church janitor. He gazed up at the stained glass window in front of the church. "Don't you just marvel at the skill of the man who created that window?"

Zachary looked up and shrugged. He wasn't impressed. The window was just a bunch of dark, dull pieces of glass.

"Wait till you see it with the sun shining through," said Mr. Barry. "Stop by after school and I'll show you something beautiful."

That afternoon, Mr. Barry led him into the church sanctuary. The sun shone brightly through the colored stained glass window; it formed a picture of Jesus blessing little children. "Quite a change when you see it from this side, isn't there?" said Mr. Barry. "I sometimes think life is like that. From our point of view it can seem dark and dull, especially when we're going through bad times. But from God's point of view, each little part fits together just right."

Zachary saw that even the dark pieces of glass used for a child's hair had a beautiful gleam. The artist knew what he was doing when he used each piece. Some day Zachary would see that God knew what he was doing, too.

HOW ABOUT YOU? Does life seem dark and dreary to you? Perhaps there has been sickness or death in your family. Perhaps your best friend has moved away or your parents are separating. Try to realize that if you could see your life as God does, you would see something beautiful forming. You may not understand until you get to heaven, but God truly is working for your best. *H.W.M.*

TO MEMORIZE: Now I know in part; then I shall know fully, even as I am fully known.
1 Corinthians 13:12 (NIV)

28 March

WATCHING LIKE A HAWK

FROM THE BIBLE:

I wrote to you as I did to find out how far you would go in obeying me. When you forgive this man, I forgive him, too. And when I forgive him (for whatever is to be forgiven), I do so with Christ's authority for your benefit, so that Satan will not outsmart us. For we are very familiar with his evil schemes. . . .

But thanks be to God, who made us his captives and leads us along in Christ's triumphal procession. Now wherever we go he uses us to tell others about the Lord and to spread the Good News like a sweet perfume. Our lives are a fragrance presented by Christ to God. But this fragrance is perceived differently by those being saved and by those perishing.

2 CORINTHIANS 2:9-11, 14-15

Let God strengthen you

ANGELA AND HER grandpa were out for a walk when they spotted a hawk circling overhead. Suddenly the hawk swooped down. It pounced on a mouse, gripped it in its claws, and carried it off.

Angela's mouth hung open. "How did the hawk see that little mouse?"

"Hawks have much sharper eyesight than ours," Grandpa explained. "That's where the expression 'watching like a hawk' comes from. That hawk saw the mouse running and caught its dinner."

"I'm glad I'm too big for a hawk's dinner," said Angela.

"Me, too." Grandpa chuckled, then looked serious. "There is an enemy who circles around looking for humans to devour. Just as that hawk looks for weaker animals to prey on, Satan looks for weak spots in our lives."

"Weak spots?"

"Weak spots are areas in our lives that aren't fully yielded to God," Grandpa said. "If a person has a bad temper and hasn't asked God for help, Satan will keep attacking that person through his temper."

"Could lying and stealing and swearing be weak spots, too?" asked Angela.

"Yes," Grandpa said. "And grumbling and disobedience, too. One of my weak spots is that I don't help Grandma enough. When I see I'm neglecting her, I tell God I'm sorry and ask for his help. Then Satan can't attack me in that weak spot."

"Fighting with my brothers is a weak spot for me," Angela decided. "I'm going to ask God to help me quit doing that."

HOW ABOUT YOU? What is your weak spot? Arguing? Laziness? Putting things off till later? Talking back? Whatever it is, talk to God about it; ask for his forgiveness and help when you fail. *C.E.Y.*

TO MEMORIZE: I wrote to you as I did to find out how far you would go in obeying me . . . so that Satan will not outsmart us. For we are very familiar with his evil schemes. *2 Corinthians 2:9, 11*

TWO KINDS OF SIN

FROM THE BIBLE:

Don't just pretend that you love others. Really love them. Hate what is wrong. Stand on the side of the good. Love each other with genuine affection, and take delight in honoring each other. Never be lazy in your work, but serve the Lord enthusiastically.

Be glad for all God is planning for you. Be patient in trouble, and always be prayerful. When God's children are in need, be the one to help them out. And get into the habit of inviting guests home for dinner or, if they need lodging, for the night.

If people persecute you because you are a Christian, don't curse them; pray that God will bless them. When others are happy, be happy with them. If they are sad, share their sorrow. Live in harmony with each other. Don't try to act important, but enjoy the company of ordinary people. And don't think you know it all!

ROMANS 12:9-16

Avoid evil: do good

WHILE BRIANNA WAS helping Dad paint the kitchen, she brought up a question that had been bothering her. "Dad, you always say it's important to confess our sins when we pray, right?"

"Yes," Dad replied, "so that our fellowship with God is not disturbed."

"Well," asked Brianna, "what if I can't think of any sins to confess? Some days I don't catch myself telling a lie or doing anything wrong. So how can I confess anything?"

Dad raised an eyebrow at her. "I wish I had that problem, Brianna," he said. "I can always think of sins to confess."

"You, Dad?" asked Brianna. "But you're such a good Christian."

Dad laughed. "Maybe I don't have 'obvious' sins. But I still sin many times a day. For example, I might have sinful thoughts. Besides, there are actually two kinds of sin."

"I thought sin was sin," Brianna said.

"In a way it is," agreed Dad. "All sin displeases God, and it hurts others and ourselves. Yet sometimes we sin by doing wrong things; other times we sin by *not* doing the right thing. The Bible says that if I know to do good and don't do it, it is sin."

Brianna thought about that. "You mean, when Mom needs help in the kitchen, but I watch TV instead, it's really a sin?" Dad nodded. "Wow!" Brianna exclaimed. "I won't have any problem thinking of things to confess from now on."

HOW ABOUT YOU? Do you confess sins such as stealing, swearing, disobeying your parents, or other things God has said you should not do? You also need to be careful to obey all that God tells you to do. Right now, stop and think about those things that you know you should do. Then determine to do them as soon as you can. *S.L.K.*

TO MEMORIZE: Anyone, then, who knows the good he ought to do and doesn't do it, sins. *James 4:17* (NIV)

30 March

DON'T BE A CHICKEN

FROM THE BIBLE:

And by that same mighty power, he has given us all of his rich and wonderful promises. He has promised that you will escape the decadence all around you caused by evil desires and that you will share in his divine nature.

So make every effort to apply the benefits of these promises to your life. Then your faith will produce a life of moral excellence. A life of moral excellence leads to knowing God better. Knowing God leads to self-control. Self-control leads to patient endurance, and patient endurance leads to godliness. Godliness leads to love for other Christians, and finally you will grow to have genuine love for everyone. The more you grow like this, the more you will become productive and useful in your knowledge of our Lord Jesus Christ. But those who fail to develop these virtues are blind or, at least, very shortsighted. They have already forgotten that God has cleansed them from their old life of sin.

2 PETER 1:4-9

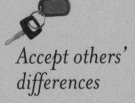

Accept others' differences

PAUL AND GRANDPA scattered grain over the floor of the chicken coop. The chickens scrambled for it. But one chicken was pecked by the others when it tried to eat. Paul noticed a red spot on the chicken's neck.

"That chicken is hurt, Grandpa!" he exclaimed.

Just then a big rooster jabbed the sore on the chicken's neck. Grandpa picked up the squawking chicken and carried it into a separate pen so that her neck could heal.

"Why do the other chickens peck this one?" Paul asked.

"I'm not exactly sure," answered Grandpa, as he rubbed medicine into the sore. "But this is typical chicken behavior. They always pick on those that are weak or hurt. And they peck right at the spot that is already sore."

"That's mean," said Paul.

"In a way, people often do the same thing," said Grandpa.

"How?" asked Paul.

"Some people make fun of others who have different-colored skin, or eyes, nose, or ears that look a little different," explained Grandpa. Paul thought of a boy named Sydney. Paul was glad now that he had not joined the other boys who teased Sydney about his bright red hair. But he hadn't tried to be friendly, either. "It's too bad when people act like chickens," said Grandpa.

Paul nodded. He decided he'd invite Sydney over to play with him when he got home.

HOW ABOUT YOU? Do you accept those who do not look or talk the way you do? Never call them names or tell jokes about them. Remember, that would be acting like a chicken! God wants you to love others and treat them kindly. Perhaps there is a "different" person in your school or neighborhood who needs your friendship. God loves that person. Will you show him or her God's love? *C.E.Y.*

TO MEMORIZE: "A new commandment I give you: Love one another. As I have loved you, so you must love one another." *John 13:34*

31 March

FOLLOW THE LEADER

FROM THE BIBLE:

Teach these things and insist that everyone learn them. Don't let anyone think less of you because you are young. Be an example to all believers in what you teach, in the way you live, in your love, your faith, and your purity. Until I get there, focus on reading the Scriptures to the church, encouraging the believers, and teaching them.

Do not neglect the spiritual gift you received through the prophecies spoken to you when the elders of the church laid their hands on you. Give your complete attention to these matters. Throw yourself into your tasks so that everyone will see your progress. Keep a close watch on yourself and on your teaching. Stay true to what is right, and God will save you and those who hear you.

1 TIMOTHY 4:11-16

Be a good example

STEVE OFTEN was impatient with his little sister, Karen. He was tired of her always copying him and following him wherever he went.

One day Mother sent Steve to Grandpa Wells with some homemade cinnamon rolls. As they sat down to visit and enjoy a roll, there was a knock at the door. "More company?" wondered Grandpa.

"Karen!" exclaimed Steve as the door opened. "Mother is going to be mad at you!" He turned to Grandpa. "Karen tries to go everywhere I go and do everything I do," he complained.

"Steve, that's probably the highest compliment she could pay you," Grandpa said. "She looks up to you. You're her example. Where you lead, she will follow."

"She looks up to me all right," said Steve. "She follows me like a shadow. And if I say I'm hungry, she says 'Me, too.' "

"Me, too," Karen said.

"Well, let's eat," said Grandpa with a chuckle.

"Thanks, Grandpa, but I have to get Karen home," Steve said. "She can share my roll on the way."

Steve glanced at Karen as she thrust her hand into his and trotted along beside him. He remembered Grandpa's words about being an example. *From now on, I'm going to be the best example for my little sister that I can be,* he decided. He knew he'd need the Lord's help for that.

HOW ABOUT YOU? Real life is a little bit like the game "Follow the Leader." Everyone is both a follower and a leader. You follow someone and someone follows you. First, be sure you are following the right leader—the Lord Jesus Christ. Second, be sure you are setting a good example for those who look up to you and follow you. *B.J.W.*

TO MEMORIZE: Don't let anyone look down on you because you are young, but set an example for the believers in speech, in life, in love, in faith and in purity. *1 Timothy 4:12* (NIV)

1 April

APRIL BIRTHDAY!

FROM THE BIBLE:

Follow God's example in everything you do, because you are his dear children. Live a life filled with love for others, following the example of Christ, who loved you and gave himself as a sacrifice to take away your sins. And God was pleased, because that sacrifice was like sweet perfume to him. . . .

For though your hearts were once full of darkness, now you are full of light from the Lord, and your behavior should show it! For this light within you produces only what is good and right and true.

Try to find out what is pleasing to the Lord. Take no part in the worthless deeds of evil and darkness; instead, rebuke and expose them. It is shameful even to talk about the things that ungodly people do in secret. But when the light shines on them, it becomes clear how evil these things are.

EPHESIANS 5:1-2, 8-13

Sin hinders your light

"HAPPY BIRTHDAY dear Daddy, happy birthday to you!" sang Chad and Stacy as their mother set the cake on the table. The children urged him to make a wish and blow out the candles.

Dad took a deep breath and blew! All the little lights on the cake went out. Suddenly one of them recovered and burned brightly again. "Oops," said Dad. He tried again. The candle flickered and appeared to go out, but then the flame came back. "Hey, wait a minute," said Dad, while the kids roared with laughter. "Whose idea was this?" he growled playfully.

"Chad got that candle at Pete's Party Store," laughed Stacy. "It's a special candle that won't blow out until you put it under water."

"That's what you get for having your birthday on April 1," teased Chad. "Happy birthday, and Happy April Fool's Day!"

The children each took turns to see if they could blow out the light. Even Mother couldn't do it. "That special candle reminds me of what God has done for us," said Dad finally. "He has given us the privilege of being lights in this world. When we allow sin to enter our lives, it blows against our lights, causing them to flicker. That makes us ineffective, but let's thank the Lord that he doesn't allow our lights to go out completely. And let's make up our minds to keep our lights free from sin so they can burn brightly for Jesus."

HOW ABOUT YOU? Is your "light" burning brightly? Or is there sin—such as disobedience, a lie, an unkind act—blowing against it? If there is, it will keep you from being a good testimony for Jesus. Confess that sin, ask God's forgiveness, and shine for him. *H.W.M.*

TO MEMORIZE: Let your light shine before men, that they may see your good deeds and praise your Father in heaven. *Matthew 5:16* (NIV)

DANGER: MOSQUITOES!

FROM THE BIBLE:

Therefore, since we are surrounded by such a huge crowd of witnesses to the life of faith, let us strip off every weight that slows us down, especially the sin that so easily hinders our progress. And let us run with endurance the race that God has set before us. We do this by keeping our eyes on Jesus, on whom our faith depends from start to finish. He was willing to die a shameful death on the cross because of the joy he knew would be his afterward. Now he is seated in the place of highest honor beside God's throne in heaven. Think about all he endured when sinful people did such terrible things to him, so that you don't become weary and give up. After all, you have not yet given your lives in your struggle against sin.

HEBREWS 12:1-4

JONATHAN PHILLIPS wanted to be a missionary when he grew up, so he was excited when Dr. Cook, a missionary from Africa, came to visit one evening. "What is it really like in the jungle, Dr. Cook? I'll bet it's exciting."

Jonathan's sister, Lisa, shuddered. "I think it would be scary, with all those lions and snakes and elephants."

"I'm not chicken!" Jonathan boasted. "If a big lion came at me, I'd just shoot him with my high-powered rifle. Bam! Bam!"

Dr. Cook laughed. "I'm glad you're so brave, Jonathan," he said. "I have seen some dangerous animals in Africa, but not the kind you're thinking of. Our biggest enemies in the jungle are mosquitoes."

"Mosquitoes?" scoffed Jonathan in unbelief. "How can you even compare a dinky, little mosquito with a big, ferocious lion? Lions can kill people."

"Actually, mosquitoes and other insects kill far more people than big animals do," said Dr. Cook. "They carry malaria, yellow fever, and other diseases. Many people have had to leave the mission field because of those tiny mosquitoes."

Jonathan's father spoke up. "That principle applies to our Christian life, too," he said. "Often it's not the big things that cause us to be discouraged. It's the little things like getting bored or not getting along with people."

"Well, I still want to be a missionary in Africa," said Jonathan, "but I'll be sure to watch out for those dangerous animals—the mosquitoes!"

HOW ABOUT YOU? You may think you'd be willing to fight great battles for Jesus' sake, but how are you handling the little problems in your life—friends who tease you, tough homework assignments, a brother or sister you can't get along with, or a parent or teacher who just doesn't seem to understand? Don't let "mosquitoes" keep you from doing God's will. *S.L.K.*

TO MEMORIZE: I can do everything with the help of Christ who gives me the strength I need. *Philippians 4:13*

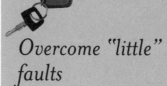

Overcome "little" faults

3 April

SUBSTITUTE TEACHER

FROM THE BIBLE:

Obey the government, for God is the one who put it there. All governments have been placed in power by God. So those who refuse to obey the laws of the land are refusing to obey God, and punishment will follow. For the authorities do not frighten people who are doing right, but they frighten those who do wrong. So do what they say, and you will get along well. The authorities are sent by God to help you. But if you are doing something wrong, of course you should be afraid, for you will be punished. The authorities are established by God for that very purpose, to punish those who do wrong. So you must obey the government for two reasons: to keep from being punished and to keep a clear conscience.

ROMANS 13:1-5

Respect authority

"HI, MOM," said Jane. "We had a substitute teacher today. You would have laughed!"

"What was so funny?"

"Well, Jarrett, Mike, and John switched seats. So all day long our sub was calling them the wrong names," Jane explained. "Then some kids told her we always get out early for recess, so we got fifteen extra minutes of recess! What a dummy!"

Mom frowned. "How was your substitute supposed to know who the kids were?" she asked.

Jane shrugged. "I suppose our teacher left her a seating chart."

"How would she know if the boys were in the right seats?" asked Mom. "And how would she know if the kids were lying about recess?"

"I don't know," answered Jane.

"It really wasn't funny, or kind, to fool her and laugh at her," Mom said.

"Well, she's just a sub," said Jane. "It doesn't matter."

"Oh yes, it does matter!" Mom exclaimed. "You are under her authority while she's in your class. That means you must respect and obey her. It's common courtesy *and* a command from God."

Jane's eyes widened. "It is? I thought the Bible just said to obey your parents."

"It also tells us to obey anyone who's in authority over us," said Mom. "That includes substitute teachers."

"She must have felt really bad," said Jane. "Hey, Mom, will you drive me back to school? She said she'd be correcting papers after school, so I could apologize to her."

"Great idea!" said Mom. "Let's go."

HOW ABOUT YOU? Have you or any of your classmates ever had a little "fun" with a substitute teacher? Have you played tricks and given the substitute a bad day? Did you think it was funny? God didn't. He tells us that we must respect and obey anyone who has authority over us. *D.S.M.*

TO MEMORIZE: "Everyone must submit himself to the governing authorities, for there is no authority except that which God has established." *Romans 13:1* (NIV)

A MESSED-UP MESSENGER

FROM THE BIBLE:

[Barnabas and Saul] preached from town to town across the entire island until finally they reached Paphos, where they met a Jewish sorcerer, a false prophet named Bar-Jesus. He had attached himself to the governor, Sergius Paulus, a man of considerable insight and understanding. The governor invited Barnabas and Saul to visit him, for he wanted to hear the word of God. But Elymas, the sorcerer (as his name means in Greek), interfered and urged the governor to pay no attention to what Saul and Barnabas said. He was trying to turn the governor away from the Christian faith.

Then Saul, also known as Paul, filled with the Holy Spirit, looked the sorcerer in the eye and said, "You son of the Devil, full of every sort of trickery and villainy, enemy of all that is good, will you never stop perverting the true ways of the Lord? And now the Lord has laid his hand of punishment upon you, and you will be stricken awhile with blindness." Instantly mist and darkness fell upon him, and he began wandering around begging for someone to take his hand and lead him.

ACTS 13:6-11

Give out God's message

MIKE AND LAURA enjoyed sending messages to each other by way of their smart dog, Duke. Mike would fasten a note on Duke's collar and say, "Go to Laura." Duke would trot down the hall to Laura's room. Then Laura would answer the note and tell Duke, "Go to Mike." Duke would obediently return to Mike's room.

One day Mike got hungry while he was doing homework. He knew Laura had some candy, so he asked for some in a note and attached it to Duke's collar. "Duke, go to Laura."

Duke trotted out of the room, but he didn't return. Mike decided to check on his messenger. "He never got here," said Laura. "I think he heard Mom open the cupboard door."

Sure enough, Duke had gone to the kitchen, and Mom had let him outside. Now Mike's messenger was running around the yard chasing a rabbit!

"So much for my messenger," Mike laughed.

"That's also the way Christians are sometimes," said Mother. "We agree to be God's messengers—but then we get sidetracked."

"Like when I was supposed to practice my trumpet for church, but I got sidetracked playing baseball," suggested Mike.

"Or when I was supposed to write a letter to a missionary as a Sunday school project but ended up playing video games instead," Laura added.

"Right," said Mother. "The message we have about the Lord is important. It takes a serious messenger to deliver a serious message."

HOW ABOUT YOU? Do you sometimes get sidetracked from giving out God's message? Do you get so busy watching TV you don't have time to memorize Bible verses or practice your special music for church? Do you forget to ask your friends to church because you're so busy talking about other things? Remember, it takes a serious messenger to deliver a serious message. *L.M.W.*

TO MEMORIZE: Go into all the world and preach the Good News to everyone, everywhere. *Mark 16:15*

5 April

HEALING THE HURT
(PART 1)

FROM THE BIBLE:

As God's messenger, I give each of you this warning: Be honest in your estimate of yourselves, measuring your value by how much faith God has given you. Just as our bodies have many parts and each part has a special function, so it is with Christ's body. We are all parts of his one body, and each of us has different work to do. And since we are all one body in Christ, we belong to each other, and each of us needs all the others.

God has given each of us the ability to do certain things well. So if God has given you the ability to prophesy, speak out when you have faith that God is speaking through you. If your gift is that of serving others, serve them well. If you are a teacher, do a good job of teaching. If your gift is to encourage others, do it! If you have money, share it generously. If God has given you leadership ability, take the responsibility seriously. And if you have a gift for showing kindness to others, do it gladly.

ROMANS 12:3-8

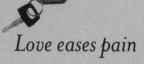

Love eases pain

"LOOK AT the assignment Miss Grice gave us in Sunday school today," said Amy, handing a paper to her mother.

Suddenly, four-year-old Megan came bursting into the room. "Mommy! That flower hurt my finger!"

Gently, Mother pulled the thorn out of Megan's finger, cleaned off the blood, and gave her a kiss. Smiling, Megan went back outside.

Mother turned back to the paper Amy had handed her. "Find a need and fill it; find a hurt and heal it," she read. "That's a good assignment."

"Sure," groaned Amy, "except I'm not a doctor. How can I heal someone?"

"Did Miss Grice explain that there are different kinds of hurts?" Mother asked.

Amy nodded. "Besides physical hurts, there are mental and spiritual hurts. But what can I do? I'm just a kid." She sighed. "I know that Karen's folks are separated. And I know that John's big brother is in jail for pushing drugs. And Mandy's dad is out of work, so she never has money for extra school activities. But I can't heal their hurts."

Mother smiled. "When Megan came crying to me a while ago, I didn't really heal her finger. I just gave her a lot of love, and she felt better," she said. "You may not be able to solve anyone else's problems, but you can encourage them. And you can point them to Jesus, the one who really can heal their hurts. Pray about it, and the Lord will show you what you can do."

HOW ABOUT YOU? Do you know someone who is hurting? You can demonstrate God's love by showing that you care. Smile at that person. Talk to him. Pray for him. Share something from God's Word. Try to heal at least one hurt this week. *B.J.W.*

TO MEMORIZE: All of you should be of one mind, full of sympathy toward each other, loving one another with tender hearts and humble minds.
1 Peter 3:8

HEALING THE HURT

(PART 2)

FROM THE BIBLE:

Brothers and sisters, we urge you to warn those who are lazy. Encourage those who are timid. Take tender care of those who are weak. Be patient with everyone.

See that no one pays back evil for evil, but always try to do good to each other and to everyone else.

Always be joyful. Keep on praying. No matter what happens, always be thankful, for this is God's will for you who belong to Christ Jesus.

Do not stifle the Holy Spirit. Do not scoff at prophecies, but test everything that is said. Hold on to what is good. Keep away from every kind of evil.

Now may the God of peace make you holy in every way, and may your whole spirit and soul and body be kept blameless until that day when our Lord Jesus Christ comes again.

1 THESSALONIANS 5:14-23

"WHAT AM I going to do?" Amy asked Kerri as they walked home from school. "It's Thursday, and I still haven't helped heal anyone's hurt."

"Me, neither," said Kerri. "Guess we'll just have to tell Miss Grice that we're not good doctors."

Amy changed the subject. "What did you make on today's math test?"

"Eighty-four," Kerri said with a sigh.

"That's not too bad. Most of the class failed," Amy said. "Julie didn't get one problem right! She's so dumb!"

"No wonder she doesn't have any friends. She . . ." Kerri stopped. "Amy, how would you feel if you failed in everything and didn't have any friends and everyone said you were dumb? You'd hurt, wouldn't you?"

Amy blinked. "Kerri, are you suggesting that we try to heal Julie's hurt?"

Kerri nodded her head solemnly.

"Well, OK," Amy agreed. "Let's stop at her house and ask if she wants to come over tonight and do homework with us. Then our assignment will be done."

"One evening won't do it," Kerri said wisely. "Remember last year when you broke your leg, Amy? You had to go to the doctor again and again, and it took months for your leg to heal. Julie has been hurting for a long time. It will take lots of care for her wounds to heal."

"Do you mean we'll have to be her friends for a long time?" Amy asked.

Kerri nodded.

"Well," Amy sighed, "here's Julie's house now. Let's get started. And we should introduce Julie to Jesus. He's the one who can really heal her hurts."

HOW ABOUT YOU? Do you know someone who needs a friend? Are you willing to be that friend? Be as helpful as you can, and don't forget to introduce him or her to your best friend, Jesus. *B.J.W.*

TO MEMORIZE: A friend loves at all times, and a brother is born for adversity. *Proverbs 17:17* (NIV)

Introduce friends to Jesus

7 April

NO LETTER TODAY

FROM THE BIBLE:

Bend down, O Lord, and hear
my prayer;
answer me, for I need your
help.
Protect me, for I am devoted to
you.
Save me, for I serve you and
trust you.
You are my God.
Be merciful, O Lord,
for I am calling on you
constantly.
Give me happiness, O Lord,
for my life depends on you.
O Lord, you are so good, so
ready to forgive,
so full of unfailing love for all
who ask your aid.
Listen closely to my prayer,
O Lord;
hear my urgent cry.
I will call to you whenever
trouble strikes,
and you will answer me.

PSALM 86:1-7

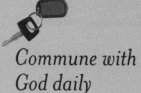

Commune with God daily

"WHERE'S PAM?" asked Dad at the breakfast table.

"She's washing her hair," Andy said.

"Doesn't she know it's time for devotions?"

"Yes, and she knows we can't wait for her," said Mother. "What bothers me is that she doesn't seem to care. I'll talk to her this afternoon."

After school Pam sat in the kitchen looking through the mail that had come. "All junk mail and bills," she complained. "I can't understand why Sherry hasn't written me. I always answer her letters right away, but she takes weeks and weeks to answer mine. Some friend she is!"

"You have one friend who might say the same thing about you," suggested Mother.

"Who?"

"Jesus," Mother replied quietly. "Lately you've been too busy to communicate with him. Many days he walks away from his 'mailbox' without having received anything from you. Do you suppose he says, 'I wonder why I haven't heard from Pam?'"

"But, Mother—" Pam began.

"And I wonder how much of the 'mail' we send him is junk mail and bills," Mother continued thoughtfully. "How often do we pray, 'Lord, I've done this for you, so you owe me this much'? And how often do we send him empty, repetitious promises?"

"I guess I'm as bad as Sherry," Pam said. "I've been disappointing the Lord, just as Sherry's been disappointing me. I think I'll go read my letter from God and talk to him."

HOW ABOUT YOU? Have you been neglecting your 'correspondence' with the Lord? Do you expect to receive a quick reply from him but often go for days without responding to his letter to you? How often is he disappointed because he doesn't hear from you? Make up your mind right now to communicate with him daily. *B.J.W.*

TO MEMORIZE: Call to me and I will answer you and tell you great and unsearchable things you do not know. *Jeremiah 33:3* (NIV)

COMPANY'S COMING

FROM THE BIBLE:

The end of the world is coming soon. Therefore, be earnest and disciplined in your prayers. Most important of all, continue to show deep love for each other, for love covers a multitude of sins. Cheerfully share your home with those who need a meal or a place to stay.

God has given gifts to each of you from his great variety of spiritual gifts. Manage them well so that God's generosity can flow through you. Are you called to be a speaker? Then speak as though God himself were speaking through you. Are you called to help others? Do it with all the strength and energy that God supplies. Then God will be given glory in everything through Jesus Christ. All glory and power belong to him forever and ever. Amen.

1 PETER 4:7-11

Entertain cheerfully

"NOT AGAIN," Tanya complained. "All we ever do is have missionaries stay at our house. Or visiting preachers—or even complete strangers, like when that family got stranded in the snowstorm last winter!"

"I thought you enjoyed having company," Mother replied.

"Sure, once in a while," Tanya admitted. "But other people don't have them as often as we do."

"That's part of our ministry," Dad explained.

"Ministry?"

"That's right," her father answered. "Mother and I wanted to go to the mission field, but my health didn't permit that."

"So, we decided we would open our home to missionaries whenever we could," finished Mother, "and we also want to use our home as a place to witness to others."

Tanya had never thought about entertaining people as a "ministry." For her it had meant doing more dishes and giving up her bedroom to guests. "Does the Bible say you're supposed to have company?"

Dad smiled. "You won't find those exact words in the Bible," he said, "but it does say we should be 'given to hospitality.' "

"It also says . . ." Mother picked up her Bible, opened it, and began to read aloud. "Let brotherly love continue. Be not forgetful to entertain strangers; for thereby some have entertained angels unawares."

"Is that like having missionaries stay with you while they're in town?" Tanya asked.

Mother nodded. "That's part of it. It's sharing your house and your love with others."

"And my room, which I guess I better clean," said Tanya, smiling.

HOW ABOUT YOU? When you have to help prepare a meal, wash extra dishes, or give up your room because your parents are entertaining, do you grumble about it, or do you think of it as sharing what you have with others? God wants you to share. Do it cheerfully for him. *R.I.J.*

TO MEMORIZE: Cheerfully share your home with those who need a meal or a place to stay. *1 Peter 4:9*

9 April

TOO MUCH SALT

FROM THE BIBLE:

You are the salt of the earth. But what good is salt if it has lost its flavor? Can you make it useful again? It will be thrown out and trampled underfoot as worthless. You are the light of the world—like a city on a mountain, glowing in the night for all to see. Don't hide your light under a basket! Instead, put it on a stand and let it shine for all. In the same way, let your good deeds shine out for all to see, so that everyone will praise your heavenly Father.

MATTHEW 5:13-16

Witness tactfully

"KEITH SURE is stupid," Mark said as he and his family ate supper. "He won't even believe the facts! After I saw him cheat on a test today, I told him he was a sinner headed for hell and that he should repent."

"Sounds like you came on a little strong," said Dad.

"I was just trying to be the salt of the earth," replied Mark. "I invited him to church, but he said he already went. I told him his church must be stupid if he wasn't a Christian yet."

"Mark!" exclaimed Dad. "If you insult the person you're talking to, he'll just get angry and be turned off to the Lord."

Mark picked up the salt shaker. "If Keith won't believe me, that's his own fault," he said as he sprinkled his food with salt. Just then, the top fell off, and all the salt poured onto his plate.

"Oh no!" cried Mother. "I must not have tightened the top when I filled the shaker this afternoon!"

"Mark," Dad said, "that's what you tried to do with Keith. Just as too much salt spoiled your food, your words today may have spoiled his interest in spiritual things."

Mark looked in dismay at the food on his plate. "I guess you're right, Dad," he admitted. "I'll apologize tomorrow, and next time I'll try to be kind and tactful."

"Good," said Mother. "Now I'll get you some more food."

HOW ABOUT YOU? Do you witness to your friends? It's important, because you may be the only Christian they know. It's also important to be careful as to how you go about it. Make sure you don't offend people. They have feelings just like you do. Pray about it, and then trust the Lord to give you the right words. *D.S.M.*

TO MEMORIZE: Let your conversation be always full of grace, seasoned with salt, so that you may know how to answer everyone. *Colossians 4:6* (NIV)

SIDETRACKED

FROM THE BIBLE:

I know the Lord is always with me.
I will not be shaken, for he is right beside me.
No wonder my heart is filled with joy,
and my mouth shouts his praises!
My body rests in safety.
For you will not leave my soul among the dead
or allow your godly one to rot in the grave.
You will show me the way of life,
granting me the joy of your presence
and the pleasures of living with you forever.

PSALM 16:8-11

Keep God first

MOTHER WAS TAKING Shania shopping for some new gym shoes. As they waited at a railroad crossing, the train moved slower and slower. Finally it stopped!

"Why would a train stop way out here on the edge of town?" Shania grumbled.

"They're probably sidetracking some cars at the grain elevator," Mother replied.

"What does sidetracking mean?"

"Well, they unfasten some of the cars from the middle of the train and pull them off onto a side track," replied Mother. "The cars being sidetracked probably are full of grain they've brought to the elevator."

After a 15-minute delay, they were finally on their way again to get the shoes.

As Shania sat in church the next day, Pastor Brown's sermon reminded her of the train. "Some Christians determine in their hearts that they will serve the Lord and do whatever he wants them to do, but somehow they get sidetracked," the pastor said, "and time is wasted."

Shania recalled how time was lost while the train was trying to maneuver the train cars onto the side track. "Sometimes the love of money will sidetrack a Christian from wanting to do God's will," said Pastor Brown. "Sometimes it's a desire for fame or pleasure. Whatever keeps us from doing what the Lord wants us to do is wrong."

Shania realized that she had been sidetracked when she begged Mother to take her shopping instead of going with her Sunday school class to pass out tracts. *Dear Jesus,* she prayed, *don't let me get sidetracked out of your will. Amen.*

HOW ABOUT YOU? Have you done what today's memory verse says? Even if you're a Christian, it's sometimes hard to put God first in your life. But when you do, you won't be sorry. Don't let anything sidetrack you from your goal. *R.E.P.*

TO MEMORIZE: I have set the Lord always before me. Because he is at my right hand, I will not be shaken. *Psalm 16:8* (NIV)

11 April

WHERE THE FISH ARE

FROM THE BIBLE:

But they all began making excuses. One said he had just bought a field and wanted to inspect it, so he asked to be excused. Another said he had just bought five pair of oxen and wanted to try them out. Another had just been married, so he said he couldn't come.

The servant returned and told his master what they had said. His master was angry and said, "Go quickly into the streets and alleys of the city and invite the poor, the crippled, the lame, and the blind." After the servant had done this, he reported, "There is still room for more." So his master said, "Go out into the country lanes and behind the hedges and urge anyone you find to come, so that the house will be full. For none of those I invited first will get even the smallest taste of what I had prepared for them."

LUKE 14:18-24

Find opportunities to witness

"OUR SUNDAY SCHOOL contest isn't fair," complained Caleb one Saturday morning. "It's called 'Fishing for Jesus,' and we're supposed to bring visitors. But my friends already go to Sunday school, so I don't have anybody to invite. The prize is a fishing rod. I sure could use that!"

"Hmmm," Dad looked thoughtful. "Speaking of fishing, want to go?"

"Yes!" yelled Caleb.

"I'll get the fishing gear," said Dad. "Meet me out in the backyard."

When Caleb ran out the back door a little later, he stopped and stared. Dad was sitting in a lawn chair, holding his fishing rod. The hook lay on the grass. "What are you doing?" asked Caleb.

"Fishing. Shhhh! Don't scare them away," Dad whispered.

"Fishing?!" exclaimed Caleb. "There aren't any fish here. C'mon, Dad. Let's go where the fish are."

Dad grinned. "Great idea." He reeled in his line and got up. "Good thing I wasn't trying to catch the most fish for a contest," he observed. "I would have lost. Let's go to Peerson's Lake. That's where the fish are."

As Caleb and Dad got into the truck, Caleb spoke. "I know what you're saying, Dad. You're telling me to go where the 'fish' are for my contest, too."

Dad nodded. "I think you'll find they're not far away."

"Yeah," said Caleb. "That new kid down the street might come. And I could ask some guys at school. I'll make some phone calls when we get home."

HOW ABOUT YOU? Do all your friends already know Jesus? It's wonderful if they do, but don't take it for granted. Talk to them about the Lord. And don't limit your witness just to those you know best. Jesus wants you to bring others to him. Look around. You probably won't have to go very far to be a fisherman for Jesus. *H.W.M.*

TO MEMORIZE: Come, be my disciples, and I will show you how to fish for people! *Mark 1:17*

THE WRONG SHOES

FROM THE BIBLE:

[Jesus said,] "You must be compassionate, just as your Father is compassionate.

"Stop judging others, and you will not be judged. Stop criticizing others, or it will all come back on you. If you forgive others, you will be forgiven. If you give, you will receive. Your gift will return to you in full measure, pressed down, shaken together to make room for more, and running over. Whatever measure you use in giving—large or small—it will be used to measure what is given back to you."

LUKE 6:36-38

Don't judge others

LORI HUNG UP the phone. "I wish I hadn't invited Kathleen over. She's in one of her moods."

"Maybe you can cheer her up," Mother suggested. "She's a new Christian in a family of unbelievers, you know."

"I get tired of trying to cheer her up," complained Lori.

Later that evening, the girls came into the kitchen. "Look, Mother," said Lori, pointing to Kathleen's feet. "Kathleen has new shoes exactly like mine."

"You must think alike," Mother said, smiling.

The girls had a great time together. The next morning Lori asked if she could go home with Kathleen after school.

"Yes," Mother answered. "Dad can pick you up on his way home from work."

That evening when Lori came in, she plopped down on the couch. "It's so depressing at Kathleen's. Her dad was in a bad mood, little Pete was crying, and Mrs. Mason was at work." Lori took off her shoes and rubbed her heel. "And my feet hurt. These new shoes rubbed a blister on my heel."

Mother looked inside Lori's shoe. "I thought you wore a size six. This is size five and a half."

"No wonder my feet were hurting!" Lori laughed. "Kathleen must have worn my shoes all day and I wore hers."

"An Indian proverb says, 'Never judge a man until you have walked a mile in his moccasins,'" Mother said. "I guess you just walked in Kathleen's."

Lori nodded. "I'm going to stop criticizing her and pray for her instead." Lori stood up. "And now I'm going to call her and see how she liked walking in my shoes."

HOW ABOUT YOU? Are you too quick to criticize others when you do not understand their behavior? Perhaps you need to "walk in their shoes" for a while. Try to understand their circumstances better. And don't judge them; pray for them. *B.J.W.*

TO MEMORIZE: Don't speak evil against each other, my dear brothers and sisters. *James 4:11*

13 April

IT'S TIME TO MOVE

FROM THE BIBLE:

For we know that when this earthly tent we live in is taken down—when we die and leave these bodies—we will have a home in heaven, an eternal body made for us by God himself and not by human hands. We grow weary in our present bodies, and we long for the day when we will put on our heavenly bodies like new clothing.

2 CORINTHIANS 5:1-2

Death is just a move

JULIE RANG the doorbell. When the door opened, she said, "Grannie, Daddy's coming to get us tomorrow!"

Grannie sighed. "I thought he was going to wait until school was out before he moved you to the coast."

"He said he couldn't wait any longer. Daddy wants us with him." Julie paused. "I wish you were really my grandma and could move with us."

"Well, I'll miss you, honey. But you need to be with your father," Grannie said.

Later, as Mother and Julie packed crates of dishes, Mother answered the phone. "Hello. . . . Yes. . . . She what?" Julie looked up in alarm. "When? Yes, thank you for calling." As Mother hung up the phone, she wiped a tear from her eye. "I have some sad news, Julie," she said. "One of the neighbors just found Grannie. She died while sitting in her rocking chair."

"No!" Julie cried out. "I just saw her a few hours ago, and she was fine."

"Apparently she had a heart attack," Mother said, hugging Julie, "and the Lord took her home."

That evening, Julie sighed as Mother tucked her in bed. "I guess God couldn't wait any longer to have Grannie with him," Julie said.

Mother nodded. "Now get some sleep. Tomorrow Daddy is coming."

"Do you think Grannie was as glad to see her heavenly Father as I will be to see Daddy tomorrow?"

"I'm sure of it," Mother replied.

HOW ABOUT YOU? Has someone you love moved to heaven lately? Of course, you will miss that person, but try not to be too sad. Think of the joy he is experiencing being with his heavenly Father. And someday you can see him again—if you are a child of God. *B.J.W.*

TO MEMORIZE: Brothers, we do not want you to be ignorant about those who fall asleep, or to grieve like the rest of men, who have no hope.
1 Thessalonians 4:13 (NIV)

14 April

GOD'S PATCHWORK QUILT

FROM THE BIBLE:

Yes, there are many parts, but only one body. The eye can never say to the hand, "I don't need you." The head can't say to the feet, "I don't need you."

In fact, some of the parts that seem weakest and least important are really the most necessary. And the parts we regard as less honorable are those we clothe with the greatest care. So we carefully protect from the eyes of others those parts that should not be seen, while other parts do not require this special care. So God has put the body together in such a way that extra honor and care are given to those parts that have less dignity. This makes for harmony among the members, so that all the members care for each other equally. If one part suffers, all the parts suffer with it, and if one part is honored, all the parts are glad.

Now all of you together are Christ's body, and each one of you is a separate and necessary part of it.

1 CORINTHIANS 12:20-27

We need one another

JANET LOOKED through a box of material scraps while her mother sewed. "Mother! Look at this gorgeous blue satin!"

"It is pretty," Mother agreed, "but there's not enough to make a dress, or even a blouse." Janet laid it back in the box.

Several weeks later, Janet found a large gift-wrapped bundle on her bed. When she tore off the wrappings, she found a pretty, handmade patchwork quilt. "Look at all the colors and designs!" Janet said. "And the border—it's made of that pretty blue satin I liked!"

"It would have been a shame not to use that material for something," said Mother. "And while I was sewing the quilt together, I realized something."

"What?" Janet asked.

"God has a patchwork quilt, too—the church!" Mom replied. "Christians can be young, old, rich, or poor. Some have many talents, others just a few. But together they make a beautiful finished product, just like this quilt."

"It is beautiful," Janet agreed. "None of the pieces would be of much use by themselves."

"No, they wouldn't," answered Mother. "There are some Christians who try to make it on their own, without even going to church or making Christian friends. But Christians need one another."

"The next time I feel like a small, unimportant scrap," Janet said, "I'll just remember that I'm an important part of God's patchwork quilt!"

HOW ABOUT YOU? If you are a Christian, you are an important part of Christ's body, the church. That means you need to serve him, and serve others. You also need the help that other Christians can give you. So don't be a loner. Go to a church where Christians study the Bible. Get involved! No matter how unimportant you may feel sometimes, God has a special place for you! *S.L.K.*

TO MEMORIZE: Now you are the body of Christ, and each one of you is a part of it.
1 Corinthians 12:27 (NIV)

15 April

DIG DEEP

FROM THE BIBLE:

No, the wisdom we speak of is the secret wisdom of God, which was hidden in former times, though he made it for our benefit before the world began. But the rulers of this world have not understood it; if they had, they would never have crucified our glorious Lord. That is what the Scriptures mean when they say,

"No eye has seen, no ear has heard,
and no mind has imagined
what God has prepared
for those who love him."

But we know these things because God has revealed them to us by his Spirit, and his Spirit searches out everything and shows us even God's deep secrets. No one can know what anyone else is really thinking except that person alone, and no one can know God's thoughts except God's own Spirit. And God has actually given us his Spirit (not the world's spirit) so we can know the wonderful things God has freely given us.

1 CORINTHIANS 2:7-12

Read the Bible thoughtfully

NATHAN YAWNED and quickly scanned the page of his Bible. Then he closed it and set it on the nightstand just as Mother came in to say good night. "Does the *plunk-plunk* of the oil well pump ever bother you at night?" she asked.

Nathan shook his head. "No, I guess I'm so used to it, I never hear it. It's been out there behind the barn as long as I can remember."

"But I can remember when it wasn't there," Mother said. "Before oil was discovered, this farm wasn't worth much. We lived in the old house, and you were a baby."

Nathan rearranged the pillow under his head as Mother continued. "That's when the oil company asked permission to drill on this land."

"And they struck oil!" Nathan declared.

"All those years while your grandparents were hardly able to make a living on this farm, there was great wealth under their feet. It wasn't discovered, though, until someone really *dug deep.*" Mother emphasized the last two words. "Son, there is also wealth in the Word of God, but you won't find it unless you dig deep. You'll never find the riches of God's Word by merely scanning the pages."

She kissed him lightly on the cheek before leaving the room. *How does Mother know I haven't been reading carefully?* Nathan wondered as the door closed behind her. He sat up in bed, turned on the lamp, and reached for his Bible.

HOW ABOUT YOU? Are you living in spiritual poverty? Do you scan the Word of God and never really think about what you're reading? Read it slowly and carefully. If you're too small to read it by yourself, listen carefully while someone reads to you. Think about what it says. Dig deep. You'll be amazed at the treasures you find. *B.J.W.*

TO MEMORIZE: O Lord, what great miracles you do! And how deep are your thoughts. *Psalm 92:5*

LOVE

FROM THE BIBLE:

Love is patient and kind. Love is not jealous or boastful or proud or rude. Love does not demand its own way. Love is not irritable, and it keeps no record of when it has been wronged. It is never glad about injustice but rejoices whenever the truth wins out. Love never gives up, never loses faith, is always hopeful, and endures through every circumstance.

Love will last forever, but prophecy and speaking in unknown languages and special knowledge will all disappear. . . .

It's like this: When I was a child, I spoke and thought and reasoned as a child does. But when I grew up, I put away childish things. Now we see things imperfectly as in a poor mirror, but then we will see everything with perfect clarity. All that I know now is partial and incomplete, but then I will know everything completely, just as God knows me now.

There are three things that will endure—faith, hope, and love—and the greatest of these is love.

1 CORINTHIANS 13:4-8, 11-13

Love is action

SHEILA'S FATHER was dropping her off at church for choir practice when he noticed a bumper sticker that read, "Have you hugged your kid today?"

Dad snorted. "That stupid bumper sticker makes me mad! I wonder how many kids have hugged their parents today!"

As Sheila jumped out of the car, she thought about her dad's words. She'd been praying for a long time that he would be saved. *I think I need to show him I love him whether he is saved or not,* she decided.

That afternoon Sheila cleaned her room and her closet. "Wow!" Dad said. "Did you clean your room without being told?"

Sheila nodded. "I just want you and Mother to know that I'm grateful for my things and that I love you," she explained.

After supper Sheila said, "Mother, I'll do the dishes. Why don't you and Daddy relax?"

"What has gotten into that child?" her father murmured as they went for a walk.

At bedtime, Sheila reached up and hugged her father, laughing as she did so. "See? Here is one kid who has hugged her parents today!" she giggled. She quickly kissed her mother's cheek and ran up the stairs.

Near the top step, she overheard her father say to her mother, "Sheila is a wonderful daughter. I think I'll go to church with you in the morning to hear her choir sing."

Sheila grinned. Love in action just might win her dad to the Lord.

HOW ABOUT YOU? Have you hugged your parents lately? Have you shown them in other ways that you love them? Maybe you know someone—a parent, a neighbor, a friend—who isn't saved and who may be won over by love in action. What can you do for them? Think about it. *R.E.P.*

TO MEMORIZE: But the fruit of the Spirit is love . . . *Galatians 5:22* (NIV)

17 April

JOY

FROM THE BIBLE:

So be truly glad! There is wonderful joy ahead, even though it is necessary for you to endure many trials for a while.

These trials are only to test your faith, to show that it is strong and pure. It is being tested as fire tests and purifies gold—and your faith is far more precious to God than mere gold. So if your faith remains strong after being tried by fiery trials, it will bring you much praise and glory and honor on the day when Jesus Christ is revealed to the whole world.

You love him even though you have never seen him. Though you do not see him, you trust him; and even now you are happy with a glorious, inexpressible joy. Your reward for trusting him will be the salvation of your souls. . . .

Always be full of joy in the Lord. I say it again—rejoice!

1 PETER 1:6-9;
PHILIPPIANS 4:4

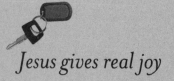

Jesus gives real joy

WHEN MICHELLE heard that Aunt Katie had a fast-growing type of cancer and wouldn't live long, she was heartbroken. Yet Aunt Katie smiled happily whenever Michelle went to visit her. "How can you be so happy?" Michelle exclaimed one day. "I feel miserable. Life will be just awful if you go away."

"Michelle, don't be afraid to use the word *die* around me," Aunt Katie answered gently. "I know I'm going to be with Jesus, and I won't have any more pain. I'm eager to go home to heaven, and I'm so glad you're going to join me there one day."

A few days later, Aunt Katie died. Many friends and relatives came to the funeral and shared words of sympathy. At first Michelle didn't think she could stand all this. She just wanted to go somewhere and cry her eyes out! She did cry—lots of times! But then she started to remember some of the things Aunt Katie had said to her, especially about going to heaven. She smiled when she thought of all the happy times they had together.

I loved her so much, and I'm not happy that she's gone, she thought. *But I do feel a certain kind of joy. I know Aunt Katie is at home with Jesus. I know she is joyful and has no more pain. And even though I miss her, I know I'll see her again when I go to heaven.*

HOW ABOUT YOU? Do you feel joy in your heart today, even when things go wrong? When you get blamed for something you didn't do, when a vacation trip "falls through," when your dog or someone you love dies, there still should be a sense of joy. All these things are temporary, but your salvation through Jesus is eternal. Real joy is found in Jesus. *R.E.P.*

TO MEMORIZE: But the fruit of the Spirit is love, joy . . . *Galatians 5:22* (NIV)

THE FIRE ALARM was ringing! But it was just ringing for a short period of time, stopping, and then starting again. Mrs. Elders said, "Children, you know what this means—it's a tornado drill! You all know what to do. Quiet now!"

James went over and opened the windows to equalize pressure inside and out, and David closed the curtains so any flying glass would not hit the children. The others filed silently into the hall. They lined up against the inside wall and crouched with their heads down to protect themselves.

Kelly wondered how long they would have to stay there when suddenly she heard a siren screaming outside. She began to tremble as the principal said over the intercom, "This is not a drill! I repeat, this is not a drill! A tornado has been spotted. Please remain calm and stay in your positions!"

Some children began to cry out in fear. However, the boy right next to Kelly seemed perfectly calm. "How can you be so calm, Michael?" Kelly asked, her voice shaking. "Listen to the wind! Aren't you afraid like the rest of us?"

"I did feel scared at first," Michael answered, "but I know Jesus as my Savior, and I asked him to help me not to be afraid. Even if I died, I know I would go to heaven. Jesus gives me peace."

Before long they realized that the tornado had missed their school. The students were allowed to return to their classrooms. Michael's calm, peaceful attitude had a big effect on Kelly.

HOW ABOUT YOU? Do storms frighten you? Are you scared in the dark? Whatever fear you have, give it to Jesus. This requires a decision on your part. Choose to let God's peace "rule in your heart." It will be a testimony to others who are fearful themselves. *R.E.P.*

TO MEMORIZE: But the fruit of the Spirit is love, joy, peace . . . *Galatians 5:22* (NIV)

PEACE

FROM THE BIBLE:

And let the peace that comes from Christ rule in your hearts. For as members of one body you are all called to live in peace. And always be thankful. . . .

Don't worry about anything; instead, pray about everything. Tell God what you need, and thank him for all he has done. If you do this, you will experience God's peace, which is far more wonderful than the human mind can understand. His peace will guard your hearts and minds as you live in Christ Jesus.

And now, dear brothers and sisters, let me say one more thing as I close this letter. Fix your thoughts on what is true and honorable and right. Think about things that are pure and lovely and admirable. Think about things that are excellent and worthy of praise. Keep putting into practice all you learned from me and heard from me and saw me doing, and the God of peace will be with you.

COLOSSIANS 3:15;
PHILIPPIANS 4:6-9

Jesus can calm fear

19 April

PATIENCE

FROM THE BIBLE:

We can rejoice, too, when we run into problems and trials, for we know that they are good for us—they help us learn to endure. And endurance develops strength of character in us, and character strengthens our confident expectation of salvation. And this expectation will not disappoint us. For we know how dearly God loves us, because he has given us the Holy Spirit to fill our hearts with his love.

ROMANS 5:3-5

Be patient with others

"DADDY, how long should I be patient with Jan?" asked Tina. Jan, who was the tallest girl in Tina's class, often made fun of her because she was a Christian.

"Well, another word for patience is long-suffering," explained Dad. "Sometimes Jesus allows us to suffer for a long time because of another person. But being patient with Jan will help you develop more patience."

The next day at school Jan shouted, "Be good, everyone! Here comes Tina, the perfect Christian. Hail to Tina! Should we bow down?" Tina wondered if the other kids laughed because they felt the same way, or because they were afraid of Jan.

At lunch Jan bumped into Tina's tray. Peas and carrots spilled all over Tina's blouse. She wanted so badly to get revenge, but she remembered that she should be willing to suffer long for the Lord.

After school, a new girl named Ramona walked beside Tina. "Tina, why do you just take all this trouble from Jan? Why don't you get even? I know I would!"

"I'm a Christian," Tina replied, "and the Bible tells me I should be willing to suffer long for Jesus' sake. I'm trying to do what God wants me to do."

Ramona looked thoughtful. "I'd like to find out more about your God if he gives you that kind of patience. I have a terrible temper!" she confessed.

"Daddy!" Tina shouted as she came in from school. "I may not ever lead Jan to Christ by learning patience, but it might help me win Ramona for the Lord!"

HOW ABOUT YOU? Do you feel like you have suffered for a long time at the hands of another person? Maybe the Lord is trying to develop the fruit of patience in your life. Then you can be an effective witness for him. *R.E.P.*

TO MEMORIZE: But the fruit of the Spirit is love, joy, peace, patience . . . *Galatians 5:22* (NIV)

KINDNESS

FROM THE BIBLE:

Then the King will say to those on the right, "Come, you who are blessed by my Father, inherit the Kingdom prepared for you from the foundation of the world. For I was hungry, and you fed me. I was thirsty, and you gave me a drink. I was a stranger, and you invited me into your home. I was naked, and you gave me clothing. I was sick, and you cared for me. I was in prison, and you visited me."

Then these righteous ones will reply, "Lord, when did we ever see you hungry and feed you? Or thirsty and give you something to drink? Or a stranger and show you hospitality? Or naked and give you clothing? When did we ever see you sick or in prison, and visit you?" And the King will tell them, "I assure you, when you did it to one of the least of these my brothers and sisters, you were doing it to me!"

MATTHEW 25:34-40

JENNY DIDN'T have many friends and sometimes got into trouble at school. Heather decided to show God's love to Jenny by being kind to her. With her mom's permission, Heather invited Jenny to come over for pizza.

After dinner, they had fun putting each other's hair up in French braids and hair clips. "Oh look, you have glitter hair gel!" Jenny said, spotting a shiny tube on the sink. "May I try some?"

"Sure," said Heather, handing her the shiny tube.

By the time Jenny went home, Heather felt good inside because she'd been kind. But then she noticed her hair gel was missing. After searching for it in all the places the girls had been, Heather suspected that Jenny had taken it. "Mom, how could she steal from me even though I was kind enough to invite her over?"

Mom put her arm around Heather. "That's a risk we take when we're kind to others. But don't let people who take advantage of your kindness keep you from being kind. When we're kind to another person, it's as though we're being kind to Jesus."

"What about my hair gel?"

"Let's pray for Jenny right now," Mom said. "We'll pray that if she did steal your gel, her conscience will hurt and she'll confess. Then call her and tell her you're missing it. Ask if she has it. If she confesses, thank her for being honest. If she denies it, let it go. We'll keep praying for her."

HOW ABOUT YOU? Do you show kindness without expecting anything in return? Do you share your toys, give clothes to needy children, or say kind words to others? Sometimes people will take advantage of your kindness. But that shouldn't stop you. If you want to be like Jesus, be kind and generous, no matter what. *L.A.P.*

TO MEMORIZE: But the fruit of the Spirit is love, joy, peace, patience, kindness . . . *Galatians 5:22* (NIV)

Be kind

21 April

GOODNESS

FROM THE BIBLE:

Jesus entered the Temple and began to drive out the merchants and their customers. He knocked over the tables of the money changers and the stalls of those selling doves. He said, "The Scriptures declare, 'My Temple will be called a place of prayer,' but you have turned it into a den of thieves!"

The blind and the lame came to him, and he healed them there in the Temple. The leading priests and the teachers of religious law saw these wonderful miracles and heard even the little children in the Temple shouting, "Praise God for the Son of David." But they were indignant.

MATTHEW 21:12-15

Love right; hate wrong

"I JUST CAN'T stand two of my best friends anymore!" declared Rachel when she came home from school. "Mom, they are being absolutely horrid to a new girl in our class just because she's a Mexican. I can't believe that Lisa and Sue can claim to be Christians and yet be so prejudiced against Maria! I know I'm not supposed to get angry with them, but what they're doing is so wrong!"

Mother put her arm around Rachel. "Honey, I'm proud of you for being angry this time! Even Jesus became angry when people did wrong things, like when he threw the moneychangers out of the temple."

"What can I do about Lisa and Sue?" Rachel asked.

"One fruit of the Spirit is goodness, and part of being good is to love what is right in the world and hate what Lisa and Sue are doing. Perhaps if you are kind to the new girl, they'll see the fruit of goodness in your life and remember that they should have the same fruit."

The next day at school, Rachel invited Maria to eat lunch with her.

"What are you doing?" whispered Sue. "She isn't like us, Rachel!"

Rachel waited until Maria was across the room before she answered Sue. "I'm just trying to do the good and right thing that I believe Jesus would want us to do," she said.

Lisa and Sue had to admit that Rachel was right. As they followed her example, they found that Maria was not so different after all. Soon all four were good friends.

HOW ABOUT YOU? Are you angered when you see something happening that you know is wrong? Part of the quality of goodness is to love the right and hate the wrong. Ask the Lord to show you the difference. *R.E.P.*

TO MEMORIZE: But the fruit of the Spirit is love, joy, peace, patience, kindness, goodness . . . *Galatians 5:22* (NIV)

FAITHFULNESS

FROM THE BIBLE:

Again, the Kingdom of Heaven can be illustrated by the story of a man going on a trip. He called together his servants and gave them money to invest for him while he was gone. He gave five bags of gold to one, two bags of gold to another, and one bag of gold to the last—dividing it in proportion to their abilities—and then left on his trip. . . .

After a long time their master returned from his trip and called them to give an account of how they had used his money. The servant to whom he had entrusted the five bags of gold said, "Sir, you gave me five bags of gold to invest, and I have doubled the amount." The master was full of praise. "Well done, my good and faithful servant. You have been faithful in handling this small amount, so now I will give you many more responsibilities. Let's celebrate together!"

MATTHEW 25:14-15, 19-21

Be dependable

PETER was trying to memorize the fruit of the Spirit listed in Galatians. "Hey, Mom, why is faith a fruit of the Spirit? I thought you needed faith before becoming a Christian."

Mother smiled. "That's true, but the Bible also tells us to have faith *after* we're Christians. For example, we should have faith that God will answer our prayers. Do you understand what *faithful* means?"

Peter nodded. "Dad calls Millie a faithful old dog. I guess that means she's always here when we need her," he said.

Mother laughed. "Yes, and we, too, should be faithful in what we do."

The next day Peter had agreed to mow Mrs. King's lawn next door for ten dollars. Just as Peter was putting gas in the mower, some of his friends approached.

"Hey, Pete! We're going to play baseball. C'mon," they urged. "We need a good third baseman."

There was nothing Peter would rather do than play baseball, so he put the gas can away. But just then old Millie came running around the corner of the garage. Stopping, Peter thought about his conversation with Mom the day before. *The fruit of the Spirit is . . . faithfulness,* he remembered. Reaching down, he patted Millie on the head and called to his friends, "You guys go on! I have a job to do right now."

HOW ABOUT YOU? When someone gives you a job to do, do you do it faithfully, no matter how large or small it is? Perhaps the job God has given you right now is to help Mom or be a good student. Are you faithful in whatever it is that God has given you to do? Be faithful so that when you stand before him someday, you will hear the words, "Well done, good and faithful servant!" *R.E.P.*

TO MEMORIZE: But the fruit of the Spirit is love, joy, peace, patience, kindness, goodness, faithfulness . . . *Galatians 5:22* (NIV)

23 April

GENTLENESS

FROM THE BIBLE:

The Lord's servants must not quarrel but must be kind to everyone. They must be able to teach effectively and be patient with difficult people.
2 TIMOTHY 2:24

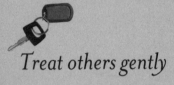

Treat others gently

ON TIM'S EIGHTH birthday, Dad and Mom surprised him with a puppy. Tim named her Sandy and soon taught her to fetch a stick and roll over. One day Tim's Dad brought home a leash and collar. "It's time to teach Sandy to walk sensibly at your side," he said.

The collar was called a choker; it tightened around Sandy's neck whenever she pulled away. She whined, and Tim knew she didn't like it at all! He didn't like it either! He complained to Mom about it.

Mother smiled and said, "Be gentle with her, Son. Give the leash a soft tug when you want her to follow. Remember, you're doing this because you love her. If she learns to walk on a leash now, you'll be able to take her anywhere with you."

Later that evening Tim read some verses from Matthew chapter eleven. When he asked what a 'yoke' was, Dad explained that it was a burden or problem Jesus might want us to bear for his sake in order to teach us a valuable lesson.

"Is it a little like Sandy's collar and leash?" Tim asked.

"Yes, it is," Dad answered. "As long as Sandy doesn't fight the collar, it's easy on her. And as long as we don't fight God's will, any yoke Jesus puts on us is easy. He's gentle with us just like you're gentle with your puppy."

"Right," agreed Mom. "And Jesus expects us to be gentle with others."

HOW ABOUT YOU? Are you ever guilty of being rough instead of gentle as you deal with other people? When a brother or sister accidentally breaks something of yours, do you become angry and shout? Remember that Jesus is gentle with us, and he expects us to be the same with our friends. *R.E.P.*

TO MEMORIZE: But the fruit of the Spirit is love, joy, peace, patience, kindness, goodness, faithfulness, gentleness . . . *Galatians 5:22* (NIV)

SELF-CONTROL

FROM THE BIBLE:

All athletes practice strict self-control. They do it to win a prize that will fade away, but we do it for an eternal prize. So I run straight to the goal with purpose in every step. I am not like a boxer who misses his punches. I discipline my body like an athlete, training it to do what it should. Otherwise, I fear that after preaching to others I myself might be disqualified. . . .

Let everyone see that you are considerate in all you do. Remember, the Lord is coming soon.

1 CORINTHIANS 9:25-27; PHILIPPIANS 4:5

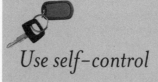

Use self-control

STEVE'S eighth-grade American history class was studying the temperance movement of the early 1900s. At that time many people who were opposed to drinking alcohol worked to get laws making its use illegal. They felt this was necessary because people often didn't use self-control (or temperance) when drinking, and they drank too much.

As Steve was reading Galatians a few days later, he found the word self-control listed as a fruit of the Spirit. "Mother," he asked, "when the Bible uses the word self-control, is it talking about drinking alcohol, like in the temperance movement?"

"Good question," said Mother. "Supporters of the temperance movement promoted self-control only with alcohol—in other words, in not getting drunk. That's one good meaning of the word, but we also need to show self-control in every other area of our lives! And we should start today."

Steve knew what his mother was getting at. Drunkenness was not his problem, but eating was. Steve loved to eat—and he hated to exercise! Even though he was only in eighth grade, he was already becoming very chubby.

His mother's words seemed to haunt him after that. Every time he wanted to eat a candy bar or drink another soda, he remembered that he was supposed to show self-control. With the Lord's help and the promptings of the Holy Spirit, Steve reached a healthier weight within six months. He had learned that one fruit of the Spirit (or evidence of salvation in our life) is self-control.

HOW ABOUT YOU? Do you display self-control in every area of your life? Are you tempted to overeat, gossip, or lose your temper? Ask the Lord to help you exercise self-control and say no. Perhaps you love to watch TV or play ball. Even in those things you need to use self-control. *R.E.P.*

TO MEMORIZE: But the fruit of the Spirit is love, joy, peace, patience, kindness, goodness, faithfulness, gentleness and self-control. *Galatians 5:22* (NIV)

25 April

INSTANT EVERYTHING

FROM THE BIBLE:

Dear brothers and sisters, if another Christian is overcome by some sin, you who are godly should gently and humbly help that person back onto the right path. And be careful not to fall into the same temptation yourself. Share each other's troubles and problems, and in this way obey the law of Christ. If you think you are too important to help someone in need, you are only fooling yourself. You are really a nobody.

Be sure to do what you should, for then you will enjoy the personal satisfaction of having done your work well, and you won't need to compare yourself to anyone else. For we are each responsible for our own conduct.

Those who are taught the word of God should help their teachers by paying them.

GALATIANS 6:1-6

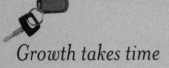

Growth takes time

SINCE MOM and Dad were going out, Chris was in charge of making supper for herself and her younger brother, Doug. "You can microwave a pizza," Mom said. "Just follow the directions on the box. And there's ready-to-eat salad in the refrigerator."

Chris had no trouble whipping up the meal. Doug even admitted it was pretty good!

The next day when Chris got home from school, she was very upset. "You know what Lana did today, Mom?" she exclaimed. "Our teacher didn't collect our homework assignments. Instead, she just asked everyone if they had it done. Lana told me this morning that she hadn't finished it, but when Miss Robinson asked her, Lana said she had it done! She lied! And she calls herself a Christian!"

"Keep in mind that Lana has only been saved for a little while," Mom responded.

"But she lied!" Chris repeated. "You make it sound like it doesn't even matter!"

"I'm not excusing what Lana did," answered Mom. "I'm just suggesting that you shouldn't be too hard on her. You do wrong things too, you know."

"I know, but—"

"Hold on," said Mom. "In this day and age we get the idea that everything should be 'instant'—like the meal you made last night. The things you fixed were easy and quick to make because they were all instant foods. But spiritual maturity isn't instant. It takes time to become mature."

"I see," said Chris thoughtfully. "I guess I was expecting too much from Lana too soon."

HOW ABOUT YOU? Do you have any friends who are new Christians? Remember, when you ask Jesus into your heart, you are instantly saved, but you aren't instantly mature. Be patient with your friends and make sure you set a good example for them to follow. *D.S.M.*

TO MEMORIZE: We should please others. If we do what helps them, we will build them up in the Lord. *Romans 15:2*

26 April

THE HIBERNATING CHRISTIAN

FROM THE BIBLE:

Another reason for right living is that you know how late it is; time is running out. Wake up, for the coming of our salvation is nearer now than when we first believed. The night is almost gone; the day of salvation will soon be here. So don't live in darkness. Get rid of your evil deeds. Shed them like dirty clothes. Clothe yourselves with the armor of right living, as those who live in the light. We should be decent and true in everything we do, so that everyone can approve of our behavior. Don't participate in wild parties and getting drunk, or in adultery and immoral living, or in fighting and jealousy. But let the Lord Jesus Christ take control of you, and don't think of ways to indulge your evil desires.

ROMANS 13:11-14

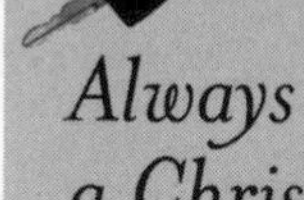

Always act like a Christian

CORY LIVED a double life. At home and church he was "Cory the Christian." He sang in the junior choir and read the Bible. At school he was "Cool Cory." He laughed at dirty jokes, used swear words, and hoped nobody would realize he went to Sunday school. But he wasn't happy. *I don't even like myself,* Cory thought as he dug rows of dirt in the garden.

"Make that row a little deeper," Dad said, interrupting his thoughts. Cory pushed the hoe in deeper. When he brought it up, he had dug up a toad. "Look, Dad!" The toad didn't move. "Is he dead?"

"No," said Dad. "Just sleepy. He's been hibernating. The ground isn't warm enough yet to wake him up."

"Wake up, silly toad." Cory pushed it with his foot. "Someone could step on you, and you'd just lie there."

"He doesn't realize danger," Dad said. "He reminds me of some Christians I know."

"How?"

"God made toads to be cold-blooded. Their blood is always the same as their surroundings. But God did not intend for his children to be cold-blooded. We are not to be controlled by our surroundings."

Cory looked at the ground.

"Some people act like Christians only when they're with Christians," Dad continued. "When they're in the world, surrounded by sin, they hibernate. Like that toad, they're unaware of danger. A hibernating Christian is easy prey for the devil."

Cory gulped. "I see what you mean, Dad." Cory put the toad in a new hole to continue his nap. "Good-bye 'Cool Cory,' " he whispered. " 'Cory the Christian' just woke up."

HOW ABOUT YOU? Is your walk with the Lord controlled by those around you? Are you living a double life? Be a warm-blooded, faithful Christian, no matter how cold the world around you. *B.J.W.*

TO MEMORIZE: Wake up, for the coming of our salvation is nearer now than when we first believed. *Romans 13:11*

27 April

IT HAPPENED TO ME

FROM THE BIBLE:

All praise to the God and Father of our Lord Jesus Christ. He is the source of every mercy and the God who comforts us. He comforts us in all our troubles so that we can comfort others. When others are troubled, we will be able to give them the same comfort God has given us. You can be sure that the more we suffer for Christ, the more God will shower us with his comfort through Christ. So when we are weighed down with troubles, it is for your benefit and salvation! For when God comforts us, it is so that we, in turn, can be an encouragement to you. Then you can patiently endure the same things we suffer. We are confident that as you share in suffering, you will also share God's comfort.

2 CORINTHIANS 1:3-7

Comfort others with God's love

KRISTY WAS SORRY when she heard that Nicole's mother had been in a car accident and was in serious condition. Many of the children avoided Nicole because they didn't know what to say. Kristy didn't know Nicole very well, but she could understand how Nicole felt because her own dad had been in a serious accident the year before. He recovered, but there were still some things he couldn't do because of the accident.

At lunchtime Kristy sat next to Nicole. "I know how hard it is," she said softly. "My father was in a car wreck last year."

"Oh," sighed Nicole, "then you understand how I feel!"

"Yes, I do," Kristy assured her. "Would you like me to pray for your mother right now?"

"Sure." Nicole smiled for the first time that day.

When Kristy got home from school, she told her dad about Nicole's mother. "I told Nicole that knowing the Lord helped me. She listened to what I had to say, because she knew I understood how she felt."

Dad smiled and nodded. "I'm glad you talked with her, Kristy," he said. "In fact, the Bible tells us that because God comforts us during bad times, we can, in turn, comfort others who are going through bad times. And one way we do this is by telling them about the Lord."

HOW ABOUT YOU? Have you experienced some hard times? Maybe your dad or mom has been seriously sick, or maybe someone close to you has died. The Lord tells us that he will comfort us during any situation, and that we, in turn, can comfort others with his love. Even if nothing really bad has happened to you, you can still pray for those who are going through a tough situation. You can still tell them about God's love. *L.M.W.*

TO MEMORIZE: He comforts us in all our troubles so that we can comfort others. *2 Corinthians 1:4*

28 April

THE DOCTOR KNOWS BEST

FROM THE BIBLE:

And remember, it is a message to obey, not just to listen to. If you don't obey, you are only fooling yourself. For if you just listen and don't obey, it is like looking at your face in a mirror but doing nothing to improve your appearance. You see yourself, walk away, and forget what you look like. But if you keep looking steadily into God's perfect law—the law that sets you free—and if you do what it says and don't forget what you heard, then God will bless you for doing it.

JAMES 1:22-25

Be doers of the Word

JULIO PEREZ and his parents went to visit Aunt Eva, who was almost eighty years old. "I feel miserable," Aunt Eva said. "That new doctor hasn't done me a bit of good. What a waste of money."

"Did he prescribe any medicine?" asked Julio's mother.

"Yes," said Aunt Eva, "but the pills didn't really help, so I stopped taking them."

"What about your nutrition?" Mr. Perez asked.

"He told me to cut down on salt," answered Aunt Eva, "but I can't stand food without lots of salt on it."

"What about exercise?" asked Mr. Perez.

Aunt Eva laughed. "The doctor told me to go for a walk once a day. At my age? Ridiculous!"

Mr. and Mrs. Perez tried to persuade Aunt Eva to follow the doctor's instructions, but she shook her head. "It wouldn't help."

On the way home, Julio said, "Aunt Eva thinks her doctor is no good. But she didn't do what he told her. No wonder she's not getting any better!"

Dad and Mom nodded. "A lot of Christians are like that, too," said Dad. "They look to God for help, but they disobey his commands. Then when they get discouraged and unhappy, they think it's God's fault. Plus, they are a poor testimony to others who need to trust Jesus Christ as Savior."

"I sure don't want to turn people away from Christ," said Julio. "I want to do what he tells me. Then everyone will see what a great 'Doctor' he really is."

HOW ABOUT YOU? When you have problems, do you blame God? Stop and think—have you obeyed all of his commands? Do you read the Bible, pray, and attend a Bible-believing church? Are there sinful habits you need to get rid of? Don't be like Aunt Eva. Follow the Doctor's orders—God always knows best! *S.L.K.*

TO MEMORIZE: Do not merely listen to the Word, and so deceive yourselves. Do what it says.
James 1:22 (NIV)

29 April

ERASING SIN

FROM THE BIBLE:

Oh, what joy for those
whose rebellion is forgiven,
whose sin is put out of sight!
Yes, what joy for those
whose record the Lord has cleared of sin,
whose lives are lived in complete honesty!
When I refused to confess my sin,
I was weak and miserable,
and I groaned all day long.
Day and night your hand of discipline was heavy on me.
My strength evaporated like water in the summer heat.
Finally, I confessed all my sins to you
and stopped trying to hide them.
I said to myself, "I will confess my rebellion to the Lord."
And you forgave me! All my guilt is gone.

PSALM 32:1-5

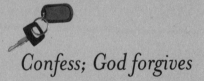

Confess; God forgives

NATHAN TOSSED and turned. Through the wall he could hear his mother typing on her computer. But the noise didn't kept him awake. It was the lie he had told that kept jabbing his conscience.

He squeezed his eyes shut. But the voice in his head continued. *Better go tell your mother you're sorry. Tell the truth.*

Finally Nathan scrambled out of bed and walked into the next room. His mother looked up in surprise as he burst into tears. "What's the matter, Nathan? Did you have a bad dream?"

"No," he choked. "I . . . I told you a lie. I said I hadn't been playing in Mr. Field's barn, but I had. I'm sorry." Nathan sniffed. "I won't play there anymore without permission."

His mother put her arm around him. "I'm sorry you lied to me, Nathan, but I'm glad you've confessed. Let me show you something. What's wrong with this word I just typed?"

Nathan looked at the computer screen. "You made a mistake," he said. "You spelled forgive f-o-r-g-e-v-e."

"Now watch," Mother said. She backspaced over the misspelled letter and typed the correct letter.

"Now it's spelled right," Nathan said.

"This reminds me of the way the blood of Jesus erases our sins when we confess them, Nathan. If I had tried to ignore this misspelled letter, it never would have been corrected. When we sin, we must do what you just did—confess. When we confess our sins to God, they are forgiven and forgotten."

Nathan yawned. "I sure feel better. I think I can sleep now."

HOW ABOUT YOU? Are you trying to ignore a sin in your life? Jesus wants to forgive you and erase it. But you have to confess. Why not do it now? *B.J.W.*

TO MEMORIZE: If you do sin, there is someone to plead for you before the Father. He is Jesus Christ, the one who pleases God completely. *1 John 2:1*

30 April

A SPECIAL DOWN PAYMENT

FROM THE BIBLE:

For we know that when this earthly tent we live in is taken down—when we die and leave these bodies—we will have a home in heaven, an eternal body made for us by God himself and not by human hands. We grow weary in our present bodies, and we long for the day when we will put on our heavenly bodies like new clothing. For we will not be spirits without bodies, but we will put on new heavenly bodies. Our dying bodies make us groan and sigh, but it's not that we want to die and have no bodies at all. We want to slip into our new bodies so that these dying bodies will be swallowed up by everlasting life. God himself has prepared us for this, and as a guarantee he has given us his Holy Spirit.

So we are always confident, even though we know that as long as we live in these bodies we are not at home with the Lord. That is why we live by believing and not by seeing.

2 CORINTHIANS 5:1-7

God gave the Holy Spirit

"HONEY, I PROMISED the car salesman that I'd bring him the down payment on our new car this afternoon," Mr. Bloss told his wife. "I'll go now, since I have some free time."

"Can I go, too?" Jennifer asked her dad.

"Sure," he said.

As they drove, Jennifer asked, "Dad, what's a down payment?"

"When we were at the car dealer the other night, your mom and I talked to the salesman about the kind of car we wanted. We told him what model, what color, and what extras we would like."

"I remember," Jennifer said. "You decided on a blue one with air conditioning."

"Right, but the salesman didn't have the car we wanted in his showroom, so he's getting it from another dealer," explained Dad. "To show him I'm serious about buying the car, I'm giving him a thousand dollars toward the price."

"Oh, I see," Jennifer said. "Because you're giving him the thousand dollars, he knows you'll come through with the rest of the payment. Otherwise, you would lose your down payment, right?"

"Right," Dad said. "You know, Jennifer, you have a down payment in you."

"In me?" asked Jennifer.

"That's right," said Dad. "Another word for down payment is deposit. The Bible says that God has given every Christian the deposit of the Holy Spirit as a guarantee that we will have a future with God in heaven."

"Really?" Jennifer asked. "Hey, that's good! God has given me a down payment—the Holy Spirit!"

HOW ABOUT YOU? Do you sometimes wonder about your relationship with the Lord? Did you know that God has given you a promise, or guarantee, that you will someday be with him? That guarantee is the Holy Spirit. Thank the Lord for giving you a special down payment! *L.M.W.*

TO MEMORIZE: He anointed us, set his seal of ownership on us, and put his Spirit in our hearts as a deposit. *2 Corinthians 1:22* (NIV)

1 May

THE BAND TRIP

FROM THE BIBLE:

Remind your people to submit to the government and its officers. They should be obedient, always ready to do what is good. They must not speak evil of anyone, and they must avoid quarreling. Instead, they should be gentle and show true humility to everyone.

Once we, too, were foolish and disobedient. We were misled by others and became slaves to many wicked desires and evil pleasures. Our lives were full of evil and envy. We hated others, and they hated us.

But then God our Savior showed us his kindness and love. He saved us, not because of the good things we did, but because of his mercy. He washed away our sins and gave us a new life through the Holy Spirit. He generously poured out the Spirit upon us because of what Jesus Christ our Savior did. He declared us not guilty because of his great kindness. And now we know that we will inherit eternal life. These things I have told you are all true. I want you to insist on them so that everyone who trusts in God will be careful to do good deeds all the time.

TITUS 3:1-8

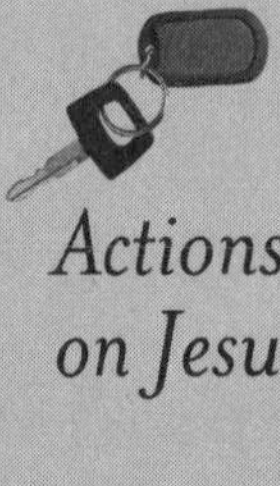

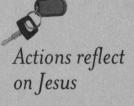

Actions reflect on Jesus

THE BAND STUDENTS from Grace Christian School were packing up to head home. "I'm glad we got a 'first' rating in our performance," Melissa said. "And staying in this motel was fun."

"I'm taking home a souvenir," said Traci as she packed a towel with "Sadybrook Motel" woven into it. "Why don't you take one too?" she suggested, tossing a towel to Melissa.

On the trip home the girls learned that some of the boys had broken a lamp during a pillow fight in their room. "We're lucky we didn't get caught," one of the boys whispered.

A week later, Mr. Palmbeck, the band director, stood solemnly before them. "Mr. Hill, the manager of our motel, came to hear our band play," Mr. Palmbeck said. "He was quite interested in Christianity. I want to share a letter I just received from him." The letter told of items missing and ruined motel furnishings.

"Mr. Hill has sent a bill for damages," said Mr. Palmbeck. "We'll pay that, but we can't pay for the damage done to your name, the school's name, or the Lord's name." There was a long silence. Then Mr. Palmbeck added, "Your instruments played beautiful music but some of your lives played sour notes. Which notes will Mr. Hill remember? Now I want those who are guilty and who are truly sorry and want to make amends to remain seated. Those who are innocent may leave."

Several students remained with bowed heads while the others filed out.

HOW ABOUT YOU? How do you act away from home? If you are a Christian, you bear Christ's name. Do your actions honor that name? Are you a testimony for Jesus in the way you behave? Now that you are saved, good works should be a part of your daily life. *J.L.H.*

TO MEMORIZE: Everyone who trusts in God will be careful to do good deeds all the time. *Titus 3:8*

2 May

DON'T GULP IT DOWN

FROM THE BIBLE:

How can a young person stay
pure?
By obeying your word and
following its rules.
I have tried my best to find
you—
don't let me wander from your
commands.
I have hidden your word in my
heart,
that I might not sin against
you.
Blessed are you, O Lord;
teach me your principles.
I have recited aloud
all the laws you have given us.
I have rejoiced in your decrees
as much as in riches.
I will study your commandments
and reflect on your ways.
I will delight in your principles
and not forget your word.

PSALM 119:9-16

Meditate on the Bible

CALVIN GRABBED his milk to wash down a large mouthful of food. "May I be excused?" he asked. "The guys are playing street hockey."

"You'll have plenty of time to play after devotions," answered Dad.

Calvin relaxed as Mother served his favorite dessert—apple pie. But she was dismayed to see his pie disappear in three large bites.

Dad passed Calvin a Bible. "Would you read to us from Psalm 119, verses 9-16?" Calvin read the passage so fast that it was hard to understand the words. "Hmmm," murmured Dad. "Cal, did you enjoy your dinner tonight?"

"Oh, yeah, sure," said Calvin.

"How about you, Karin?" asked Dad.

"It was delicious!" exclaimed Karin. "The chicken was tender, and the corn was so buttery, and I loved the pie!"

Dad laughed. "I have a feeling you enjoyed it more than your brother did. Does anyone know why?"

"Karen took her time," Mother answered, "while Cal gulped his down."

Dad nodded. "You know, it's the same with the Word of God. To get as much out of it as possible, we need to take time when we read it. Food that is gulped isn't well digested; neither does the Bible mean much to us when we hurry through it. Cal, read that passage to us once again. This time let's chew it well—that is, let's take time to think about what we're reading."

Cal nodded as he began to read carefully.

HOW ABOUT YOU? Do you hurry through the Scripture passage each day so you can get on to the story? If you do, you're missing the most important part. Read God's Word carefully—maybe you should read it again after the story. Meditate on it as you go through the day and as you go to sleep as well. *H.W.M.*

TO MEMORIZE: But his delight is in the law of the Lord, and on his law he meditates day and night. *Psalm 1:2* (NIV)

3 May

NO TRESPASSING

FROM THE BIBLE:

He was despised and rejected—a man of sorrows, acquainted with bitterest grief. We turned our backs on him and looked the other way when he went by. He was despised, and we did not care.

Yet it was our weaknesses he carried; it was our sorrows that weighed him down. And we thought his troubles were a punishment from God for his own sins! But he was wounded and crushed for our sins. He was beaten that we might have peace. He was whipped, and we were healed! All of us have strayed away like sheep. We have left God's paths to follow our own. Yet the Lord laid on him the guilt and sins of us all.

ISAIAH 53:3-6

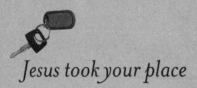

Jesus took your place

TIM AND HIS MOTHER had a grouchy old neighbor named Mr. Crossley. He hated dogs, so Tim kept his dog, Pudge, locked in the yard. Mr. Crossley had been losing chickens lately, and he threatened to shoot any dog he saw on his property.

One day when Tim arrived home, Pudge didn't come when called. Tim saw a package on the steps and realized the postman had been there. He'd failed to close the gate properly! Tim heard some barking near Mr. Crossley's property, so he headed that way. He arrived just in time to see Mr. Crossley taking aim at Pudge. "Stop!" screamed Tim.

He threw himself at his pet just as the gun went off. Tim was wounded in the leg!

Later Mr. Crossley was talking to Mother at the hospital. "I feel just awful!" he said. "I never shot a kid before. He jumped right in the way to save his dog!"

Tim's mother nodded. "Tim loves Pudge so much! But thank God, it was only a flesh wound. The doctor says Tim can come home tonight." She paused, then added thoughtfully, "You know, Mr. Crossley, Pudge trespassed, but Tim was wounded. This reminds me of myself. I trespassed against God—I sinned. I was doomed to die, but Jesus lovingly stepped into my place. The Bible says, 'He was wounded and crushed for my sins.' He took my place on the cross—and he took *your* place, too, Mr. Crossley."

Mr. Crossley was listening intently. "I never realized anyone loved me that much," he said. "I'd like to hear more about this."

HOW ABOUT YOU? Do you realize how much Jesus loves you? You, too, have trespassed, or sinned, against God. But Jesus took the punishment you deserve. He was wounded for you. Have you thanked him and asked him to be your Savior? Do it today. *B.J.W.*

TO MEMORIZE: He was wounded and crushed for our sins. *Isaiah 53:5*

4 May

TICKET TROUBLE

FROM THE BIBLE:

I am a real Jew if there ever was one! What's more, I was a member of the Pharisees, who demand the strictest obedience to the Jewish law. And zealous? Yes, in fact, I harshly persecuted the church. And I obeyed the Jewish law so carefully that I was never accused of any fault.

I once thought all these things were so very important, but now I consider them worthless because of what Christ has done. Yes, everything else is worthless when compared with the priceless gain of knowing Christ Jesus my Lord. I have discarded everything else, counting it all as garbage, so that I may have Christ and become one with him. I no longer count on my own goodness or my ability to obey God's law, but I trust Christ to save me. For God's way of making us right with himself depends on faith. As a result, I can really know Christ and experience the mighty power that raised him from the dead. I can learn what it means to suffer with him, sharing in his death.

PHILIPPIANS 3:5-10

AS KEVIN approached the gate at the athletic field, he noticed a boy from his school arguing with one of the men taking tickets. "Sorry," the gatekeeper said. "This is a ticket for last week's game. I can't let you in."

"Oh, come on," argued George. "I just grabbed the wrong one by mistake. My dad will pay for a new one when he gets here."

"You'll have to wait for him," the man said.

"Don't you know who I am?" George demanded. "My dad's the principal of the high school!"

"You can be president of the United States, but if you don't have a proper ticket, you don't go in," the man replied.

Back home Kevin told his dad about the ticket incident. "Will that man be in trouble because he wouldn't let the principal's son in?" asked Kevin.

Dad shook his head. "The gatekeeper was right," he said. "He looks at the ticket, not the person who wants to get into the ball game. If it's the correct one, the person has the right to proceed. If not, he can't go in."

Dad reached for his Bible for family devotions. "That's kind of the way God works, too," he added. "Christ, and Christ alone, is our ticket to heaven. God won't look at who we are. He will only look to see if we have Christ in our heart. We'll get into heaven only if we trust him as Savior and Lord."

HOW ABOUT YOU? Do you have your "ticket" to heaven? Have you given Jesus Christ control of your life? You can never say, "Look at me, God. I am holy." You can only say, "Look upon Christ, who is my 'ticket' to heaven." If you've never received him, don't wait. Do it today. *H.M.*

TO MEMORIZE: I no longer count on my own goodness or my ability to obey God's law, but I trust Christ to save me. *Philippians 3:9*

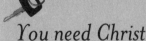

You need Christ

5 May

NO STAINS

FROM THE BIBLE:

For you know that God paid a ransom to save you from the empty life you inherited from your ancestors. And the ransom he paid was not mere gold or silver. He paid for you with the precious lifeblood of Christ, the sinless, spotless Lamb of God. God chose him for this purpose long before the world began, but now in these final days, he was sent to the earth for all to see. And he did this for you.

Through Christ you have come to trust in God. And because God raised Christ from the dead and gave him great glory, your faith and hope can be placed confidently in God.

1 PETER 1:18-21

Jesus' blood washes away sin

"LOOK, MOM," said Sandi as she picked up a bottle of laundry detergent in the grocery store. "The label says it removes the most difficult stains. Could we try it on my yellow shirt? There's a stain on the sleeve."

"Well, it's pretty expensive," said Mother, "but I guess we can try it."

That afternoon, Sandi washed her shirt, following the directions carefully. But the stain remained. "I can't believe it!" she exclaimed. "They can send men to the moon, but they can't find a way to get out a little spot."

Mother laughed, then looked thoughtfully at the shirt. "This reminds me of another area where everyone's best efforts fail. Everyone is born a sinner. It's as though the stain of sin is on a person's 'garment of life.' People often try to hide their sin by being good, and sometimes they try to keep it out of sight."

"You mean like when I roll up my shirt sleeve to hide the stain?" Sandi asked.

"Yes, the spot is still there. And nothing we can do is able to remove it," said Mother. "There is something that can wash sin away, though."

"What?"

"The blood of Jesus," Mother said. "And we don't have to pay a thing for it—Jesus paid it all. God offers it freely to all who will admit their need and accept Jesus as Savior. It's the only thing that can cleanse a person's soul."

HOW ABOUT YOU? Are you still trying to cover up your sins or get rid of them through your own efforts? Or have they been washed away by Jesus' blood? If not, admit your failure today and allow Jesus to cleanse your heart and life. *H.W.M.*

TO MEMORIZE: To him who loves us and has freed us from our sins by his blood . . . to him be glory and power for ever and ever! Amen.
Revelation 1:5-6 (NIV)

6 *May*

THE WARNING

FROM THE BIBLE:

And I saw a great white throne, and I saw the one who was sitting on it. The earth and sky fled from his presence, but they found no place to hide. I saw the dead, both great and small, standing before God's throne. And the books were opened, including the Book of Life. And the dead were judged according to the things written in the books, according to what they had done. The sea gave up the dead in it, and death and the grave gave up the dead in them. They were all judged according to their deeds. And death and the grave were thrown into the lake of fire. This is the second death—the lake of fire. And anyone whose name was not found recorded in the Book of Life was thrown into the lake of fire.

REVELATION 20:11-15

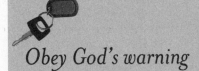

Obey God's warning

CARRIE AND DAN, who didn't usually attend church, were visiting Uncle Bob and Aunt Ellen for the weekend. On Sunday they went to church, but they didn't like it much. Pastor Hanover's sermon was about hell.

"This is too much!" muttered Dan.

"All they do here is try to scare us," Carrie added.

Later that day, Uncle Bob lifted a round, white, plastic object out of a box.

"What's that?" Dan asked.

"Just wait till I get the batteries in," replied their uncle. "We'll see if it works." He pressed a small button on the case. Immediately an ear-splitting shriek filled the room! Carrie and Dan covered their ears. Uncle Bob took his finger off the button, and the noise stopped.

"It's a smoke detector," he said, smiling. "Whenever there's smoke in the house, the alarm will go off."

"Why does it have to be so loud and scary?" Carrie asked.

"Its purpose is not to scare us," Uncle Bob replied. "It's to warn us of danger so we can avoid it." He paused, then added thoughtfully, "That reminds me of church this morning. Sometimes we think sermons about hell are intended to scare us, but actually they are only meant to warn us."

Carrie and Dan looked at each other. "Well, that warning about hell this morning did scare me," Carrie said. "I don't want to go to hell. I'd like to be saved."

Dan nodded. "Me, too."

HOW ABOUT YOU? Have you been warned about hell? Did you heed that warning? Hell isn't a pleasant subject, and yes, it is scary! But it is also real. The good news is that you don't need to go there. Receive Jesus as your Savior. Then your name will be written in the Book of Life, and you will spend eternity in heaven. *S.K.*

TO MEMORIZE: Anyone whose name was not recorded in the Book of Life was thrown into the lake of fire. *Revelation 20:15*

7 May

BY MYSELF, DADDY

FROM THE BIBLE:

So we have continued praying for you ever since we first heard about you. We ask God to give you a complete understanding of what he wants to do in your lives, and we ask him to make you wise with spiritual wisdom. Then the way you live will always honor and please the Lord, and you will continually do good, kind things for others. All the while, you will learn to know God better and better.

We also pray that you will be strengthened with his glorious power so that you will have all the patience and endurance you need. May you be filled with joy, always thanking the Father, who has enabled you to share the inheritance that belongs to God's holy people, who live in the light. For he has rescued us from the one who rules in the kingdom of darkness, and he has brought us into the Kingdom of his dear Son. God has purchased our freedom with his blood and has forgiven all our sins.

COLOSSIANS 1:9-14

"Walk" with God's help

SAM ENJOYED helping his little brother, Josiah, learn to walk. But whenever Sam let go of his hand, Josiah would fall down with a thud. "Dad, how long will it be till Josiah can walk alone?" Sam asked.

"He needs a little more time," Dad replied. "I remember when you were learning to walk. You fell, too, but you seldom let me help you. If I tried, you said, 'No! By myself, Daddy!' "

Sam grinned. "Are you sure you're not mixing me up with somebody else?"

"It was you all right," Dad smiled. "You were stubborn. But you taught me something."

"I did?" Sam was surprised.

Dad nodded. "I was a new baby Christian at that time. And I was trying to walk the Christian life all by myself. I seldom read my Bible or prayed. I rarely went to church. I accepted no help from my heavenly Father or from other Christians. And like you, I was falling. I always wanted my own way and had a hard time controlling my temper. As I watched you resist my help, I suddenly realized I was resisting the Lord's help. In my spiritual life I was saying, 'By myself, Daddy.' It's a lesson I never forgot."

HOW ABOUT YOU? Are you struggling to "walk" as a Christian should? Do you have problems with a temper? Fears? Laziness? Pride? Sooner or later you will "fall" spiritually if you try to walk alone. Study God's Word. Meet regularly with other Christians. Take time to pray. You need to depend on your heavenly Father's help in order to be the honest, kind, helpful person he wants you to be. *D.S.M.*

TO MEMORIZE: To him who is able to keep you from falling and to present you before his glorious presence without fault and with great joy—to the only God our Savior be glory, majesty, power and authority through Jesus Christ our Lord. *Jude 1:24-25* (NIV)

LISA'S DEMONSTRATION

FROM THE BIBLE:

I pray that your love for each other will overflow more and more, and that you will keep on growing in your knowledge and understanding. For I want you to understand what really matters, so that you may live pure and blameless lives until Christ returns. May you always be filled with the fruit of your salvation—those good things that are produced in your life by Jesus Christ—for this will bring much glory and praise to God.
PHILIPPIANS 1:9-11

Demonstrate God's love

"GUESS WHAT?" Lisa bounded into the room, followed by Amy. "Amy and I are going to give a demonstration at the next 4-H Club meeting."

"Great," said Mother. "What will you demonstrate?"

"We were thinking of giving a demonstration on flower arranging," Lisa said. "You have a book that will show us how, and we have lots of spring flowers in the garden."

"That's a lovely idea," Mother said.

All afternoon the girls studied and practiced arranging flowers. Finally, they came into the living room, carrying a bouquet. "Beautiful!" Mother exclaimed.

"We're still working on our speech. We have three weeks to practice," Lisa said. "May I go with Amy to her aunt's house tomorrow morning? We want to give this arrangement to her. She's disabled and can't even get out of bed now." Mother smiled with approval. The next morning the girls took the flowers to the elderly lady and spent an hour visiting with her.

"How did your demonstration go?" Mother asked when Lisa returned home.

"That's not for a few weeks yet," Lisa replied. She was surprised that her mother had forgotten.

Mother smiled. "I'm talking about the demonstration you performed this morning." she said. "The flowers you arranged are beautiful, but not nearly as beautiful as the love you girls showed by taking the flowers to Amy's aunt and spending time with her. I'm sure it meant a lot to her. You girls are demonstrating something far more important than flower arranging."

Lisa raised her eyebrows. "We are?"

"Yes," Mother said, smiling. "You're demonstrating God's love by your thoughtfulness."

HOW ABOUT YOU? Do you show the world the love of God by your actions? Are you kind and thoughtful? Do you help whenever you can? Demonstrate God's love to someone today. *B.J.W.*

TO MEMORIZE: Dear children, let us stop just saying we love each other; let us really show it by our actions. *1 John 3:18*

9 May

KEEP ON ASKING

FROM THE BIBLE:

Then, teaching them more about prayer, he used this illustration: "Suppose you went to a friend's house at midnight, wanting to borrow three loaves of bread. You would say to him, 'A friend of mine has just arrived for a visit, and I have nothing for him to eat.' He would call out from his bedroom, 'Don't bother me. The door is locked for the night, and we are all in bed. I can't help you this time.' But I tell you this—though he won't do it as a friend, if you keep knocking long enough, he will get up and give you what you want so his reputation won't be damaged."

LUKE 11:5-8

Don't give up praying

KYLE WAS opening a birthday present from his parents. "A chemistry set!" he exclaimed. "It's just what I wanted!"

His parents chuckled. "We know." Mother smiled. "How could we help but know with all the hints you've given?"

"Have I been hinting?" Kyle said.

"Ever since you saw that chemistry set at the store, you've been talking about it," Dad said, grinning.

"And before I went out to buy your present," Mother added, "I found a note in my purse that said, 'Don't forget the C.S.! Love, Guess Who.' "

Kyle laughed. "I guess I have been kind of a pest."

"You weren't rude about it, just persistent," his father replied.

"I can't wait to show Steve," said Kyle.

"That reminds me—you were going to pray for an opportunity to witness to Steve," said Dad. "How'd it turn out?"

Kyle looked uncomfortable. "Well, I did pray about it for a while, but nothing happened, so I kinda forgot about it."

"Speaking of prayer," Mother said, "you were going to pray for money to go to the church youth camp this summer. Have you got it yet?"

Kyle shook his head, "I saved about ten dollars, but I guess I quit praying about that, too."

Dad looked serious. "You're persistent when it comes to asking for birthday presents," he said. "It's a shame you haven't applied that principle to your praying. Too often we say a half-hearted prayer and then forget about it. Who knows how many wonderful answers to prayer we'd receive if only we'd keep asking!"

HOW ABOUT YOU? Is there a problem or a need in your life that you've prayed about? Don't forget to keep on praying. In his Word, God sets down several conditions for powerful, effective prayer. One of them is being earnest. So keep on asking and believing.
S.L.K.

TO MEMORIZE: The earnest prayer of a righteous person has great power and wonderful results.
James 5:16

IMPERFECT PARENTS

FROM THE BIBLE:

You who are slaves must accept the authority of your masters. Do whatever they tell you—not only if they are kind and reasonable, but even if they are harsh. For God is pleased with you when, for the sake of your conscience, you patiently endure unfair treatment. Of course, you get no credit for being patient if you are beaten for doing wrong. But if you suffer for doing right and are patient beneath the blows, God is pleased with you.

This suffering is all part of what God has called you to. Christ, who suffered for you, is your example. Follow in his steps. He never sinned, and he never deceived anyone. He did not retaliate when he was insulted. When he suffered, he did not threaten to get even. He left his case in the hands of God, who always judges fairly.

1 PETER 2:18-23

Forgive your parents

JEREMY WAS walking out the door to play baseball with his friends. Just then Dad came in. "Jeremy Robert," he said sternly, "I've told you to put the garden tools away when you're done using them." He held up a rusty rake and hoe. "These must have been left out during the last rain."

"But, Dad," Jeremy said. "I didn't—"

"Don't make excuses," his father said. "Go to your room until suppertime."

Unfair! thought Jeremy as he flopped onto his bed. Not only would he miss playing baseball, but he was being punished for something he didn't do. How could God let this happen?

Finally his bedroom door opened, and his father came in. "I need to apologize, Son," he said sheepishly. "I just remembered I was the one who left the tools in the garden. I'd come in for a phone call. Then I forgot all about them. Will you forgive me?"

"I guess so," Jeremy mumbled.

"Something like this happened to me when I was a boy," said Dad. "My father gave me a licking for something he thought I'd done."

"Really?" said Jeremy.

Dad nodded. "At first I was bitter and questioned God. Then I realized God wanted me to forgive my father. I've never forgotten that lesson of forgiveness."

"I suppose I shouldn't expect you to be perfect," Jeremy said. "Just think of all the things you've forgiven me for! I'm going to tell that story to my own kids some day. I'm sure their father won't be perfect either!"

HOW ABOUT YOU? How do you feel when your parents make a mistake? Do you become bitter and critical? Or do you forgive them and try to learn from the experience? Parents aren't perfect, but God still expects you to love and obey them, for his sake. *S.K.*

TO MEMORIZE: But if you suffer for doing good and you endure it, this is commendable before God. *1 Peter 2:20* (NIV)

11 May

MOTHERING

FROM THE BIBLE:

Come, my children, and listen to me,
and I will teach you to fear the Lord.
Do any of you want to live
a life that is long and good?
Then watch your tongue!
Keep your lips from telling lies!
Turn away from evil and do good.
Work hard at living in peace with others.
The eyes of the Lord watch over those who do right;
his ears are open to their cries for help.
But the Lord turns his face against those who do evil;
he will erase their memory from the earth.
The Lord hears his people when they call to him for help.
He rescues them from all their troubles.

PSALM 34:11-17

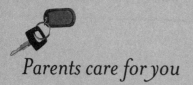

Parents care for you

LIZ GLARED at her mother. "You have no good reason to make me miss Sara's slumber party this Friday," she insisted. "You don't even know her. I think you're being very unfair."

"Perhaps it's because I don't know Sara that I feel you shouldn't go," Mom said. "I'm not trying to ruin your fun. I'm trying to protect you from a possible bad influence. Why don't you invite Sara over for dinner so I can get to know her?"

Liz agreed, and Sara came to dinner the next evening. Afterwards, they played a game together and giggled a lot.

"Sara seems like a nice girl," said Mother after Sara had been taken home, "but I still feel uneasy about the slumber party. I really need to meet Sara's parents, or find out more about them, before I can allow you to spend the night there." Liz sighed. She knew there would be no slumber party for her this week.

After school the next day, Liz's dog, GG (short for "Good Girl"), was making a terrible commotion. "Mother, what is wrong with GG?" asked Liz. "Ever since she had puppies she's been barking every time someone comes to the door. She never used to bark at people so much."

"GG isn't going to take any chances with her puppies," explained Mother. "She'll try to keep anyone who isn't family away from them." She paused, then added, "I guess all mothers are that way, so please be patient with GG—and me—as we mother our children!"

HOW ABOUT YOU? Do you sometimes wonder why your parents seem so protective of you? Do you feel like they just won't let you grow up? God has given them the great responsibility of keeping you from evil influences. They're just doing their job. Be patient with them. *P.R.*

TO MEMORIZE: Come, my children, and listen to me, and I will teach you to fear the Lord. *Psalm 34:11*

FOR STEPMOTHER
(PART 1)

FROM THE BIBLE:

How wonderful it is, how pleasant,
when brothers live together in harmony!
For harmony is as precious as the fragrant anointing oil
that was poured over Aaron's head,
that ran down his beard
and onto the border of his robe.
Harmony is as refreshing as the dew from Mount Hermon
that falls on the mountains of Zion.
And the Lord has pronounced his blessing,
even life forevermore.

PSALM 133:1-3

Accept what God allows

JUANITA was not happy about her dad's new wife.

"I wish you would try to accept your stepmother," suggested Dad. "I think you would find her kind and loving."

"I've never said she wasn't nice," Juanita protested. "It's just that she isn't my mother, so I'm not going to treat her as if she is."

"No, she's not your mother," Dad admitted, sadly. "But your mother has died and there is nothing we can do about that."

"But why did you have to bring Marian here?" Juanita asked, choking back tears. "And just before Mother's Day!"

Dad nodded, understandingly. "Tomorrow is going to be a difficult day for all of us," he admitted. "But just remember, it's going to be a difficult day for Marian, too."

"Marian!" Juanita snapped. "Why should this be a hard day for her? You and Julio both act like you've forgotten all about Mom. Julio even bought a Mother's Day card!"

A light tap on the door interrupted their conversation. It was Marian. "Look what was just delivered," she beamed, bringing in a small flowering plant. "It's lovely. Thank you!" The card that came with it was signed in Julio's handwriting. It read "Your new family."

Juanita bit her lower lip to keep herself under control. Quickly she slipped out the door. She knew the anger building up inside her was wrong. She felt guilty. Somehow, she knew she would eventually have to accept Marian for who she was—not her real mother, but someone who was willing to step in and take on a new family.

HOW ABOUT YOU? Is there someone you are not accepting? God has brought that person into your life for a purpose. Ask him to help you to show love, kindness, and thoughtfulness at all times. Look for the good in the situation. *R.I.J.*

TO MEMORIZE: How wonderful it is, how pleasant, when brothers live together in harmony! *Psalm 133:1*

13 May

FOR STEPMOTHER
(PART 2)

FROM THE BIBLE:

I look up to the mountains—
does my help come from there?
My help comes from the Lord,
who made the heavens and the earth!
He will not let you stumble and fall;
the one who watches over you will not sleep.
Indeed, he who watches over Israel
never tires and never sleeps.
The Lord himself watches over you!
The Lord stands beside you as your protective shade.
The sun will not hurt you by day,
nor the moon at night.
The Lord keeps you from all evil
and preserves your life.
The Lord keeps watch over you as you come and go,
both now and forever.

PSALM 121:1-8

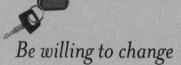

Be willing to change

JUANITA WENT outside and called loudly for her brother. She wanted to let Julio know what she thought about his really dumb idea—sending a flowering plant to a woman who wasn't their mother.

"But tomorrow is Mother's Day," protested Julio. "I thought our new mom should get flowers just like everybody else."

"She's not our mom," Juanita replied. "She's Dad's wife."

Julio shrugged his shoulders. "Well, she lives here and she's really nice," he said, "so I just wanted to do it."

"But you didn't have any right putting my name on that card!" Juanita fumed.

"I didn't put your name on the card," said Julio. "I just wrote that it was from her new family."

"Well, she thinks I'm in on it," Juanita insisted.

"Actually, that's what I wanted her to think," Julio admitted. "I overheard her and Dad praying last night. And she asked God to help you to love her soon."

Suddenly Juanita felt ashamed—very ashamed! Even little Julio acted more mature than she did. Juanita sat under a tree and prayed. "I'm sorry, Lord," she whispered. "Help me to love her as you would." Maybe she wouldn't be able to call Marian "Mother"—at least not right away. But with God's help she was going to be like a daughter, a Christian daughter.

Hurrying into the house, she called for Julio. "Here," she said, pulling some money from her pocket. "If the 'new family' is going to send flowers, I'd better pitch in and pay for my share." Suddenly Juanita felt a lot better inside.

HOW ABOUT YOU? Do you sometimes know your attitude is wrong, but you refuse to change? That makes you unhappy, doesn't it? Admit when you are wrong. Then make a definite effort to correct those wrongs. You'll feel better. And remember, God is there to help you. *R.I.J.*

TO MEMORIZE: My help comes from the Lord, who made the heavens and the earth! *Psalm 121:2*

A GIFT FOR MOTHER

ONE SATURDAY morning, Jasmine asked her brother to help her shop for a gift for their mom because the next day was Mother's Day. "Can't," David said crossly. "Mom says I can't leave the house."

"Why not?" Jasmine asked. "What did you do?"

"I cleaned my closet, just like Mom told me," David grumbled. "She said I wasn't finished. I told her it was my closet, and it suited me just fine! She made me do it over. So I did. Then I said, 'Now does it suit you?' She said my closet did, but not my attitude. So I have to stay home today."

"This spoils everything," moaned Jasmine. "I'll go ask her if you can go to the store with me."

When Mom said no, Jasmine stomped her foot and talked back to her. So she got grounded too.

The next day, Mom gave a beautiful sweater to Grandma Pratt, who was spending the day with them. "Mom, we would have bought you something yesterday," Jasmine said, "but you wouldn't let us go to the store."

"I didn't want a gift from you children," said Mom.

"You didn't?" asked David. "You gave Grandma a present."

"Well, I love her," answered Mom. "How do you show your love for a parent?"

"Give presents and stuff?" said David.

"Oh, Dave, that's not right," Jasmine realized. "First we need to obey our parents, because that pleases the Lord. I guess we didn't act like we loved Mom or Jesus yesterday. I'm sorry, Mom."

"Me, too," added David. "Will you forgive us?"

"Of course I will," answered Mom.

HOW ABOUT YOU? Can your parents tell by your actions that you love them? Have you told them lately—not by words, but by quick and cheerful obedience—that they are precious to you? Right now ask God to help you obey. *A.G.L.*

TO MEMORIZE: Children, obey your parents in the Lord, for this is right. *Ephesians 6:1*

FROM THE BIBLE:

You children must always obey your parents, for this is what pleases the Lord. Fathers, don't aggravate your children. If you do, they will become discouraged and quit trying.

You slaves must obey your earthly masters in everything you do. Try to please them all the time, not just when they are watching you. Obey them willingly because of your reverent fear of the Lord. Work hard and cheerfully at whatever you do, as though you were working for the Lord rather than for people. Remember that the Lord will give you an inheritance as your reward, and the Master you are serving is Christ. But if you do what is wrong, you will be paid back for the wrong you have done. For God has no favorites who can get away with evil.

COLOSSIANS 3:20-25

Obedience shows love

15 May

MALNOURISHED CHRISTIANS

FROM THE BIBLE:

Is anyone thirsty? Come and drink—even if you have no money! Come, take your choice of wine or milk—it's all free! Why spend your money on food that does not give you strength? Why pay for food that does you no good? Listen, and I will tell you where to get food that is good for the soul!

Come to me with your ears wide open. Listen, for the life of your soul is at stake. I am ready to make an everlasting covenant with you. I will give you all the mercies and unfailing love that I promised to David. . . .

The rain and snow come down from the heavens and stay on the ground to water the earth. They cause the grain to grow, producing seed for the farmer and bread for the hungry. It is the same with my word. I send it out, and it always produces fruit. It will accomplish all I want it to, and it will prosper everywhere I send it.

ISAIAH 55:1-3, 10-11

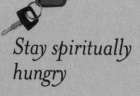

Stay spiritually hungry

CRAIG AND his mother were watching a TV program showing malnourished children in an African country. "They must be so hungry!" he exclaimed.

"Well, in some cases they may not always feel as hungry as they actually are," said Mother. "When you don't eat for a long time, the hunger pangs go away after a while. So starving people may not feel terribly hungry, even though they desperately need food."

That night after dinner Dad said, "Instead of our usual devotions, we could each share something we've learned from our own personal devotions recently. Craig, why don't you start?"

Craig squirmed in his chair. "I haven't been keeping up with my devotions lately."

"Why not?" asked Dad.

"I don't know. I guess the Bible's just too hard to understand, and . . . ," Craig hesitated. "And sometimes it's boring."

"Craig," Mother said, "do you remember the starving people we saw on TV today?" He nodded and she continued. "Even though they were starving to death and hadn't eaten for days, they possibly didn't feel hungry. It's the same with the Bible—if you stop reading it faithfully, your hunger for God's teaching will fade, even though you need it more than ever. But the more you read it, the more interesting you'll find it, and the more you'll want to read it."

"Really?" said Craig. "I guess I haven't been very hungry for it lately. I'm going to start reading my Bible to work up my appetite again!"

HOW ABOUT YOU? How hungry are you for God's Word? Do you sometimes feel like you don't need to read your Bible? Don't become an undernourished Christian. Be sure to keep your appetite sharp by reading your Bible every day. The more you read it, the more interested in it you'll become. *D.S.M.*

TO MEMORIZE: Blessed are those who hunger and thirst for righteousness, for they will be filled. *Matthew 5:6* (NIV)

16 May

THE RACE OF LIFE

(PART 1)

FROM THE BIBLE:

Endure suffering along with me, as a good soldier of Christ Jesus. And as Christ's soldier, do not let yourself become tied up in the affairs of this life, for then you cannot satisfy the one who has enlisted you in his army. . . .

Therefore, since we are surrounded by such a huge crowd of witnesses to the life of faith, let us strip off every weight that slows us down, especially the sin that so easily hinders our progress. And let us run with endurance the race that God has set before us. We do this by keeping our eyes on Jesus, on whom our faith depends from start to finish. He was willing to die a shameful death on the cross because of the joy he knew would be his afterward. Now he is seated in the place of highest honor beside God's throne in heaven.

2 TIMOTHY 2:3-4; HEBREWS 12:1-2

"GRANDPA!" Joey called. "Our school is sponsoring a big race in four weeks, and I'm going to run in it!"

Grandpa Jones chuckled. "Good for you, Joey."

"First prize is twenty dollars! That would buy lots of candy!"

"If you're serious about running, you'd better cut down on junk foods," Grandpa advised.

"But how can I ever live without candy bars and taco chips for four whole weeks?" he said, groaning.

"There's no law against a runner eating junk food," Grandpa replied. "It's just that if you're really serious about winning, you'll cut out anything that doesn't help you reach your goal."

Joey thought for a moment. "I really do want to win that race," he said. "I guess candy and snacks aren't as important to me as the prize. There's no sense running if I don't do everything I can to try to win."

"That's an important truth, Joey," Grandpa said, nodding. "Sometimes I hear you complain because you can't do some of the things your unsaved friends do. But if we want to reach the ultimate goal—that of becoming like Jesus—we'll gladly stay away from harmful or unnecessary activities in order to please the Lord."

"You're right," said Joey. "I need to start being as serious about serving the Lord as I am about winning that race!"

HOW ABOUT YOU? Are there things that keep you from doing your best in your Christian "race"? Places you want to go? TV programs and movies you want to watch? Some things may not in themselves be sinful, but if they keep you from serving the Lord, they're wrong for you. Decide today to get serious about serving God. Put away those things that get in the way. *S.L.K.*

TO MEMORIZE: Let us strip off every weight that slows us down . . . and let us run with endurance the race that God has set before us. *Hebrews 12:1*

Be serious about serving God

17 May

THE RACE OF LIFE
(PART 2)

FROM THE BIBLE:

As for me, my life has already been poured out as an offering to God. The time of my death is near. I have fought a good fight, I have finished the race, and I have remained faithful. And now the prize awaits me—the crown of righteousness that the Lord, the righteous Judge, will give me on that great day of his return. And the prize is not just for me but for all who eagerly look forward to his glorious return.

2 TIMOTHY 4:6-8

Death can be blessed

JOEY WAS HAPPY to win second place and ten dollars in the big race at school. But he was solemn a few days later when Grandpa Jones had to be taken to the hospital. After school, Joey went to visit him.

"Hi, Joey," said Grandpa, weakly.

"I wish you'd get better and come home, Grandpa," Joey said.

Grandpa sighed. "I do want to go home—to my heavenly home, I mean," he said softly.

Joey frowned. "You mean you want to . . . to die? Why?"

"When your body is worn-out like mine, you'll look forward to having a new body and going to be with Jesus in your new home," Grandpa said.

"Not me!" Joey said. "I don't ever want to get old and sick."

Grandpa smiled. "Joey, when you ran that race, how did you feel when you were almost to the finish line?"

"Pretty bad," he replied. "My legs were sore, my chest hurt, and I was hot, sweaty, and thirsty. But in a way I felt great because I knew the race was almost over, and I'd done my best."

"That's how I feel," Grandpa said gently. "Even though my body is tired and hurting, I'm happy because I can see the finish line up ahead. I've been saved by grace through Jesus Christ. I can't wait to finally see him and the wonderful things he has prepared for me."

HOW ABOUT YOU? Do you ever think about growing old and dying? You shouldn't be afraid if you know Jesus as your Savior. Then dying will just be a matter of "crossing the finish line" and receiving a reward for the work you have done for God. *S.L.K.*

TO MEMORIZE: I have finished the race, and I have remained faithful. And now the prize awaits me—the crown of righteousness that the Lord, the righteous Judge, will give me on that great day of his return. *2 Timothy 4:7-8*

CAUSE FOR FEAR

FROM THE BIBLE:

For this has been decreed by the messengers; it is commanded by the holy ones. The purpose of this decree is that the whole world may understand that the Most High rules over the kingdoms of the world and gives them to anyone he chooses—even to the lowliest of humans.
DANIEL 4:17

The unsaved are in danger

"MY TEACHER told us to watch that TV special about nuclear war," said Laura. "We're going to discuss it tomorrow."

"Let's all watch it together," said Mother.

The program showed fire and destruction, with entire cities, buildings, and families wiped out in seconds by a nuclear blast. "Why would people want to destroy each other that way?" Laura asked when the show ended.

"Without Christ, a person's heart is evil," Dad explained. "The unbeliever thinks only of himself. He wants to control and run things his way."

Laura shivered. "I don't think I'll be able to sleep tonight."

"Remember that God is in control of everything," Mother reminded her. "Man can do only what God allows him to do. God has the final say as to when and how the world will end."

"That reminds me of Matthew chapter 10, verse 28," Dad said. "It tells us not to fear those who can kill the body, but rather to fear him who can destroy the body and soul."

"Isn't that a verse for missionaries?" asked Laura.

"It's a good verse for all of us," Dad replied. "It's a warning to those who are not Christians. If someone kills their bodies, their souls will go to hell where they will be in torment forever—much worse than nuclear warfare. For us who are Christians, the verse reminds us that all we can suffer is physical death. And then our souls will go to heaven."

"I'm glad I'm a Christian," said Laura, yawning. "I guess I'll sleep after all."

HOW ABOUT YOU? Does the thought of nuclear war frighten you? Remember that nothing can happen without God's permission. But if you're not a Christian, you should be afraid. The minute after you die will be too late to accept Christ. Salvation is for today. Don't put it off. *J.L.H.*

TO MEMORIZE: How shall we escape if we ignore such a great salvation? *Hebrews 2:3* (NIV)

19 May

SHOULD I TELL?

FROM THE BIBLE:

Saul now urged his servants and his son Jonathan to assassinate David. But Jonathan, because of his close friendship with David, told him what his father was planning. "Tomorrow morning," he warned him, "you must find a hiding place out in the fields. I'll ask my father to go out there with me, and I'll talk to him about you. Then I'll tell you everything I can find out."

The next morning Jonathan spoke with his father about David, saying many good things about him. "Please don't sin against David," Jonathan pleaded. "He's never done anything to harm you. He has always helped you in any way he could. Have you forgotten about the time he risked his life to kill the Philistine giant and how the Lord brought a great victory to Israel as a result? You were certainly happy about it then. Why should you murder an innocent man like David? There is no reason for it at all!"

So Saul listened to Jonathan and vowed, "As surely as the Lord lives, David will not be killed."

1 SAMUEL 19:1-6

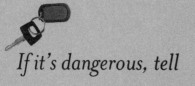

If it's dangerous, tell

BRAD WAS walking to the grocery store when he saw his friend Kevin with some other boys—smoking! Kevin tried to hide his cigarette behind his back.

"Hi," Brad said as he quickly walked into the store. When he came out, Kevin was gone. But Brad couldn't get him out of his mind. Kevin was a Christian!

Later, Kevin telephoned. "Look, Brad," he said, "just pretend you didn't see me tonight, OK? I only smoke when I'm with those guys. They think you're really out of it if you don't smoke!"

"Then don't hang around with them!" yelled Brad.

"Yeah, well . . . just promise me you won't tell anyone," said Kevin.

Brad didn't promise, but he did pray about Kevin that night. He didn't normally tell secrets when a friend asked him not to, but this was different. Kevin needed help. He knew Kevin's parents wouldn't want him smoking. It was bad for Kevin's health.

Brad thought of the Bible verse that says Christians are to share each other's troubles. First, he'd tell Kevin that he'd be willing to go with him to talk to his parents. If Kevin said no, then he'd tell Kevin he was going to an adult himself. Yes, there was a time not to break a confidence, but there was also a time when someone had to reach out and help.

HOW ABOUT YOU? Have you ever been in a situation when you couldn't decide whether or not it was right to tell something you knew? If a person shares something with you in confidence, but that "something" is dangerous, you should tell. First tell your friend that you must share the problem with an adult. Then offer to go with your friend to get help from a parent, a pastor, or a Sunday school teacher. *L.M.W.*

TO MEMORIZE: Share each other's troubles and problems, and in this way obey the law of Christ. *Galatians 6:2*

BAD BOWLING

FROM THE BIBLE:

Since God chose you to be the holy people whom he loves, you must clothe yourselves with tenderhearted mercy, kindness, humility, gentleness, and patience. You must make allowance for each other's faults and forgive the person who offends you. Remember, the Lord forgave you, so you must forgive others. And the most important piece of clothing you must wear is love. Love is what binds us all together in perfect harmony. And let the peace that comes from Christ rule in your hearts. For as members of one body you are all called to live in peace. And always be thankful.

Let the words of Christ, in all their richness, live in your hearts and make you wise. Use his words to teach and counsel each other. Sing psalms and hymns and spiritual songs to God with thankful hearts. And whatever you do or say, let it be as a representative of the Lord Jesus, all the while giving thanks through him to God the Father.

COLOSSIANS 3:12-17

"DAD, MAY I go bowling tonight?" Connie asked. "Everyone's going to Bowl & Bar, and it's only three dollars."

Dad spread cheese on a mousetrap and set it. "I've heard bad reports about that bowling alley, so we don't want you to go there."

"You never let me do anything!" yelled Connie. "What's wrong with bowling?"

Dad pointed to the cheese in the trap. "What's wrong with the cheese?"

"Nothing, I guess," said Connie, surprised.

"You're right," said Dad. "It's good, wholesome cheese. When a mouse takes a bite, he doesn't notice the trap." Dad took a pencil and touched the cheese. *Snap!* "But he'll be caught."

Dad set the trap aside. "There's nothing wrong with bowling," he said. "The trouble is, it could lure you into a trap. That place sells alcohol and attracts bad company. Kids smoke and use swear words. We've heard about fights and illegal drug use at that alley. You or your friends could be influenced to do things displeasing to God. If you want to bowl, you can go to the local alley with an adult chaperone."

Connie sighed. But as she looked at the mousetrap, she knew her father was right. Going to Bowl & Bar sounded exciting, but it wasn't worth getting caught in a trap.

HOW ABOUT YOU? Do you like to bowl? Good—unless it puts you in a place displeasing to the Lord. Do you like to go to the mall? Fine—unless the people you're with tempt you to do wrong things. Do you like to play soccer? Great—unless it keeps you from church on Sunday. Do you like to talk with friends? Fine—unless they tempt you to gossip. Make sure the wholesome activity you choose does not lure you into a trap where you'll be tempted to sin. *H.W.M.*

TO MEMORIZE: Whatever you eat or drink or whatever you do, you must do all for the glory of God. *1 Corinthians 10:31*

Choose activities carefully

21 May

JUST LIKE TOOTHPASTE

FROM THE BIBLE:

Dear brothers and sisters, not many of you should become teachers in the church, for we who teach will be judged by God with greater strictness.

We all make many mistakes, but those who control their tongues can also control themselves in every other way. We can make a large horse turn around and go wherever we want by means of a small bit in its mouth. And a tiny rudder makes a huge ship turn wherever the pilot wants it to go, even though the winds are strong. So also, the tongue is a small thing, but what enormous damage it can do. A tiny spark can set a great forest on fire. And the tongue is a flame of fire. It is full of wickedness that can ruin your whole life. It can turn the entire course of your life into a blazing flame of destruction, for it is set on fire by hell itself.

People can tame all kinds of animals and birds and reptiles and fish, but no one can tame the tongue. It is an uncontrollable evil, full of deadly poison.

JAMES 3:1-8

Speak kindly

JASON WAS babysitting his little brother, Josh, when the phone rang. It was Jason's friend Toby. The boys talked quite a while before Jason returned to the kitchen where he had left Josh. But his brother was no longer there. Jason heard suspicious noises coming from the bathroom. He found Josh trying desperately to push toothpaste back into the tube.

"You dummy, Josh!" exclaimed Jason. "Why can't you leave things alone? I could swat you!" As he began to clean up the mess, he continued to scold his little brother.

"I'm sorry," whimpered Josh. "I'll put it back."

"You can't," growled Jason. "Once toothpaste is out, it stays out!"

When Jason saw how upset his little brother was, he wished he hadn't been so harsh. "I'm sorry, Josh," he said. "You aren't a dummy."

"But you said . . . ," began Josh.

"Forget that." Jason rumpled his little brother's hair. "I shouldn't have said it in the first place."

When their parents arrived, they heard all about the toothpaste episode. "Jason said I'm a dummy," said Josh.

"I told you you're not," protested Jason, "and I said I was sorry."

"Josh, you were very naughty," said Mother, "and, Jason, you were too hasty with your tongue. I'm glad you apologized, but there's a lesson here. Just as you can't get toothpaste back into the toothpaste tube, you can't take back words that have come out of your mouth. So make sure all your words are pleasing to God."

HOW ABOUT YOU? Do you sometimes say things in anger? Or do you sometimes say things jokingly, but you know they really hurt the person you're talking to? Words can never be unsaid. The Bible says your speech is to be always with grace. Then you won't have to worry about taking back mean words you have spoken. *L.M.W.*

TO MEMORIZE: Don't use foul or abusive language. Let everything you say be good and helpful. *Ephesians 4:29*

MARY'S DISCIPLE

FROM THE BIBLE:

Then he said to the crowd, "If any of you wants to be my follower, you must put aside your selfish ambition, shoulder your cross daily, and follow me. If you try to keep your life for yourself, you will lose it. But if you give up your life for me, you will find true life. And how do you benefit if you gain the whole world but lose or forfeit your own soul in the process? If a person is ashamed of me and my message, I, the Son of Man, will be ashamed of that person when I return in my glory and in the glory of the Father and the holy angels."

LUKE 9:23-26

"MARY HAD a little lamb, little lamb. . . ." Kelly stopped singing as she entered the kitchen. "Hi, Mom. May I go next door to Josie's house?"

"As soon as you finish your Sunday school lesson," Mother said. Kelly resumed her song as she went to her room and got out her Sunday school book. "It followed her to school one day, school one day, school one day. . . ." Then there was silence as she got busy with her lesson.

Soon the song began again. "It made the children laugh and play, laugh and play . . . Mom, I'm all done." Kelly stood in the doorway, grinning. "Mary had a good disciple, didn't she?"

"A good what?"

"My lesson was about the twelve disciples of Jesus. It said a disciple is a follower—and Mary's lamb followed her wherever she went," explained Kelly. "It was a good disciple."

Mother laughed. "You're right. The lamb even followed her into the school. It didn't seem bothered by the children's laughter or jokes."

"Yeah," Kelly said. "We should follow Jesus like that, shouldn't we? We should do what he wants, even if other kids think we're weird." She stood at the door. "I'm going over to Josie's now. I'll tell her I'm Jesus' disciple. Then I'll see if she wants to come with me to Sunday school tomorrow."

HOW ABOUT YOU? Do your classmates think you're a little strange when you bow your head and pray before you eat your lunch? Do they laugh if you talk about Jesus? Do they think you're a goody-goody because you go to church and Sunday school regularly? Be a good disciple—a good follower—of Jesus. Do the things that please him, no matter what anyone says. *H.W.M.*

TO MEMORIZE: If any of you wants to be my follower, you must put aside your selfish ambition, shoulder your cross daily, and follow me. *Luke 9:23*

Be a good disciple

23 May

NEEDED: SMALL LIGHTS

FROM THE BIBLE:

Unless you are faithful in small matters, you won't be faithful in large ones. If you cheat even a little, you won't be honest with greater responsibilities. And if you are untrustworthy about worldly wealth, who will trust you with the true riches of heaven? And if you are not faithful with other people's money, why should you be trusted with money of your own?
LUKE 16:10-12

Your task is important

PASTOR JAMES had come for dinner. The grown-ups discussed their church's campaign to reach every family in their small town with the gospel. Dad was overseeing an upcoming men's breakfast. Mother was going to sing at a women's luncheon. Stephen, Shannyn's big brother, was making posters to advertise a citywide youth rally. *I wish I were big enough to help,* Shannyn thought with a sigh.

Just then, Pastor James turned to Shannyn. "Will you invite your friends to our special meetings?" he asked.

Shannyn shrugged and nodded. "I suppose," she said, "but I wish I could do something important."

Later, Mother tucked Shannyn into bed. "Would you please plug in the night-light, Mom?" said Shannyn.

"Sure," said Mother, walking into the hall. Suddenly, a bright light filled the hall, spilling over into Shannyn's room.

Shannyn jumped out of bed and ran to the door. She saw a bright lamp plugged into the outlet. "Mom, that light's too bright."

Mother turned back. "You're right," she agreed. She turned off the lamp and plugged in the usual night-light. "You see," she said, "little lights are needed, just as big ones are. And little jobs need to be done, just as big ones do. Little people, as well as big ones, need to be invited to come to Jesus."

Shannyn smiled. "OK, I'll invite all my friends," she decided. "I'll invite my whole class. I'll be a night-light."

HOW ABOUT YOU? Are you too young to preach? To organize meetings? To prepare a dinner? That's all right. Someday the Lord may ask you to do those things. Right now, perhaps you can be a friend to the lonesome child down the block. You can invite the teacher and classmates to come to church. Whatever God asks you to do, do it for his glory. *H.W.M.*

TO MEMORIZE: Unless you are faithful in small matters, you won't be faithful in large ones.
Luke 16:10

BEHIND PRISON BARS

FROM THE BIBLE:

Then many who heard him say these things believed in him.

Jesus said to the people who believed in him, "You are truly my disciples if you keep obeying my teachings. And you will know the truth, and the truth will set you free."

"But we are descendants of Abraham," they said. "We have never been slaves to anyone on earth. What do you mean, 'set free'?"

Jesus replied, "I assure you that everyone who sins is a slave of sin. A slave is not a permanent member of the family, but a son is part of the family forever. So if the Son sets you free, you will indeed be free."

JOHN 8:30-36

Avoid Satan's trap

JUSTIN'S EYES widened as he watched a TV documentary on prison life. It showed a big room with over fifty beds in it. And some men in solitary confinement were interviewed.

"Boy, Dad, I sure wouldn't want to end up in a place like that!" Justin said afterward.

"You, know, Justin, those prisoners probably said the same thing when they were your age. I doubt they planned to be in a prison with no freedom." Dad paused for a few moments. "Remember when we were having trouble with rats in the barn?"

"Sure," Justin said. "You went to the store and bought a really big mousetrap."

"That was a rat trap," said Dad. "I baited it with some peanut butter and set it in the middle of the barn floor. Those rats never thought about the danger. They only focused on getting the peanut butter."

"And those prisoners never thought about the trouble they would get into when they committed their crimes, right?" said Justin.

"That's right! Satan baited his trap with things that looked attractive to them, and they were caught," said Dad. "The good news is that God still loves those prisoners. I've read of several men who turned to the Lord while behind prison bars."

"But it would have been better if they had accepted Christ as Savior while they were young," said Justin thoughtfully. "Then they could have avoided going to prison at all."

HOW ABOUT YOU? Do you sometimes think it would be fun to see if you could get away with drinking? Trying drugs? Stealing? Hurting someone? Remember that every criminal behind bars was once young like you. Don't let Satan catch you in his trap of doing "little" bad things now. Accept Jesus as your Savior and pattern your life after him. Enjoy the freedom he provides. *C.V.M.*

TO MEMORIZE: If the Son sets you free, you will be free indeed. *John 8:36*

25 May

TOOLS AND TALENTS

FROM THE BIBLE:

Each of us has different work to do. And since we are all one body in Christ, we belong to each other, and each of us needs all the others.

God has given each of us the ability to do certain things well. So if God has given you the ability to prophesy, speak out when you have faith that God is speaking through you. If your gift is that of serving others, serve them well. If you are a teacher, do a good job of teaching. If your gift is to encourage others, do it! If you have money, share it generously. If God has given you leadership ability, take the responsibility seriously. And if you have a gift for showing kindness to others, do it gladly.

Don't just pretend that you love others. Really love them. Hate what is wrong. Stand on the side of the good. Love each other with genuine affection, and take delight in honoring each other.

ROMANS 12:5-10

God gives different talents

"DID YOU KNOW Jana refuses to join our junior choir?" Adrienne asked her friend Drew. The two girls were baking cookies at Adrienne's house. "Isn't that terrible?"

"Yes," Drew sighed. "I asked Mary to help with posters. She said she's not artistic."

"It's too bad when no one wants to do things for the Lord," said Adrienne as her mother walked in. "Mom, do you know where the cookie cutters are?"

"Use this," Mom said, handing her a cheese cutter.

"Mom," she laughed, "you can't cut out cookies with a cheese cutter."

Mom acted surprised. "Well, here then." She handed Drew a kitchen scissors.

"Mom!" said Adrienne. "We need the cookie cutters!"

"I'm just trying to show you something," Mom confessed. "In a way, these tools all have the same job—they cut. Yet their jobs are all different; each is good for its own particular purpose."

She found a cookie cutter and handed it to Drew. "Christians all have the same task—to glorify the Lord and bring others to him. But that doesn't mean we all have to do exactly the same thing."

"Did you hear us talking?" asked Adrienne.

Mother nodded. "Jana's mother told me that Jana doesn't sing well because of a hearing problem. But she can draw beautiful pictures! Maybe she'd like to help you with posters, Drew. As for Mary, her Sunday school teacher said she brought more visitors to class this year than any other person."

"So we each should serve, using our unique abilities, right?" said Drew. "I'll try to remember that."

HOW ABOUT YOU? Scripture tells us that we each have gifts (talents and skills)—all important, all useful for the glory of God. What is *your* gift? What is someone else's? When we combine our gifts to do the Lord's work, good things happen! *H.W.M.*

TO MEMORIZE: God has given each of us the ability to do certain things well. *Romans 12:6*

26 May

CATHY'S CREATION

FROM THE BIBLE:

By faith we understand that the entire universe was formed at God's command, that what we now see did not come from anything that can be seen.
HEBREWS 11:3

God created the world

THE HUM OF the sewing machine sounded throughout the house. "My creation is almost ready for you to see," said 12-year-old Cathy. She had been measuring and cutting and stitching ever since she arrived home from school, only taking time for supper.

Mother smiled. "I'm eager to see it—whatever it is," she said. "You've certainly spent a lot of time on it."

"Oh, you'll like it," said Cathy as she stood up and shook out the material she was using. "Tada! Here it is—my own special creation! It's an apron for Dad to use when he barbecues hamburgers or steak this summer."

"Hey, just what he needs," said Mother, "especially one that has flowered pockets and a polka-dot bib."

Cathy laughed. "Some creation, isn't it?"

"You keep saying 'creation,' Cathy, and I know what you mean," said Mother. "But the dictionary says the main meaning of *create* is 'to cause to exist.' In other words, *create* means to make something out of nothing. I like to remember this because it reminds me of God's awesome power. He's the only One who can really create anything in that sense."

Cathy nodded. "I hadn't thought of that," she said as she looked at the apron she was holding. "OK, Mom. I'm a fashion designer, not a creator."

"Now that I can agree with!" Mother said, smiling. "Let's wrap it up so you can give it to Dad."

HOW ABOUT YOU? Do you realize what a great thing God did when he created the world and everything in it? When you draw a picture, sew something unusual, or cook some concoction no one ever heard of, remind yourself that you are not creating in the same way God did. Only he can create something from nothing. *G.W.*

TO MEMORIZE: In the beginning God created the heavens and the earth. *Genesis 1:1*

27 May

WE REMEMBER
(PART 1)

FROM THE BIBLE:

Obey the government, for God is the one who put it there. All governments have been placed in power by God. So those who refuse to obey the laws of the land are refusing to obey God, and punishment will follow. For the authorities do not frighten people who are doing right, but they frighten those who do wrong. So do what they say, and you will get along well. The authorities are sent by God to help you. But if you are doing something wrong, of course you should be afraid, for you will be punished. The authorities are established by God for that very purpose, to punish those who do wrong. So you must obey the government for two reasons: to keep from being punished and to keep a clear conscience.

Pay your taxes, too, for these same reasons. For government workers need to be paid so they can keep on doing the work God intended them to do.

ROMANS 13:1-6

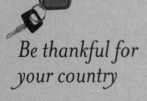

Be thankful for your country

REBECCA AND her brother waved as old cars, fire engines, floats, and bands went by in the Memorial Day parade. Men in uniform carried flags, and Rebecca saw "VFW" on one. "What is 'VFW'?" she asked her uncle.

"It stands for Veterans of Foreign Wars," Uncle Phil answered. "Remembering the soldiers is the whole reason we celebrate Memorial Day."

Afterwards they went to the cemetery where Uncle Phil's friend Don, who died in battle, was buried. Uncle Phil placed flowers on Don's grave. "Doing this helps me remember that Don—and many soldiers—fought and died so you and I can enjoy freedom in the United States," he said.

Rebecca just shrugged, so Uncle Phil continued. "They died so we could worship where we want to worship and spend our money the way we'd like—on houses, church, or even on chocolate milkshakes," he said. "Let's stop for a shake on the way home."

As they sipped their shakes, Rebecca said, "I never realized the meaning of Memorial Day. I've heard about fighting for democracy, but nobody told me to be grateful to those soldiers for my milkshakes and candy bars."

"We should be grateful to those who died for our country," Uncle Phil said, "and we should also be grateful to God. He's the one who has given us the blessing of living in a free land."

HOW ABOUT YOU? Memorial Day is more than just a day off from school and a nice parade. It's time to remember, with gratitude, those brave men who gave their lives so that you can enjoy many good things. You can't thank the soldiers who died. But maybe you know someone who fought for our country and is still alive. If so, say thank you. And thank God, too. *C.E.Y.*

TO MEMORIZE: Give everyone what you owe him: . . . if respect, then respect; if honor, then honor. *Romans 13:7* (NIV)

WE REMEMBER

(PART 2)

FROM THE BIBLE:

For this is what the Lord himself said, and I pass it on to you just as I received it. On the night when he was betrayed, the Lord Jesus took a loaf of bread, and when he had given thanks, he broke it and said, "This is my body, which is given for you. Do this in remembrance of me." In the same way, he took the cup of wine after supper, saying, "This cup is the new covenant between God and you, sealed by the shedding of my blood. Do this in remembrance of me as often as you drink it." For every time you eat this bread and drink this cup, you are announcing the Lord's death until he comes again.

1 CORINTHIANS 11:23-26

Be reverent during communion

THE LORD'S SUPPER was being served, but Rebecca wasn't paying attention to the minister. Instead, she was thinking about all the fun she'd had on Memorial Day.

After the service Rebecca looked for her uncle. "Hi, Uncle Phil," she said. "I liked all the things we did on Memorial Day—the parade and visiting the cemetery and everything. I'm still thankful to God for my freedom—and my milkshakes!"

"Great!" Uncle Phil smiled. "We did have fun last Monday. And today is an even more important memorial day."

"It is?" Rebecca was puzzled.

"Today we celebrated the Lord's Supper, or Communion," said Uncle Phil. "When we do this, we remember that our Lord Jesus willingly suffered and died to free our souls from sin and death forever."

"I never thought of it as a memorial day, but I will from now on," said Rebecca. She planned to listen better during the service next time.

"It's a good time to thank God for the freedom he gave you when he washed your sins away," said Uncle Phil. "Thank him, too, for all the spiritual blessings and privileges you have because of that freedom."

"I will," promised Rebecca. "On Monday I learned the meaning of our country's Memorial Day, and today I learned about the Christian's 'memorial day.' That's even more important—after all, chocolate shakes are good, but heaven is the best!"

HOW ABOUT YOU? Does the Lord's Supper have meaning for you, or doesn't it hold your interest? Jesus died and paid the price for your freedom from sin. Because of that, you may have your sins forgiven, peace in any circumstance, God's watchful care over you, and best of all, eternity in heaven. You should remember what he's done for you with reverence and thanksgiving. The communion service is a special time for doing that. *C.E.Y.*

TO MEMORIZE: You will know the truth, and the truth will set you free. *John 8:32*

29 May

IRON SHOES

FROM THE BIBLE:

And of Asher he said: "Asher is most blessed of sons; let him be favored by his brothers, and let him dip his foot in oil. Your sandals shall be iron and bronze; as your days, so shall your strength be. There is no one like the God of Jeshurun, who rides the heavens to help you, and in His excellency on the clouds. The eternal God is your refuge, and underneath are the everlasting arms."

DEUTERONOMY 33:24-27 (NKJV)

God takes care of you

"I NEED NEW gym shoes. My old ones are worn out," announced Jeff one evening.

"So they are!" exclaimed Mother. "I believe you go through more shoes than a centipede!"

Dad laughed. "Maybe you need shoes of iron and bronze, like Asher, the man we read about in devotions."

Jeff sighed. "My shoes are the least of my problems. Everything is going wrong lately. I can't understand my math. I have to sit between two girls in band, and my best friend, Ian, is moving out of town because his parents split up."

"Oh, bless your heart," sympathized Mother, putting her arm around Jeff.

"You really do need iron shoes to get across those hard places," said Dad soberly, "and they're available!"

He smiled at Jeff. "I'm not talking about literal shoes. But Asher was assured that God would not only provide sturdy shoes for the rough and hilly terrain, but also *spiritual shoes* needed for life's battles. The Bible speaks of the greatness of God and the 'everlasting arms' he uses to hold his children."

"That promise applies to us, too," Mother added. "We can rest in God's arms and trust him in everything."

"Would you like to pray about your problems right now, Jeff?" asked Dad. Jeff nodded and they prayed together.

"Let's go pick out some new gym shoes," said Mother when they had finished. "Each time you see them, they'll remind you that God will provide the needed 'shoes' to take care of your other problems, too."

HOW ABOUT YOU? Are your problems piling up? Too much homework? Someone ill? A divorce? A death? Does everything seem to be more than you can bear? God cares. He wants to hold and comfort you in his "everlasting arms." Trust him to provide whatever you need to face your problems and to help you through them. *H.W.M.*

TO MEMORIZE: The eternal God is your refuge, and his everlasting arms are under you.
Deuteronomy 33:27

30 May

DECISIONS! DECISIONS!

FROM THE BIBLE:

"So honor the Lord and serve him wholeheartedly. . . . But if you are unwilling to serve the Lord, then choose today whom you will serve. . . . But as for me and my family, we will serve the Lord."

The people replied, "We would never forsake the Lord and worship other gods. For the Lord our God is the one who rescued us and our ancestors from slavery in the land of Egypt. He performed mighty miracles before our very eyes. As we traveled through the wilderness among our enemies, he preserved us. It was the Lord who drove out the Amorites and the other nations living here in the land. So we, too, will serve the Lord, for he alone is our God."

Then Joshua said to the people, "You are not able to serve the Lord, for he is a holy and jealous God." . . .

But the people answered Joshua, saying, "No, we are determined to serve the Lord!"

"You are accountable for this decision," Joshua said. "You have chosen to serve the Lord."

"Yes," they replied, "we are accountable."

JOSHUA 24:14-19, 21-22

"I REALLY WANT to take gymnastics," said Alicia as she shopped for groceries with her mother and brother. "But if I do, I'll have to quit the church quiz team."

"I guess you'll just have to weigh the cost and decide which to do," Mother said.

"The cost?" asked Alicia. "The gymnastics lessons are free and so is quiz team."

"I mean the cost in terms of what you have to give up and what you'll receive in return," said Mother. "If you choose quiz team, you'll give up the gymnastic lessons and possible friendships with the other girls. If you choose gymnastics, it will cost you the enjoyment and value of studying the Bible and meeting new Christian friends."

Alicia wondered if it might be possible to do both things. *Maybe I could leave gymnastics early and get to quiz practice late. Would that work?*

Her little brother, Jimmy, tugged at her sleeve. "Show me the candy," he begged. "I have birthday quarters."

Alicia helped Jimmy pick out some candy. Then they went to the cashier. But Jimmy shoved his money inside his pocket. "Give the money to the lady," Alicia whispered.

Jimmy shook his head. "I want to keep my quarters—and the candy."

The cashier laughed. "We'd all like to buy things and still keep our money."

Alicia nodded. She was learning that it wasn't easy to wisely count the cost of her choices. But decisions did have to be made.

HOW ABOUT YOU? Do you have difficult choices to make? Pray about your decision. Then count the cost. What will you give up and what will you gain by your choice? There's always a price for choices and actions, but there are rewards, too. Choose the way you believe will please the Lord. *C.R.*

TO MEMORIZE: Choose today whom you will serve. . . . But as for me and my family, we will serve the Lord. *Joshua 24:15*

Consider the cost of decisions

31 May

UGLY BUT BEAUTIFUL

FROM THE BIBLE:

The king then asked him, "Is anyone still alive from Saul's family? If so, I want to show God's kindness to them in any way I can."

Ziba replied, "Yes, one of Jonathan's sons is still alive, but he is crippled." . . .

So David sent for him and brought him from Makir's home. His name was Mephibosheth; he was Jonathan's son and Saul's grandson. When he came to David, he bowed low in great fear and said, "I am your servant."

But David said, "Don't be afraid! I've asked you to come so that I can be kind to you because of my vow to your father, Jonathan. I will give you all the land that once belonged to your grandfather Saul, and you may live here with me at the palace!" . . .

And from that time on, Mephibosheth ate regularly with David, as though he were one of his own sons.

2 SAMUEL 9:3, 5-7, 11

Be "blind" to outward appearance

KEITH NUDGED Levi and pointed to a lady coming down the walk. She was wearing sunglasses and was walking a large dog in a special harness. "Have you ever seen such an ugly mutt?" Keith said.

Levi shrugged. He realized the lady was blind, and he knew this must be a Seeing Eye dog. "I think he's neat," Levi said.

To the boys' surprise, the lady stopped. "This is Shawnee," she said, "and he's been taking me places for six years now. He's saved my life at least twice that I know of. He's always there when I need him."

"Wow," said Levi.

"I've been told that Shawnee is not a pretty dog," the lady said, "but even if he's the ugliest thing in the world, he's still beautiful to me. I'm very blessed," she said.

"Blessed!" Keith blurted out. "But you're blind."

The lady nodded. "Yes, but the accident that took away my physical sight gave me a different kind of sight. I no longer judge animals or people on what they look like. I'm blind to all that. Instead, I look at what they're like on the inside. That's what really counts."

As the boys headed home, Levi said, "That lady was nice, and so was her dog. Never again will I make fun of the way another person looks."

"Me, neither," agreed Keith. "I won't even make fun of how a *dog* looks."

HOW ABOUT YOU? Do you ever laugh at people because they don't look as nice as you do? Do you look down on them because of scars or other physical handicaps? In a sense, God is "blind" to outward appearances. He cares about what is on the inside. You should, too. Never laugh at anyone for what he looks like. He may be more beautiful than you on the inside. *D.S.M.*

TO MEMORIZE: You alone know the human heart. *1 Kings 8:39*

1 June

THE OPEN UMBRELLA

FROM THE BIBLE:

The law of the Lord is perfect,
reviving the soul.
The decrees of the Lord are trustworthy,
making wise the simple.
The commandments of the Lord are right,
bringing joy to the heart.
The commands of the Lord are clear,
giving insight to life.
Reverence for the Lord is pure,
lasting forever.
The laws of the Lord are true;
each one is fair.
They are more desirable than gold,
even the finest gold.
They are sweeter than honey,
even honey dripping from the comb.
They are a warning to those who hear them;
there is great reward for those who obey them.

PSALM 19:7-11

Read your Bible

AS JERRY LEFT Mike's house, Mike's mother handed him a large paper bag. "Here are a few things your mother can put in her garage sale," she said.

"Thanks," Jerry replied. Taking the bag in his arms, he started down the street. He felt a raindrop hit his face, then another. Clutching the bag, he started to run. Then the wet paper bag broke, scattering items over the ground. Jerry quickly gathered everything up and kept running. When he got home, his mother looked at him in surprise.

"What are all those things you're carrying?" she asked.

Jerry dumped his wet armload onto the table. "Some things from Mike's mom." Jerry stared at the table. There lay a perfectly good umbrella.

Mom laughed. "You carried this umbrella all the way home in the rain without even opening it?"

"I guess I only thought of it as something to carry," Jerry said with a grin. He went to change into dry clothes. When he came back, Mom was drying the umbrella.

"You know, Son," she said, "God has used this incident to teach me that it's not enough to carry my Bible to church. It won't do me any good unless I open it and read it."

"That goes for me too, Mom," said Jerry.

"How about reading a passage together right now?" Mom suggested.

"OK!" said Jerry. "I'll help you clear off the table."

HOW ABOUT YOU? Do you have a Bible? Do you carry it with you to church? That's great, but a closed Bible won't do you any good. It must be opened and read in order to help you. If you haven't been reading God's Word like you should, why not start today? You'll be glad you did! *S.L.K.*

TO MEMORIZE: The commandments of the Lord are right, bringing joy to the heart. The commands of the Lord are clear, giving insight to life. *Psalm 19:8*

2 June

THE SNAPPING TURTLE

FROM THE BIBLE:

Fools get into constant quarrels; they are asking for a beating.
The mouths of fools are their ruin; their lips get them into trouble.
What dainty morsels rumors are—but they sink deep into one's heart. . . .
Those who love to talk will experience the consequences, for the tongue can kill or nourish life. . . .
There are "friends" who destroy each other, but a real friend sticks closer than a brother.

PROVERBS 18:6-8, 21, 24

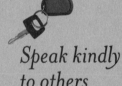

Speak kindly to others

LINDY LAY on her bed, sniffing. "Go away!" she snapped when her father tapped on her door.

"Don't you want to go fishing with me?" asked Dad.

Lindy jumped to her feet. "Oh, I do! Wait for me!"

Later as they sat on the riverbank, Dad asked, "What's been bothering you, honey?"

"Oh, Daddy," wailed Lindy, "nobody wants to be my friend anymore."

"Do you have any idea why?" Dad asked.

"No!" snapped Lindy. "I—oh! Get away! Get away!"

A few feet away a turtle sat glaring at Lindy and snapping furiously. "Not too friendly, is he?" laughed Dad. "Leave him alone, and he won't hurt you."

Lindy shuddered. "Let's move."

When they were settled in a new spot, Dad asked, "Could it be that everyone is leaving you alone because you've been acting like a snapping turtle—glaring and snapping at everyone?"

"But, Daddy," Lindy began, "I—"

"No, let me finish," Dad interrupted. "When that turtle started snapping at us, what did we do?"

"We got out of his way," Lindy answered.

"And that's what your friends are doing—getting out of your way," Dad replied. "The Bible says in order to have friends, you must be friendly."

The next day when Lindy came home from school, she was smiling. "You were right, Daddy," she said. "When I stopped snapping at my friends, they stopped getting out of my way."

HOW ABOUT YOU? Have people been avoiding you? Is it because you've been snapping at them? God's Word is filled with practical wisdom, and one thing it teaches is that your tongue can cause you all kinds of trouble. Check your attitude and your tongue. Ask God to help you use it to make friends instead of driving people away. *B.J.W.*

TO MEMORIZE: I will watch what I do and not sin in what I say. I will curb my tongue when the ungodly are around me. *Psalm 39:1*

3 *June*

PASS THE POTATOES

FROM THE BIBLE:

When you pray, don't be like the hypocrites who love to pray publicly on street corners and in the synagogues where everyone can see them. I assure you, that is all the reward they will ever get. But when you pray, go away by yourself, shut the door behind you, and pray to your Father secretly. Then your Father, who knows all secrets, will reward you.

When you pray, don't babble on and on as people of other religions do. They think their prayers are answered only by repeating their words again and again. Don't be like them, because your Father knows exactly what you need even before you ask him!

MATTHEW 6:5-8

Mean what you pray

"WHY DID it have to rain today?" grumbled Brian. "Our first softball game of the season was cancelled—all because of this silly storm!"

"Want to play a game with me?" his sister, Jill, offered.

"No," Brian snapped. "That's boring."

At suppertime, Brian's dad asked him to give thanks for the food. Brian bowed his head. "Dear heavenly Father, thank you for this food and the beautiful day you've given us. Amen. Pass the potatoes."

"Oh, Brian," Jill said. "You always say the same thing!"

"I'm afraid Jill's right," said Mother. "It's become a routine with you. You don't even think about what you are saying."

"I do so," Brian argued.

"Brian, ever since you got home from school, you've been complaining about the rain. Then you prayed and thanked the Lord for the 'beautiful' day!"

Brian looked sheepish. "I guess I didn't think."

"The Bible tells us not to repeat prayers over and over when they have no meaning," said Dad. "I don't think thanking the Lord for the nice day had very much meaning for you, Son. You could have thanked the Lord for sending the rain for the farmers' crops, but it certainly wasn't honest to say you were thankful for the day."

"You're right," he admitted. "Shall I pray again?"

Supper waited while Brian again led the family in prayer.

HOW ABOUT YOU? Do you rattle off the same things each time you pray? Wouldn't it become sort of boring if your friends said the same thing every time they talked to you? The Lord desires that you talk to him about what you're thinking. He is a friend who has done much for you. Think about what you are saying when you pray. *L.M.W.*

TO MEMORIZE: When you pray, don't babble on and on as people of other religions do. They think their prayers are answered only by repeating their words again and again. *Matthew 6:7*

4 June

OWE NO ONE

FROM THE BIBLE:

Give to everyone what you owe them: Pay your taxes and import duties, and give respect and honor to all to whom it is due.

Pay all your debts, except the debt of love for others. You can never finish paying that! If you love your neighbor, you will fulfill all the requirements of God's law.

ROMANS 13:7-8

Pay your debts

"ALLOWANCE TIME!" Dad said as he entered his son's room.

Mark sighed. "Just put it on the dresser."

"What's wrong?" Dad asked. "Usually you're eager to get your allowance."

"What's the use?" said Mark sadly. "I can't buy anything anyway."

"Tell me about it," Dad said.

So Mark explained. "A few weeks ago, Scott loaned me some money to buy a new video game. I meant to pay him back the next day, but I never got around to it." Dad frowned as Mark went on. "The next Saturday all the guys were going to play laser tag, and I didn't want to be left out, so . . ."

"So you spent your allowance on laser tag instead," finished Dad.

Mark nodded. "Yeah," he said glumly, "and now I have to pay Scott back."

"I hope you learned a lesson from all this," said Dad solemnly. "It's a biblical principle that it's best to go without something until you have the money to pay for it. You should borrow money only when it's absolutely necessary. Then you should repay it as quickly as possible."

"What should I do now?" Mark asked.

"Set aside money for your church offering, then put the rest toward what you owe. Do that until you've paid Scott in full."

"Sounds good, Dad," Mark said as he picked up his money. "By the way, do you have any odd jobs I could do? I want to pay off my debt as quickly as I can!"

HOW ABOUT YOU? Have you been in the habit of borrowing money—a quarter here or a dollar there? Many people, even adults, have gotten into trouble because they borrowed money. It's far better to wait—and work—for the things you want. You'll be happier if you do. *S.L.K.*

TO MEMORIZE: Pay all your debts, except the debt of love for others. You can never finish paying that! *Romans 13:8*

DAILY BENEFITS

FROM THE BIBLE:

Praise the Lord, I tell myself;
with my whole heart, I will
praise his holy name.
Praise the Lord, I tell myself,
and never forget the good
things he does for me.
He forgives all my sins
and heals all my diseases.
He ransoms me from death
and surrounds me with love
and tender mercies.
He fills my life with good things.
My youth is renewed like the
eagle's!

PSALM 103:1-5

Don't forget the benefits

BRAD RUBBED his eyes hard with his fists. Just because he couldn't go to summer camp was no reason to cry. He stuffed the application in his pocket, straightened his shoulders, and entered the house.

"Your dad has gone to apply for a job." Mrs. Nelson smiled at her son as he came in.

"But he has gone to so many interviews, Mom! Why doesn't God give Dad a job? We're God's children. I thought he took care of his children."

Mom nodded. "He does. Our bills are paid. We still have our home. We have each other. There may not be money for extras like summer camp, Brad, but God has given us many benefits."

"I can't see—" Brad stopped as Dad burst in.

"I got it!" He swung his wife around and around. "I got the job! The pay is good, and the benefits are great!"

"What are benefits?" Brad questioned.

"You might call them added blessings," Dad explained. "I mean things like health insurance and paid holidays."

"What did you mean when you said God has given us many benefits, Mom?" Brad looked puzzled.

"I was talking about health, love, joy, eternal life, the promise that he will supply all our needs—things like that," she explained. "Every day he gives us benefits."

HOW ABOUT YOU? Are you so busy looking at what you do not have, that you forgot to be thankful for what God has given you? Every day we receive benefits (added blessings) from the Lord. You may not always have as much money as you want, but there are many things more important than money. Right now make a list of at least five benefits God has given to you. *B.J.W.*

TO MEMORIZE: Praise be to the Lord, to God our Savior, who daily bears our burdens. *Psalm 68:19* (NIV)

6 June

AN UNJOYFUL SOUND

FROM THE BIBLE:

Shout with joy to the Lord, O earth!
Worship the Lord with gladness.
Come before him, singing with joy.
Acknowledge that the Lord is God!
He made us, and we are his.
We are his people, the sheep of his pasture.
Enter his gates with thanksgiving;
go into his courts with praise.
Give thanks to him and bless his name.
For the Lord is good.
His unfailing love continues forever,
and his faithfulness continues to each generation.

PSALM 100:1-5

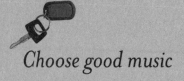

Choose good music

AS ERIC AND DARRIN worked together painting a raft they had built, Darrin started singing. "Where in the world did you learn that?" Eric asked.

"Oh, it's the latest album by the Mid-Knight Witches," answered Darrin. "I bought it yesterday."

Eric looked up. "But you're a Christian!"

"So? The Bible doesn't say you can't listen to Mid-Knight Witches' songs," replied Darrin. "Besides, I don't pay attention to the words."

Eric looked surprised. "You must pay some attention to them! You just sang them—'I'm going to steal you, kill you, chill you.' "

"The words don't mean anything," protested Darrin.

The conversation still bothered Eric that night. As he sat down to supper, he told his parents what Darrin had said. "That's interesting," said Dad. "I just read an article in the paper about Mid-Knight Witches. The lead singer says he enjoys the power the group has over young people's minds."

Eric was thoughtful for a few moments, and then he said, "Darrin told me that the Bible doesn't say anything about listening to Mid-Knight Witches' music, but it does! God tells us to make a joyful noise, and the Mid-Knight Witches' album certainly isn't joyful!"

"It also says we are to make melody in our heart to the Lord," his mother reminded him. Eric smiled and nodded. He had some important verses to show Darrin!

HOW ABOUT YOU? What kind of music do you listen to on your radio? What kind of tapes and CDs do you buy? Do you think rock music is OK because you don't pay any attention to the words? Be careful! Often the lyrics in rock songs are not pleasing to the Lord. There are many good songs that are fun to sing. Listen to the right kind of music! *L.M.W.*

TO MEMORIZE: Sing psalms and hymns and spiritual songs among yourselves, making music to the Lord in your hearts. *Ephesians 5:19*

7 June

SMILE, GOD LOVES YOU

FROM THE BIBLE:

If you live a life guided by wisdom, you won't limp or stumble as you run. Carry out my instructions; don't forsake them. Guard them, for they will lead you to a fulfilled life.

Do not do as the wicked do or follow the path of evildoers. Avoid their haunts. Turn away and go somewhere else, for evil people cannot sleep until they have done their evil deed for the day. They cannot rest unless they have caused someone to stumble. They eat wickedness and drink violence!

The way of the righteous is like the first gleam of dawn, which shines ever brighter until the full light of day. But the way of the wicked is like complete darkness. Those who follow it have no idea what they are stumbling over.

Pay attention, my child, to what I say. Listen carefully. Don't lose sight of my words. Let them penetrate deep within your heart, for they bring life and radiant health to anyone who discovers their meaning.

Above all else, guard your heart, for it affects everything you do.

PROVERBS 4:12-23

BRUCE frowned as he came to the breakfast table. His sister, Carin, and his parents were talking cheerfully. Sliding onto his chair, Bruce scowled. "Not oatmeal again! I hate oatmeal, I hate school, I hate everything," he growled.

The cheerful look left Carin's face, and the corners of her mouth drooped. "I hate a few things myself," she announced, "like this shirt. Do I have to wear it?"

Mom looked dismayed. "But it's practically new!" she exclaimed.

"I like it," said Dad. He turned to Bruce. "By the way, how about going to a ball game tonight?"

"Bruce always gets to do things," complained Carin. "Mom, why can't we do something for once, like go shopping?"

"And get another shirt you don't like," Bruce said with a sneer.

"Whoa!" called Dad. "Hold on here!" He turned to Bruce. "It occurs to me that we were all sitting happily at the table until you came with that big frown on your face. Your gloom has spread over the whole family."

"That's true," agreed Mom. "No part of your body can influence others as much as your face."

Bruce lifted his head. "I never thought of it that way."

As Mother set bowls of hot cereal before them, Dad added, "Since our faces affect others so much, we should keep them as cheerful as possible. Before we eat this morning, let's ask the Lord to give us happy hearts so we are better able to smile."

HOW ABOUT YOU? Do you spread happiness and goodwill with a cheerful face? Or do you spread unhappiness and depression with scowls and frowns? What you feel in your heart usually shows on your face, so it's important to keep your heart right with the Lord. Before facing the world each day, spend time with God. *C.E.Y.*

TO MEMORIZE: A glad heart makes a happy face; a broken heart crushes the spirit. *Proverbs 15:13*

Spread happiness

8 June

THE COUNSELOR HUNT

FROM THE BIBLE:

I can never escape from your spirit!
I can never get away from your presence!
If I go up to heaven, you are there;
if I go down to the place of the dead, you are there.
If I ride the wings of the morning,
if I dwell by the farthest oceans,
even there your hand will guide me,
and your strength will support me.
I could ask the darkness to hide me
and the light around me to become night—
but even in darkness I cannot hide from you.
To you the night shines as bright as day.
Darkness and light are both alike to you.

PSALM 139:7-12

God is listening

JAMIE WAS having a wonderful time at camp with her best friend, Dawn. Their counselor, Mary, was just like a friend to all the girls.

During supper one evening, the counselors disappeared from the dining hall. Then Mr. Ken, the camp director, explained that the counselors were hiding and the campers had a half hour to find them.

"Where shall we look first?" asked Jamie as they ran out of the building.

"Why don't we try looking near our cabin?" said Dawn.

Half an hour later, the kids and most of the counselors were back. Mr. Ken rang the bell, signaling the counselors who hadn't been found to come out of hiding. Jamie and Dawn were astonished to see Mary pop out of a garbage can nearby.

"We must have walked past there a dozen times," Jamie moaned.

Mary giggled. "I thought for sure you'd find me!"

When the girls in the cabin gathered for devotions that evening, Mary talked about the counselor hunt. "I heard some kids talking as they walked by my hiding place. I don't think some of them would have talked the way they did if they had known a counselor was nearby," she said. "I think I got a little idea of how God must feel when people forget he's listening. It's important to remember that he can always hear. He's always there even though we can't see him."

HOW ABOUT YOU? How do you talk when there are no parents, teachers, or other adults around? When you're with your friends, do you say words that you're careful to avoid when your parents are with you? Make sure your speech is clean no matter who is nearby. God can hear you even when you're all alone. He's always listening! *D.S.M.*

TO MEMORIZE: "Can anyone hide from me? Am I not everywhere in all the heavens and earth?" asks the Lord. *Jeremiah 23:24*

9 June

DARKNESS OR LIGHT

FROM THE BIBLE:

The light shines through the darkness, and the darkness can never extinguish it.

God sent John the Baptist to tell everyone about the light so that everyone might believe because of his testimony. John himself was not the light; he was only a witness to the light. The one who is the true light, who gives light to everyone, was going to come into the world.

But although the world was made through him, the world didn't recognize him when he came.

JOHN 1:5-10

Walk in God's light

MICHAEL'S cat, Fluffy, spied a moth fluttering around the living room lamp. Fluffy couldn't reach the moth, but he watched intently as it circled the lampshade. "The moth wants the light, and Fluffy wants the moth," Dad said, chuckling.

"What makes moths want the light?" asked Michael.

"It's something God built into them," answered Dad. "They fly at night, so they have to find food at night. Most night-blooming flowers are white, and the white shows up in the darkness, especially when the moon is out. The moths are attracted by the light flowers."

"So the fact that they want light helps them find food?" asked Michael.

"That's right." Dad nodded. "He's setting a good example for you, too."

"How?" Michael asked, puzzled.

Dad smiled. "Well, we need the light of God just as the moth needs the light to find the flowers. What would you think about a moth who hungrily flew around in the dark and wouldn't come to the light flowers for food?"

"I'd think something was wrong with a moth like that," answered Michael.

"Yet some people stay away from God and stumble around in darkness spiritually," said Dad.

"You'd think people would at least know as much as moths!" Michael said with a grin.

HOW ABOUT YOU? Do you know that staying close to God is what the Bible calls "walking in the light"? Forgetting about God and going your own way is like "walking in the darkness." Stay in the light by reading your Bible, praying, obeying God, and keeping him in your thoughts. *C.E.Y.*

TO MEMORIZE: For though your hearts were once full of darkness, now you are full of light from the Lord, and your behavior should show it!
Ephesians 5:8

10 June

DOING YOUR BEST

FROM THE BIBLE:

My children, listen to me. Listen to your father's instruction. Pay attention and grow wise, for I am giving you good guidance. Don't turn away from my teaching. For I, too, was once my father's son, tenderly loved by my mother as an only child.

My father told me, "Take my words to heart. Follow my instructions and you will live. Learn to be wise, and develop good judgment. Don't forget or turn away from my words. Don't turn your back on wisdom, for she will protect you. Love her, and she will guard you. Getting wisdom is the most important thing you can do! And whatever else you do, get good judgment. If you prize wisdom, she will exalt you. Embrace her and she will honor you. She will place a lovely wreath on your head; she will present you with a beautiful crown."

My child, listen to me and do as I say, and you will have a long, good life.

PROVERBS 4:1-10

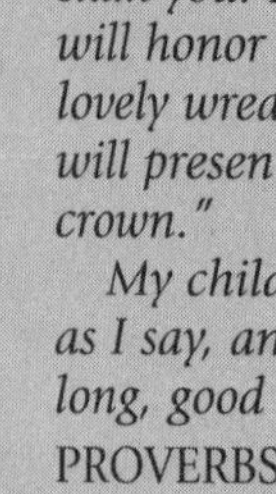

Work cheerfully

"OH, YUCK! I hate this job," mumbled Corrie. She slammed the bathroom door. Every Saturday morning it was one of her chores to scrub the bathroom, and she absolutely detested it. Corrie groaned as she knelt down to scour the tub. "Why can't Mom do this? She has longer arms." She stood up and looked in the mirror. Next she got out the brush and tried styling her hair a different way—anything to forget cleaning the bathroom.

Mom poked her head through the doorway. "Corrie, this is a twenty-minute job," she said, "and you've been in here an hour already!"

Corrie started scouring again, then she stopped. Everything was quiet except for her dad and mother talking in the living room.

"Don't forget," she heard her mother say, "next week Corrie's orthodontist bill is due. That's another hundred fifty."

"Right, and we need to send in her summer camp fee before the end of the month."

"She really needs some new tennis shoes, too," Mom added.

Corrie felt bad. All the bills her parents were talking about were for her. "I'm sorry, Lord," she prayed silently. "I'm sorry I grumbled so much about a little job. Dad and Mom do so much for me, and I know cleaning the bathroom is one of the ways I can show them how much I appreciate their love. Help me not to complain about my chores anymore."

HOW ABOUT YOU? Do you have regular chores you are to do each week? Do you sometimes complain and grumble about them? Your dad and mom do a lot for you. They feed you and clothe you and provide a place for you to live. Thank the Lord for your parents. Show them how much you love and appreciate them by cheerfully helping around the house. *L.M.W.*

TO MEMORIZE: "Honor your father and mother." This is the first of the Ten Commandments that ends with a promise. *Ephesians 6:2*

11 June

TWO BUCKETS

FROM THE BIBLE:

But God's truth stands firm like a foundation stone with this inscription: "The Lord knows those who are his," and "Those who claim they belong to the Lord must turn away from all wickedness."

In a wealthy home some utensils are made of gold and silver, and some are made of wood and clay. The expensive utensils are used for special occasions, and the cheap ones are for everyday use. If you keep yourself pure, you will be a utensil God can use for his purpose. Your life will be clean, and you will be ready for the Master to use you for every good work.

Run from anything that stimulates youthful lust. Follow anything that makes you want to do right. Pursue faith and love and peace, and enjoy the companionship of those who call on the Lord with pure hearts.

2 TIMOTHY 2:19-22

Keep your thoughts pure

"I'LL GO GET some water," volunteered Carl. He grabbed the bucket and headed for the spring. He and his parents were "roughing it" at a cottage for the weekend. When Carl returned with the fresh water, his dad asked him to fill another bucketful.

"Here's another bucket," said Dad.

"But, Dad, this bucket is filthy!" Carl exclaimed. "You don't want to drink out of this dirty bucket, do you?"

"Oh, no!" answered Dad. "Mom and I will use the clean one, but I thought you might want to use the dirty one. Since you don't care what you put in your mind, I didn't think you'd care what you put in your stomach, either."

"My mind?" Carl asked.

"Mom just told me that when she was packing for you this morning, she found some dirty joke books," Dad explained. Carl looked guilty as Dad continued. "When I was a boy on the farm, we had two buckets. One was the water bucket. The other was the slop bucket where we threw all our garbage. Every night I carried it out to the pigs. We didn't even try to keep the slop bucket clean." He paused. "Carl, your mind can be a water bucket or a slop bucket."

"I'm really sorry," admitted Carl. "What should I do?"

"Ask the Lord to forgive you," Dad replied. "Then stay away from evil influences—like dirty books, bad pictures, or the wrong crowd."

"I'll be careful from now on," said Carl. "I certainly don't want my mind to be a slop bucket!"

HOW ABOUT YOU? What are you putting in your mind? Has it become a slop bucket? Memorize today's verse, and ask the Lord to help you do what it says. *B.J.W.*

TO MEMORIZE: Fix your thoughts on what is true and honorable and right. Think about things that are pure and lovely and admirable. Think about things that are excellent and worthy of praise. *Philippians 4:8*

12 June

CAUGHT IN A TRAP

FROM THE BIBLE

In those days, when you were slaves of sin, you weren't concerned with doing what was right. And what was the result? It was not good, since now you are ashamed of the things you used to do, things that end in eternal doom. But now you are free from the power of sin and have become slaves of God. Now you do those things that lead to holiness and result in eternal life. For the wages of sin is death, but the free gift of God is eternal life through Christ Jesus our Lord.

ROMANS 6:20-23

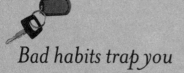

Bad habits trap you

RON REYNOLDS and his Uncle George were buddies. Ron could talk to Uncle George about anything—like he did the day they were out in the woods looking for berries. "Did you ever smoke, Uncle George?" Ron wanted to know.

"Nope, never did," his uncle answered.

"How come?" Ron asked.

A smile crossed Uncle George's face. "First, because I knew if I ever got caught, my dad would give me a good thrashing! Later, because I knew it was bad for me."

"Most of the guys in my class smoke," continued Ron.

"And does it look pretty tempting to you?" asked Uncle George.

"Well, the guys say it's fun, and they look kinda neat when they take a big drag, and—hey!" Ron interrupted himself. "Here is one of Mr. Hobson's traps! Can he really catch anything with just a piece of smelly fish? Do you think it ever dawns on the animals that the trap will hurt them?"

"The fish does seem to work, and the animals don't seem to sense danger. That sort of reminds me of your friends at school," said Uncle George. "They go after those smelly cigarettes, not thinking about the harm they can do to their bodies, or that they will be trapped by the habit."

"Some people aren't much smarter than dumb animals, are they?" asked Ron. "I don't plan to get trapped like that!"

HOW ABOUT YOU? Are you being lured into a trap by cigarettes, drugs, or alcohol? They can only do you harm. They can even kill you! If you have been trapped, you will need help to overcome these habits. Seek help from your parents, Sunday school teacher, or pastor—and most important, ask Jesus to set you free. *B.J.W.*

TO MEMORIZE: These evil desires lead to evil actions, and evil actions lead to death. *James 1:15*

13 June

TO RAIN OR NOT TO RAIN

TOBY AWOKE to the sound of rain. "If this rain keeps up, Dan and I won't be able to go to Fun Island this afternoon!" he exclaimed.

After breakfast Toby's little brother, Timmy, begged him to play. At the same time, Toby's sister, Taryn, approached him. "You promised to help me with my math, remember?"

"I can't please you both," Toby sighed, "but Taryn needs help. I'll play with you later, Timmy."

Just then Dan arrived. "Isn't this rain awful?" Toby complained.

"We need the rain, though," replied Dan. "We've been praying for it for weeks. It's been so dry that the farmers' crops were drying up."

"But it could ruin our day," complained Toby. "I'm praying that it'll stop."

Timmy had been listening. "Toby's praying that it will stop, and Dan's praying that it won't. God can't give you both what you want, can he?"

Toby looked at his little brother. Just a few minutes earlier, Toby had had to decide whether to do what Timmy wanted or what Taryn wanted. Now he thought about his prayer and about Dan's. Somehow, he thought it wouldn't be hard for God to decide what to do. Toby knew that God did not want people to pray selfishly. And he knew he hadn't prayed with the right attitude.

Forgive me, Lord, for being selfish, Toby prayed silently. Aloud he said, "I guess I hope he answers Dan's prayer. God will give us another sunny day for our trip."

HOW ABOUT YOU? Do you want things to go your way no matter what hardships it brings to others? We cannot expect God to give us what we want when we pray with that attitude. Learn to pray unselfishly, asking God to send you what he knows is best. *A.G.L.*

TO MEMORIZE: And even when you do ask, you don't get it because your whole motive is wrong—you want only what will give you pleasure. *James 4:3*

FROM THE BIBLE:

Since we believe human testimony, surely we can believe the testimony that comes from God. And God has testified about his Son. All who believe in the Son of God know that this is true. Those who don't believe this are actually calling God a liar because they don't believe what God has testified about his Son.

And this is what God has testified: He has given us eternal life, and this life is in his Son. So whoever has God's Son has life; whoever does not have his Son does not have life.

I write this to you who believe in the Son of God, so that you may know you have eternal life. And we can be confident that he will listen to us whenever we ask him for anything in line with his will. And if we know he is listening when we make our requests, we can be sure that he will give us what we ask for.

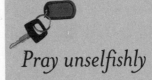

1 JOHN 5:9-15

Pray unselfishly

A LETTER FOR YOU

FROM THE BIBLE:

Now is the time to get rid of anger, rage, malicious behavior, slander, and dirty language. Don't lie to each other, for you have stripped off your old evil nature and all its wicked deeds. In its place you have clothed yourselves with a brand-new nature that is continually being renewed as you learn more and more about Christ, who created this new nature within you. . . .

Since God chose you to be the holy people whom he loves, you must clothe yourselves with tenderhearted mercy, kindness, humility, gentleness, and patience. You must make allowance for each other's faults and forgive the person who offends you. Remember, the Lord forgave you, so you must forgive others. And the most important piece of clothing you must wear is love. Love is what binds us all together in perfect harmony. And let the peace that comes from Christ rule in your hearts. For as members of one body you are all called to live in peace. And always be thankful.

Let the words of Christ, in all their richness, live in your hearts and make you wise. Use his words to teach and counsel each other. Sing psalms and hymns and spiritual songs to God with thankful hearts.

COLOSSIANS 3:8-16

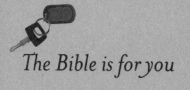

The Bible is for you

"EAT A WELL-BALANCED meal, get to bed early, and be sure to—" Kim stopped. "Who's this from anyway?" she asked her brother, Tom.

"My track coach," replied Tom. "Tomorrow's the track meet, so he sent a letter to everybody on the team. He wants us to stay healthy. It's good advice for everybody, though, don't you think?"

"It's your letter, so the advice is for you. I wouldn't want to miss my pizza party at church tonight in order to eat healthy," Kim said with a grin.

Kim went to the church party that night. At the end, Pastor Blake led a devotional time. "How many of you like to get mail?" he asked. All hands went up. "What do you do when you get a letter?" he continued.

"Open it and read it," the children chorused.

Pastor Blake nodded and held up his Bible. "This is God's letter to you," he said. "Do you open it and read it? Do you apply what God says to your life, or do you read it as though you were reading someone else's mail?"

It was easy for Kim to see what Pastor Blake was getting at. When she had read the track coach's letter to Tom, she hadn't thought much about the advice it contained. *But do I read the Bible that way, too?* she wondered. *I'm going to be careful, after this, to see what God is telling me.*

HOW ABOUT YOU? When you read today's Scripture, did you think, *Oh, my friend should read this* or *My brother ought to pay attention to that?* Don't read the Bible as if it were someone else's mail. Realize that it is God's letter to you. Go back over the verses you read today and see what good advice God is giving you. *H.W.M.*

TO MEMORIZE: Let the words of Christ, in all their richness, live in your hearts and make you wise. *Colossians 3:16*

15 June

SMELLY PRESENTS

FROM THE BIBLE:

Once we, too, were foolish and disobedient. We were misled by others and became slaves to many wicked desires and evil pleasures. Our lives were full of evil and envy. We hated others, and they hated us.

But then God our Savior showed us his kindness and love. He saved us, not because of the good things we did, but because of his mercy. He washed away our sins and gave us a new life through the Holy Spirit. He generously poured out the Spirit upon us because of what Jesus Christ our Savior did. He declared us not guilty because of his great kindness. And now we know that we will inherit eternal life.

TITUS 3:3-7

Good works are not enough

LITTLE SARAH HIGGINS came into the living room holding an armful of paper-wrapped bundles. "Look!" she cried happily. "I made you all some presents!"

As she handed out the packages, her brother Ted wrinkled up his nose. "Something stinks!" he said. Unwrapping his package, he found a small object made from an old newspaper. It was yellow and slightly damp, and it smelled terrible!

"See? It's an airplane," announced Sarah. "We learned to fold them in nursery school. And I made one for Ann, too. And see, I folded hats for Mommy and Daddy."

"They're very nice," said Mother with a faint smile. "But, uh, Sarah, where did you get the newspapers?"

"I found them in the basement."

"Oh, no!" groaned Dad. "I've been meaning to take those to the dump. The pile probably got damp. That's why they smell so bad."

"Sarah, I'll find you some nice construction paper. Then we can make some new presents," soothed Mom.

"Sarah meant well," sighed Dad. "She thought her gifts were so nice, but we saw them as smelly junk. It reminds me of a verse in Isaiah: 'All our righteous acts are like filthy rags.' The things we do that look so good to us God sees as filthy rags. Until we let Christ wash away our sins with his blood, all our good works are no better than those smelly presents."

HOW ABOUT YOU? Do you think God will be pleased with good things you try to do? If you haven't trusted Jesus as your Savior, God won't accept your good works. They look—and smell—like "filthy rags" to him. Ask Jesus to save you and give you a clean heart. *S.L.K.*

TO MEMORIZE: All of us have become like one who is unclean, and all our righteous acts are like filthy rags. *Isaiah 64:6* (NIV)

16 June

A FUNNY KIND OF LOVE

FROM THE BIBLE:

And have you entirely forgotten the encouraging words God spoke to you, his children? He said,
"My child, don't ignore it when the Lord disciplines you,
and don't be discouraged when he corrects you.
For the Lord disciplines those he loves,
and he punishes those he accepts as his children."

As you endure this divine discipline, remember that God is treating you as his own children. . . . If God doesn't discipline you as he does all of his children, it means that you are illegitimate and are not really his children after all. Since we respect our earthly fathers who disciplined us, should we not all the more cheerfully submit to the discipline of our heavenly Father and live forever? . . .

God's discipline is always right and good for us because it means we will share in his holiness. No discipline is enjoyable while it is happening—it is painful! But afterward there will be a quiet harvest of right living for those who are trained in this way.

HEBREWS 12:5-11

Appreciate correction

RANDY SAT on the front porch, sniffling. "It was just a little fib," he told his dog, Lucky. "And now I'm being punished. 'I'm doing this because I love you.' " He mimicked his mother's voice. "Funny kinda love that is!"

Johnny came into the yard with his dog, Marcus. "What's the matter with you?" Johnny asked.

"Nothin'," said Randy. Then he added, "My mom is punishing me because I told a little fib."

Suddenly, the two dogs noticed another dog in the street and took off. Down the street they raced. "Come, back here, Marcus!" Johnny yelled as he started after his dog.

Randy went to the gate and called, "Lucky, come here!" Lucky stopped as though he had seen a red light. He turned and came back to Randy while Johnny continued down the street, begging his dog to stop. Once Marcus ran right in front of a car. He went three blocks before he decided to let Johnny catch him.

"I punished Lucky when he didn't obey," Randy told Johnny when they got back. "I hated to do it, but Dad said that was part of my responsibility. Lucky soon learned to obey."

"I couldn't do that to Marcus," Johnny said. "I love him too much."

"Marcus almost got run over," Randy reminded Johnny. "I love Lucky, too, that's why I pun—" Randy stopped as he remembered what his mother had said. Maybe her love wasn't such a funny kind, after all.

HOW ABOUT YOU? Do your parents punish you and then tell you they love you? They are telling you the truth. God says it's their responsibility to train you and even spank you when you need it. They know that a little correction now can save you a lot of trouble later. *B.J.W.*

TO MEMORIZE: For the Lord corrects those he loves, just as a father corrects a child in whom he delights. *Proverbs 3:12*

A BETTER PERSON

FROM THE BIBLE:

You younger men, accept the authority of the elders. And all of you, serve each other in humility, for

"God sets himself against the proud,
but he shows favor to the humble."

So humble yourselves under the mighty power of God, and in his good time he will honor you. Give all your worries and cares to God, for he cares about what happens to you.

1 PETER 5:5-7

Be glad for correction

ADAM WATCHED his father cut branch after branch off the fruit trees in the backyard. "Won't that ruin the trees?" he asked after a time.

Dad stepped away from his work. "Just the opposite," he replied. "If I do this now, these trees will grow into straight, strong, and productive trees."

"That doesn't make sense," Adam retorted.

Dad grinned. "Neither does the punishment I give you from time to time, but it's necessary."

Adam scratched his head in wonderment. "What do punishments have to do with pruning trees?" he asked.

Dad answered, "They make you a better person, just as pruning results in better trees. When you take something that doesn't belong to you, as you did this morning, punishment is important."

That morning, Adam had taken a baseball that belonged to the boy next door. As a result, he had been punished.

Dad continued, "If I let you get away with stealing little things now, you may grow up and try to steal bigger things. The punishment you'd get then would be a whole lot worse."

Adam knew his father was right. It seemed strange to think that he was "lucky" to be punished. His father spoke again. "I punish you because I love you, Son. You're something like the trees I'm pruning. If you let the bad things in your life be cut away, you will grow to be a better person."

Adam nodded. Though it hurt a little now, he knew it would pay off later.

HOW ABOUT YOU? Do you get angry when you are corrected? Try to realize that it is helpful. It is done because someone loves you and wants you to be the very best person you can possibly be. *R.I.J.*

TO MEMORIZE: No discipline is enjoyable while it is happening—it is painful! But afterward there will be a quiet harvest of right living for those who are trained in this way. *Hebrews 12:11*

18 June

DO I HAVE TO?

FROM THE BIBLE:

After dark one evening, a Jewish religious leader named Nicodemus, a Pharisee, came to speak with Jesus. "Teacher," he said, "we all know that God has sent you to teach us. Your miraculous signs are proof enough that God is with you."

Jesus replied, "I assure you, unless you are born again, you can never see the Kingdom of God."

"What do you mean?" exclaimed Nicodemus. "How can an old man go back into his mother's womb and be born again?"

Jesus replied, "The truth is, no one can enter the Kingdom of God without being born of water and the Spirit. Humans can reproduce only human life, but the Holy Spirit gives new life from heaven. So don't be surprised at my statement that you must be born again."

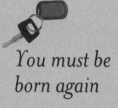

JOHN 3:1-7

You must be born again

DAVE HAD just taken a practice swing when he heard his mother's voice. "Dave," she called, "it's time to come in and do your reading."

"Aw, Mom," Dave moaned. It was summer, and Dave's teacher had suggested that he read one story each day to help improve his reading. But although Dave sat down, he didn't read. He watched a fly climbing up the wall. "Mom, what if I clean my room instead?"

"No, Dave, you must read that story," Mom answered.

Dave counted the tiles on the ceiling. "What if I wash the dishes?"

"No, Son, I want you to obey me and read that story. That's the one thing you have to do," said Mom, "and then you may go outside." She sat down beside him. "Do you know what this reminds me of? Most people want very much to go to heaven. God has clearly told us there is only one way to get there. John 3:3 says, 'Except a man be born again, he cannot see the kingdom of God.' They say, 'I'll join the church and I'll give money.' God says, 'No, you must be born again.' 'I'll obey the Ten Commandments. I'll be baptized.' 'No, you must be born again.' "

"And God won't change his mind, will he?" said Dave. He knew his mother wouldn't change her mind, either, so he settled down to read. In 15 minutes he was outdoors again.

HOW ABOUT YOU? Are you one of the people who try different ways to gain eternal life? Do you think you can be saved by being good, getting baptized, or going to church? These are good things, but they are man's ways, not God's ways. They do not lead to eternal life. You must accept Jesus as Savior and be born again. *N.G.H.*

TO MEMORIZE: Jesus replied, "I assure you, unless you are born again, you can never see the Kingdom of God." *John 3:3*

HOW CAN YOU TELL?

FROM THE BIBLE:

All who believe in the Son of God know that this is true. Those who don't believe this are actually calling God a liar because they don't believe what God has testified about his Son.

And this is what God has testified: He has given us eternal life, and this life is in his Son. So whoever has God's Son has life; whoever does not have his Son does not have life.

I write this to you who believe in the Son of God, so that you may know you have eternal life.

1 JOHN 5:10-13

Be sure you know Christ

UNCLE JOE was working in his garden one afternoon when Brandon came to visit. After talking about the weather, Brandon said, "I know I trusted Jesus to be my Savior, but sometimes I don't feel like a Christian. How can I tell if I am one?"

Uncle Joe smiled as he bent down by a row of tiny green sprouts and pointed to one of them. "That's a beet plant," he said. "But how can you tell, Brandon?"

"Well, if you planted beet seeds there, that's what will grow."

"Good!" said Uncle Joe. "The seed that produces Christians is the gospel. Someone planted that seed in you when you believed."

Uncle Joe continued, "There's another way to tell what kind of plant that is—by the fruit it bears," replied his uncle. "If this is truly a beet plant, then eventually it will produce a beet. In the same way, Christians are known by their fruit—good works that come as a result of their faith in Christ."

"I know the best reason of all to know it's a beet plant," said Brandon. "You said it was, and I believe you."

Uncle Joe smiled. "And God tells us in his Word that if we receive Jesus as Savior, we are his children. Also, his Spirit dwells in us and tells us that we belong to him, although it's not in words we can hear. We must believe what he says."

HOW ABOUT YOU? Do you ever wonder if you're really saved? Make sure you understand the gospel and that you have trusted Jesus Christ to be your own Savior from sin. Remember—it's not what you do that saves you—it's what Christ did for you on the cross. *S.L.K.*

TO MEMORIZE: I write this to you who believe in the Son of God, so that you may know you have eternal life. *1 John 5:13*

20 June

NO DOUBT ABOUT IT

FROM THE BIBLE:

Jesus replied, "All those who love me will do what I say. My Father will love them, and we will come to them and live with them. Anyone who doesn't love me will not do what I say. And remember, my words are not my own. This message is from the Father who sent me. I am telling you these things now while I am still with you."

JOHN 14:23-25

You can know you're saved

"MOM," called Jon, "can I help carry Mrs. Emmet's groceries home?"

"It's nice you're so eager to help," Mother teased. She knew that Mrs. Emmet always treated Jon to an ice-cream cone.

As Jon walked beside his elderly neighbor, she asked him, "Jon, are you a Christian?"

Jon shrugged. "I sure hope so," he said.

They stopped at the ice-cream shop. As Jon took the first lick of his chocolate fudge ice-cream cone, his friend Zac came in. "Hi, Jon," greeted Zac. "You got an ice-cream cone?"

To Jon's surprise, Mrs. Emmet answered for him. "He sure hopes so," she said. Both boys looked at her rather strangely. The boys chatted, and then Jon and Mrs. Emmet went on their way.

"Why did you say I hoped I had an ice-cream cone?" Jon asked as they walked along. "I have one—no hoping about it."

Mrs. Emmet laughed. "That was silly—almost as silly as your saying you 'hoped' you were a Christian." She paused. "Jon, when you have something, you don't need to hope you have it. You can know for sure. The question is, do you believe in the Lord Jesus Christ?"

Slowly Jon nodded. "I asked him to forgive me and to save me," he said. "But sometimes I feel like I should do something more."

"There's nothing more you can do for salvation," Mrs. Emmet assured him. "The Bible says that if you believe in Jesus, you have eternal life—you're a Christian. There's no doubt about it."

HOW ABOUT YOU? Are you a Christian? You don't have to hope or guess so. You can know. Jesus paid the price for your sin. Accept what he has done for you. Take him as your Savior. When you do that, you have eternal life. *H.W.M.*

TO MEMORIZE: Whoever has God's Son has life; whoever does not have his Son does not have life. *1 John 5:12*

DON'T FENCE ME IN

FROM THE BIBLE:

For the Lord's sake, accept all authority—the king as head of state, and the officials he has appointed. For the king has sent them to punish all who do wrong and to honor those who do right.

It is God's will that your good lives should silence those who make foolish accusations against you. You are not slaves; you are free. But your freedom is not an excuse to do evil. You are free to live as God's slaves. Show respect for everyone. Love your Christian brothers and sisters. Fear God. Show respect for the king.

1 PETER 2:13-17

Rules help you

"I'M SO TIRED of rules," complained Matt. "It's always, 'If you don't do this, you can't do that.' That's all I hear at home, at school, at church, even at play! Even dogs are no longer free! It says here that they have to be confined to their owner's property. Tag won't like being fenced in."

Matt was right—Tag didn't like being kept inside a fence, and time after time he dug out of the yard. One day when Matt and his mother came home from town, they discovered that Tag was missing once again. A neighbor had seen the dogcatcher picking him up. Matt was in tears. "We can get him back, can't we?" he asked.

"Oh, yes," Mother said, "but he'll just get out again."

"If only he could understand that the yard is a place of safety and protection for him!" sighed Matt. "Then he would know why we fence him in."

"You're right," agreed Mother, "and you know, Matt, we're a little like Tag. We sometimes feel 'fenced in' too—fenced in by rules we don't like. But God has given us parents, teachers, policemen, yes, even rules, to provide safety and protection for us."

"That makes sense," agreed Matt slowly. "I guess we do need rules and laws. But what about Tag, Mom?"

The solution to the problem was found when Dad came home. He made arrangements to pick up Tag and take him out to Uncle Frank's farm. "We'll miss him, but we can visit him," he said. "There he can run free."

HOW ABOUT YOU? Do you rebel at having rules you must follow? You never outgrow the "do's" and "don'ts" of living. All your life there will be those who have authority over you. God says to obey them. *B.J.W.*

TO MEMORIZE: Obey your leaders and submit to their authority. *Hebrews 13:17* (NIV)

THE RIGHT TOOLS

FROM THE BIBLE:

These are the words of Jeremiah son of Hilkiah, one of the priests from Anathoth, a town in the land of Benjamin. The Lord first gave messages to Jeremiah during the thirteenth year of King Josiah's reign in Judah. . . .

The Lord gave me a message. He said, "I knew you before I formed you in your mother's womb. Before you were born I set you apart and appointed you as my spokesman to the world."

"O Sovereign Lord," I said, "I can't speak for you! I'm too young!"

"Don't say that," the Lord replied, "for you must go wherever I send you and say whatever I tell you. And don't be afraid of the people, for I will be with you and take care of you. I, the Lord, have spoken!"

Then the Lord touched my mouth and said, "See, I have put my words in your mouth!"

JEREMIAH 1:1-2, 4-9

God gives strength

JEREMY WAS UPSET as he pedaled his bike into the garage.

Dad looked up from his workbench. "Jeremy, I'd like you to help paint the lawn furniture this afternoon."

"OK," Jeremy replied, taking a paintbrush. As they painted, Jeremy poured out his worries. "Brian Parker wasn't in school today, Dad," he said, "and his grandmother is dying. I know I should go see him, but I'm afraid to. I don't know what to say to him." Jeremy sniffed loudly.

"I understand how you feel, Jeremy," said Dad, "but Brian needs you. In difficult situations like this you often don't have to say anything. Just be there and listen."

"But, Dad, I'm just a kid," said Jeremy.

"That's what the prophet Jeremiah said, but God told him that was no excuse," Dad reminded him. "You know, when I asked you to paint the lawn furniture just now, I supplied all the tools and the paint for you to do the job. When God has a job for us, he always supplies whatever is necessary to get the job done, too. He gives us the grace to do it." Jeremy still looked doubtful. "Mom and I can go with you after dinner," suggested Dad. "Will that help?"

Jeremy grinned. "It sure will."

Later as they returned from the Parkers', Jeremy said, "You were right, Dad. I'm glad I went. Brian needed me."

HOW ABOUT YOU? Is there something you feel God wants you to do, like visit a sick person or witness to a friend? Have you been saying, "But I'm just a kid. I can't do that?" If God asks you to do a job, he will give you the necessary tools to handle it. Stop making excuses and go do it. You'll feel a lot better after you do. *B.J.W.*

TO MEMORIZE: My grace is sufficient for you, for my power is made perfect in weakness.
2 Corinthians 12:9 (NIV)

JUST A MITE

FROM THE BIBLE:

While Jesus was in the Temple, he watched the rich people putting their gifts into the collection box. Then a poor widow came by and dropped in two pennies. "I assure you," he said, "this poor widow has given more than all the rest of them. For they have given a tiny part of their surplus, but she, poor as she is, has given everything she has."
LUKE 21:1-4

Serve in love

IT WAS JOSE'S ambition to be a missionary someday, but he wondered if he'd ever be big enough to serve the Lord.

One evening, Jose went with his father to Mr. Baker's house. He liked the old gentleman, so while Dad fixed a leaky faucet, Jose talked with Mr. Baker. "I wish I could be a big help to others like my dad is," Jose said wistfully.

"Why, Jose, I think you're a very helpful person. Isn't it a useful thing to make an old man like me happy by talking with me?" he said, chuckling.

"Yeah," he said slowly, "but I'd like to be a missionary myself. Then I'd really be helpful to God and others."

"Ever hear of the 'widow's mite'?" asked Mr. Baker.

"A bug?" Jose asked, surprised.

Mr. Baker slapped his knee and laughed. "There is an insect called a mite, but I was thinking of another meaning of the word," he said. "It can mean a small amount of something. The phrase *a widow's mite* comes from a story Jesus told about a widow who dropped just two small coins in the collection box. Jesus said that in God's sight she gave more than anyone else because she gave all she could."

Jose sat quietly thinking about what Mr. Baker had said. He didn't have to grow up before he could serve God, after all! Right now he could give "a widow's mite."

HOW ABOUT YOU? Does the amount of money you can give seem very small? Do the things you do for Jesus seem little and not worth much? God looks at your heart and counts the smallest acts done in love as special gifts from you. Even a friendly smile given to a lonely person is a precious gift to God. He sees the love that's in your heart. Serve God now.
C.E.Y.

TO MEMORIZE: "Do everything in love."
1 Corinthians 16:14 (NIV)

24 June

A NOISY WITNESS

FROM THE BIBLE:

Then he said to the crowd, "If any of you wants to be my follower, you must put aside your selfish ambition, shoulder your cross daily, and follow me. If you try to keep your life for yourself, you will lose it. But if you give up your life for me, you will find true life. And how do you benefit if you gain the whole world but lose or forfeit your own soul in the process? If a person is ashamed of me and my message, I, the Son of Man, will be ashamed of that person when I return in my glory and in the glory of the Father and the holy angels."

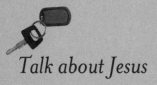

LUKE 9:23-26

Talk about Jesus

JOANNE WENT to the store with her two-year-old sister, Lena, who liked riding in the grocery cart. As they rounded a corner in the store, they saw an elderly lady picking up the contents of her purse that had spilled. Joanne helped her. "Thank you," said the lady. "Most young people wouldn't stop to help. Why did you help?"

Joanne knew she should talk about Jesus, but she was embarrassed. "Uh, I guess I just like helping people," she said, walking away quickly.

After a while, Lena began loudly singing "Jesus Loves Me." People were looking and smiling at them, and Joanne felt embarrassed. "Hush, Lena! Don't be so noisy!"

Soon the lady that Joanne had helped walked up. "I heard what the little one was singing," she said. "You must be a Christian!"

"Well, uh, yes, I am," Joanne mumbled.

The woman smiled. "I thought there was something different about you. My neighbor is a Christian, too, and she's always trying to talk to me about Jesus. I think I'll listen more next time."

After the lady walked away, Joanne said to her sister, "Lena, you're a sweetheart! I've been wrong to keep quiet about Jesus. Thank you for showing me how important it is to be a 'noisy witness'!"

HOW ABOUT YOU? Are you embarrassed to have someone notice that you're a Christian? Perhaps you are a "silent witness"—you try to show by your life and actions that you're a Christian. That's good, but talking is important too. Others won't be persuaded to come to the Lord unless they know why you do the things you do. Don't be ashamed to talk about Jesus. *S.L.K.*

TO MEMORIZE: If a person is ashamed of me and my message in these adulterous and sinful days, I, the Son of Man, will be ashamed of that person when I return in the glory of my Father with the holy angels. *Mark 8:38*

READY OR NOT

FROM THE BIBLE:

In the last days there will be scoffers who will laugh at the truth and do every evil thing they desire. This will be their argument: "Jesus promised to come back, did he? Then where is he?" . . .

They deliberately forget that God made the heavens by the word of his command, and he brought the earth up from the water and surrounded it with water. Then he used the water to destroy the world with a mighty flood. And God has also commanded that the heavens and the earth will be consumed by fire on the day of judgment, when ungodly people will perish.

But you must not forget, dear friends, that a day is like a thousand years to the Lord, and a thousand years is like a day. The Lord isn't really being slow about his promise to return, as some people think. No, he is being patient for your sake. He does not want anyone to perish, so he is giving more time for everyone to repent.

2 PETER 3:3-9

Jesus will come again

"PLEASE CALL Crystal and then sit down for breakfast, Kevin," said Mother.

"Sure," agreed Kevin with a grin. "Crystal!" he called. "Fire! Get up! There's a fire!"

"What? Where? Oh, you're not funny, Kevin," she scolded. "You scared me!"

Dad looked up from his newspaper. "Talk about being scared," he said, "listen to this. 'Doomsday Prophet Warns End of World Coming Next Tuesday!' This article will scare a lot of people."

Crystal was wide-eyed. "Is the world really going to end next Tuesday, Daddy?" she asked.

Dad smiled at Crystal. "No, the world won't end Tuesday, but the Lord Jesus might come before then."

Kevin added, "My history teacher says people have been saying that Jesus will come back for hundreds of years. He's not so sure Jesus will ever come."

"Kevin," said Mother, "the very fact that people are doubting is a sign of Jesus' soon return. The apostle Peter wrote that in the last days scoffers would be questioning Jesus' promise because the world continues as it always has. But God surely will keep his promise."

"One thing is certain," said Dad, "no one knows the day or hour when Jesus will come. It could be sooner than Tuesday. Then again, it could be next year or years from now. Only God knows. We need to be ready for him anytime."

HOW ABOUT YOU? Do you think that because Jesus hasn't come yet, it isn't going to happen? He's patiently waiting, giving people more opportunities to be saved. But time is running out. You may be sure that when the time is right according to God's timetable, Jesus will come. *B.J.W.*

TO MEMORIZE: You also must be ready, because the Son of Man will come at an hour when you do not expect him. *Matthew 24:44* (NIV)

26 June

BALLOONS FOR ALL
(PART 1)

FROM THE BIBLE:

But when the Pharisees heard that he had silenced the Sadducees with his reply, they thought up a fresh question of their own to ask him. One of them, an expert in religious law, tried to trap him with this question: "Teacher, which is the most important commandment in the law of Moses?"

Jesus replied, " 'You must love the Lord your God with all your heart, all your soul, and all your mind.' This is the first and greatest commandment. A second is equally important: 'Love your neighbor as yourself.' All the other commandments and all the demands of the prophets are based on these two commandments."

MATTHEW 22:34-40

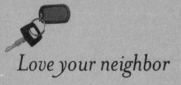

Love your neighbor

HARDY'S DEPARTMENT STORE was having a grand opening, and Mother had let Mike walk downtown to see what was going on. Mike watched a clown blowing up helium balloons and giving them away to each child. Mike wanted one too! He also knew his little sister, Sara, would love one. But Sara was sick, and Mike noticed that no child was allowed to have more than one balloon. Well, she could look at his. Marching up to the clown, he asked politely, "May I have a balloon, please?"

"Sure," boomed the clown. "What's your favorite color?"

"Blue," answered Mike without hesitation. Then, Mike made a sudden decision. "Please, sir, may I have a red one instead? It's for my little sister. She's sick, and she likes red."

The clown looked at him in surprise. "Well, well," he said, as he filled a blue balloon and then a red balloon. "The rule is one balloon to a child, but I'm going to make an exception. Every girl should have a brother like you!"

Sara was delighted with her balloon, and so was Mom. "I'm so pleased—not just because you both got a balloon, but because you were willing to give up your own balloon so Sara could have one," she told Mike. "I know God is pleased too. You truly followed his command to love your neighbor—in this case, your sister—as yourself."

HOW ABOUT YOU? The Bible teaches that our neighbor may be anyone we come in contact with, not only the person next door. If you're a Christian, you are to love that neighbor as you love yourself. Do you do that? See how many ways you can find to show that you truly love your neighbor as yourself. It sounds like a hard thing to do, but it will bring you joy. *H.W.M.*

TO MEMORIZE: Love your neighbor as yourself. *Matthew 22:39* (NIV)

BALLOONS FOR ALL
(PART 2)

FROM THE BIBLE:

And the Holy Spirit helps us in our distress. For we don't even know what we should pray for, nor how we should pray. But the Holy Spirit prays for us with groanings that cannot be expressed in words. And the Father who knows all hearts knows what the Spirit is saying, for the Spirit pleads for us believers in harmony with God's own will. And we know that God causes everything to work together for the good of those who love God and are called according to his purpose for them.

ROMANS 8:26-28

Keep praying

ONE-YEAR-OLD Andy loved Sara's red balloon. He made a pest of himself, pulling on the string and then trying to take hold of the balloon itself. Finally, Mike had an idea. "I'll take him to the store to get one of his own."

When they arrived, the clown smiled when he saw Mike with Andy. "Brought me a new customer, did you?" Turning to Andy, he asked, "And what would you like, young man?"

"Wahyo boon!" shouted Andy.

The clown smiled as he selected a green balloon.

"No! Wahyo boon," insisted Andy.

At the clown's puzzled look, Mike laughed. "He wants a yellow balloon."

Grinning, the clown handed one to Andy. "I hope your brother and sister appreciate you."

When Dad arrived home, he admired the balloons as Mike recounted the day's events. Dad said, "It's a good thing for Andy that you can understand him." He paused, then continued, "That reminds me of something God does for us. Often we have trouble praying. We sometimes don't know what to say or even what to ask God for. But God has given us his Holy Spirit to help us and to pray for us. He makes our requests clear and 'just right' before God."

HOW ABOUT YOU? Do you think your prayers are too weak to be of any worth? Does it seem that the prayers of Mom and Dad—or better still, the prayers of pastors—would accomplish more than yours ever could? Don't be discouraged because you can't pray as well as you would like to. If you're a Christian, the Holy Spirit will take your prayers and make them perfect before God's throne. Keep praying. *H.W.M.*

TO MEMORIZE: We do not know what we ought to pray for, but the Spirit himself intercedes for us. *Romans 8:26* (NIV)

28 June

DO IT YOURSELF

FROM THE BIBLE:

You have heard that the law of Moses says, "Do not murder. If you commit murder, you are subject to judgment." But I say, if you are angry with someone, you are subject to judgment! If you call someone an idiot, you are in danger of being brought before the high council. And if you curse someone, you are in danger of the fires of hell.

So if you are standing before the altar in the Temple, offering a sacrifice to God, and you suddenly remember that someone has something against you, leave your sacrifice there beside the altar. Go and be reconciled to that person. Then come and offer your sacrifice to God.

MATTHEW 5:21-24

Humble yourself

AS MOTHER arranged the new curtains, Angela looked proudly around her room. "Redecorating is fun, isn't it, Mother? I'm almost glad we didn't have the money to buy everything new and ready-made," said Angela. "My quilt and curtains are so unique, and they match the wall color perfectly. Even my old bedroom furniture looks nice refinished."

Mother nodded. "Do-it-yourself jobs are hard work, but they're worth the effort. Why don't you call Carly and invite her over to see your room?"

Angela snorted. "She wouldn't come. She's not speaking to me."

Mother raised her eyebrows. "Are you speaking to her?"

"Of course not! She'll have to speak to me first. She's the one who's mad, and I didn't do a thing to her. I asked God to make her apologize to me, but she still hasn't done it."

"Maybe he wants you to apologize to Carly," suggested Mother.

"But I didn't do anything to her!" Angela wailed.

"Are you sure? It usually takes two to quarrel," Mother reminded her daughter. "We often want God to take care of our problems when there is something he expects us to do for ourselves. One thing he wants us to do is 'humble ourselves.' Apologizing is certainly humbling. Remember our Scripture reading this morning? Carly has something 'against you,' so you should go to her."

"But that's hard!" Angela cried.

Mother nodded. "It's a hard 'do-it-yourself' job, but the results are worth it." As Angela dialed Carly's number, Mother smiled.

Later Angela showed Carly her room, and Mother heard her say, "Do-it-yourself jobs are usually hard, but they're worth it."

HOW ABOUT YOU? Does God want you to apologize to someone? It's not easy to humble yourself, but it's God's way and it's worth the effort. An apology is a small price to pay for a friend. *B.J.W.*

TO MEMORIZE: Be completely humble and gentle; be patient, bearing with one another in love. *Ephesians 4:2* (NIV)

AN EXCITING LETTER

FROM THE BIBLE:

Oh, how I love your law!
I think about it all day long.
Your commands make me wiser
than my enemies,
for your commands are my
constant guide.
Yes, I have more insight than my
teachers,
for I am always thinking of
your decrees.
I am even wiser than my elders,
for I have kept your
commandments.
I have refused to walk on any
path of evil,
that I may remain obedient to
your word.
I haven't turned away from your
laws,
for you have taught me well.
How sweet are your words to my
taste;
they are sweeter than honey.
Your commandments give me
understanding;
no wonder I hate every false
way of life.

PSALM 119:97-104

"HOW ARE YOU doing in the Sunday school contest?" Mrs. Anderson asked her daughter.

"Pretty good," said Patty. "I haven't done this week's questions yet, but I'll do them later. I don't feel like studying the Bible right now."

The mailman came just then. "Oh, Mom, look! Here's a letter from the Walters. May I open it?"

The Walters and the Andersons had been close friends for a long time. It had been very difficult for both families when Mr. Walters had been transferred far away. But now Patty was excited. Maybe they had good news!

"A letter from the Walters?" Mom seemed to show little interest. "Maybe I'll have time to read it later."

"Later? But why not now?" Patty asked.

"Well, Patty, I just don't feel like reading it right now."

Patty looked at her mother strangely. Suddenly she understood. "I see, Mom. I know the Bible is God's letter to us and that it also contains good news. Yet I keep postponing the time when I'll read it. I'll go do those questions right now!"

Mom smiled as she picked up the letter from the Walters. "Good idea! But I think it will be all right if you wait just long enough to read this letter first!"

HOW ABOUT YOU? Do you study the Bible? Do you read the good things God has to say to you, or do you think "someday when I'm bigger I'll study God's Word"? The Bible is God's letter to you. In it there is good news—how Christ died and rose again and is someday coming back for his own. Be excited about the Bible. *L.M.W.*

TO MEMORIZE: Oh, how I love your law! I think about it all day long. *Psalm 119:97*

Read the Bible

30 June

A SMALL LIGHT

FROM THE BIBLE:

You are the salt of the earth. But what good is salt if it has lost its flavor? Can you make it useful again? It will be thrown out and trampled underfoot as worthless. You are the light of the world—like a city on a mountain, glowing in the night for all to see. Don't hide your light under a basket! Instead, put it on a stand and let it shine for all. In the same way, let your good deeds shine out for all to see, so that everyone will praise your heavenly Father.

MATTHEW 5:13-16

Be a light

GREG AND MELISSA watched from the window as lightening streaked across the sky, followed by a loud crash of thunder. Suddenly it was pitch dark in the house.

"What happened?" cried Greg, stumbling over a footstool in the dark.

"Oh, it's so dark!" Melissa exclaimed. "Mom, please come here!"

Mom came into the room with a lighted candle. "The lightning must have knocked the electricity out," she said. "We'll have to see by candlelight for a while."

"It's surprising how much light that one little flame gives," said Melissa as they sat watching the flickering light in the otherwise dark room.

Greg was quiet, then blurted out, "You are the light of the world." He grinned as he added, "My Sunday school verse just popped into my mind because of that candle!"

Melissa nodded. "Our teacher said that if we've received Jesus as Savior, he lives in us. When we do things that please him, others see Jesus in us, so they have light to see him."

"I always figured that the little bit I could do didn't amount to much," added Greg. "For the first time, I think I know what a lot of difference one small light can make."

Just then the lights came back on. "I'm glad to have electricity again, but I'll always remember what I learned tonight from the candle," said Greg.

HOW ABOUT YOU? Do you feel as though there's not much you can do to let your light shine for Jesus? That isn't true! Obeying parents and teachers, being kind, showing love, forgiving others, and being patient are just some of the ways to let your life shine. Anything you are able to do for Jesus is worthwhile. *C.E.Y.*

TO MEMORIZE: You are the light of the world—like a city on a mountain, glowing in the night for all to see. *Matthew 5:14*

IT'S BORING

FROM THE BIBLE:

So we must listen very carefully to the truth we have heard, or we may drift away from it. The message God delivered through angels has always proved true, and the people were punished for every violation of the law and every act of disobedience. What makes us think that we can escape if we are indifferent to this great salvation that was announced by the Lord Jesus himself? It was passed on to us by those who heard him speak, and God verified the message by signs and wonders and various miracles and by giving gifts of the Holy Spirit whenever he chose to do so.

HEBREWS 2:1-4

Give attention to Bible study

"I WISH I didn't have to go to Sunday school today," Jody sighed as she slowly ate her cereal.

Her mother looked, surprised. "Why, Jody! I thought you liked church!"

"I do like church. It's Mrs. Darnell's class I don't like!" Jody explained. "She's so boring! I wish I was back in third grade so I could still be in Mr. Richards's class."

"Mr. Richards was a good teacher," agreed Mom, "and I'm glad you learned so much from him. But Jody, Mrs. Darnell is a good teacher too. Many children have come to know Christ through her teaching."

"Her class is no fun, though," protested Jody. "I practically fall asleep listening to her!"

"Mrs. Darnell might not be as entertaining as Mr. Richards, but she does know God's Word," Mom insisted. "Remember this, too—nowhere does the Bible say that studying the Scripture is supposed to be 'fun.' Sometimes Bible study is simply hard work." Jody still didn't look convinced. "In 2 Corinthians we're told to bring our thoughts into captivity," continued Mom. "We're to turn them toward the things of Christ."

Jody thought about it. Then she grinned. "OK, Mom. If my thoughts start to wander today, I'll grab hold of them and turn them toward the Lord! Right?"

"Right!" Mom smiled. "While in Mrs. Darnell's class, make yourself listen to what she is saying. Be interested in learning about God's Word."

HOW ABOUT YOU? Are you sometimes bored in church or Sunday school? Sometimes it will take concentration on your part to understand the lesson God is teaching, but it will be worth it. Bible study is often hard, but it is important. If you are bored, it could be because you are not capturing your thoughts and turning them toward the Lord. Think about it. *L.M.W.*

TO MEMORIZE: We take captive every thought to make it obedient to Christ. *2 Corinthians 10:5* (NIV)

2 July

AUNT SUE'S GIFT

FROM THE BIBLE:

Forever, O Lord,
your word stands firm in heaven.
Your faithfulness extends to every generation,
as enduring as the earth you created.
Your laws remain true today,
for everything serves your plans.
If your law hadn't sustained me with joy,
I would have died in my misery.
I will never forget your commandments,
for you have used them to restore my joy and health.
I am yours; save me!
For I have applied myself to obey your commandments.
Though the wicked hide along the way to kill me,
I will quietly keep my mind on your decrees.
Even perfection has its limits,
but your commands have no limit.

PSALM 119:89-96

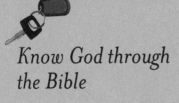

Know God through the Bible

KEVIN WAVED the brown package excitedly. "Look what came in the mail! I think it's a birthday present from Aunt Sue!" He ripped open the package, then frowned. "A book of missionary stories," he said unhappily. "Sounds boring." Kevin put the book on his shelf.

A month later, Kevin's family provided dinner for Mr. Jackson, a missionary speaker at their church. Kevin listened attentively when Mr. Jackson told a story about a leopard that had once stalked his trail. "Several Indians and I were on our way to preach in one of the villages," said Mr. Jackson. "We expected that leopard to attack at any moment."

"What happened?" Kevin's eyes were wide.

"The leopard just quit following us," said Mr. Jackson. "I know God answered many people's prayers."

All too soon Mr. Jackson was gone. "Sure wish I could get to know him better," Kevin said.

Weeks later, he took a book from the shelf and idly turned the first few pages, then suddenly sat erect. "Mom! This book from Aunt Sue is written by Mr. Jackson!" When bedtime came, he could hardly put the book down. "I feel like Mr. Jackson is a good friend," he said.

"You got to know him through his book." Mother smiled, then looked thoughtful. "You know, Kevin, that's something like God and the Bible. We sometimes feel we don't know God, but it's because we don't read his book—the Bible."

HOW ABOUT YOU? Do you sometimes wish you knew God better—like your Sunday school teacher or your pastor does? Are you willing to do your part to know him? Be sure to do your Sunday school lessons. And listen to your pastor. There's a book to help you, too—the Bible. Read it daily. Then you'll get to know God. *G.W.*

TO MEMORIZE: I will delight in your principles and not forget your word. *Psalm 119:16*

3 July

READY FOR FISHING

FROM THE BIBLE:

From then on, Jesus began to preach, "Turn from your sins and turn to God, because the Kingdom of Heaven is near."

One day as Jesus was walking along the shore beside the Sea of Galilee, he saw two brothers—Simon, also called Peter, and Andrew—fishing with a net, for they were commercial fishermen. Jesus called out to them, "Come, be my disciples, and I will show you how to fish for people!" And they left their nets at once and went with him.

A little farther up the shore he saw two other brothers, James and John, sitting in a boat with their father, Zebedee, mending their nets. And he called them to come, too. They immediately followed him, leaving the boat and their father behind.

MATTHEW 4:17-22

Witness patiently

SAMANTHA GOT the fishing gear together and put it in the car. This was her first fishing trip with her father, and she was excited. As they traveled to the lake, Samantha told Dad about a girl she had witnessed to last weekend. "But I guess it didn't do any good," she finished. "Carol didn't want to come to Christ."

"Well," Dad replied, "fishing and witnessing are a lot alike, so maybe you'll learn something today."

After they had reached the lake, Dad baited his hook and showed Samantha how to bait hers.

"Now what?" Samantha asked.

"Now you throw in the line and then sit back and wait," Dad answered.

Samantha followed his instructions, but soon she became restless. "How long do I have to wait?"

"Until you get a bite," Dad said pleasantly.

Samantha frowned. "I don't like that part," she grumbled. "I thought you could just throw out the line and get a fish right away."

"No," her father replied. "The fish don't just jump in the boat. You do everything you can, and then you use patience. Lots of patience. When and if you get a bite, you pull in the line, and you may find a fish on the end of it. Now, remember that I told you fishing and witnessing were a lot alike? Do you see why?"

Samantha nodded. She had talked with Carol about accepting Christ; now she needed to show patience. While she waited, she would pray for Carol every day. Maybe God would let Samantha "pull in the line" someday.

HOW ABOUT YOU? Have you witnessed to someone thinking they would come to Jesus right away? It often takes time, patience, persistence, and prayer. Keep witnessing and waiting for God to work. *H.W.M.*

TO MEMORIZE: "Come, follow me," Jesus said, "and I will make you fishers of men." *Matthew 4:19* (NIV)

4 July

CONSIDER THE COST
(PART 1)

FROM THE BIBLE:

What joy for the nation whose
God is the Lord,
whose people he has chosen for
his own.
The Lord looks down from
heaven
and sees the whole human
race. . . .
He made their hearts,
so he understands everything
they do.
The best-equipped army cannot
save a king,
nor is great strength enough to
save a warrior.
Don't count on your warhorse to
give you victory—
for all its strength, it cannot
save you.
But the Lord watches over those
who fear him,
those who rely on his unfailing
love.
He rescues them from death
and keeps them alive in times
of famine.
We depend on the Lord alone to
save us.
Only he can help us,
protecting us like a shield.
PSALM 33:12-13, 15-20

Honor the flag

ON THE FOURTH of July, Tom and his sister, Amy, sat on a curb, watching the parade. "There's our school band," said Tom. "There goes Jack, beating on the drum."

"And look at Old Glory. Isn't she beautiful?" said an elderly man who was sitting in a wheelchair.

"Old Glory?" asked Tom. "What's she playing?"

"Don't be silly," giggled Amy. "He means the flag."

"Yes," said the man, "and you two forgot to stand at attention as the flag passed by!"

"But almost no one does that," protested Amy.

"No," agreed the man, "only a few. I imagine they're the ones who know the price of that flag."

"Price?" wondered Tom.

"To me the flag has a price," answered the old man. "If I could stand, I certainly would. I was wounded while fighting for that flag and for what it represents—all the blessings and freedoms we enjoy in this country. I like to believe that I am in this wheelchair today so the flag can go down the street. I and many others know the cost of the flag because we helped pay the price."

Tom and Amy felt ashamed. "We're sorry, sir," said Tom. "We didn't realize what our freedom cost. Our flag and our freedom will mean more to us now."

HOW ABOUT YOU? Do you stand at attention when the Pledge of Allegiance is given and when the national anthem is sung? Remember that many brave men and women gave their lives or were wounded so that you can enjoy all the blessings your flag represents. Show proper respect for your flag and your country. Thank God for the privilege of living in a country where he is recognized. As the Pledge of Allegiance says, it is "under God" that you have the liberty which you enjoy. *B.J.W.*

TO MEMORIZE: Blessed is the nation whose God is the Lord. *Psalm 33:12* (NIV)

CONSIDER THE COST
(PART 2)

FROM THE BIBLE:

For you know that God paid a ransom to save you from the empty life you inherited from your ancestors. And the ransom he paid was not mere gold or silver. He paid for you with the precious lifeblood of Christ, the sinless, spotless Lamb of God. God chose him for this purpose long before the world began, but now in these final days, he was sent to the earth for all to see. And he did this for you.

Through Christ you have come to trust in God. And because God raised Christ from the dead and gave him great glory, your faith and hope can be placed confidently in God.

1 PETER 1:18-21

Jesus paid for salvation

WHEN TOM and Amy returned home from the parade, they asked their parents if they could go to the fireworks that night.

"Sure, and we've asked the Greens to join us," Mom told him. "Your dad has been witnessing to Mr. Green for some time."

"That's right," said Dad. "He's interested, but he feels he should do something to earn his salvation—says you can't get something for nothing. I'm hoping to talk with him again tonight. Did you enjoy the parade?"

The children told them about the man in the wheelchair. "We never appreciated the flag and our freedom because it never cost us anything," Amy explained. "But it cost some people a whole lot."

Dad looked thoughtful. "It's so easy for all of us to take our blessings for granted, forgetting that someone paid a big price for them. And you've given me an idea for reaching Mr. Green, too."

"Tell us," said Mom.

"As I said, Mr. Green feels that salvation should cost something," said Dad. "Perhaps I can show him that, although it's free to us—like the liberties we enjoy in America—a big price was paid for it. It cost God his only Son. It cost Jesus his life. We can enjoy the privilege of being a child of God because of the price he was willing to pay for us."

HOW ABOUT YOU? Do you realize that salvation cost a great deal? Jesus had to leave the glories of heaven and die on the cross. He had to suffer punishment—all this to pay the price of your salvation. There is nothing more you can do. You must simply believe he paid the price for you and accept the free gift of salvation that he offers. Accept him today. *B.J.W.*

TO MEMORIZE: He was chosen before the creation of the world, but was revealed in these last times for your sake. *1 Peter 1:20* (NIV)

6 *July*

CONSIDER THE COST
(PART 3)

FROM THE BIBLE:

And you husbands must love your wives with the same love Christ showed the church. He gave up his life for her to make her holy and clean, washed by baptism and God's word. He did this to present her to himself as a glorious church without a spot or wrinkle or any other blemish. Instead, she will be holy and without fault.
EPHESIANS 5:25-27

Appreciate your church

"UP AND AT 'EM, kids!" Dad called up the stairs one Sunday morning.

Tom and Amy soon appeared at the breakfast table, looking sleepy-eyed. "Ooooh! I wish I could sleep in just one Sunday," moaned Amy.

"Yeah," agreed Tom. "Do we have to go to church every week? Is church that important?"

"Apparently Christ thought it was important," Dad told them. "The Bible says he loved the church and gave himself for it. Of course, it's not the building that he died for. It's the people who make up his church."

"I was just thinking," Mom added. "We often take for granted the privilege of going to church. It's interesting how we always value things more if they cost us something."

Tom looked thoughtful. "You mean, like the man in the wheelchair appreciated the flag and our country because he fought for it?" he asked.

"Right," agreed Dad. "Many take living in this country for granted, and we take the privilege of going to church for granted. But even today in some countries, people risk their lives to meet with other believers."

"In some places, people walk many miles to go to church," Mom added. "Usually they don't have beautiful buildings or comfortable seats. But they come anyway because they love God and want to worship him."

"All it cost me to go to church is a few minutes of sleep," commented Amy. "That's not much, is it?"

"I'm spoiled too," admitted Tom. "Hey, let's get ready for church."

HOW ABOUT YOU? Do you sometimes grumble because you have to go to church and Sunday school each week? Instead, thank God for the privilege. Thank him for your church building, your pastor, your Sunday school teacher. Attend services faithfully. Don't take them for granted. *B.J.W.*

TO MEMORIZE: Christ loved the church and gave himself up for her. *Ephesians 5:25* (NIV)

7 July

SMART BIRDS

FROM THE BIBLE:

I have given them your word. And the world hates them because they do not belong to the world, just as I do not. I'm not asking you to take them out of the world, but to keep them safe from the evil one. They are not part of this world any more than I am. Make them pure and holy by teaching them your words of truth. As you sent me into the world, I am sending them into the world. And I give myself entirely to you so they also might be entirely yours.

JOHN 17:14-19

Keep far from sin

BRENT AND HIS DAD sat on the beach and watched the waves come in and go out again. Brent observed the sandpipers on the moist sand picking for food. They seemed to sense when the big waves were about to hit. Seconds before the water reached them, they flew away. The birds returned when the tide went back out, once more finding food. Over and over they repeated the action. "Those are smart birds," Brent said with a laugh. "When the waves go out, they come for food, but when the waves come in, they leave even before the first drop of water can touch their feet."

Dad nodded. "Too bad Christians aren't always that smart." Brent looked at him quizzically. "We live in the world, and there's sin all around us," explained Dad, "but we ought to model those sandpipers. They leave before the water comes close. As Christians we should not allow sin to come close to us."

"Sometimes we can't help it if we get pulled into something that's not good," Brent reasoned. "It's not always our fault."

"I know what you're saying," answered Dad. "But maybe if we had prayed about the situation and looked for God's leading, we would never have gotten close enough to the sin so that there was a danger of being pulled in."

"Good point," Brent said. "Who'd have thought sandpipers could give a lesson from God?" he said with a laugh.

HOW ABOUT YOU? Do you find yourself trying to get so close to "worldly things" that Satan is able to trap you and pull you under? Or do you try to live so close to God that when temptation comes, you're able to rely on his strength to resist the evil? God's Word teaches us to resist. *R.I.J.*

TO MEMORIZE: You do not belong to the world, but I have chosen you out of the world. *John 15:19* (NIV)

8 July

LITTLE THINGS

FROM THE BIBLE:

Again, the Kingdom of Heaven can be illustrated by the story of a man going on a trip. He called together his servants and gave them money to invest for him while he was gone. He gave five bags of gold to one, two bags of gold to another, and one bag of gold to the last—dividing it in proportion to their abilities—and then left on his trip. . . .

After a long time their master returned from his trip and called them to give an account of how they had used his money. The servant to whom he had entrusted the five bags of gold said, "Sir, you gave me five bags of gold to invest, and I have doubled the amount." The master was full of praise. "Well done, my good and faithful servant. You have been faithful in handling this small amount, so now I will give you many more responsibilities. Let's celebrate together!"

MATTHEW 25:14-15, 19-21

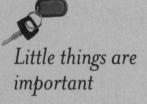

Little things are important

"THERE WERE LOTS of kids at vacation Bible school today," observed Linda as she left the church with her parents.

"Yes, it was a good morning," said her father, who was pastor of the church. "I appreciate all your help, Linda."

"I wish I could do more," she said. "I only do little things—like pick up after the kids or show the little ones where they have to go. Nothing important like teaching."

That evening, Mom handed Linda a note. "This is from your dad and me," she said.

"A thank-you note," Linda said, and began reading it out loud, but very slowly. "Thank you Linda for your help at vbs each day the little things you do really are important and were proud youre our daughter we love you very much"

Linda was quiet a moment. "This is hard to read."

"Oh?" asked Mom, looking surprised. "Why is that?"

"You didn't capitalize words or put periods and commas in the note," Linda answered.

"Oh," Mom said, "they're just little things that don't really matter."

Linda laughed. "They're little, but they're important."

"That's true," Mom agreed. "And guess what? It's the same with little jobs—especially those done for the Lord. Any time you begin thinking the little things you do aren't important, just think about this note."

"Thanks," Linda said. "Little things really do matter!"

HOW ABOUT YOU? Do you sometimes feel as though the jobs you do aren't important? In God's sight it doesn't matter whether a job is big or little, exciting or boring. The most important thing is that you faithfully do it. Whether it's washing dishes, mowing the lawn, or even opening a door for someone, do it in such a way that God himself would say to you, "Well done." *S.L.N.*

TO MEMORIZE: The most important thing about a servant is that he does just what his master tells him to. *1 Corinthians 4:2* (TLB)

THE RIGHT BAIT
(PART 1)

FROM THE BIBLE:

So humble yourselves under the mighty power of God, and in his good time he will honor you. Give all your worries and cares to God, for he cares about what happens to you.

Be careful! Watch out for attacks from the Devil, your great enemy. He prowls around like a roaring lion, looking for some victim to devour. Take a firm stand against him, and be strong in your faith. Remember that your Christian brothers and sisters all over the world are going through the same kind of suffering you are.

In his kindness God called you to his eternal glory by means of Jesus Christ. After you have suffered a little while, he will restore, support, and strengthen you, and he will place you on a firm foundation. All power is his forever and ever. Amen.

1 PETER 5:6-11

Resist Satan

LINDSAY SLAMMED her books on the table. "That Colton!" she exclaimed. "I know he accepted Jesus as his Savior last month, and I know I can't expect him to become a mature Christian overnight. But when I hear the bad language he uses, I wonder if he's really a Christian after all!"

"Maybe you should speak to him about it," said Mom. "And be sure to pray for him."

"But why would he even want to talk like that?" said Lindsay.

"Perhaps he does it out of habit," Mom suggested. "I'm glad you're not tempted to use bad language, but you're probably tempted by things that don't tempt him."

"What do you mean?"

"When Dad went fishing for bluegills last week, what kind of bait did he use?" asked Mom.

Lindsay made a face. "Yucky worms," she said. "He says bluegills like them, but if I were a bluegill, I'd rather have a nice little minnow."

Mom laughed. "But the bluegills wouldn't, and that's my point. A good fisherman knows the right bait to use." She paused. "In a way, Satan is a good 'fisherman.' Maybe he tempts you to be discontent unless you can have the latest thing in fashion. Yet fashion trends may not tempt Colton at all."

Lindsay blushed as she recalled how she had pouted when her mother refused to buy her a short skirt. "You're right," she admitted. "I'll ask God to help Colton—and me."

HOW ABOUT YOU? What bait does Satan place before you? Clothes? Good grades? Skipping a responsibility if you just don't feel like doing it? Satan knows your weakness and will use it to his advantage. But even more importantly, God is your strength. Ask him to help you when you're tempted to do wrong. *H.W.M.*

TO MEMORIZE: The devil prowls around like a roaring lion looking for someone to devour. Resist him, standing firm in the faith. *1 Peter 5:8-9* (NIV)

10 July

THE RIGHT BAIT
(PART 2)

FROM THE BIBLE:

Jesus replied with an illustration: "A Jewish man was traveling on a trip from Jerusalem to Jericho, and he was attacked by bandits. They stripped him of his clothes and money, beat him up, and left him half dead beside the road.

"By chance a Jewish priest came along; but when he saw the man lying there, he crossed to the other side of the road and passed him by. A Temple assistant walked over and looked at him lying there, but he also passed by on the other side.

"Then a despised Samaritan came along, and when he saw the man, he felt deep pity. Kneeling beside him, the Samaritan soothed his wounds with medicine and bandaged them. Then he put the man on his own donkey and took him to an inn, where he took care of him. . . .

"Now which of these three would you say was a neighbor to the man who was attacked by bandits?" Jesus asked.

The man replied, "The one who showed him mercy."

Then Jesus said, "Yes, now go and do the same."

LUKE 10:30-37

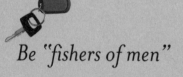

Be "fishers of men"

LINDSAY climbed into the car after church. "I'm going fishing this afternoon, OK?" She grinned. "My teacher said I should."

Dad laughed. "And why is that?"

"Well, our Sunday school lesson was about being 'fishers of men,' " explained Lindsay. "I remembered the talk Mom and I had this week about using the right bait for fishing, so I told the class about the bait Satan uses to tempt us. We decided to think about what 'bait' we should use when we 'fish for men,' too."

"Hmmm," murmured Dad. "And what did you come up with?"

Lindsay went on excitedly. "We decided we should use special bait that will make people want to listen when the way of salvation is explained. Can you guess what it is?"

"What?" asked Mom.

"Love," replied Lindsay. "Mrs. Parsons says that love is the bait we should use, but it can take different forms. It will take the form of a party this Saturday. The way to salvation will be explained during our devotional time. We're supposed to bring an unsaved friend, so I plan to start 'fishing' by going to Joy's house and inviting her to the party."

"Good," approved Dad, "but I hope the 'fishing' won't end at the party."

"No," said Lindsay. "Mrs. Parsons says the party is just a start. Afterwards we still need to offer the 'bait' of loving acts if we want to see our friends come to know Jesus."

HOW ABOUT YOU? Are you "fishing for men"? What are you using for bait? Winning someone to Jesus often begins with being a friend. Something as simple as a cheerful smile, helping with a problem, or sharing a special treat may cause a person to listen when you tell him about Jesus or invite him to church. Will you go "fishing" by using a loving act today?
H.W.M.

TO MEMORIZE: Love your neighbor as yourself.
Matthew 19:19

SHARING THE RIGHT WAY

FROM THE BIBLE:

Son of man, I have appointed you as a watchman for Israel. Whenever you receive a message from me, pass it on to the people immediately. If I warn the wicked, saying, "You are under the penalty of death," but you fail to deliver the warning, they will die in their sins. And I will hold you responsible, demanding your blood for theirs. If you warn them and they keep on sinning and refuse to repent, they will die in their sins. But you will have saved your life because you did what you were told to do.

EZEKIEL 3:17-19

Warn your friends

SHAYNE WAS unusually quiet after she returned home from church. Her pastor had preached about the return of the Lord Jesus. Shayne knew that she was on her way to heaven, but she wondered about her friends. None of them had accepted Jesus as Savior, yet she seldom shared God's plan of salvation with her friends.

That night, Shayne had a strange dream. She and her friends were lost in a dark cave. Shayne had a map showing exactly where to go to get out safely, but she refused to share it with the others. In her dream, Shayne watched the others start off in many wrong directions, but she didn't say anything to them. She looked at her map again and then started out by herself. Finally she reached the exit and waved to the crowd of people waiting for the group.

"Where are the others?" someone asked.

Shayne shrugged her shoulders. "They were going all kinds of ways," she replied carelessly.

Shayne spotted her pastor standing with the others. "But you knew they were going the wrong way," he stated pointedly. "Why didn't you show them the right way?"

Shayne awoke, glad it was only a dream. Then a thought struck her. In the cave her friends were lost. In life they were lost, too. She was glad that she would have another chance to tell them that Jesus is the only way to heaven.

HOW ABOUT YOU? Do you have some friends who think they'll get to heaven by being good, by going to church, or by being baptized? Are there others who don't seem to be concerned about finding the way at all? Maybe God is giving you an opportunity to share God's way—his Son, the Lord Jesus Christ. Warn them that all other ways lead to eternal death. *R.I.J.*

TO MEMORIZE: Give them warning from me. *Ezekiel 3:17* (NIV)

12 July

A FAITHFUL FRIEND

FROM THE BIBLE:

The unfailing love of the Lord never ends! By his mercies we have been kept from complete destruction. Great is his faithfulness; his mercies begin afresh each day. I say to myself, "The Lord is my inheritance; therefore, I will hope in him!"

The Lord is wonderfully good to those who wait for him and seek him. So it is good to wait quietly for salvation from the Lord.

LAMENTATIONS 3:22-26

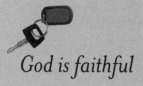

God is faithful

NATHAN CAREFULLY made his bed, then swept his bedroom floor. "Company's coming," he explained to his dog, Rags, who was watching every move Nathan made. Nathan's friend, Dan, was coming to spend the night.

Rags pushed his cool, damp nose into Nathan's hand, his special way of showing love. Nathan loved Rags. Nathan remembered the time Rags had gotten very sick. Nathan had been afraid his dog would die, and he'd prayed that God would make Rags well again. When Rags got better, Nathan had thanked God over and over. Since then, his dog's cool, wet nose always made Nathan think of God's faithfulness. "Great is your faithfulness," quoted Nathan. "It's just like the Bible says, Rags." The dog wagged his tail as though he fully agreed.

Nathan jumped at the sound of the telephone and ran to answer it. "Hi, Dan." There was a pause. Then, "Your uncle got tickets to the football game tonight? Oh, uh, sure, I understand. Well, OK. Bye."

Nathan ran into his room with Rags at this heels. He flung himself on his bed, feeling mad and sad at the same time. He felt a cool, wet nose push into his hand. He put his arm around the dear, old dog, and he thought about God's love.

"It's true, Rags, God is faithful," he murmured. "My friend disappointed me, but God is here with me just as sure as you are. I didn't get what I wanted this time, but I know God loves me and cares for me just the same."

HOW ABOUT YOU? Has a friend or relative disappointed you? Have you been lonely, sick, or had other trouble? God is always with you. He is faithful and will never leave you. When you're feeling sad, remember God loves you and faithfully cares for you—in good times and in bad. *C.E.Y.*

TO MEMORIZE: Great is your faithfulness. *Lamentations 3:23* (NIV)

13 July

LOUDMOUTH LYNN

FROM THE BIBLE:

To hide hatred is to be a liar;
to slander is to be a fool.
Don't talk too much, for it
fosters sin. Be sensible and
turn off the flow!
The words of the godly are like
sterling silver; the heart of a
fool is worthless.
The godly give good advice,
but fools are destroyed by
their lack of common
sense. . . .
The godly person gives wise
advice, but the tongue that
deceives will be cut off.
The godly speak words that
are helpful, but the wicked
speak only what is corrupt.

PROVERBS 10:18-21, 31-32

Think before you speak

LYNN REALLY was a sweet little girl, but she had one very bad habit—she talked loud and long! As a result, she earned the nickname "Loudmouth Lynn."

One day Lynn was setting the table for dinner and began a long story as she talked with her mother. She looked up to see that her mother had returned to cooking, "Mom!" Lynn wailed. "You're not even listening!"

"I'm listening," Mother assured her. "Your story is getting long, and I want to finish cooking these vegetables. Your father will soon be home from his fishing trip."

Dad arrived home disappointed that he had only caught a few small panfish. Mother cooked them anyway, and Lynn was eager to try them. She found that the meat was delicious, but the fish were full of tiny, white bones.

"I'm tired of picking through these fish to find the good parts," she said finally, pushing her plate away.

Mother nodded. "You know, Lynn, that's the feeling I get sometimes when I'm listening to you talk. Some of the things you say are quite interesting and worthwhile. But some is chatter, complaining, or even gossip. After a while I get tired of picking through for the good things."

Lynn sighed. "You've told me before that I talk too much, and other people have too," she said with a long face.

"Cheer up." Mother smiled. "You don't have to stop talking entirely! Just make sure to take the 'bones' out—your silly, unless speech—before you say anything. You'll find that your speech will be more pleasing to others—and to God as well."

HOW ABOUT YOU? Are you a loudmouth? Do you like to talk and talk? People who talk too much tend to gossip, complain, or exaggerate to get attention. Think before you speak.

TO MEMORIZE: Being a fool makes you a blabbermouth. *Ecclesiastes 5:3*

14 July

WHERE IN THE WORLD IS HABAKKUK?

FROM THE BIBLE:

How can a young person stay pure?
By obeying your word and following its rules.
I have tried my best to find you—
don't let me wander from your commands.
I have hidden your word in my heart,
that I might not sin against you.
Blessed are you, O Lord;
teach me your principles.
I have recited aloud
all the laws you have given us.
I have rejoiced in your decrees
as much as in riches.
I will study your commandments
and reflect on your ways.
I will delight in your principles
and not forget your word.

PSALM 119:9-16

Memorize the books of the Bible

"OK, BOYS," Mr. Paterson said to his Sunday school class, "please turn in your Bibles to Habakkuk, chapter one, verse two."

"You're kidding!" exclaimed David. "Haba-who?"

"That's not really a book, is it?" Jason laughed.

"Sure, it's a book," Tim spoke up. "It goes 'Jonah, Micah, Nahum, Habakkuk.' "

"Wow! You sure can rattle those off, Tim," said Jason. "I tried learning them once, but they're just too hard! It's not worth it when your Bible has a table of contents."

"It is worth it!" declared Mr. Paterson. "It's difficult to study any book without knowing how to find things in it. Besides, if someone asks you a question about the Bible, you should know where to find the answers. No one will be very patient if you spend a lot of time fumbling around, searching for a particular book."

After class, David said, "Hey, Jason, did you get that new comic book?"

"Sure did," replied Jason. "I have all twenty-seven in the series! And I can tell you what every single one of them is about."

Mr. Paterson overheard him. "You can do that, yet you can't learn a list of Bible books?"

Jason looked embarrassed. "I never thought about that," he mumbled. "I guess I could learn the books of the Bible." Suddenly he turned to David. "Bet I can learn them quicker than you!"

In answer, David opened his Bible and began memorizing the list of Bible books.

HOW ABOUT YOU? Do you know the books of the Bible? Maybe you think it's too hard to learn those "funny-sounding" names. If you learn a little about each book, it will make it easier for you to remember them. It is important to study the Bible; part of that study is to know the books. *L.M.W.*

TO MEMORIZE: I rejoice in following your statutes as one rejoices in great riches. *Psalm 119:14* (NIV)

THE SECOND MILE

FROM THE BIBLE:

You have heard that the law of Moses says, "If an eye is injured, injure the eye of the person who did it. If a tooth gets knocked out, knock out the tooth of the person who did it." But I say, don't resist an evil person! If you are slapped on the right cheek, turn the other, too. If you are ordered to court and your shirt is taken from you, give your coat, too. If a soldier demands that you carry his gear for a mile, carry it two miles. Give to those who ask, and don't turn away from those who want to borrow.

MATTHEW 5:38-42

Do a little extra

"WILL SOMEONE please volunteer to stay and help me after school?" Mrs. Harris asked her fifth-grade class.

Eric started to raise his hand but remembered his mother was taking him shopping after school.

Gina thought, *I would stay, but I'm tired.*

Tony and Ricky glanced at each other, a reminder that they had scheduled a ball game after school.

Patti raised her hand. "Mrs. Harris, I'll help."

The next day when Mrs. Harris made the math assignment, she pointed out twenty extra credit problems on the board. Eric, Tony, and Ricky decided they would not have time to do the work. Gina decided she did not have enough energy. Only Patti copied the problems.

And so it went. Time after time, Patti did the little extra, and the other children made excuses.

"Class, the local radio station is planning a special program next week in honor of National Education Week," Mrs. Harris announced one day. "Each teacher has been asked to choose one student to be interviewed and give a brief report of the class activities." She smiled as the students suddenly gave her their undivided attention. "I have chosen Patti," Mrs. Harris went on.

At lunch Patti was met with jealous glares and catty remarks. "Teacher's pet!" "Apple polisher!" Everyone had forgotten the little extras Patti always did—everyone, that is, except Mrs. Harris.

HOW ABOUT YOU? Do you think pastors, Sunday school teachers, and parents seem to have favorites? How long has it been since you did a little extra for someone else? Like picking up the songbooks or volunteering some help at church? Washing dishes or taking out the trash without being asked? Go the second mile. Do a little bit extra. *B.J.W.*

TO MEMORIZE: If someone forces you to go one mile, go with him two miles. *Matthew 5:41* (NIV)

16 July

THE SCENTED CANDLE

FROM THE BIBLE:

In everything you do, stay away from complaining and arguing, so that no one can speak a word of blame against you. You are to live clean, innocent lives as children of God in a dark world full of crooked and perverse people. Let your lives shine brightly before them. Hold tightly to the word of life, so that when Christ returns, I will be proud that I did not lose the race and that my work was not useless.

PHILIPPIANS 2:14-16

Be a sweet witness

"MMMMM!" Sharla took a deep breath as she closed the front door behind her. "Coconut." She hurried into the kitchen. "I want a piece of that coconut cake, Mom."

A frown wrinkled her mother's forehead. "Coconut cake? I don't have any."

"Are you making coconut pie then?" Sharla opened the oven door. "I smell coconut."

"No, I'm not," Mom answered. Then she grinned. "You smell the coconut candle that's burning, Sharla."

"Ooohhh! It sure is making me hungry." She sat down at the table and watched as her mother tossed a salad. "Jason witnesses to the kids at school all the time," she said abruptly.

Mom smiled. "That's good."

Sharla frowned. "I don't know if it is or not."

Mom looked up in surprise. "You don't know if it's good or not?" she repeated.

"It's the way he witnesses," Sharla explained. "He is such a—such a smarty witness. It's like he's bragging because he knows Jesus and the other kids don't. He's not a very good example of a Christian. His attitude is wrong."

"A witness with a wrong attitude is like a floodlight shining in someone's eyes," said Mom as she set the salad on the table. "It blinds people. On the other hand, a witness with a sweet spirit is like a scented candle."

Sharla took a deep breath and smiled. "I know what you mean. Like the scented candle made me hungry, a sweet witness will cause people to hunger to know Jesus. That's the kind of witness I want to be." Then she added, "Mom, could we make a coconut cake after dinner?"

HOW ABOUT YOU? What kind of witness are you? Are you like a floodlight or a scented candle? Do you blind people with a know-it-all attitude, or do you cause them to hunger for Christ? *B.J.W.*

TO MEMORIZE: My true disciples produce much fruit. This brings great glory to my Father. *John 15:8*

17 July

HIS SHEEP AM I
(PART 1)

ERIC WAS visiting his Uncle Joe and Aunt Sue at their ranch in Montana. He had never seen so many sheep. "They all look so fat and woolly!"

"Not all of them," said Uncle Joe, as he stopped his jeep outside the fence of a neighboring ranch. "Take a look at those sheep."

Eric saw a large number of very thin sheep. "Uncle Joe, they look like they may have a disease!"

Uncle Joe started the jeep again. "Their owner is away," he sighed, "and the manager doesn't really care about them. He doesn't move them to green pastures or to areas with clean water."

After dinner that evening, Uncle Joe read some verses from John 10. He ended the reading with the verse, "I am the good shepherd. The good shepherd lays down his life for the sheep."

Thoughtfully Eric spoke. "I think you're really a good shepherd, Uncle Joe," he said. "I'll bet your sheep are glad they belong to you. Are people who belong to Jesus glad, too?"

Uncle Joe nodded. "How about you, Eric? Do you belong to Jesus? If you don't belong to Jesus, you belong to Satan, and that means you belong to someone who doesn't really care for you—kind of like those sick sheep."

"Jesus, the Good Shepherd, gave his life so you could belong to him," added Aunt Sue. "If you accept him as your Savior, he will be your shepherd."

"I'll do that," agreed Eric. Together they bowed their heads to pray.

HOW ABOUT YOU? Do you belong to Jesus, the Good Shepherd, or do you belong to Satan? Jesus loves you and wants to take care of you and guide you. Accept him as your Savior, and then you can look to him for care and help, no matter what life may bring. *G.W.*

TO MEMORIZE: The Lord is my shepherd. I shall not want. *Psalm 23:1* (NKJV)

FROM THE BIBLE:

"I assure you, anyone who sneaks over the wall of a sheepfold, rather than going through the gate, must surely be a thief and a robber! For a shepherd enters through the gate. The gatekeeper opens the gate for him, and the sheep hear his voice and come to him. He calls his own sheep by name and leads them out. After he has gathered his own flock, he walks ahead of them, and they follow him because they recognize his voice. . . ."

Those who heard Jesus use this illustration didn't understand what he meant, so he explained it to them. "I assure you, I am the gate for the sheep," he said. "All others who came before me were thieves and robbers. But the true sheep did not listen to them. Yes, I am the gate. Those who come in through me will be saved. . . . The thief's purpose is to steal and kill and destroy. My purpose is to give life in all its fullness.

"I am the good shepherd. The good shepherd lays down his life for the sheep."

JOHN 10:1-11

You can belong to Jesus

18 July

HIS SHEEP AM I
(PART 2)

FROM THE BIBLE:

Yet true religion with contentment is great wealth. After all, we didn't bring anything with us when we came into the world, and we certainly cannot carry anything with us when we die. So if we have enough food and clothing, let us be content.

1 TIMOTHY 6:6-8

Be content

"ERIC! WAKE UP!" Uncle Joe whispered loudly. "I know it's the middle of the night, but it's raining so hard that there's danger of flooding in the south pasture. The sheep have to be moved. Want to help?"

Three hours later after much hard work, the sheep were high and dry. Eric tumbled back into bed, and Aunt Sue let him sleep late the next morning.

That afternoon, Eric and Uncle Joe drove out to check on the flock of sheep that had just been moved. "Wow!" exclaimed Eric when he saw the rich, green pasture. "What a great place for the sheep!"

Uncle Joe pointed. "See that sheep over by the fence? She'll try to get to the other side, even though it isn't good pasture there."

Eric looked surprised. "Why would she do that when she's in such a great pasture?"

Uncle Joe smiled. "You're never like that, are you?" he asked. "You never want something more when God has already given you many good things, do you?"

Suddenly Eric remembered that just yesterday, he had not been content. Instead of being happy with the many things that he could do on the ranch, he had been crabby when he hadn't been allowed to ride Uncle Joe's favorite horse. And then Aunt Sue had asked him to do the dishes! At bedtime, he didn't thank God for the day. He was a new Christian, but he would try to remember that everything needed in a Christian's life is provided by the Good Shepherd.

HOW ABOUT YOU? Are you a Christian who finds yourself wanting things that God hasn't given you? Do you want a bigger allowance? More clothes? Better health? More permissive parents? Pray about your needs and your wants, but stay content with what God provides. *G.W.*

TO MEMORIZE: He restores my soul; He leads me in the paths of righteousness for His name's sake. *Psalm 23:3* (NKJV)

RESCUED
(PART 1)

FROM THE BIBLE:

[Jesus said,] "And as Moses lifted up the bronze snake on a pole in the wilderness, so I, the Son of Man, must be lifted up on a pole, so that everyone who believes in me will have eternal life.

"For God so loved the world that he gave his only Son, so that everyone who believes in him will not perish but have eternal life. God did not send his Son into the world to condemn it, but to save it.

"There is no judgment awaiting those who trust him. But those who do not trust him have already been judged for not believing in the only Son of God."

JOHN 3:14-18

Jesus rescues sinners

THIRTEEN-YEAR-OLD Sean and his father were walking down Main Street and noticed an unusual display in a shop window. "There's a dog in that cage!" A large hand-lettered sign on the cage read: "Death row! This animal has one more day to live." Sean stopped and looked at the small, brown-eyed puppy inside. "What does that sign mean, Dad?" he asked.

"It's a new program that the animal shelter is trying out," said Dad. "They can't take care of all the stray dogs and cats. This display lets people know about the problem and gives the animals one last chance to be adopted. If no one takes the puppy, he'll be put to sleep."

"You mean this little puppy is going to be killed?" moaned Sean. He stared though the glass at the unfortunate puppy. "Poor little guy," he said sadly. "Oh, Dad, can't we take him home? Look—he likes us already."

Dad sighed. "We already have two hamsters."

"But this is different," Sean insisted. "This dog needs us, Dad. It sort of reminds me of Jesus."

"What do you mean?" asked Dad.

"Well, you told me we were already condemned—on 'death row' in a way—before Jesus saved us from our sins," explained Sean. "If Jesus hadn't rescued me, I'd still be on my way to hell. I want to rescue this dog like Jesus rescued me."

Dad nodded his head thoughtfully. "When you put it that way, how can I refuse?"

Sean grinned. "Thanks, Dad! And the puppy thanks you, too!"

HOW ABOUT YOU? Have you come to the place in your life where you realize that you are a sinner and on your way to hell? If you haven't accepted Jesus as your Savior, you're condemned already. Don't wait till tomorrow. Be saved today! *S.L.K.*

TO MEMORIZE: Whoever believes in him is not condemned, but whoever does not believe stands condemned already. *John 3:18*

20 July

RESCUED
(PART 2)

FROM THE BIBLE:

If God is for us, who can ever be against us? Since God did not spare even his own Son but gave him up for us all, won't God, who gave us Christ, also give us everything else? . . .

Can anything ever separate us from Christ's love? Does it mean he no longer loves us if we have trouble or calamity, or are persecuted, or are hungry or cold or in danger or threatened with death? . . . No, despite all these things, overwhelming victory is ours through Christ, who loved us.

And I am convinced that nothing can ever separate us from his love. Death can't, and life can't. The angels can't, and the demons can't. Our fears for today, our worries about tomorrow, and even the powers of hell can't keep God's love away. Whether we are high above the sky or in the deepest ocean, nothing in all creation will ever be able to separate us from the love of God that is revealed in Christ Jesus our Lord.

ROMANS 8:31-39

God can be trusted

WHEN SEAN and his dad arrived home with the new puppy, Mother lined a box with an old, soft blanket. "What will you name him, Sean?"

"I think I'll call him Little Guy," Sean answered. Opening the refrigerator, he asked, "Mom, can I give him some of this leftover chicken?"

"Well, I guess he can have it this once," she agreed, "but make sure you take it off the bones, so he won't choke."

Sean set the saucer of meat near the dog, and Little Guy began to eat it greedily. "Uh-oh, there's still a piece of bone in there."

"Take it away from him," Dad said, "or it might get caught in his throat." Sean reached out to pick up the bone, but as he did so, Little Guy growled and snapped at his hand. "Ow!" shouted Sean. "He nipped me! I was only trying to help him! Little Guy," he scolded, "you know you can trust me!"

"No, he doesn't," said Dad. "You know, Sean, some Christians don't have any more sense than that dog. They're afraid to trust God completely. They think he's going to take something away from them or tell them to do something that will make them unhappy. They forget that it was God who saved them in the first place by sacrificing his own Son, Jesus. He only wants what's best for them!"

Sean nodded. "I'd better trust God just like I want Little Guy to trust me."

HOW ABOUT YOU? Are you a Christian but afraid to trust God with your daily life? Don't be! Remember, God sent his own Son to save your life. He certainly will not change his mind now and try to make you miserable! *S.L.K.*

TO MEMORIZE: Since God did not spare even his own Son but gave him up for us all, won't God, who gave us Christ, also give us everything else?
Romans 8:32

RESCUED
(PART 3)

FROM THE BIBLE:

But God is so rich in mercy, and he loved us so very much, that even while we were dead because of our sins, he gave us life when he raised Christ from the dead. (It is only by God's special favor that you have been saved!) For he raised us from the dead along with Christ, and we are seated with him in the heavenly realms—all because we are one with Christ Jesus. And so God can always point to us as examples of the incredible wealth of his favor and kindness toward us, as shown in all he has done for us through Christ Jesus.

God saved you by his special favor when you believed. And you can't take credit for this; it is a gift from God. Salvation is not a reward for the good things we have done, so none of us can boast about it. For we are God's masterpiece. He has created us anew in Christ Jesus, so that we can do the good things he planned for us long ago.

EPHESIANS 2:4-10

Saved to serve

SEAN'S PUPPY seemed to grow bigger every day. Sean took good care of Little Guy, and they loved to play together.

But Little Guy was more than a playmate. He also went along when Sean delivered papers. If a paper didn't land right on the porch, he learned to pick it up in his mouth and carry it there. Little Guy was an excellent watchdog, too.

One evening Dad said, "You must be glad you saved Little Guy from 'Death Row.' "

Sean smiled and patted the dog. "I sure am!" he said. "You know, I think Little Guy is glad too."

"I think Little Guy is happy," said Dad, "because he has a loving master who cares for him and whom he can serve. Some dogs are pampered by their owners but never contribute anything in return."

"I don't think Little Guy would like sitting on a pillow all day, getting fat. I don't think I would, either," Sean added.

"Human beings were created to serve God," Dad remarked. "They're never really happy until they do. Some people accept Christ as Savior and then don't do anything more about it. They sit around on pillows, so to speak, waiting for others to serve them. They have forgotten that they were saved to serve!"

HOW ABOUT YOU? If you are a Christian, are you really serving Christ the way you should? God didn't save you just so you could go to heaven. He wants to use you in this life, too. Get involved in your church. Witness to your friends. Do kind things for your family and others. Read the Bible and pray. Give up your bad habits. It's only right for you to want to serve the One who saved you! *S.L.K.*

TO MEMORIZE: Christian friends, I plead with you to give your bodies to God. Let them be a living and holy sacrifice—the kind he will accept. *Romans 12:1*

22 July

THE REPRESENTATIVE

FROM THE BIBLE:

Pray at all times and on every occasion in the power of the Holy Spirit. Stay alert and be persistent in your prayers for all Christians everywhere.

And pray for me, too. Ask God to give me the right words as I boldly explain God's secret plan that the Good News is for the Gentiles, too. I am in chains now for preaching this message as God's ambassador. But pray that I will keep on speaking boldly for him, as I should.

EPHESIANS 6:18-20

Be faithful

LIONEL HAD WANTED a paper route ever since he was old enough to qualify. So when Richard asked him to be his substitute for a month, Lionel accepted excitedly.

Each afternoon Lionel hurriedly delivered the papers to the houses on Richard's route. At the end of the month, he was thrilled to collect his earnings.

But at the first house, the man didn't pay him in full. "I subtracted for the paper that went on the garage roof and the two that fell into the wet flower garden," the man explained. "I couldn't read those."

Lionel reluctantly left the house without even saying thanks. Boy, some people were impossible!

At the next house, the lady paid for the full month but reminded Lionel that Richard was always careful to put the paper inside the screen door on rainy days.

By the time Lionel returned home, he was not in a good mood. "Talk about crabby people," he said, telling his dad what had happened.

"Well, Son," said Dad, "those people had a right to expect good service from you, just as they get from Richard," he reminded. "After all, you were his representative."

Lionel's father's words were almost the same words his Sunday school teacher had used last Sunday. "We are God's representatives here on earth," his teacher had explained. "He has a right to expect us to be faithful."

HOW ABOUT YOU? Can the Lord trust you to be his representative? If you're a Christian, all you do and say reflects on the Lord as well as on yourself. If you tell a lie, cheat, snub someone, or do a sloppy job, others may decide that "if that's the way Christians act, I don't care to be one." But a cheerful smile, an honest life, and a job well done are a good testimony for your Lord. *R.I.J.*

TO MEMORIZE: We are Christ's ambassadors.
2 Corinthians 5:20

A PICKY WITNESS

FROM THE BIBLE:

When the apostles were with Jesus, they kept asking him, "Lord, are you going to free Israel now and restore our kingdom?"

"The Father sets those dates," he replied, "and they are not for you to know. But when the Holy Spirit has come upon you, you will receive power and will tell people about me everywhere—in Jerusalem, throughout Judea, in Samaria, and to the ends of the earth."

ACTS 1:6-8

Don't be a picky witness

"I'M GOING to be a missionary pilot overseas when I grow up," said Jim as he watched a small plane circle the Jordan ranch.

"Not me," declared his best friend, A.J. "I'm going to stay right here in the good old U.S.A.! I like . . ." His words were drowned out by the noise of the Piper Cub plane.

When the sound had faded, A.J. said, "I'm going to show Jose how to hit a baseball. Want to come along?"

Jim frowned. "No! I can't stand that guy. He talks funny. He's dumb, and his clothes are always dirty."

A.J. shrugged. "You're not so clean yourself."

Jim looked down at his ragged jeans and dirty hands. "Yeah, but . . ."

"I imagine Jose thinks we talk funny too," added A.J.

"At least we talk English!" Jim argued. "He speaks a mixture of two languages."

"Then he's smarter than we are. We can speak only one," said A.J. "You know, Jim, you called Jose dumb, but you aren't so smart yourself. I think you would be a better crop duster than a missionary pilot. How do you think you can tell people in foreign lands about the love of Jesus when you won't even be friends to a guy who is a little different from you? You're a mighty picky witness."

"I . . . I . . ." Jim hung his head. His eyes watered. "I never thought about it that way, A.J." Then he looked up. "I'll go get my baseball glove. Maybe Jose will teach me some Spanish."

HOW ABOUT YOU? Do you have visions of doing great things for God someday? What about today? How do you treat those around you? Salvation is for "whosoever will." Are you willing to witness to anyone and everyone? *B.J.W.*

TO MEMORIZE: The Good News about the Kingdom will be preached throughout the whole world, so that all nations will hear it. *Matthew 24:14*

24 July

SECRET SERVICE

FROM THE BIBLE:

Take care! Don't do your good deeds publicly, to be admired, because then you will lose the reward from your Father in heaven. When you give a gift to someone in need, don't shout about it as the hypocrites do—blowing trumpets in the synagogues and streets to call attention to their acts of charity! I assure you, they have received all the reward they will ever get. But when you give to someone, don't tell your left hand what your right hand is doing. Give your gifts in secret, and your Father, who knows all secrets, will reward you.

MATTHEW 6:1-4

God rewards service

MRS. BRIMLEY unlocked the front door and walked wearily into her kitchen with her children. It had been a long day at the department store. She was tired, but she had to get supper for the kids. She'd just picked them up from a neighbor down the street.

She sniffed the air. What was that good smell? In the oven she found a potato-and-ham casserole. Mrs. Brimley was startled. *Who could have done this?* she wondered. Then on the kitchen counter, Mrs. Brimley noticed a small card. It simply said, "I did it in the name of the Lord." There was no signature.

That evening as they ate the lovely supper, her children talked about the secret helper. "I bet it was Mrs. James," said David, the youngest.

"No," said Karen. "How could she have gotten in? It must have been Gloria, our neighbor."

"But she was with us all day," argued David.

"Children," Mom interrupted, "whoever made supper for us didn't want us to know who he or she is. Shouldn't we respect that wish? It wasn't done for praise. It was done as a service to God, and he'll give the reward. It's nice to be appreciated for what we do, but which is better—a reward of thanks from people, or a reward from God?"

"Both would be nice." David grinned. "But you're right. A thank you from God is more important."

HOW ABOUT YOU? Can you think of someone for whom you could do a kind deed? Would you be willing to let God receive all the thanks and praise and wait until you reach heaven to get your reward? Acts of Christian service that are done in secret often bring people's attention to God and his workings. Why not be one of God's "secret servants"? Don't wait—do that service today. *C.R.*

TO MEMORIZE: Your Father, who sees what is done in secret, will reward you. *Matthew 6:4* (NIV)

25 July

THE HAND IN THE GLOVE

FROM THE BIBLE:

I am the true vine, and my Father is the gardener. He cuts off every branch that doesn't produce fruit, and he prunes the branches that do bear fruit so they will produce even more. You have already been pruned for greater fruitfulness by the message I have given you. Remain in me, and I will remain in you. For a branch cannot produce fruit if it is severed from the vine, and you cannot be fruitful apart from me.

Yes, I am the vine; you are the branches. Those who remain in me, and I in them, will produce much fruit. For apart from me you can do nothing.

JOHN 15:1-5

God gives power

"YOU'RE SO QUIET, Son. What's on your mind?" asked Ben's father as he stopped at Ben's room to pray with him.

Ben sighed. "Oh, I've just been wondering if I should be a missionary," he said. "I'd like to, but what if I try and I'm no good at it? What if God calls me to do something I can't do?"

Ben's father thought for a moment, then reached over to Ben's desk and picked up his baseball glove. He walked to the corner of the room, propped the glove against the wall, found a baseball, and threw it at the glove. Though the ball hit the center of the glove, it rolled to the floor. Dad picked up the glove and looked at it in disgust. "This glove is a total failure," he said.

Ben laughed. "Oh, Dad, you know it can't catch by itself! It has to have a hand inside."

Dad smiled at Ben. "You're just like this glove," he said. "God has a purpose for your life, Ben, just as there is a purpose for this glove. Your hand inside the glove gives it guidance, strength, and power. Don't worry, Ben. God will never prop you in a corner and leave you alone. It's his mighty hand that does the work when you are willing to be used."

HOW ABOUT YOU? Have you thought about God's plan for your life? Are you learning to accept his guidance and use his power right now? If he asks you to witness to somebody, he'll help you do it. If he asks you to be cheerful when things go wrong, he'll help you with that. Never be afraid of God's calling. He will use you if you are willing. *C.R.*

TO MEMORIZE: I am the vine; you are the branches. Those who remain in me, and I in them, will produce much fruit. For apart from me, you can do nothing. *John 15:5*

26 July

MISSING MEN

FROM THE BIBLE:

But God made our bodies with many parts, and he has put each part just where he wants it. . . . Yes, there are many parts, but only one body. The eye can never say to the hand, "I don't need you." The head can't say to the feet, "I don't need you."

In fact, some of the parts that seem weakest and least important are really the most necessary. And the parts we regard as less honorable are those we clothe with the greatest care. So we carefully protect from the eyes of others those parts that should not be seen, while other parts do not require this special care. So God has put the body together in such a way that extra honor and care are given to those parts that have less dignity. This makes for harmony among the members, so that all the members care for each other equally. If one part suffers, all the parts suffer with it, and if one part is honored, all the parts are glad.

1 CORINTHIANS 12:18-26

Do your part on God's team

"WANT TO PLAY Foosball, Jack?" asked Tim, the camp counselor.

"Sure!" Jack agreed. They took their places on opposite sides of the table. "I'm missing a man on this rod," Jack said.

"Yes, but we're even," observed Tim. "I have a man who has no legs. He can't help his team very much either. Let's play."

Jack twisted the rod, making one of his men push the ball toward Tim's men. Tim took careful aim and spun the metal pole. The ball shot through the hole where the missing man should have been. *Clunk!*

"Let's try again," said Jack, picking up the ball and putting it back into play. This time he won the point. "That was fun," he exclaimed when the game was over. "Sure wish I'd had the missing man, though."

"It hurts to have one missing," agreed Tim. "It reminds me that as Christians we're on God's team. If we're missing from church, we're like the missing man on your pole. If we're in church but not doing what we should be doing for God, we're like the legless figure. The whole team suffers when one person doesn't do his part. Others have to try and fill in the empty area, and sometimes they can't move fast enough."

"Wow," said Jack. "I never thought about being on God's team and how important each person is."

HOW ABOUT YOU? Are you on God's team? You are if you're a Christian. How well do you get along with your teammates? Are you in your place each time you're needed? Are you doing what God would like you to do? His team is the best there is, and each team member is needed. Always be ready to do your part. *V.L.C.*

TO MEMORIZE: If one member suffers, all the members suffer with it; or if one member is honored, all the members rejoice with it. *1 Corinthians 12:26* (NKJV)

WRONG NOTES

FROM THE BIBLE:

And now, may the God of peace, who brought again from the dead our Lord Jesus, equip you with all you need for doing his will. May he produce in you, through the power of Jesus Christ, all that is pleasing to him. Jesus is the great Shepherd of the sheep by an everlasting covenant, signed with his blood. To him be glory forever and ever. Amen.

I urge you, dear brothers and sisters, please listen carefully to what I have said in this brief letter. . . .

May God's grace be with you all.

HEBREWS 13:20-22, 25

God won't give up on you

AMBER GOT out her cello. As she drew her bow across the strings, the notes were shaky and unsure. "I'll never get this right," she wailed. "This song sounds horrible!"

"Try it again," said Mom, coming into the room. With a sigh, Amber did so, and by the end of the practice session, the song had definitely improved.

During family devotions that evening, Amber told about a neighborhood ball game. "John lost his temper and went home mad," she said in disgust. "He's a Christian, but he sure blew it today."

"That's too bad," replied Dad. "Try to be patient with him, though. He's still a new Christian."

"Remember that new song you were trying to play on your cello?" Mom asked.

"Yeah, it still needs a lot of work."

"That's true," agreed Mom, "but it's improving, so don't give up. We all need a lot of improvement in our Christian lives, too, and I'm glad that God doesn't give up on us."

"That's true," said Dad. "When we accept Jesus, God begins to change us. This takes time, but God has promised that he will continue to work in our lives."

"Right," said Mom. "Every time we sin, we sound like a 'wrong note,' and our harmony with God is gone. But when we confess our sin and ask for forgiveness, we get back in tune."

"I'll think about that whenever I practice my cello," Amber said, grinning. "And I'll be more patient with John, too."

HOW ABOUT YOU? Have you or your friends been making "wrong notes" lately? Maybe you've heard the saying "Be patient, God isn't finished with me yet." Be patient with your friends, too. Ask forgiveness for your own sins. Try each day to learn more about God's word and grow more like him. Thank him for his patient work in your life. *J.A.G.*

TO MEMORIZE: Be patient in trouble, and always be prayerful. *Romans 12:12*

28 July

FEED YOURSELF

FROM THE BIBLE:

Teach these things and insist that everyone learn them. Don't let anyone think less of you because you are young. Be an example to all believers in what you teach, in the way you live, in your love, your faith, and your purity. Until I get there, focus on reading the Scriptures to the church, encouraging the believers, and teaching them.

Do not neglect the spiritual gift you received through the prophecies spoken to you when the elders of the church laid their hands on you. Give your complete attention to these matters. Throw yourself into your tasks so that everyone will see your progress. Keep a close watch on yourself and on your teaching. Stay true to what is right, and God will save you and those who hear you.

1 TIMOTHY 4:11-16

Read your Bible

"MOM, LOOK at Christopher," Cally said, laughing. Her one-year-old brother waved his spoon and rubbed mashed potatoes all over his face. He dipped the spoon back into his bowl and then put it in his mouth. "Big boy!" cheered Cally. "You got it all in that time!"

"Soon he'll be eating all by himself," said Mom.

After a busy evening, Mom reminded Cally that it was nearly bedtime. "Save time to have your devotions," she said.

"Sometimes I think I might as well skip devotions," Cally sighed. "I don't understand the Bible very well when I read it by myself. Why can't I just wait till I'm older?"

"Cally, what would you think if Christopher refused to try to feed himself?" asked Mom. "Would you be happy to see that?" Cally slowly shook her head. Mom continued, "We're glad to help him when he needs help, but we're also glad to see him attempt to feed himself. And as he practices, he'll become better at it."

"I know what you're saying," said Cally. "You're saying that as a Christian, I should feed myself too, by reading the Bible for myself."

"That's right," agreed Mom. "It's fine for you to be fed by going to church and Sunday school and by having devotions with the rest of us, but you also need to feed yourself. Sometimes you may 'miss your mouth' and not understand what you've read. Then you can ask for help. But don't stop trying. Learn to get some spiritual food all by yourself."

HOW ABOUT YOU? Are you learning to feed yourself spiritually? You should be. You may not understand everything, but as you work at it, you'll find you understand more and more. Take time to read God's Word every day. *H.W.M.*

TO MEMORIZE: We have not stopped praying for you and asking God to fill you with the knowledge of his will. *Colossians 1:9* (NIV)

A SUPER SONGWRITER

FROM THE BIBLE:

Now the Spirit of the Lord had left Saul, and the Lord sent a tormenting spirit that filled him with depression and fear. Some of Saul's servants suggested a remedy. "It is clear that a spirit from God is tormenting you," they said. "Let us find a good musician to play the harp for you whenever the tormenting spirit is bothering you. The harp music will quiet you, and you will soon be well again."

"All right," Saul said. "Find me someone who plays well and bring him here."

One of the servants said to Saul, "The son of Jesse is a talented harp player. Not only that; he is brave and strong and has good judgment. He is also a fine-looking young man, and the Lord is with him."

So Saul sent messengers to Jesse to say, "Send me your son David, the shepherd." . . .

And whenever the tormenting spirit from God troubled Saul, David would play the harp. Then Saul would feel better, and the tormenting spirit would go away.

1 SAMUEL 16:14-19, 23

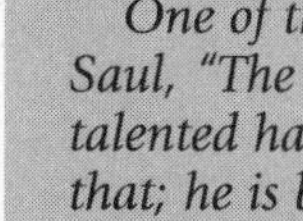

Use abilities for God

ERIKA SAT at the window, watching the birds flit around the feeder. "What's on your mind?" her mother asked.

"The church newsletter," replied Erika. "Pastor Hamilton came to our Sunday school class last week and asked us all to do something for next month's issue. Gary is drawing a picture of the church, and Sue is writing a thank-you note to all the Sunday school teachers, but I can't think of anything!"

"You like to write poetry," Mom suggested.

Suddenly Erika broke into a smile. "I could write a song! Maybe Jenny could help me with a tune." Erika's older sister was an accomplished pianist.

Erika started writing a verse to praise God for his creation—especially the beautiful birds. She worked all morning and finally finished it. Jenny helped to compose a tune. After supper, the girls sang the song for their parents.

"My daughters, the songwriters," Dad said, smiling. "Maybe songwriting will be your career!"

"Oh, Dad," Erika laughed, "we're still so young!"

"Have you heard of the hymn writer, Isaac Watts?" asked Dad. "He started writing poetry when he was very young, and in his lifetime he wrote over six hundred hymns. Fanny Crosby wrote seven thousand songs of praise to God!"

"Wow!" Erika said. Maybe this would be the first song of many for her. Maybe she would be able to serve the Lord by being a songwriter! That was an exciting thought!

HOW ABOUT YOU? Every Sunday at church you sing different hymns and songs. Have you ever wondered who wrote all that music? It was written by people who had a special God-given talent to express themselves through poetry and music. If you are interested in poetry, practice putting your thoughts about the Lord in rhyme. Perhaps someday a hymnbook will have your name in it! *L.M.W.*

TO MEMORIZE: Sing to the Lord a new song; sing to the Lord, all the earth. *Psalm 96:1* (NIV)

30 July

IT STILL HURTS

FROM THE BIBLE:

The Lord is king!
Let the nations tremble!
He sits on his throne between the cherubim.
Let the whole earth quake!
The Lord sits in majesty in Jerusalem,
supreme above all the nations.
Let them praise your great and awesome name.
Your name is holy!
Mighty king, lover of justice,
you have established fairness.
You have acted with justice
and righteousness throughout Israel.
Exalt the Lord our God!
Bow low before his feet, for he is holy!
Moses and Aaron were among his priests;
Samuel also called on his name.
They cried to the Lord for help,
and he answered them.
He spoke to them from the pillar of cloud,
and they followed the decrees and principles he gave them.

PSALM 99:1-7

Sin has consequences

OH, HOW TERRY wished he had listened to his mother when she told him not to jump his bike over the ramp he had built. As soon as her back was turned, Terry had done it again. The planks had flown up in his face as he hit the ramp, and then all he could remember was the pain!

"Mom, I'm sorry," he cried after the doctor set the two broken bones in his arm. "I shouldn't have disobeyed."

Terry's mother accepted his apology. But she also reminded him that he had not only disobeyed her—he had disobeyed God's command to honor his father and mother. "You need to ask God's forgiveness too," she said. After he and Mom prayed together, he felt much better, knowing he was forgiven.

The next morning, Terry felt down in the dumps. The pain in his arm had kept him awake much of the night. "I prayed that God would take the pain away, but he didn't," Terry told his mom. "If God forgave me for disobeying, why doesn't he heal the pain?"

"Oh, Terry, God always is willing to forgive sin," explained Mom, "but he doesn't always take away the consequences of our sin. Because God is a God of justice, he often allows us to face the consequences. He knows that we'll learn our lesson better by having to suffer because of what we've done. The pain will eventually ease, but God wants you to remember what it cost you to disobey."

HOW ABOUT YOU? Have you ever had to face the nasty consequences of sin? Perhaps you've had to take a zero on a test when you confessed that you cheated. Or perhaps, like Terry, you've disobeyed your parents and suffered physical injury. God always forgives confessed sin, but he does not always remove the consequences of your sins! *R.E.P.*

TO MEMORIZE: Your throne is founded on two strong pillars—righteousness and justice. *Psalm 89:14*

31 *July*

THE FAMILY PARROT

FROM THE BIBLE:

You brood of snakes! How could evil men like you speak what is good and right? For whatever is in your heart determines what you say. A good person produces good words from a good heart, and an evil person produces evil words from an evil heart. And I tell you this, that you must give an account on judgment day of every idle word you speak. The words you say now reflect your fate then; either you will be justified by them or you will be condemned.

MATTHEW 12:34-37

Choose your words wisely

WHEN DAD FINISHED saying the blessing at suppertime, two-year-old Joey called out, "Yay-men!"

Cindy laughed. "Joey's learning new words." Just then Mother lifted the cover off the casserole dish. "Yuck!" Cindy said. "Green beans. I hate them!"

"Yuck!" came the echo from the high chair. "Hate dem."

Cindy clapped her hand over her mouth. "Sorry, Mom! I shouldn't have said that."

"Would you pass the beans, please?" Dad said, and he put some on Joey's plate.

"Pwease!" Joey shouted. "Pwease!" He began to eat his beans heartily, a big smile on his face. "Yuck!"

Cindy laughed. "He doesn't even know what he's saying!"

"That's true." Mother nodded. "Joey is like a parrot. If he hears a word often enough, he learns to say it."

"I don't think he's the only one in the family like that," observed Dad. "I've noticed a few expressions creeping into your speech, Cindy. You've just heard them and let them seep into your mind."

Cindy blushed as she remembered several times her parents had corrected her language lately. "That's true," she admitted. "I hear kids at school say these things over and over again. I guess, as a Christian, I ought to be more careful."

Dad nodded. "We have a big responsibility to spread good words for those around us to hear. And we have a responsibility to ourselves to repeat only those words we want to become part of our thoughts and hearts."

HOW ABOUT YOU? Are you careful to use only words that you would not be embarrassed to have repeated? Do you think carefully about the meaning of the popular expressions your friends use before you repeat them? Are you embarrassed to have your parents or your pastor hear you using them? God hears them. *C.R.*

TO MEMORIZE: I tell you this, that you must give an account on judgment day of every idle word you speak. *Matthew 12:36*

1 August

TRANSPLANTED TREE

FROM THE BIBLE:

Oh, the joys of those
who do not follow the advice
of the wicked,
or stand around with sinners,
or join in with scoffers.
But they delight in doing
everything the Lord wants;
day and night they think
about his law.
They are like trees planted along
the riverbank,
bearing fruit each season
without fail.
Their leaves never wither,
and in all they do, they
prosper.
But this is not true of the wicked.
They are like worthless chaff,
scattered by the wind.
They will be condemned at the
time of judgment.
Sinners will have no place
among the godly.
For the Lord watches over the
path of the godly,
but the path of the wicked
leads to destruction.

PSALM 1:1-6

Grow spiritually

DAVID CARRIED a water jug to a tiny black spruce tree in the backyard and gently watered it. In spite of his efforts, more and more needles were turning brown each day. "It's not going to live, is it, Mom?" he asked.

"No, David," his mother answered. "I don't think so."

"But I've been taking good care of it!" David said.

"I know, Son," Mom said. "But Grandpa told you he didn't think a black spruce would grow in our yard."

"I don't see why not!" David insisted. "Other trees do."

"That's true, but black spruce trees usually grow where it's extremely damp," Mom explained. "We live in a dry area." David and his mother stood looking at the scraggly tree. "You know, David, that seedling reminds me of some Christians."

"Christians?" asked David.

His mother nodded. "To grow in the Lord, they should pray and read their Bibles and be friends with other Christians. Instead, some Christians spend their time in the wrong environment—with people who don't love the Lord. They ignore their Bibles, skip church, and don't take time to pray. Then they wonder why they don't grow spiritually."

"Oh, I get it!" exclaimed David. "It's as important for a Christian to be in the right environment as it is for a tree to be in the right environment." He grinned. "Well, even if this tree doesn't live, I've learned a lesson from it."

HOW ABOUT YOU? Are you growing spiritually? Are you in the right environment? Do your friends love the Lord and live according to what is taught in the Bible? Are you getting nourishment from God's Word? You cannot grow spiritually in the wrong conditions. Make sure you are a healthy Christian! *L.M.W.*

TO MEMORIZE: Let your roots grow down into him and draw up nourishment from him, so you will grow in faith, strong and vigorous in the truth you were taught. *Colossians 2:7*

THE ROUGH EDGES

FROM THE BIBLE:

So make every effort to apply the benefits of these promises to your life. Then your faith will produce a life of moral excellence. A life of moral excellence leads to knowing God better. Knowing God leads to self-control. Self-control leads to patient endurance, and patient endurance leads to godliness. Godliness leads to love for other Christians, and finally you will grow to have genuine love for everyone. The more you grow like this, the more you will become productive and useful in your knowledge of our Lord Jesus Christ. But those who fail to develop these virtues are blind or, at least, very shortsighted. They have already forgotten that God has cleansed them from their old life of sin.

So, dear brothers and sisters, work hard to prove that you really are among those God has called and chosen. Doing this, you will never stumble or fall away.

2 PETER 1:5-10

"MORNIN', BRIAN. What have you got there?" called Mr. Walker.

Oh, brother, Brian thought. "This is a porch swing, Mr. Walker," he said aloud.

"Looks a bit worn-out," Mr. Walker observed. "You fixin' to paint it?"

"Yes, sir," Brian replied.

"Paintin' it white, eh? I'd paint it green. Match your house better."

"My mother wants it white," Brian said.

"You gonna paint wearin' that good shirt, boy? When I was a kid I only had two shirts to my name."

As Brian dipped his brush into the paint, Mr. Walker added, "Wait a minute there, young 'un. You can't paint yet. Where's your sandpaper?"

Brian was getting irritated. "I don't need sandpaper."

"Sure you do. Look how that old paint's peelin'. You've gotta sand it down before you put on the new paint."

Brian was about to tell the old man to mind his own business when he heard the phone ringing inside. After the phone call, Brian groaned.

"What's wrong?" Mother asked.

"You should paint the porch swing green," Brian mimicked. "You shouldn't wear that good shirt! You shouldn't paint without sanding first."

"Hmmm." Mother nodded. "Good advice. Go change your shirt, Brian. And you should sand off the rough spots and peeling paint. If you don't, the new paint won't last long."

"You're as critical as Mr. Walker."

"Criticism isn't always bad, Brian," explained Mother. "Often it's the sandpaper God uses to smooth rough spots in our character."

"Between you and Mr. Walker, I ought to become pretty smooth," Brian said as he went to change his shirt and look for sandpaper.

HOW ABOUT YOU? Do you resent criticism? It's a sign of spiritual maturity when you can take it with a good attitude. The Lord will often use others to show you where you should change. *B.J.W.*

TO MEMORIZE: Fools think they need no advice, but the wise listen to others. *Proverbs 12:15*

Heed constructive criticism

3 August

GOOD ADVICE

FROM THE BIBLE:

When you arrive in the land the Lord your God is giving you, be very careful not to imitate the detestable customs of the nations living there. For example, never sacrifice your son or daughter as a burnt offering. And do not let your people practice fortune-telling or sorcery, or allow them to interpret omens, or engage in witchcraft, or cast spells, or function as mediums or psychics, or call forth the spirits of the dead. Anyone who does these things is an object of horror and disgust to the Lord. It is because the other nations have done these things that the Lord your God will drive them out ahead of you. You must be blameless before the Lord your God.
DEUTERONOMY 18:9-13

Don't read horoscopes

DAN EAGERLY opened the newspaper and read his horoscope for the next day. No one else in his family read the horoscopes. In fact, Dan's father said that the Bible was against anything that tries to foretell the future. "God is the only one who knows what is in the future," Dad had said. "In the Bible, we find all the advice we need on how to live." But the horoscope fascinated Dan.

"You stand a good chance of winning an argument," Dan read in the evening paper. That sounded good to him. He had lost an argument in the neighborhood ball game just that day. He thought he touched home base before the ball got there, but the other boys said he was out.

The next day, the boys played baseball again. When Dan got up to bat, he hit the ball and ran. He got to first base just as Jim, the first baseman, yelled, "Out!"

"I am not out!" protested Dan. Remembering his horoscope, he decided he wouldn't give in until he won the argument. But Jim didn't give in either. In anger, Dan pushed Jim to the ground. The other boys took Jim's side and said Dan couldn't play anymore.

Dan walked slowly away from the ball field. *I never should have believed that dumb horoscope,* he thought. *I guess Dad's right. The Bible does give much better advice.*

HOW ABOUT YOU? Do you read your horoscope? It's a dangerous thing to do. Maybe you think you're reading it just for fun, but God wants to be our source of advice, comfort, and help. He sternly forbids the use of things like fortune-telling or witchcraft to try to find out what will happen in the future. Listen to him and leave the horoscope alone. *C.E.Y.*

TO MEMORIZE: It is better to trust the Lord than to put confidence in people. *Psalm 118:8*

4 August

NO WAVES TOO ROUGH

FROM THE BIBLE:

Those who live in the shelter of
the Most High
will find rest in the shadow of
the Almighty.
This I declare of the Lord:
He alone is my refuge, my
place of safety;
he is my God, and I am
trusting him.
For he will rescue you from
every trap
and protect you from the
fatal plague.
He will shield you with his
wings.
He will shelter you with
his feathers.
His faithful promises are your
armor and protection.
Do not be afraid of the terrors of
the night,
nor fear the dangers of the
day,
nor dread the plague that stalks
in darkness,
nor the disaster that strikes
at midday.
Though a thousand fall at your
side,
though ten thousand are dying
around you,
these evils will not touch you.
But you will see it with your
eyes;
you will see how the wicked
are punished.

PSALM 91:1-8

CALVIN STUMBLED into the water. The rolling waves cooled his warm body and relaxed his troubled mind. Because it felt so good and soothing to him, he swam out to deeper water. "I wish I could stay here forever," he sighed, "and not think about anything."

But Calvin had a lot to think about. He had a tumor on his left leg, and in two more days he would be admitted to a hospital where a specialist would perform the surgery. It wasn't known yet how serious the tumor was. Calvin's mind was filled with questions. *How would the operation go?*

His little sister, Cindy, shrieked, interrupting his thoughts.

"Daddy, I can't go swimming here!" she squealed. "The waves are too big! I don't like this ocean. It's scary!"

"Look," Dad said, "the waves aren't too rough for me. They aren't moving me. Here! Take my hand, and we'll swim together. You'll be safe."

Cindy was hesitant. Then she looked at her dad. He was strong! He would protect her! Cindy put her little hand into her daddy's big hand. Soon she was enjoying the water as it splashed around her.

Calvin swam back to Cindy. "See, Cal," she shouted. "I'm not afraid now. Daddy's holding my hand. He won't let go."

Calvin smiled at Cindy and at himself. If she could trust their father in the rolling waves, he decided he could trust his heavenly Father. The days ahead might be rough, but God would hold him and give him strength. That's all he needed to know to give him peace.

HOW ABOUT YOU? Are you facing a difficult time in your life? Are you ready to give up? Don't! Tell Jesus about your struggles. Ask him for wisdom, strength, and courage. Ask him to hold you safely through it all. He will. *J.L.H.*

TO MEMORIZE: Hold me up, and I shall be safe. *Psalm 119:117* (NKJV)

God holds you

5 August

PENGUINS AND PEOPLE

FROM THE BIBLE:

I look up to the mountains—
does my help come from there?
My help comes from the Lord,
who made the heavens and the earth!
He will not let you stumble and fall;
the one who watches over you will not sleep.
Indeed, he who watches over Israel
never tires and never sleeps.
The Lord himself watches over you!
The Lord stands beside you as your protective shade.
The sun will not hurt you by day,
nor the moon at night.
The Lord keeps you from all evil
and preserves your life.
The Lord keeps watch over you
as you come and go,
both now and forever.

PSALM 121:1-8

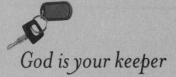

God is your keeper

DIANE WAS SO excited! She and her parents were going to the city zoo. She loved watching all the animals, but the penguins were her favorites.

The tour guide told how the zookeepers kept the penguin room cold so the birds would be comfortable. "Otherwise," explained the guide, "the birds would get sick and possibly die from the change of climate."

During family devotions that evening, Diane's father said, "Remember how careful the zookeepers are in taking care of the penguins?"

Diane nodded. "They have to have certain foods, and just the right temperature, and even special lights!"

"Right," said Dad. "God does the same thing for us. Just think what would happen if it hailed all the time, or if the temperature suddenly went from below freezing to as hot as an oven. God controls our environment because he knows what conditions we need to live in."

"I never thought of that," said Diane. "God must love us very much to take care of us so well."

"He certainly does," replied her father, smiling. "He not only controls our physical environment but also all the things that come into our lives. He is our keeper, and he allows only what is good for us, whether it seems that way to us or not."

Diane nodded. Then a twinkle came to her eye. "Hey, Dad, we should go to the zoo real often so I'll be reminded of that!"

HOW ABOUT YOU? Did you know that God keeps you day by day? He provides the air you breathe, the food and water you need, the type of environment in which you can survive. He also provides for your spiritual needs. All the things he allows in your life work together to make you the person you should be. Thank him for being your keeper. *D.S.M.*

TO MEMORIZE: The Lord is your keeper; the Lord is your shade at your right hand. *Psalm 121:5* (NKJV)

6 August

NO MISTAKE!

FROM THE BIBLE:

You made all the delicate, inner parts of my body
and knit me together in my mother's womb.
Thank you for making me so wonderfully complex!
Your workmanship is marvelous—and how well I know it.
You watched me as I was being formed in utter seclusion,
as I was woven together in the dark of the womb.
You saw me before I was born.
Every day of my life was recorded in your book.
Every moment was laid out before a single day had passed.
How precious are your thoughts about me, O God!
They are innumerable!
I can't even count them;
they outnumber the grains of sand!
And when I wake up in the morning,
you are still with me!

PSALM 139:13-18

You're not a mistake

GARY WALKED up to home plate. The pitcher threw the ball. "Strike one!" the umpire called. The next pitch went right over home plate while Gary just stood there. "Strike two!" the umpire shouted. The third time Gary tapped the ball lightly. He was out before he got halfway to first base.

"Another out!" Rob complained. "It's all because of Gary. It was a mistake to let him play ball with us."

"He *is* a mistake," Dan joined in.

Red-faced, Gary picked up his gear and ran off toward home. He was in such a hurry that he didn't even see his neighbor, Mr. Radcliffe, walking out to the mailbox. Gary collided with him. Mr. Radcliffe noticed the tears in Gary's eyes. "Hey, you seem a bit shaken," Mr. Radcliffe said. "Come inside for some lemonade."

Gary went inside and soon the incident on the ball field spilled out. "And it's true—I *am* a mistake," Gary blurted. "I never should have been born! My mother wasn't married when she had me!"

"Gary, you're not a mistake!" Mr. Radcliffe said positively. "God created you. Psalm 139 tells us that God knew you and scheduled your days before you were even born."

"Really?" Gary asked hopefully.

"Really," said Mr. Radcliffe as he poured another glass of lemonade. "Don't use the circumstances of your birth as an excuse to be less than what God intended you to be. God loves you and has a wonderful plan for your life."

HOW ABOUT YOU? Don't ever call yourself a mistake! Your birth was no surprise to God. You are very special to him. You aren't responsible for your parents' actions, but you are responsible for the way you live your life. Make it pleasing to God. *J.L.H.*

TO MEMORIZE: Your eyes saw my unformed body. All the days ordained for me were written in your book before one of them came to be. *Psalm 139:16* (NIV)

7 August

THE FALL

FROM THE BIBLE:

So why do you condemn another Christian? Why do you look down on another Christian? Remember, each of us will stand personally before the judgment seat of God. For the Scriptures say,

" 'As surely as I live,' says the Lord,
'every knee will bow to me
and every tongue will confess allegiance to God.' "

Yes, each of us will have to give a personal account to God. So don't condemn each other anymore. Decide instead to live in such a way that you will not put an obstacle in another Christian's path.

ROMANS 14:10-13

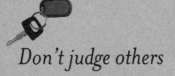

Don't judge others

"I DON'T THINK Anna is a Christian at all," declared Jason as he rode his bike up the driveway. "In fact, I'm sure she's not. She lied to me!" He turned his bike around.

Mom looked up from her flower garden. "I'm sorry to hear that," she replied. "But don't you think you're making an awfully hasty judgment?"

A moment later, his howl pierced the air as he skidded and fell. "Oh, my elbow hurts," he groaned.

"I'm sure it does," sympathized Mom. "Let's go fix it up."

When Jason and his mother went back out a little later, Jason got ready to mount his bike. "Oh," said Mom, taking hold of the handlebars, "you're not going to try to ride again, are you?"

"Sure," Jason replied.

"But, Jason," protested Mom, "I just don't think you can ride. Tell you what—let's put the training wheels back on."

"Mom!" Jason was indignant. "Just because I fell doesn't mean I can't ride!"

"Hmmm," said Mom thoughtfully, "slipping and falling with your bike doesn't mean you're not really a bike rider?" Jason shook his head.

"Well, guess what?" Mom said. "Slipping and falling in your Christian life doesn't mean you're not really a Christian either. It does mean you need to confess what you've done and ask God to forgive you." Mom smiled at Jason. "But be careful not to judge people. Instead, help them get back on track."

HOW ABOUT YOU? Are you disappointed in someone who says he's a Christian? Don't judge the person who slips and falls into sin. Leave that to God. Pray for that person. Let him know you love him, though you don't like what he did. Let him know that God will forgive and you will too. *H.W.M.*

TO MEMORIZE: Why do you condemn another Christian? . . . Remember, each of us will stand personally before the judgment seat of God. *Romans 14:10*

8 August

WRONG CONCLUSION

ABIGAIL AND STACI slowly walked past Mr. Mitchell's rundown house. Empty wine bottles could be spotted on the porch. Mr. Mitchell was an alcoholic.

"I bet Mr. Mitchell doesn't have any friends," said Abigail.

"Not unless they're drunks too," said Staci.

At that moment Mr. Mitchell and another man walked out the front door, laughing. "Hey!" exclaimed Abigail. "That's Mr. Horton! Could Mr. Horton be an alcoholic, too?"

"He must be if he's a friend of Mr. Mitchell!" replied Abigail. Staci nodded in agreement.

"Bye, John. I'll see you tomorrow then!" Mr. Horton waved to Abigail and Staci. "Hi, girls! What's up?"

"We're just going for a walk," mumbled Staci.

"We didn't know you and Mr. Mitchell were friends," blurted Abigail.

Mr. Horton smiled broadly. "I've tried to be a friend to him, and that has given me the chance to tell him about Jesus," he said. "Just this morning he asked Jesus to save him and forgive his sins! What's more, Mr. Mitchell said he'd be in church tomorrow. Praise the Lord!"

Abigail knew she had to explain. "When we saw you at his house, we thought you must be a drunk too. I mean, it just seemed like if you were there . . ." She didn't know how to finish.

"I see," said Mr. Horton. "Let this experience be a reminder that you should never jump to conclusions about other people, girls. But now that you know the truth, just praise the Lord! See you tomorrow!"

HOW ABOUT YOU? Are you quick to criticize others? Do you make judgments before you know all the facts? It's better to put off forming an opinion until you're sure you know the whole story. Give others the benefit of the doubt, and leave the judging to the Lord. *V.L.R.*

TO MEMORIZE: There is one Lawgiver, who is able to save and to destroy. Who are you to judge another? *James 4:12* (NKJV)

FROM THE BIBLE:

So humble yourselves before God. Resist the Devil, and he will flee from you. Draw close to God, and God will draw close to you. Wash your hands, you sinners; purify your hearts, you hypocrites. Let there be tears for the wrong things you have done. Let there be sorrow and deep grief. Let there be sadness instead of laughter, and gloom instead of joy. When you bow down before the Lord and admit your dependence on him, he will lift you up and give you honor.

Don't speak evil against each other, my dear brothers and sisters. If you criticize each other and condemn each other, then you are criticizing and condemning God's law. But you are not a judge who can decide whether the law is right or wrong. Your job is to obey it. God alone, who made the law, can rightly judge among us. He alone has the power to save or to destroy. So what right do you have to condemn your neighbor?

JAMES 4:7-12

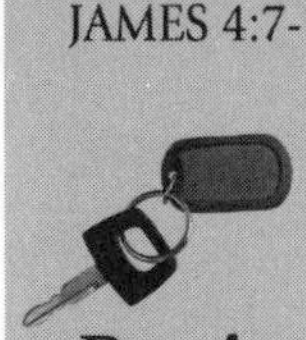

Don't jump to conclusions

9 August

THE SUNDAY SCHOOL LESSON

FROM THE BIBLE:

Stop judging others, and you will not be judged. For others will treat you as you treat them. Whatever measure you use in judging others, it will be used to measure how you are judged. And why worry about a speck in your friend's eye when you have a log in your own? How can you think of saying, "Let me help you get rid of that speck in your eye," when you can't see past the log in your own eye? Hypocrite! First get rid of the log from your own eye; then perhaps you will see well enough to deal with the speck in your friend's eye.

MATTHEW 7:1-5

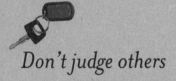

Don't judge others

AS STEVE WALKED out of the Sunday school classroom, he was glad Mr. Sanders had taught the lesson about not judging others. Some of the kids were really guilty of doing that.

Like Theresa, who was always raising her hand to answer all the questions. She probably thought that made her a better Christian than anybody else.

Or Shelley, who always dressed in trendy clothes. She probably thought the rest of the kids were hicks because nobody else wore such expensive clothes.

Or Scott, who never listened in class or brought his Bible. But his dad was the chief of police, and Scott probably thought he was the best.

Even Tom, Steve's best friend, would whisper all through Sunday school if anyone would listen. Tom probably thought he deserved to be the center of attention.

Wow! Steve thought as he settled into his seat in church. *That lesson could be good for almost anyone in my class.* He took a snapshot of the class from his Bible. *It would even be good for . . .* He stopped suddenly as his eyes fell on his own face smiling back at him from the picture. *Me?* He blushed as he thought about it. Ever since he had left the classroom, he had been judging his classmates. He had forgotten that he had plenty of faults of his own. He decided to get his own problem—a critical attitude—under control before he worried about the faults of anybody else!

HOW ABOUT YOU? Do you sometimes see all the faults of others and none of your own? In today's Scripture, Jesus is simply teaching that you must check your own life before you try to straighten out others. First take care of the sins in your own life. You may find there's no time left to judge anyone else. *L.M.W.*

TO MEMORIZE: For with what judgment you judge, you will be judged. *Matthew 7:2* (NKJV)

A LIVING WITNESS

KATHY ARRIVED home from Bible camp determined to be a witness. She promptly told her family that the best thing about camp was that she had become a Christian. "A Christian?" exclaimed her sister, Kim. "Aren't we already Christians?"

"You aren't a Christian just because you call yourself one," began Kathy.

"Kathy, if you want to be religious, that's fine," Dad told her, "but don't ask us to join you."

That evening Dad said that their family reunion was next Sunday. "Sunday!" exclaimed Kathy. "I can't go! I don't want to skip church!"

"If this religion of yours means hurting your family, we want none of it!" growled Dad.

Kathy felt bad because she had offended her family. She talked to Pastor Randall about it. "It's great that you're witnessing, Kathy," he said, "but guard against a 'holier-than-thou' attitude. Witnessing is more than talking. You must also be a living witness. Let your actions and attitude show that Jesus has changed you."

Kathy nodded. "I'll try again."

Kathy found many opportunities to be a living witness. She willingly gave in when she and Kim disagreed about which game to play. She mowed the lawn without being told. She even gave up going to play volleyball with the church youth group in order to help Kim finish a school project that was due the next day. As they finished, Kim turned to her. "I'll go with you to church this week," she said. "I have to see what Christianity is all about. It sure changed you."

HOW ABOUT YOU? Have you heard that "actions speak louder than words"? Attitudes also speak louder than words. Watch yourself today. Is your attitude cheerful, humble, and willing? If not, ask God to help you make the needed changes, so you may be a living witness for him. *J.L.H.*

TO MEMORIZE: Live wisely among those who are not Christians, and make the most of every opportunity. *Colossians 4:5*

FROM THE BIBLE:

Since God chose you to be the holy people whom he loves, you must clothe yourselves with tenderhearted mercy, kindness, humility, gentleness, and patience. You must make allowance for each other's faults and forgive the person who offends you. Remember, the Lord forgave you, so you must forgive others. And the most important piece of clothing you must wear is love. Love is what binds us all together in perfect harmony. And let the peace that comes from Christ rule in your hearts. For as members of one body you are all called to live in peace. And always be thankful.

Let the words of Christ, in all their richness, live in your hearts and make you wise. Use his words to teach and counsel each other. Sing psalms and hymns and spiritual songs to God with thankful hearts. And whatever you do or say, let it be as a representative of the Lord Jesus, all the while giving thanks through him to God the Father.

COLOSSIANS 3:12-17

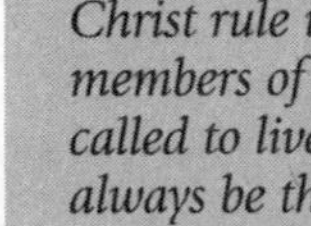

Witness through attitudes

11 August

THE UNFINISHED MODEL
(PART 1)

FROM THE BIBLE:

And I saw a great white throne, and I saw the one who was sitting on it. The earth and sky fled from his presence, but they found no place to hide. I saw the dead, both great and small, standing before God's throne. And the books were opened, including the Book of Life. And the dead were judged according to the things written in the books, according to what they had done. The sea gave up the dead in it, and death and the grave gave up the dead in them. They were all judged according to their deeds. And death and the grave were thrown into the lake of fire. This is the second death—the lake of fire. And anyone whose name was not found recorded in the Book of Life was thrown into the lake of fire.
REVELATION 20:11-15

There's life after death

"HAPPY BIRTHDAY, Micah!" exclaimed Anita, handing a gift to her brother. Micah looked pleased when he opened it and discovered a model airplane kit.

"Hurry up, kids," Mom exclaimed impatiently. "Your dad is here to take you both for the weekend. You better take your Bibles like he always wants you to!"

Anita sighed, hating the reminder that her mom and dad were getting divorced.

Dad tooted the horn. Anita grabbed her suitcase and math book. She sighed again. If she didn't understand fractions soon, she wouldn't pass!

That evening, Anita saw Micah's model airplane in the wastebasket. "It's no good," Micah grumbled when she asked about it. "The pieces don't fit!"

In bed, Anita cried and cried, brooding over her hurts and problems. Getting up to get a tissue, she slipped on a throw rug and tumbled down the stairs. "Oh, my leg!" she screamed in pain.

Her dad and brother rushed her to the hospital. The next day, Anita wore a cast on her leg. She shared her feelings with Dad. "I've been crying about everything," she sobbed, "and God doesn't seem to care."

"Anita," said Dad gently, "you know this life isn't all there is. Jesus does care. For those who trust in him, he promises life after death in heaven, where there will be no more tears."

Anita looked up. "Daddy, will you help me make sure I'll go to heaven?"

HOW ABOUT YOU? Have you ever thought things were so awful that life was hardly worth living? Have you cried and cried over your problems? If you're a Christian, Jesus promises to take you with him one day where there will be no more crying. If you haven't done so, won't you accept Jesus today and trust him with your life? *J.L.H.*

TO MEMORIZE: He will wipe every tear from their eyes. There will be no more death or mourning or crying or pain. *Revelation 21:4* (NIV)

THE UNFINISHED MODEL
(PART 2)

FROM THE BIBLE:

All honor to the God and Father of our Lord Jesus Christ, for it is by his boundless mercy that God has given us the privilege of being born again. Now we live with a wonderful expectation because Jesus Christ rose again from the dead. For God has reserved a priceless inheritance for his children. It is kept in heaven for you, pure and undefiled, beyond the reach of change and decay. And God, in his mighty power, will protect you until you receive this salvation, because you are trusting him. It will be revealed on the last day for all to see. So be truly glad! There is wonderful joy ahead, even though it is necessary for you to endure many trials for a while.

These trials are only to test your faith, to show that it is strong and pure. It is being tested as fire tests and purifies gold—and your faith is far more precious to God than mere gold. So if your faith remains strong after being tried by fiery trials, it will bring you much praise and glory and honor on the day when Jesus Christ is revealed to the whole world.

1 PETER 1:3-7

TWO DAYS after Anita asked Jesus to save her and take charge of her life, she was again talking things over with her father. "I'm glad I'm a Christian now," she told him, "but I still feel so discouraged. I still can't do fractions, and you and Mom are still getting divorced. Now I have this cast from falling off my bike and—oh, I don't know! Everything still seems hopeless."

"Anita, things may not always go like we want them to," Dad replied, "but life isn't hopeless! God has a plan for us. And I love you very much. Your mother loves you, too, and so does Micah."

As Dad finished speaking, Micah walked in the door. He held something behind his back. "Surprise!" he exclaimed, holding out the model Anita had given him. It was finished. "I just got impatient when I couldn't get it together right away," he told her sheepishly. "I'm sorry. Doesn't it look great now?"

Anita was smiling when Micah left. Dad smiled too. "Micah's plane does look good," he said, "and your life can be good too. Anita, the pieces are all there, and with God's help they will work out in time. God is the perfect Creator."

"I guess I don't want to give up too soon," admitted Anita. "I'm ready to work at it again—with God's help and yours."

HOW ABOUT YOU? Are there times when you feel like everything and everybody is against you? That isn't true. God loves you very much. Ask him to help you. There are others who care, too. Seek a Christian adult—perhaps a parent, pastor, or Sunday school teacher—to help you work out your problems. You are very important to them and to God. *J.L.H.*

TO MEMORIZE: "I know the plans I have for you," says the Lord. "They are plans for good and not for disaster, to give you a future and a hope."
Jeremiah 29:11

God gives hope

13 August

ONLY BUBBLES

FROM THE BIBLE:

For no one can lay any other foundation than the one we already have—Jesus Christ. Now anyone who builds on that foundation may use gold, silver, jewels, wood, hay, or straw. But there is going to come a time of testing at the judgment day to see what kind of work each builder has done. Everyone's work will be put through the fire to see whether or not it keeps its value. If the work survives the fire, that builder will receive a reward. But if the work is burned up, the builder will suffer great loss. The builders themselves will be saved, but like someone escaping through a wall of flames.

1 CORINTHIANS 3:11-15

"Things" don't last

"STOP CRYING, Jill. I'll blow more bubbles for you." Deborah dipped the red plastic wand into the soap solution, then blew gently. Her little sister Jill clapped her hands and giggled when the colorful bubbles appeared, but as they drifted away or broke, she began crying again.

Deborah sighed as her mother came out on the porch. "Jill cries whenever the bubbles break," Deborah complained. "She doesn't realize that bubbles are pretty but they don't last!"

"I wonder if God feels that way sometimes," Mom said, picking up Jill to soothe her.

"What do you mean?" asked Deborah.

"Remember how badly I felt when I broke that antique bowl last week?" she said. "God's Word tells us that some of the things we treasure most on earth are just like bubbles. In God's sight they're worthless, but we care about them so much! We complain and cry when they are gone."

"I think I understand," responded Deborah. "I cried when I got my hair cut. That was silly because it grew back."

"And remember how upset Dad and I became when we loaned our new car to Aunt Dori and she put a dent in it?" reminded Mom. "My, how easy it is to think of 'bubbles' that we cry over. But it's only the loving deeds we do for Christ that will be of value in eternity."

HOW ABOUT YOU? What do you value most in life? Your bicycle? Some jewelry? A favorite toy? God has given you many things to use and enjoy, but don't spend all your time and energy on "bubbles" that are going to burst and disappear. Remember the old saying "Only one life, 'twill soon be past. Only what's done for Christ will last." *P.R.*

TO MEMORIZE: After all, we didn't bring anything with us when we came into the world, and we certainly cannot carry anything with us when we die. *1 Timothy 6:7*

BOSS BOYS?

FROM THE BIBLE:

Brothers and sisters, we urge you to warn those who are lazy. Encourage those who are timid. Take tender care of those who are weak. Be patient with everyone.

See that no one pays back evil for evil, but always try to do good to each other and to everyone else.

Always be joyful. Keep on praying. No matter what happens, always be thankful, for this is God's will for you who belong to Christ Jesus.

Do not stifle the Holy Spirit. Do not scoff at prophecies, but test everything that is said. Hold on to what is good. Keep away from every kind of evil.

Now may the God of peace make you holy in every way, and may your whole spirit and soul and body be kept blameless until that day when our Lord Jesus Christ comes again.

1 THESSALONIANS 5:14-23

"I WAS ELECTED to the Boss Boys Club," Barry proudly announced one night. "They have meetings and talk about stuff and do things together."

"Better check them out before you get involved with them," suggested Dad.

Barry shrugged. "They sound good to me." He looked at the plate of food Mom set before him. "What is this?"

"It's called Super Supper," said Mom. "Sounds good, doesn't it?"

"Sounds OK, but I'll check it out and see for myself," insisted Barry. He took a very small bite, then tried a little more. "It's good," he said, "but I don't like the mushrooms."

"I gave you only a few," said Mom. "If you want another helping, you can avoid them."

"You 'checked it out' so you could take the good and leave the bad," observed Dad. "That's just what the Bible tells us to do. In 1 Thessalonians, Paul says to test—or check out—everything. I think Paul is warning us about jumping into things we haven't checked out," said Dad.

"Like the Boss Boys," said Barry.

The following evening Barry was rather quiet. "I learned that the Boss Boys aren't so cool," he said. "I talked to one of them, and he let it slip that they buy cigarettes and alcohol with part of the club money. I'm glad I found out before I turned over half of my allowance for dues."

"I'm glad you took the apostle Paul's advice," said Dad.

HOW ABOUT YOU? Are you so eager to join a club, read a popular book, watch a certain movie, or buy a best-selling CD that you plunge ahead without checking to see if it will do you harm or good? Will it help you love the Lord, or will it draw you away from him? Check it out. Keep only the good. *H.W.M.*

TO MEMORIZE: Test everything. Hold on to the good. Avoid every kind of evil.
1 Thessalonians 5:21-22 (NIV)

Test things; keep the good

15 August

I DON'T WANT TO GO!

FROM THE BIBLE:

But on the way, Naomi said to her two daughters-in-law, "Go back to your mothers' homes instead of coming with me. And may the Lord reward you for your kindness to your husbands and to me. May the Lord bless you with the security of another marriage." Then she kissed them good-bye, and they all broke down and wept. . . .

And Orpah kissed her mother-in-law good-bye. But Ruth insisted on staying with Naomi. "See," Naomi said to her, "your sister-in-law has gone back to her people and to her gods. You should do the same."

But Ruth replied, "Don't ask me to leave you and turn back. I will go wherever you go and live wherever you live. Your people will be my people, and your God will be my God. I will die where you die and will be buried there. May the Lord punish me severely if I allow anything but death to separate us!" So when Naomi saw that Ruth had made up her mind to go with her, she stopped urging her.

RUTH 1:8-18

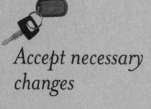

Accept necessary changes

"ENGLAND!" Amanda was stunned. "We're really moving to England?"

"That's right, honey," said Dad. "The company wants to start a branch overseas, and they've chosen me to get it started. We'll be living in England for at least five years."

Amanda looked out the living room window at the familiar street. She had lived in this same house ever since she was a baby. She'd have to leave her friends, her school, and her church. "I don't think I want to move." Tears trickled down Amanda's cheeks.

Amanda's dad put his arm around her. "You do have a choice," he said. "You can be upset and bitter about moving, or you can look at it as a special experience. It's up to you. Remember, too, that no matter where we move, God will be with us, and he promises to take care of us."

Amanda thought about what her dad had said. She knew they were going to England whether she liked it or not, so she might as well choose to like it. She certainly didn't want to be bitter and unhappy for five years! Amanda called her best friend, Julie, that very night. "Guess what! We're moving to England!" she said.

"How neat!" Julie squealed after Amanda explained. "You can send me lots of letters, and I can put the stamps in my stamp collection!"

Amanda smiled. Moving to England could be a good adventure. She was glad she had changed her attitude.

HOW ABOUT YOU? Does your family move a lot? Have you had to change schools? It isn't easy to move away from everything familiar. Remember that the Lord promises to be with you anytime or anywhere. Try to see the advantages of living in different places. Learn to enjoy the unique experiences and the wide array of friends. Be content wherever God places you. *L.M.W.*

TO MEMORIZE: I have learned to be content whatever the circumstances. *Philippians 4:11* (NIV)

16 August

BLANK PAPER

FROM THE BIBLE:

We live our lives beneath your wrath.
We end our lives with a groan.
Seventy years are given to us!
Some may even reach eighty.
But even the best of these years are filled with pain and trouble;
soon they disappear, and we are gone.
Who can comprehend the power of your anger?
Your wrath is as awesome as the fear you deserve.
Teach us to make the most of our time,
so that we may grow in wisdom.
O Lord, come back to us!
How long will you delay?
Take pity on your servants!
Satisfy us in the morning with your unfailing love,
so we may sing for joy to the end of our lives.
Give us gladness in proportion to our former misery!
Replace the evil years with good.

PSALM 90:9-15

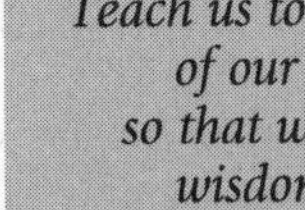

Don't waste time

"HEATHER," said Mom as she stood in the doorway of her daughter's room one Saturday, "you've spent half the day in here just wasting time. How about doing something constructive, like writing a letter to Grandma Nelson?"

Heather went off to find some writing paper. A few minutes later, Mom heard Heather scolding two-year-old Jody. "Jody scribbled on all the pages of my new writing tablet," Heather exclaimed. "They're ruined!"

Heather flipped through the tablet and found one clean page. "Here's one Jody missed. It's still good," she said.

But Mom shook her head. "No, the way it is now, it's really no better than the ones Jody scribbled on," she said.

"What do you mean?" asked Heather.

"It's empty," Mom answered. "Nothing has been done with it that is of any real value to anyone."

Heather grinned. "I'll use it to write Grandma."

"Good." Mom smiled. "A day of your life is like a blank piece of paper, honey. You can use it thoughtlessly with silly or harmful activities, and it would be like these pages Jody scribbled on. Or you can waste it by simply neglecting to use it for anything worthwhile."

"Like I wasted my morning," said Heather thoughtfully. "Well, the day's not over yet, so I still have time to make something out of it. I'll start by writing that letter."

HOW ABOUT YOU? Do you waste time with unnecessary activities or through laziness? If you're a Christian, you should be "making the most of every opportunity." Use your time carefully in ways that please the Lord. This may include being friendly, helping your mother, studying God's Word, reading a good book, getting needed rest, witnessing to a friend. Start now to make each day of your life worthwhile! *S.L.K.*

TO MEMORIZE: Be very careful, then, how you live—not as unwise but as wise, making the most of every opportunity, because the days are evil. *Ephesians 5:15-16* (NIV)

17 August

OVER AND OVER

FROM THE BIBLE:

These are the proverbs of Solomon, David's son, king of Israel.

The purpose of these proverbs is to teach people wisdom and discipline, and to help them understand wise sayings. Through these proverbs, people will receive instruction in discipline, good conduct, and doing what is right, just, and fair. These proverbs will make the simpleminded clever. They will give knowledge and purpose to young people.

Let those who are wise listen to these proverbs and become even wiser. And let those who understand receive guidance by exploring the depth of meaning in these proverbs, parables, wise sayings, and riddles.

Fear of the Lord is the beginning of knowledge. Only fools despise wisdom and discipline.

Listen, my child, to what your father teaches you. Don't neglect your mother's teaching.

PROVERBS 1:1-8

Learn from repetition

"COURTNEY!" called Mother. "Come in and do your Sunday school lesson. You've been working with King for an hour already!"

Courtney frowned. "If I don't train King every chance I get, he won't be ready for the show next week," she told her mother. "Besides, it's the story about Daniel and the lions. I've heard it a million times!"

"I don't think it's been quite that many. It won't take that long, and you may be surprised—you might learn something new."

Courtney grumbled as she plunked down at the table with her Sunday school book and her Bible. Fifteen minutes later, she was done and back outside with King.

That evening, Cindy talked about how well King was learning. "I guess it's because I've been teaching him since he was a puppy. I've made him do things over and over until he got them right."

"You know," said Mother, "like King, you have been taught things since you were young. But, just like King, you have to be taught things over and over. Everything you're learning in church now will be helpful to you in later years."

"So it doesn't really matter if they give us the same lesson more than once?" asked Courtney.

Mother laughed. "You give King the same lessons every day!" she said.

"Yeah, you're right," responded Courtney. "I think I'll do my lesson over this evening. I did it pretty fast this afternoon; maybe I missed something."

HOW ABOUT YOU? Do you get tired of hearing the same Bible stories over and over? Remember, you seldom learn all there is to know by hearing it only once. Thank God for parents and teachers, who patiently teach you God's Word. If you learn your lessons well, you'll be rewarded by being able to use them in later years. *D.S.M.*

TO MEMORIZE: Apply your heart to instruction and your ears to words of knowledge. *Proverbs 23:12*

18 August

IT DIDN'T JUST HAPPEN

FROM THE BIBLE:

And God said, "Let the waters swarm with fish and other life. Let the skies be filled with birds of every kind." So God created great sea creatures and every sort of fish and every kind of bird. And God saw that it was good. Then God blessed them, saying, "Let the fish multiply and fill the oceans. Let the birds increase and fill the earth." . . .

And God said, "Let the earth bring forth every kind of animal—livestock, small animals, and wildlife." And so it was. . . . And God saw that it was good.

Then God said, "Let us make people in our image, to be like ourselves. They will be masters over all life—the fish in the sea, the birds in the sky, and all the livestock, wild animals, and small animals."

So God created people in his own image;
God patterned them after himself;
male and female he created them.

God blessed them and told them, "Multiply and fill the earth and subdue it. Be masters over the fish and birds and all the animals."

GENESIS 1:20-28

BECKY'S SCIENCE teacher didn't believe in the biblical record of creation. He told the class that all animals evolved from lower forms of life. When Becky asked where the lower forms of life had come from, Mr. Matthews shrugged. "They just happened." Becky believed God had created the heavens and earth, but how could she convince her teacher?

The next day, Becky brought a beautiful carved cardinal that she had received as a gift. When it was time for science class, Becky put the wooden bird on her desk. The other students admired it, and even Mr. Matthews came back to where she was sitting and looked at the cardinal. "Whoever carved this bird certainly knew what he was doing," he observed. "This is beautiful! Who did it?"

Becky shrugged. "Nobody. I woke up this morning, and there it was. It just happened!"

The teacher looked surprised. "You mean you don't know who made it?"

"Nobody made it. I told you, it just happened!" insisted Becky.

Mr. Matthews raised his eyebrows. "Sure it did," he said sarcastically. "What are you getting at?"

Becky grinned at him. "Mr. Matthews, you'd think I was silly if I really believed that no one made this wooden cardinal, yet you told me that no one made the real cardinals."

Mr. Matthews gave her a thoughtful look. Becky silently thanked the Lord that she had at least made the teacher think.

HOW ABOUT YOU? Do your teachers sometimes teach things that go against God's Word? God did create all things, including all life. The Bible teaches that, and you can see evidence of God's creation in this beautiful world around you. Just as it takes a talented artist to create a pretty picture, it took the Master Designer, God, to create the awesome world in which you live. *L.M.W.*

TO MEMORIZE: By my great power I have made the earth and all its people and every animal. *Jeremiah 27:5*

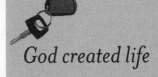

God created life

19 August

EVERYWHERE AT ONCE

FROM THE BIBLE:

O Lord, you have examined my heart
and know everything about me.
You know when I sit down or stand up.
You know my every thought when far away.
You chart the path ahead of me
and tell me where to stop and rest.
Every moment you know where I am.
You know what I am going to say
even before I say it, Lord.
You both precede and follow me.
You place your hand of blessing on my head.
Such knowledge is too wonderful for me,
too great for me to know!
I can never escape from your spirit!
I can never get away from your presence!
If I go up to heaven, you are there;
if I go down to the place of the dead, you are there.
If I ride the wings of the morning,
if I dwell by the farthest oceans,
even there your hand will guide me,
and your strength will support me.

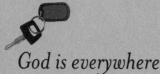

PSALM 139:1-10

God is everywhere

ALAN AND ROB were discussing their Sunday school lesson before lunch. "I believe in God as much as you do," Alan declared, "but if he were everywhere, we would see him."

"He's here just the same," insisted Rob. "Like Mr. Malloy said, He's onima . . . ominen . . ."

"Omnipresent." Dad helped him out. "Mom has dinner ready, so let's not keep her waiting." After giving thanks, Dad turned to Alan. "Now, what was the disagreement about?"

"Oh, I just think too scientifically to believe that God is everywhere at once," Alan said smugly. He changed the subject. "Can we listen to Children's Bible Hour while we eat? Please?"

"Sure." Mom smiled. "But first, Mr. Science, tell me what makes it possible to hear people on the radio? We can't see them."

Alan grinned. "No, not unless they're on TV," he agreed. "You see, there are radio waves, or sound waves, in the air—picture waves, too, and—"

"You don't mean right here in this room, do you?" interrupted Dad, waving his arms. "I can't see any. I can't feel any either. You must mean they're inside the radio and TV sets."

"Nope, they're all around you," stated Alan.

"Maybe we should skip Children's Bible Hour today," Mom suggested. "That way we won't use up all those sound waves and keep others from listening."

"Oh, Mom," laughed Alan, "Those same sound waves are everywhere."

"Just like God!" interjected Rob suddenly. "He's here and everywhere all at once."

HOW ABOUT YOU? Is it hard to understand that God is omnipresent—everywhere at once? This is part of his greatness. You cannot escape him. He is there when you tell a lie. He is with you when you're afraid. He is present when you're lonely. What a great God! *H.W.M.*

TO MEMORIZE: Where can I go from your Spirit? Where can I flee from your presence? *Psalm 139:7* (NIV)

THE ANSWERED PRAYER

FROM THE BIBLE:

Dear brothers and sisters, what's the use of saying you have faith if you don't prove it by your actions? That kind of faith can't save anyone. Suppose you see a brother or sister who needs food or clothing, and you say, "Well, good-bye and God bless you; stay warm and eat well"—but then you don't give that person any food or clothing. What good does that do?

So you see, it isn't enough just to have faith. Faith that doesn't show itself by good deeds is no faith at all—it is dead and useless.

Now someone may argue, "Some people have faith; others have good deeds." I say, "I can't see your faith if you don't have good deeds, but I will show you my faith through my good deeds."

JAMES 2:14-18

Help one another

EMILY WAS TRYING on her new school clothes when Mother came in. "This dress is my favorite of all my new clothes," Emily said. "And I love these new shoes."

Mother smiled. "I'm glad you like them. Now come on. It's Joey's bedtime, and we haven't had our family prayer time yet."

When Dad asked for prayer requests, Emily said, "Let's pray that Sheryl will get some new shoes. She's worn the same worn-out, old shoes all summer. I know they're the only ones she has."

As Emily prayed for Sheryl, she had a funny feeling that she was forgetting something. She still had that feeling as she put her new clothes and shoes in the closet. Even when she crawled into bed, the feeling stayed with her.

Emily screwed up her forehead and stared into the dark, trying to remember what she was forgetting. She reviewed the day, starting with breakfast and their daily Bible reading. "Suppose you see a brother or sister who needs food or clothing, and you say, 'Well, good-bye and God bless you; stay warm and eat well'—but then you don't give that person any food or clothing. What good does that do?" Dad had read.

Emily sat right up in bed and laughed. She jumped out of bed and ran into the living room. "Mother, God wants me to answer my own prayer and buy Sheryl's shoes with my baby-sitting money."

Mother looked surprised, then smiled as she said, "Why, Emily, what a generous idea! We'll go shopping tomorrow."

HOW ABOUT YOU? Are you asking God to do something that you can do yourself? God often uses people to answer prayers, and he may even use you to answer your own prayers. Be ready to obey if God prompts you to do something. *B.J.W.*

TO MEMORIZE: Whenever we have the opportunity, we should do good to everyone, especially to our Christian brothers and sisters. *Galatians 6:10*

21 August

A TIME TO FORGET

FROM THE BIBLE:

There is a time for everything,
a season for every activity
under heaven.
A time to be born and a
time to die.
A time to plant and a time
to harvest.
A time to kill and a time to heal.
A time to tear down and a
time to rebuild.
A time to cry and a time
to laugh.
A time to grieve and a
time to dance.
A time to scatter stones and a
time to gather stones.
A time to embrace and a
time to turn away.
A time to search and a
time to lose.
A time to keep and a
time to throw away.
A time to tear and a time
to mend.
A time to be quiet and
a time to speak up.
A time to love and a time
to hate.
A time for war and a
time for peace.
ECCLESIASTES 3:1-8

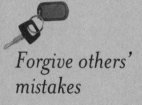

Forgive others' mistakes

"MOM, GUESS what I just heard about our new neighbors? The dad just got out of prison!" Before his mother could reply, Mark rushed on. "He stole a whole lot of money from his employer, and he had to spend five years in prison! I wonder if we should tell Mr. Wilson that he has a thief working for him."

"I'm sure Mr. Wilson knows all about Mr. Smith," Mom replied calmly.

Mark's eyes snapped. "I'm going to be more careful about locking up my bicycle. I told the other guys to watch theirs, too."

"Mark, you should not be talking about Mr. Smith to others. You don't really know anything about it," Mom scolded. "Now, are you going to play at Nathan's?"

"Yeah." Mark nodded. Then he ran down the hall to his big brother's room. As Mom followed she heard him ask, "Brad, can I take your telescope over to Nathan's?"

"No. I can't trust you," snapped Brad. "You lost my calculator last month."

"But I paid you for it," Mark reminded him.

"Yeah," admitted Brad, "but if you lose my telescope or break it, it'll take you months to pay for it."

"But, Brad," wailed Mark, "it's not fair to hold that one mistake against me forever."

Mom spoke quickly. "Neither is it fair to hold Mr. Smith's mistake against him," she said. "He has paid for it. Jesus said if we want mercy, we must be merciful. If we want to be forgiven, we must be forgiving."

HOW ABOUT YOU? When Jesus forgives us for our sins, he forgets them. Is there something about someone that you need to forget? Then do it. How? Stop talking about it and soon you will forget it too. *B.J.W.*

TO MEMORIZE: I—yes, I alone—am the one who blots out your sins for my own sake and will never think of them again. *Isaiah 43:25*

22 August

WHAT GOD WON'T SHARE

FROM THE BIBLE:

Don't brag about tomorrow, since you don't know what the day will bring.

Don't praise yourself; let others do it! . . .

As the Scriptures say, "The person who wishes to boast should boast only of what the Lord has done."

When people boast about themselves, it doesn't count for much. But when the Lord commends someone, that's different!

PROVERBS 27:1-2;
2 CORINTHIANS 10:17-18

Give God the glory

". . . AND THANK YOU, Lord, that the guys seemed so convicted by what I said when I witnessed to them at school," prayed Ryan in his Sunday school class. "Amen."

Several boys exchanged glances. Dan nudged Kyle. "I timed him," he whispered. "He prayed for three minutes—and all about his wonderful witnessing."

Their teacher, Mr. Burton, asked for any announcements. Ryan jumped up. "Next week at school we're supposed to give an oral report on our favorite book, so I'm going to do mine on the Bible. I'm sure I'll be a great witness."

After class Mr. Burton called Ryan aside. "I'm glad to see your enthusiasm for witnessing," he said, "but don't brag when you tell how the Lord is using you. Talk more about Jesus, less about yourself."

But during the next week, Ryan spent more time talking about the terrific witness his book report would be than he spent working on the report. When he gave the report, he stumbled miserably through it. "Next time, talk about something more familiar to you," his teacher suggested. Ryan blushed with shame.

The following Sunday, Ryan talked to Mr. Burton. "Doesn't God want me to be a good witness?"

"Yes," said Mr. Burton, "but he wants you to glorify *him,* not yourself," he said. "Perhaps you just needed a lesson in humility."

Ryan agreed. "I'll try to remember that I'm just the instrument. God does the real work."

HOW ABOUT YOU? Are you ever tempted to brag about some good work you've done—or plan to do—for the Lord? Good things done to impress others or to make you feel important often end in failure. It's an honor and a privilege to be used of God, but the glory belongs to him. It's one thing God won't share! *S.L.K.*

TO MEMORIZE: I am the Lord; that is my name! I will not give my glory to anyone else. *Isaiah 42:8*

23 August

CALM IN THE STORM

FROM THE BIBLE:

But now, O Israel, the Lord who created you says: "Do not be afraid, for I have ransomed you. I have called you by name; you are mine. When you go through deep waters and great trouble, I will be with you. When you go through rivers of difficulty, you will not drown! When you walk through the fire of oppression, you will not be burned up; the flames will not consume you. For I am the Lord, your God, the Holy One of Israel, your Savior. I gave Egypt, Ethiopia, and Seba as a ransom for your freedom."
ISAIAH 43:1-3

Trusting God brings peace

AS RAIN PATTERED against Dana's bedroom window, two big tears dampened her pillow. The storm inside her heart seemed far greater than the one outside. Her dad had lost his job and money was very tight for her family. They were worried that they might have to sell their home.

A few minutes later, Dana heard her door opening, and her mother came in. "Is the storm bothering you, honey?" Mom asked.

Dana sniffed. "No, I hardly noticed it," she said.

Mom smiled. "That's good. When you were small, you were terribly afraid of lightning."

"I was?" asked Dana.

Mom sat in the rocker next to the bed. "When there was a bad storm, I used to come and sit in this chair. Just having me here seemed to make your fears go away."

Dana looked at her mom and grinned. "I'll be OK tonight."

"I know you will," replied Mom as she stood up. "I know how upset you've been lately, and I've been praying that God's presence will help you through this tough time. He'll make sure the storms of life never really hurt you."

After Mom left, Dana looked at the empty rocking chair. She tried to imagine the Lord sitting there, watching over her during this difficult time. Suddenly she knew that even though the problems in her life were still there, she could trust God to take care of her. Dana rolled over and was soon sound asleep.

HOW ABOUT YOU? Are there some difficult problems in your life right now? God is able to change your situation, but he may let you go through hard times so that you'll learn to trust in him completely. Learning to trust God, no matter what happens, is the secret to real happiness. Remember, he's always there! *S.L.K.*

TO MEMORIZE: You will keep in perfect peace all who trust in you, whose thoughts are fixed on you! *Isaiah 26:3*

BROKEN PROMISES

FROM THE BIBLE:

When you make a vow to the Lord your God, be prompt in doing whatever you promised him. For the Lord your God demands that you promptly fulfill all your vows. If you don't, you will be guilty of sin. However, it is not a sin to refrain from making a vow. But once you have voluntarily made a vow, be careful to do as you have said, for you have made a vow to the Lord your God.

DEUTERONOMY 23:21-23

Keep your promises

MIGUEL LIKED the missionary who was speaking in his church. "In my country, there are many orphan children," Mr. Rathbun was saying. "We are asking Christians to pray earnestly about our building a new home for them. We're also asking you to give up just one cup of coffee or one can of pop per week and give the price of it to the Lord for this home. If you can help, raise your hand." Miguel's hand shot up, as did those of his friends, Greg and Marcus.

The following Saturday, the three boys were biking home after ball practice. "Let's get some pop at the gas station," said Greg.

As they were getting out their coins, Miguel exclaimed, "Hey, wait! We promised to give up one pop a week, and I haven't given up one yet. Have you?"

"Nah," said Greg. "I'll give up two next week."

"Yeah," agreed Marcus. "I'm too thirsty now."

That evening Miguel told his father about his friends and then added, "I was mad until I remembered I was just as bad as they were. I promised to pray for Mr. Rathbun's orphanage, but I haven't done it much."

"I'm glad you see your own faults, Miguel," Dad told him. "The Lord says it's better not to make a promise than to make one and not keep it. Now if you keep your promise, then you can pray that God will work in your friends' hearts so they will want to do their part too."

HOW ABOUT YOU? Have you made promises to God that you haven't kept? God keeps all his promises, and he expects you to keep yours. Be careful about making promises. Ask God to help you keep the ones you make. *A.G.L.*

TO MEMORIZE: When you make a promise to God, don't delay in following through, for God takes no pleasure in fools. Keep all the promises you make to him. *Ecclesiastes 5:4*

25 August

THE KIWI

FROM THE BIBLE:

Charm is deceptive, and beauty does not last; but a woman who fears the Lord will be greatly praised. Reward her for all she has done. Let her deeds publicly declare her praise. . . .

Don't be concerned about the outward beauty that depends on fancy hairstyles, expensive jewelry, or beautiful clothes. You should be known for the beauty that comes from within, the unfading beauty of a gentle and quiet spirit, which is so precious to God.

PROVERBS 31:30-31;
1 PETER 3:3-4

Be content with your looks

LINDSEY FROWNED as she looked at herself in the full-length mirror. "I'm ugly," she sighed sadly.

"That's nonsense," Mom said. She and Lindsey's dad had noticed that Lindsey was not her usual friendly, cheerful self lately. "You're changing," Mom continued, "but you are definitely not ugly. Come on, let's go to the grocery store."

At the store, Mom asked, "Would you get two kiwi for me, please?" She pointed toward the strange, brown fruit.

"I've never seen kiwi before," said Lindsey. "Are you sure you want these funny-looking things?"

After dinner that evening, Mom set out a colorful bowl of fruit for dessert. "What a pretty green fruit this is, Mom," observed Lindsey. "What is it?"

"It's kiwi," Mom informed her, smiling.

"You're kidding!" Lindsey exclaimed. "You mean those ugly, fuzzy, brown things we bought?"

"That's right." Her dad spoke up. "You know, honey, you've been putting too much value on the way you look lately. The Bible says beauty is vain. Just like with the kiwi, it's what's inside that counts. Keep working on that. Look your best, and then be content with the way you're made. Ever since you've become so concerned about your looks, all your inside sweetness has been covered up. And I really miss my old Lindsey."

"I think I like the old Lindsey better too," Lindsey said. She grinned at her mother. "You can serve me kiwi, Mom, whenever you think I need a reminder."

HOW ABOUT YOU? Are you unhappy with the way you look? Learn to accept the way God made you and be content. Most of all, work at becoming a beautiful person inside by living the way God's Word tells you to live. *S.L.N.*

TO MEMORIZE: Charm is deceptive, and beauty does not last, but a woman who fears the Lord will be greatly praised. *Proverbs 31:30*

26 August

TURN AROUND

FROM THE BIBLE:

Oh, what joy for those
whose rebellion is forgiven,
whose sin is put out of sight!
Yes, what joy for those
whose record the Lord has
cleared of sin,
whose lives are lived in
complete honesty!
When I refused to confess
my sin,
I was weak and miserable,
and I groaned all day long.
Day and night your hand of
discipline was heavy on me.
My strength evaporated like
water in the summer heat.
Finally, I confessed all my sins
to you
and stopped trying to hide
them.
I said to myself, "I will confess
my rebellion to the Lord."
And you forgave me! All my
guilt is gone.

PSALM 32:1-5

MEOW! Mother could hear the cat crying from the living room. "Andy, what are you doing to Muffy?" she asked.

"Nothing, Mom," answered Andy. "I was just petting her the wrong way, and it made her fur all stand up funny. She didn't like it."

"I'll bet she didn't!" answered Mother with a smile. "I'm sure it makes a cat feel funny to have its fur rubbed the wrong way. Try to be a little more careful."

The next day Andy looked unhappy when he got home from school. "Is something wrong?" asked Mother.

"Just about everybody in my class cheated on a test today," replied Andy. "John asked why I didn't cheat too. I told him it makes me feel funny to do that kind of stuff. Why do I feel bad about cheating if nobody else feels bad?"

"Well, it's a little like rubbing Muffy's fur the wrong way," Mother replied. "You're a Christian, so the Holy Spirit convicts you when you do something wrong. It's as if God were rubbing your fur the wrong way to make you feel uncomfortable. You feel guilty. But you feel right again after you turn around and go in the right direction—after you've repented of your sin and confessed it."

Andy grinned at his mother. "I get it!" he said.

"When you do what you should," added Mother, "you feel safe and happy instead of guilty and afraid."

HOW ABOUT YOU? Do you feel unhappy and guilty about something you've done? That's the Holy Spirit working to convict you and your sin. It's as though your "fur is being rubbed the wrong way." When you feel guilty about something, confess that sin to God and tell him you're sorry. Then ask him to give you the power to not repeat that sin. *D.S.M.*

TO MEMORIZE: He who conceals his sins does not prosper, but whoever confesses and renounces them finds mercy. *Proverbs 28:13* (NIV)

God convicts of sin

27 August

GUILTY CONSCIENCE

FROM THE BIBLE:

So Christ has now become the High Priest over all the good things that have come. He has entered that great, perfect sanctuary in heaven, not made by human hands and not part of this created world. Once for all time he took blood into that Most Holy Place, but not the blood of goats and calves. He took his own blood, and with it he secured our salvation forever.

Under the old system, the blood of goats and bulls and the ashes of a young cow could cleanse people's bodies from ritual defilement. Just think how much more the blood of Christ will purify our hearts from deeds that lead to death so that we can worship the living God. For by the power of the eternal Spirit, Christ offered himself to God as a perfect sacrifice for our sins.

HEBREWS 9:11-14

Listen to the Holy Spirit

DUSTIN WHISTLED as he sauntered out of Brown's grocery store. Then he jumped on his bicycle and raced down the street. Nervously, he glanced over his shoulder. Only when he was nine blocks from the store did he stop and pull a package of chocolate-covered nuts from his pocket. He ate them all before he got home.

"Dustin," Mother said, "will you run to Brown's store and get me some sugar, please?"

"B-B-Brown's? But I don't feel good," stammered Dustin. "Can't Michelle go?" Concerned, Mother agreed.

When Mother answered the phone a bit later, Dustin heard her say, "Yes, Mr. Brown." After that he could hear only snatches of the conversation. Soon she hung up and went out to the garage to talk to Dad.

When Dad came in, Dustin exclaimed, "I didn't think Mr. Brown saw me in the store, but he told Mother, didn't he? I'm sorry."

Dad looked puzzled. "Mr. Brown told Mother that Michelle left her wallet at the store. We're upset that Michelle keeps forgetting things. What are you talking about?"

"I s-s-stole some c-c-candy today," stammered Dustin. "I've been sick about it ever since."

Dad shook his head. "You were trying to run from a guilty conscience. There's a Bible verse that says, 'The wicked man flees though no one pursues.' That's what you were doing."

"I'm glad I confessed," said Dustin. "I'd hate to spend the rest of my life with a guilty conscience running from nobody."

"Good," said Dad, "because now you're going to go apologize and pay Mr. Brown for that candy."

HOW ABOUT YOU? God has given each one of us a conscience. If you have accepted Jesus, the Holy Spirit will work through your conscience. Listen to him. Obey him. He will keep you from sin. *B.J.W.*

TO MEMORIZE: The wicked man flees though no one pursues, but the righteous are as bold as a lion. *Proverbs 28:1* (NIV)

28 August

THE BUG LIGHT

FROM THE BIBLE:

Don't you realize that all of you together are the temple of God and that the Spirit of God lives in you? God will bring ruin upon anyone who ruins this temple. For God's temple is holy, and you Christians are that temple.

Stop fooling yourselves. If you think you are wise by this world's standards, you will have to become a fool so you can become wise by God's standards. For the wisdom of this world is foolishness to God. As the Scriptures say,

"God catches those who think they are wise
in their own cleverness."
And again,
"The Lord knows the thoughts of the wise,
that they are worthless."
So don't take pride in following a particular leader. Everything belongs to you.

1 CORINTHIANS 3:16-21

"LET'S SIT ON the back porch, Rob, and watch the sun go down," Dad suggested one evening. They sat several minutes without talking, then Dad spoke. "Rob, you're usually cheerful, but you've been very quiet lately."

"Everything's fine—really! We don't need to talk about anything," Rob answered quickly, not looking at his dad.

Soon the sun was down, and the only sound they heard was the *zzzztt!* of the bug light.

"Dad," Rob finally said, "everything isn't fine." Then Rob told how a friend had offered him a cigarette. After saying no a few times, he had smoked one. Since then he had smoked several times, and now he was starting to want a cigarette more often.

Dad put his arm around Rob. "Thanks, Rob, for telling me," he said.

"I've been watching the bugs fly into that bug light," continued Rob. "They don't realize it's drawing them to their death. Now I realize that it's the same with smoking. I took the first cigarette because some friends smoked. Then I thought it made me feel good. But I could get addicted if I don't stop now."

"Smart thinking, Rob," Dad said. "Sin often looks attractive to us. It's easy to get involved in it, but it can destroy us."

"This afternoon I told God I'm not going to smoke again—and I'll stop hanging around bad friends," said Rob quietly.

HOW ABOUT YOU? Has anyone ever asked you to smoke a cigarette? God's Word says Christians are not to defile (do anything to hurt) their bodies. A person who encourages you to smoke or take drugs is not a true friend. Don't try those things—not even once. Keep your body pure for the Lord Jesus. *D.K.*

TO MEMORIZE: Don't you know that your body is the temple of the Holy Spirit, who lives in you and was given to you by God? You do not belong to yourself. *1 Corinthians 6:19*

Stay away from sin

29 August

BREAKING POINT

FROM THE BIBLE:

In the last days there will be scoffers who will laugh at the truth and do every evil thing they desire. This will be their argument: "Jesus promised to come back, did he? Then where is he? . . . Everything has remained exactly the same since the world was first created."

They deliberately forget that God made the heavens by the word of his command, and he brought the earth up from the water and surrounded it with water. Then he used the water to destroy the world with a mighty flood. And God has also commanded that the heavens and the earth will be consumed by fire on the day of judgment, when ungodly people will perish.

But you must not forget, dear friends, that a day is like a thousand years to the Lord, and a thousand years is like a day. The Lord isn't really being slow about his promise to return, as some people think. No, he is being patient for your sake. He does not want anyone to perish, so he is giving more time for everyone to repent.

2 PETER 3:3-9

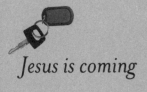

Jesus is coming

"MOM, IS JESUS really coming back someday?" asked Joseph as he and his little sister, Amanda, rode home after church.

"Of course he is," said Mother. "Why do you ask?"

"My teacher talked about that today," said Joseph. "It seems like I've heard it all my life—from you and the church—but it never happens."

"See what I got in Sunday school," said Amanda, holding up a balloon. "Blow it up for me, Joe."

Joseph took the balloon and blew air into it.

"Blow it bigger," Amanda instructed, and Joseph blew more air into the balloon.

"There," he said. "That's as big as it will go. I'll tie it for you."

"No," said Amanda. "Blow it more."

"It will burst," warned Joseph, but Amanda wouldn't listen. "OK, then," said Joseph. Finally it happened. *Bang!*

"It's too bad, honey, but it's your own fault," Mother told Amanda firmly. "Joe warned you." Mother turned to Joseph. "This reminds me of your question, Son. The Lord hasn't returned because he is patient and loving, wanting everyone to have an opportunity to be saved. That balloon stretched to the point where it would burst, and Jesus' patience will one day be stretched to the point where the last person who is going to accept him will do so. Then he will come again."

"So then we should be patient too," Joseph decided.

HOW ABOUT YOU? Does it seem strange that people have been talking about the return of Jesus for two thousand years? He has been very patiently giving men and women and boys and girls the chance to accept him as Savior. But the time will come when he will return as he promised. Will you be waiting? *H.W.M.*

TO MEMORIZE: The Lord is not slow in keeping his promise, as some understand slowness. He is patient with you, not wanting anyone to perish, but everyone to come to repentance. *2 Peter 3:9* (NIV)

30 August

THE MESSENGERS

FROM THE BIBLE:

"Now listen to this story. A certain landowner planted a vineyard, built a wall around it, dug a pit for pressing out the grape juice, and built a lookout tower. Then he leased the vineyard to tenant farmers and moved to another country. At the time of the grape harvest he sent his servants to collect his share of the crop. But the farmers grabbed his servants, beat one, killed one, and stoned another. So the landowner sent a larger group of his servants to collect for him, but the results were the same.

"Finally, the owner sent his son, thinking, 'Surely they will respect my son.'

"But when the farmers saw his son coming, they said to one another, 'Here comes the heir to this estate. Come on, let's kill him and get the estate for ourselves!' So they grabbed him, took him out of the vineyard, and murdered him.

"When the owner of the vineyard returns," Jesus asked, "what do you think he will do to those farmers?"

MATTHEW 21:33-40

"I'M TIRED of being preached at all the time!" Matt complained one day. "I get preached at in Sunday school and in church and even at home."

Dad raised his eyebrows. "Son, God gives us teachers, pastors, and parents to teach and help us."

Matt shrugged. "Maybe so. But who are they to lay down the laws?"

"They don't lay down the laws," answered Dad. "They're God's messengers. They simply bring his laws to us."

Matt jumped to his feet. "Well, I don't like messengers! Think I'll go for a bike ride." Dad sighed.

The next evening when Matt came in from helping Mr. Bentley at the corner grocery store, his face was red. "Some people make me so mad!" he fumed. "I made a delivery today to old Mrs. Carrington. Mr. Bentley told me to tell her she wouldn't be able to charge anything else to her account until she paid her bill. And would you believe that the old lady bawled me out? She called me a smart-aleck teenager. Why should she yell at me? Why doesn't she yell at Mr. Bentley? I just took her the message."

A funny look crossed Matt's face when his dad smiled and said, "Well, I seem to remember that you don't like messengers either."

Matt looked down in embarrassment, then said thoughtfully, "I guess I'm just like old Mrs. Carrington. I guess it's not the message or the messengers that are wrong; it's me. I don't know if Mrs. Carrington will ever change, but I will—starting now!"

HOW ABOUT YOU? Do you gripe and grumble when the preaching convicts you? Or when the teaching applies to you? When others bring you God's message, you had better listen. Don't get mad at them. They are simply the messengers. Listen to them. *B.J.W.*

TO MEMORIZE: We speak as messengers who have been approved by God to be entrusted with the Good News. *1 Thessalonians 2:4*

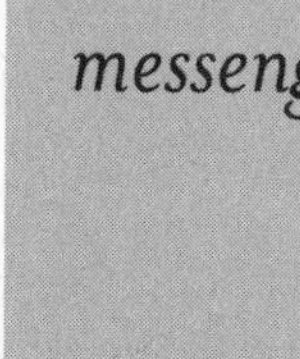

Listen to God's messengers

31 August

LOST GRADES

FROM THE BIBLE:

We work together as partners who belong to God. You are God's field, God's building—not ours.

Because of God's special favor to me, I have laid the foundation like an expert builder. Now others are building on it. But whoever is building on this foundation must be very careful. For no one can lay any other foundation than the one we already have—Jesus Christ. Now anyone who builds on that foundation may use gold, silver, jewels, wood, hay, or straw. But there is going to come a time of testing at the judgment day to see what kind of work each builder has done. Everyone's work will be put through the fire to see whether or not it keeps its value. If the work survives the fire, that builder will receive a reward. But if the work is burned up, the builder will suffer great loss. The builders themselves will be saved, but like someone escaping through a wall of flames.

1 CORINTHIANS 3:9-15

Work for rewards

"MOM, GUESS what happened!" called Tyler after school. "Someone stole my teacher's grade book. She can't find it, and she's sure somebody took it because she had it this morning and now it's gone. She hasn't decided what to do about it." He stopped to bite into an apple. "Just think—all our grades are lost!" Tyler rolled his eyes and took another bite of his apple.

At suppertime Dad heard all about the missing grade book. "I guess we can't get report cards if she doesn't find it," said Tyler.

"Oh, I think your teacher will manage to come up with some grades," Mom said.

"Some of the kids are mad," said Tyler, "and some think it's funny—especially some of the guys who are always getting bad grades."

Dad nodded. "I guess people who do poorly always like to have their grades forgotten," he agreed. He reached for the Bible. "Read for us tonight, will you, Tyler? How about 1 Corinthians 3. Read verses 9-15."

Tyler read the verses. "Wow, it sounds like God is keeping records too!" he said.

"That's right," Dad said, nodding. "And you can be sure no one will ever be able to steal or destroy God's grade book. His records will be accurate, and he won't fail to reward those Christians who have worked for him."

"In that case," said Tyler, "I plan to get good grades!"

HOW ABOUT YOU? Is your name in God's "grade book"? It is if you're a Christian. What kind of grade did you get today? Were you kind? Loving? Helpful? Did you do your best at school? With your chores? With your brothers and sisters? Be very careful to please the Lord in your daily life so that someday you may receive his reward. *H.W.M.*

TO MEMORIZE: If the work survives the fire, that builder will receive a reward. *1 Corinthians 3:14*

HIGH SWING, LOW SWING

FROM THE BIBLE:

Your attitude should be the same that Christ Jesus had. Though he was God, he did not demand and cling to his rights as God. He made himself nothing; he took the humble position of a slave and appeared in human form. And in human form he obediently humbled himself even further by dying a criminal's death on a cross. Because of this, God raised him up to the heights of heaven and gave him a name that is above every other name, so that at the name of Jesus every knee will bow, in heaven and on earth and under the earth, and every tongue will confess that Jesus Christ is Lord, to the glory of God the Father.

PHILIPPIANS 2:5-11

Put others first

ON THE FIRST day of second grade, David and his friend, Brett, noticed two empty swings on the playground during recess. "Hey, let's go swing!" yelled Brett.

The boys ran toward the swings, and as they got closer, David realized that one swing was higher than the other. *I want that one,* he thought. *It'll probably go a lot higher than the low one.* So he grabbed the higher swing and both boys began pumping. David looked at Brett and frowned. *Brett's going higher than I am,* he thought, so he pumped harder. But no matter how hard David worked, he could not get as high as Brett.

At dinner that evening, David told his family about his first day of school and about the swings. "I thought the higher swing would go higher than the lower one. That's why I wanted it," he admitted.

Dad smiled. "No, the lower swing has longer chains, so it can swing out further and higher than a swing with short chains," he explained.

"You know," commented Mother, "most people think they'll be happy with the 'first,' the 'biggest,' the 'best,' or the 'most' things in life. But the Bible doesn't teach that. It tells us that as Christians we should think of others before ourselves."

Dad smiled at David. "That's right. Just like that low swing lifted Brett high in the air, God will lift us up if we humble ourselves and put others first."

HOW ABOUT YOU? Are you often interested in getting the best for yourself? That's being selfish. The Bible teaches that Jesus humbled himself by leaving heaven and becoming a man. It also teaches that Christians should be humble as he was. Put others first instead of putting yourself first. God blesses those who do. *S.L.N.*

TO MEMORIZE: When you bow down before the Lord and admit your dependence on him, he will lift you up and give you honor. *James 4:10*

2 September

MONEY THAT FLEW AWAY

FROM THE BIBLE:

True religion with contentment is great wealth. After all, we didn't bring anything with us when we came into the world, and we certainly cannot carry anything with us when we die. So if we have enough food and clothing, let us be content. But people who long to be rich fall into temptation and are trapped by many foolish and harmful desires that plunge them into ruin and destruction. For the love of money is at the root of all kinds of evil. And some people, craving money, have wandered from the faith and pierced themselves with many sorrows.

1 TIMOTHY 6:6-10

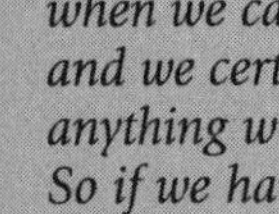

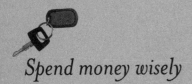

Spend money wisely

IT WAS CARNIVAL TIME! Megan was so excited! Fingering the ten-dollar bill in her pocket, she walked through the midway, where barkers called out to her to try her luck at the games. She stopped at one booth that displayed prizes such as big teddy bears, watches, and radios. Megan decided to try the game just once before she went over to the rides.

Soon Megan had played the game several times and still had not won a prize. She tried again and again. Before she knew it, she'd spent all her money and had won nothing but a cheap plastic toy. She could have bought that little plastic toy at the store for a quarter! She was still upset when she arrived home and confessed to her parents what had happened. "Boy, was I dumb!" she said. "I wasted ten dollars."

"Oh, I don't know," Mom said slowly. "You may have gotten something worth a lot more than that—like a good lesson."

"That's right," agreed Dad. "When we buy something without thinking it over, or when our greed causes us to try to get things without earning them, we find that our money takes wings and flies away."

"I wish I'd known that before," said Megan sadly. "Then the money I had would still be in my pocket instead of flying away!"

HOW ABOUT YOU? Do you love to buy things? Young people are often tempted to spend money foolishly. When you grow up, you'll need to know how to spend money carefully. Now is the time to learn! Get a notebook and write down how you spend your money. Spend it only on things you've planned to buy. Be sure to set aside your offering to God first. Learn to be responsible with the money God has given to you. *S.L.K.*

TO MEMORIZE: Riches can disappear as though they had the wings of a bird! *Proverbs 23:5*

3 September

THE WATER'S TOO COLD!

FROM THE BIBLE:

People who cover over their sins will not prosper. But if they confess and forsake them, they will receive mercy.

Blessed are those who have a tender conscience, but the stubborn are headed for serious trouble.

PROVERBS 28:13-14

Don't get numb to sin

ROBBIE'S EYES wandered over to Sue's paper. There was the word he was trying to spell. *I really knew how to spell it. I just forgot,* Robbie thought to himself. *So it isn't really cheating.* But deep down inside, Robbie knew he had cheated, and it made him feel awful!

The next week Robbie copied from Sue's paper again. He felt funny, but since he knew most of the words, he decided he hadn't really cheated.

When the next Friday rolled around, Robbie copied again. Now it didn't really bother him at all.

That weekend Robbie's family went swimming at the lake. Dad yelled, "C'mon in! The water's fine!" But when Robbie's toes touched the water, he stopped. It felt like ice water!

"It's cold, Dad!" Robbie exclaimed.

"Not after you get used to it," encouraged Dad.

As Robbie slowly walked in, the water didn't seem so cold. Finally Robbie dove into the waves. Now the water didn't seem cold at all.

Back home Robbie said, "I wonder why the lake water seems so icy cold when you first get in. After you get wet, it's fine!"

Dad nodded thoughtfully. "It's a lot like sin, isn't it, Robbie? At first it really bothers a Christian to sin, but then we get almost numb to it and it hardly bothers us at all. In fact, it feels fine!"

Robbie thought about his cheating at school and he went to his bedside to confess it to God.

HOW ABOUT YOU? Have you allowed yourself to commit the same sin so often that your spirit is numb to it? Confess and forsake sin at the very beginning. If you don't it may not bother you after a while. But it's still sin. Don't continue in it. *R.E.P.*

TO MEMORIZE: Blessed are those who have a tender conscience, but the stubborn are headed for serious trouble. *Proverbs 28:14*

4 September

THE GOLF LESSON

FROM THE BIBLE

While we live, we live to please the Lord. And when we die, we go to be with the Lord. So in life and in death, we belong to the Lord. Christ died and rose again for this very purpose, so that he might be Lord of those who are alive and of those who have died.

So why do you condemn another Christian? Why do you look down on another Christian? Remember, each of us will stand personally before the judgment seat of God. For the Scriptures say,

" 'As surely as I live,' says the Lord,
'every knee will bow to me
and every tongue will confess allegiance to God.' "

Yes, each of us will have to give a personal account to God. So don't condemn each other anymore. Decide instead to live in such a way that you will not put an obstacle in another Christian's path.

ROMANS 14:8-13

Show love to everyone

"DID YOU SEE that new kid at school?" Josh was talking to Tim on the phone. "I know he's tall, but we don't want him on our team," Josh continued. "He's probably never played sports, and he doesn't even speak good English. Anyway, I have to go. Dad's going to teach me to play golf."

Josh hung up and saw his father standing at the door. "I changed my mind, Josh. You don't look like a very good golfing prospect. You're not dressed right. You don't know any golfer's language. I don't think you can learn."

"That's not fair!" Josh gasped. "You can't tell what kind of golfer I am by looking at me."

"Who's the new boy in your school?" Dad asked.

"Oh, a kid named Ricardo. He's Hispanic—he has an accent, and he doesn't look like us, and . . . and . . . You heard me on the phone, didn't you?"

Dad nodded. "Yes, Josh, I did. You judged Ricardo without knowing him."

"Just like you judged me about playing golf," said Josh.

"God tells us not to judge others," said Dad. "What are you going to do about this?"

"I'll have to apologize for what I said to Tim," Josh replied. "Then I'll ask Ricardo to come over and shoot baskets. I need to ask God to forgive me too."

"Good," said Dad. "Now I think we should go see what kind of golfer you really are."

HOW ABOUT YOU? Do you form opinions about others based on how they look or talk? God loves every person in the world so much that he gave his Son to die for them. What can you do to show love for someone different from you? Can you give him a smile? Invite him to play? Think of at least one way to share God's love today. *D.K.*

TO MEMORIZE: So don't condemn each other anymore. *Romans 14:13*

5 September

ITS PROPER PLACE
(PART 1)

FROM THE BIBLE:

O my people, listen to my
teaching.
Open your ears to what
I am saying,
for I will speak to you in
a parable.
I will teach you hidden lessons
from our past—
stories we have heard and
know,
stories our ancestors handed
down to us.
We will not hide these truths
from our children
but will tell the next
generation about the
glorious deeds of the Lord.
We will tell of his power and
the mighty miracles he did.
For he issued his decree to Jacob;
he gave his law to Israel.
He commanded our ancestors
to teach them to their
children,
so the next generation might
know them—
even the children not
yet born—
that they in turn might teach
their children.

PSALM 78:1-6

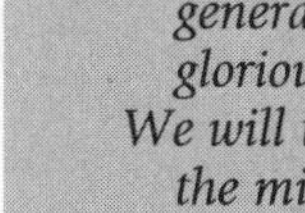

Honor your parents

ERIN WAS EXCITED! She was almost certain she was going to be named captain of the cheerleading squad!

"That's really important to you, isn't it?" her mother asked as they talked about it.

"Important!" Erin cried out. "Mom, this is the most important thing in my whole life! If I'm elected, all the kids will treat me special!"

Erin's mother took a deep breath and let it out slowly. "That's what worries me, honey. I think it's great to have this opportunity if you don't allow it to go to your head or to replace more important things."

"What could be more important?" Erin countered, trying to keep her voice steady.

"I'm talking about priorities," her mother said simply. "The Bible says we are to seek 'first the kingdom of God' and to 'set our affection on things above.' " Then Mom went back to the kitchen.

Erin stood there for a long time. Her mother always quoted Scripture to her. It made her so mad! As Erin sat down on the couch, she noticed her mother's Bible. Suddenly she felt ashamed of herself. She really knew why Mom cautioned her about things and quoted Scripture so often. Just last week in Sunday school they had talked about the responsibility of parents to teach their children the things that God had taught them. And children have a responsibility to listen. Maybe she should think about what Mom had said.

HOW ABOUT YOU? Do you sometimes feel as though your parents are always "preaching" at you? Next time it happens, remember that they are doing their best to teach you as they should. Don't be angry with them. Instead, honor them by listening and by thinking about what they say. Ask the Lord to teach you through them. *R.I.J.*

TO MEMORIZE: Honor your father and mother, as the Lord your God commanded you.
Deuteronomy 5:16

6 *September*

ITS PROPER PLACE
(PART 2)

FROM THE BIBLE:

Since you have been raised to new life with Christ, set your sights on the realities of heaven, where Christ sits at God's right hand in the place of honor and power. Let heaven fill your thoughts. Do not think only about things down here on earth. For you died when Christ died, and your real life is hidden with Christ in God. And when Christ, who is your real life, is revealed to the whole world, you will share in all his glory.
COLOSSIANS 3:1-4

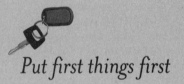

Put first things first

ERIN WAS STILL thinking about her chances of being the cheerleading captain as she and her mother left for a missionary conference at church. But by the time the meeting was over, Erin was no longer thinking about the school group. She had heard about great needs in various places and actually found herself thinking about the responsibility to let people know about Jesus. She remembered once telling her mother she wanted to be a missionary someday, but that was probably just a childish whim.

Back home, Erin said, "Those missionary pictures made me wonder."

Her mother looked over at her. "About what, honey?"

"Maybe *wonder* isn't the word," Erin began slowly, "but I've been thinking of what you said this afternoon about needing to keep things in their proper place. Now after seeing those pictures and hearing about all those needy people, being the cheerleading captain just doesn't seem so important anymore."

Just then the telephone rang, and Erin went to answer it. "Congratulations," a voice said enthusiastically. "You've just been elected captain of the cheerleaders."

Though Erin was thrilled to get the news, the last few hours had made her realize there were many things in life that were more important than being the captain of the cheerleaders. She would do her best at the job, but some other things would receive equal or more attention. She wondered if perhaps God would call her to the mission field someday after all.

HOW ABOUT YOU? What is most important to you? Is it good grades? Popularity? Athletics? Pretty clothes? Cars or trucks? The list goes on and on. It may be OK for these things to be important in your life, but they should never be most important. Put God and his will first, and other things will fall into their rightful places. *R.I.J.*

TO MEMORIZE: Set your mind on things above, not on things on the earth. *Colossians 3:2* (NKJV)

7 September

SIZE ISN'T EVERYTHING

FROM THE BIBLE:

I am the true vine, and my Father is the gardener. He cuts off every branch that doesn't produce fruit, and he prunes the branches that do bear fruit so they will produce even more. You have already been pruned for greater fruitfulness by the message I have given you. Remain in me, and I will remain in you. For a branch cannot produce fruit if it is severed from the vine, and you cannot be fruitful apart from me.

Yes, I am the vine; you are the branches. Those who remain in me, and I in them, will produce much fruit. For apart from me you can do nothing. Anyone who parts from me is thrown away like a useless branch and withers. Such branches are gathered into a pile to be burned. But if you stay joined to me and my words remain in you, you may ask any request you like, and it will be granted! My true disciples produce much fruit. This brings great glory to my Father.

JOHN 15:1-8

Do your best

"THIS WILL probably be the last picking of tomatoes," said Nicholas's mother as he followed her into the garden. "It's about time for a frost." Mother glanced at Nicholas. "What's wrong?" she asked.

"Nothing," Nicholas mumbled. But Mother knew better. She had seen Nicholas measuring himself against the door frame several times lately. She also knew his friends sometimes teased him about being the runt of the class.

"Look at this little plant," commented Mother. "It didn't grow as fast as the others, but look at the tomatoes on it. It has probably produced more tomatoes than any of the others."

"I don't know how it could," said Nicholas. "It's about half the size of the others."

"Size isn't everything." Mother stood and stretched. "Some of these plants put all their energy into getting taller, but this little plant produced fruit. You don't have to be the tallest or the biggest to be the most productive."

"Yeah, right," Nicholas sighed.

"Don't worry about being short, Nicholas," Mother said. "God made us all different. Instead, you can be the kindest and the most courageous. The important thing is to bring forth fruit for God—to do what he wants you to do. Who knows? By next year, you may be the tallest."

Nicholas grinned. "Maybe," he said, "but I doubt it. I know you're right, though. I'll try to quit worrying about my size and think more about the things I can do—especially the things I can do for God."

HOW ABOUT YOU? Have you been fretting because you're different from your friends? Remember, we're all different. Don't waste your energy worrying about your size or looks. Think about bearing fruit, doing something for the Lord. What are you going to do today to bear fruit? *B.J.W.*

TO MEMORIZE: Remain in me and I will remain in you. No branch can bear fruit by itself; it must remain in the vine. *John 15:4* (NIV)

8 September

HOMEWORK SOLUTION

FROM THE BIBLE:

A mob quickly formed against Paul and Silas, and the city officials ordered them stripped and beaten with wooden rods. They were severely beaten, and then they were thrown into prison. The jailer was ordered to make sure they didn't escape. So he took no chances but put them into the inner dungeon and clamped their feet in the stocks.

Around midnight, Paul and Silas were praying and singing hymns to God, and the other prisoners were listening. Suddenly, there was a great earthquake, and the prison was shaken to its foundations. All the doors flew open, and the chains of every prisoner fell off! The jailer woke up to see the prison doors wide open. He assumed the prisoners had escaped, so he drew his sword to kill himself. But Paul shouted to him, "Don't do it! We are all here!"

ACTS 16:22-28

A right attitude is important

"THIS SCIENCE experiment is just not working out," Lucas moaned. "I've done it four times, and each time it comes out differently."

Dad had just come into the kitchen. "I know schoolwork isn't easy. Remember, I'm taking a night school class."

"Do you like to do homework?" Lucas asked.

"Well, not always," Dad said with a chuckle. "It can be frustrating. I find that it helps to pray about it before I start. Since I know I have to study, I ask the Lord to give me a right attitude. I work much better with the right attitude."

Lucas looked at his dad thoughtfully. "I guess maybe I should pray about my science experiment," he decided.

During family devotions that night, Dad read the story of Paul and Silas, who were singing in prison. "I've often wondered what would have happened if they had grumbled and complained instead of praying and singing," said Dad. "That wouldn't have been much of a testimony to the other prisoners, and perhaps the jailer would not have been saved. But they had a joyful attitude, and great things happened." He looked at Lucas. "Reminds me of your homework problems," he said. "When you prayed this afternoon, how did your homework go afterward?"

Lucas grinned. "Great things happened then, too," he said. "I calmed down and read the directions again. And I had forgotten one part. I even found it interesting."

Dad nodded knowingly. "God helped Paul, and he will help us to have a good attitude too."

HOW ABOUT YOU? Do you begin your homework with a bad attitude? If so, ask God to change that attitude so you can do your best work for him. Then try again. A bad attitude keeps you from doing your best. Jesus understands this and wants to help you. *J.A.G.*

TO MEMORIZE: Around midnight, Paul and Silas were praying and singing hymns to God, and the other prisoners were listening. *Acts 16:25*

REPORT CARDS

FROM THE BIBLE:

For no one can lay any other foundation than the one we already have—Jesus Christ. Now anyone who builds on that foundation may use gold, silver, jewels, wood, hay, or straw. But there is going to come a time of testing at the judgment day to see what kind of work each builder has done. Everyone's work will be put through the fire to see whether or not it keeps its value. If the work survives the fire, that builder will receive a reward. But if the work is burned up, the builder will suffer great loss. The builders themselves will be saved, but like someone escaping through a wall of flames.
1 CORINTHIANS 3:11-15

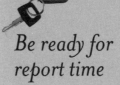

Be ready for report time

IAN DRAGGED his feet as he headed home. Spunky, a neighbor's dog, noticed him and dashed over for some attention. He raced around Ian and danced in front of him until Ian almost tripped over him. "Go away, you dumb dog!" yelled Ian. He kicked Spunky, and the dog yelped.

Mr. Edwards, who owned the dog, was raking leaves and witnessed the scene. "Ian, what has gotten into you? Why did you kick Spunky?" Ian hung his head, embarrassed that Mr. Edwards had seen his actions. "What put you in such a bad mood today?" asked Mr. Edwards.

"Report cards," groaned Ian.

Mr. Edwards looked sympathetic. "Not so good, huh?"

"No," muttered Ian. "My parents will ground me for sure. They'll say I'm not doing my best."

"Are you?" Mr. Edwards asked.

Ian blushed. "No, I guess not." He paused, then added, "I wish adults got report cards too. Then maybe they'd be more understanding."

Mr. Edwards smiled. "Well, in a sense, those of us who are Christians are earning grades, or marks."

"What do you mean?" asked Ian.

"Well, Christians aren't saved by their works, but they will be judged for the works they do after they're saved." Mr. Edwards explained. "Christians should be concerned about getting 'good grades' in such things as obedience, faith, and love."

"I forgot all about that," said Ian. "I could remind my folks about it, but they'd probably point out that it applies to me, too. Well, guess I'd better get home. I've got a lot of work to do to improve my record—for my parents and for the Lord."

HOW ABOUT YOU? What kind of grades are you getting in your Christian life? Are you trying to be more kind, faithful, and obedient? Someday you will have to give an account. Will you have a good "report card"? *J.L.H.*

TO MEMORIZE: Yes, each of us will have to give a personal account to God. *Romans 14:12*

10 September

TEAMMATES

FROM THE BIBLE:

So you are all children of God through faith in Christ Jesus. And all who have been united with Christ in baptism have been made like him. There is no longer Jew or Gentile, slave or free, male or female. For you are all Christians—you are one in Christ Jesus. And now that you belong to Christ, you are the true children of Abraham. You are his heirs, and now all the promises God gave to him belong to you.
GALATIANS 3:26-29

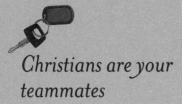

Christians are your teammates

"GO, JON! GO!" yelled Alec, as he jumped up and down. "All right!" He cheered wildly as his teammate scored the first touchdown of the game.

At dinner that evening, Alec gave his family a blow-by-blow account of the afternoon's game. Over and over they heard the name "Jon" as Alec described the various plays. Finally Alec's sister, Sophia, looked at her brother in disgust. "I am sick of hearing about Jon," she declared. "I thought you didn't even like him."

"Well, he may not be my favorite person," admitted Alec, "but he's on our team. We're fighting for the same cause. We're both Coreyville Cougars, the 'best in the west!' " You should have seen him run this afternoon—"

"Oh, brother," moaned Sophia. "Here comes another chapter of 'Jon, the Football Player.' "

Mother laughed. "I'm glad you enjoyed your game so much, Alec," she said. "It's nice that you've found something to admire in Jon. We should always look for positive things in others."

"I think Alec has given us a good example of how we should view other Christians," observed Dad. "We don't have to like everything about them, and they don't all have to be our best friends. But we should remember that we're on the same team, fighting for the same cause—that of winning others to Jesus and bringing glory to God. We should love them, and I believe we can find something to admire in each of them. We should regard them as teammates."

HOW ABOUT YOU? Is there a fellow Christian whom you dislike? Look for some good quality in him, and then concentrate on that rather than on the things that annoy you. Remember, you both belong to Christ, and that should bind you together. You are teammates. As such, work together to glorify the Lord. *H.W.M.*

TO MEMORIZE: You are all children of God through faith in Christ Jesus. *Galatians 3:26*

PRACTICE, PRACTICE!

FROM THE BIBLE:

In everything you do, stay away from complaining and arguing, so that no one can speak a word of blame against you. You are to live clean, innocent lives as children of God in a dark world full of crooked and perverse people. Let your lives shine brightly before them. Hold tightly to the word of life, so that when Christ returns, I will be proud that I did not lose the race and that my work was not useless. But even if my life is to be poured out like a drink offering to complete the sacrifice of your faithful service (that is, if I am to die for you), I will rejoice, and I want to share my joy with all of you. And you should be happy about this and rejoice with me.

PHILIPPIANS 2:14-18

Practice your joy

"JEREMY, DON'T STOP practicing your trumpet yet!" Mom called from the kitchen.

"But, Mom, I've played each of the songs."

"Then play them each again. You promised you would practice 20 minutes every day," his mother replied.

"But I never get any better at it," Jeremy grumbled.

"Some things take lots of practice to be able to do them well," Mom said. "Nothing worthwhile in life comes easily."

To Jeremy, the idea of being in band had seemed like fun. But now the fun had turned to work! He almost wished he could get out of the whole thing, including his promise to practice 20 minutes a day. But Dad had paid to rent a trumpet for him, so he knew he had to stick with it.

During family devotions, Dad read from Philippians. Then Dad said, "Did any of you children notice a theme in those verses?"

Nine-year-old Sara knew. "The same words are used over again and again—*joy* and *rejoice!*"

"Right!" Dad agreed. "Why do you suppose the apostle Paul repeated those words so much?"

"Maybe joy is a bit like practicing the trumpet," Mom suggested. "We have to practice being joyful over and over, even when we may not feel like being joyful. Someday rejoicing will get easier for us, just like your trumpet playing will get easier for you, Jeremy. Let's all start practicing joy in this house, OK?"

As Dad closed their discussion with prayer, Jeremy determined in his heart to practice his trumpet and his joy every day!

HOW ABOUT YOU? Are you often gloomy with your family? When things go wrong, do you pout and grumble? If you do, you need to practice finding something to rejoice about. If you're a Christian, Scripture demands that you do this, and the end result is a happier you! *R.E.P.*

TO MEMORIZE: Rejoice in the Lord always. I will say it again: Rejoice! *Philippians 4:4* (NIV)

12 September

PRAISE WORKS WONDERS
(PART 1)

FROM THE BIBLE:

Always be full of joy in the Lord. I say it again—rejoice! Let everyone see that you are considerate in all you do. Remember, the Lord is coming soon.

Don't worry about anything; instead, pray about everything. Tell God what you need, and thank him for all he has done. If you do this, you will experience God's peace, which is far more wonderful than the human mind can understand. His peace will guard your hearts and minds as you live in Christ Jesus.
PHILIPPIANS 4:4-7

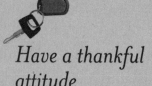

Have a thankful attitude

BETH SLAMMED the door as she came in from school. "What an awful day," she moaned. "Why I was so lucky to get Mrs. Hodges for two classes a day, I'll never know. She's a grouch! Nobody likes her. Junior high school is going to be awful!"

"Remember the verse we read this morning?" reminded Mother. "It says, 'With thanksgiving, present your requests to God.' I'm sure the Lord has some lessons to teach you in her classes."

"I'm sure I'll learn lots of lessons before I get out of there," grumbled Beth. "Like 'no talking during class,' and 'stay in your seats.' Why should I give thanks for that?"

"No matter what our circumstances are, we should always praise the Lord," explained Mother. "He tells us to pray about what is happening and to include thanksgiving in those prayers."

"Well," said Beth, "it will be hard to praise the Lord for a class that meets two hours a day, five days a week, all year long! Oh, I can't stand it!" She clapped her hand to her head and fell into a soft chair.

"Now, Beth, don't get dramatic," said Mother, laughing. "You'll be able to stand it. You can even win Mrs. Hodges's respect and friendship if your attitude is right. Pray about it, and let the Holy Spirit control you. I think you'll be surprised."

HOW ABOUT YOU? Have you talked to the Lord about the circumstances you face each day? Perhaps there's a teacher, a classmate, or even a parent you think you can't stand. Talk to God about it; pray for that person; ask the Lord to give you a proper attitude toward him or her. Then thank God for the opportunities and lessons you can learn right where you are. *B.J.W.*

TO MEMORIZE: Do not be anxious about anything, but in everything, by prayer and petition, with thanksgiving, present your requests to God.
Philippians 4:6 (NIV)

13 September

PRAISE WORKS WONDERS

(PART 2)

FROM THE BIBLE:

When the ways of people please the Lord, he makes even their enemies live at peace with them. . . .

Those who listen to instruction will prosper; those who trust the Lord will be happy.

The wise are known for their understanding, and instruction is appreciated if it's well presented.

Discretion is a life-giving fountain to those who possess it, but discipline is wasted on fools.

From a wise mind comes wise speech; the words of the wise are persuasive.

Kind words are like honey—sweet to the soul and healthy for the body.

PROVERBS 16:7, 20-24

Give honest praise to others

ONE SATURDAY morning as Beth was raking the lawn, her little brother, Casey, came out of the house with Mother. "It worked, Beth!" Casey called excitedly. "We're going to the store!"

Mother looked puzzled. "What worked?"

Beth laughed. "Casey was pouting because he wanted to go to the store but you said you were too busy," she explained. "I told him to quit fussing and to start being kind to you."

"But she said to tell only the truth," interrupted Casey, "so I did. You're a good housekeeper, and a good mama."

Mother laughed. "Hey, Beth. That might be the solution to your problem with your teacher, Mrs. Hodges. Why not try telling her the things you honestly appreciate about her?"

The next Monday when Beth walked into Mrs. Hodges's room, she said, "That's a pretty dress you have on, Mrs. Hodges." The teacher looked startled but pleased. Later when Beth was having trouble with an assignment, she went to Mrs. Hodges. "I know you explained this in class," she said, "but for some reason, I still don't understand. Could you explain it once more?"

As time passed, Beth was surprised to find out she was beginning to like Mrs. Hodges, and Mrs. Hodges seemed to like Beth, too. She even paid her a compliment now and then. "It's strange," mused Beth. "When you say nice things about people, they say nice things about you, too."

HOW ABOUT YOU? Did you know that praise works wonders? Perhaps it's the answer to your problem with a teacher, a critical neighbor, or a relative. Try it—just be careful to always tell them the truth. Don't flatter. Ask the Lord to help you see the good things in people, and then be genuine in your compliments. *B.J.W.*

TO MEMORIZE: When a man's ways are pleasing to the Lord, he makes even his enemies live at peace with him. *Proverbs 16:7* (NIV)

14 September

THE GAME OF LIFE
(PART 1)

FROM THE BIBLE:

Obey the government, for God is the one who put it there. All governments have been placed in power by God. So those who refuse to obey the laws of the land are refusing to obey God, and punishment will follow. For the authorities do not frighten people who are doing right, but they frighten those who do wrong. So do what they say, and you will get along well. The authorities are sent by God to help you. But if you are doing something wrong, of course you should be afraid, for you will be punished. The authorities are established by God for that very purpose, to punish those who do wrong. So you must obey the government for two reasons: to keep from being punished and to keep a clear conscience.

Pay your taxes, too, for these same reasons. For government workers need to be paid so they can keep on doing the work God intended them to do.

ROMANS 13:1-6

Obey those in authority

PAUL STRETCHED and yawned. "I gotta get to bed early tonight," he stated. "Coach's orders. He says it's important to work hard and eat right, but that nothing will take the place of a good night's sleep."

"Well, then, by all means get to bed early—after you work hard and eat right, that is," teased his sister, Amanda. "Be sure to do whatever your football coach says."

"You surely are putting a lot into the game, Paul," said Dad. He looked thoughtful. "You know, the game of football reminds me of the game of life. God has provided a big, beautiful field on which to play the game. He created the earth and everything in it."

Amanda grinned. "Oh, and here's an important part—the coaches we must listen to are our Bible teachers and especially our parents, as well as the Lord. I bet that's the thing Dad wanted to get across to us."

Dad gave her a playful swat with his newspaper. "You got it." He smiled. "You two are getting good at figuring out the lessons I'm trying to teach. Don't forget how important it is to follow the advice of your coaches!"

"Right, Dad." Paul laughed. He stood up and yawned again. "I'm going to do that now by getting to bed. Good night, everybody."

HOW ABOUT YOU? Do you listen to your "coaches" in the game of life? God has given you parents, Sunday school teachers, pastors, and other Christian leaders and friends to help you make right choices. Listen carefully to what they have to say. God says to obey them. *H.W.M.*

TO MEMORIZE: Submit yourselves for the Lord's sake to every authority instituted among men. *1 Peter 2:13* (NIV)

THE GAME OF LIFE
(PART 2)

FROM THE BIBLE:

Your decrees are wonderful.
No wonder I obey them!
As your words are taught,
they give light;
even the simple can
understand them.
I open my mouth, panting
expectantly,
longing for your commands.
Come and show me your mercy,
as you do for all who love your
name.
Guide my steps by your word,
so I will not be overcome by
any evil.
Rescue me from the oppression
of evil people;
then I can obey your
commandments.
Look down on me with love;
teach me all your principles.
PSALM 119:129-135

God's word is right

"THAT WAS A GOOD game this afternoon, Paul," observed Dad at dinner. "You did a good job."

"When those two coaches went at it, I thought they were going to have a big fight," said Amanda. "Then the referee looked at some book. What was that?"

"That was the National Football League Rule Book," said Paul. "When there's a disagreement, they can look up the rule about it. Whatever the book says, that's it! No more arguing."

"It's the final authority in the game of football," said Dad. He paused, then added, "God has supplied a book that is the final authority in the game of life, too."

"This is an easy one," said Paul. "The final authority in life is—"

"The Bible," interrupted Amanda.

Dad nodded. "Sometimes our 'coaches' disagree on something," he said. "A preacher says one thing; a well-known Christian leader says another. A parent or teacher says something different still. It can get very confusing. Then we need to turn to the Bible and see what God says."

"But he doesn't talk about some subjects," said Amanda, "like if it's OK for a twelve-year-old girl to wear makeup." She glanced at Mom.

Dad smiled. "No, but he does say you are to obey your parents, so they'll decide on the makeup issue. God will show us principles to help us in all our decisions. We have to read his Word to know those principles, though." He reached for his Bible. "Let's do that right now."

HOW ABOUT YOU? Do you get confused when there is disagreement among your parents or Christian leaders as to what is right or wrong? Find out what God says about it. He's always right. Look for principles in his Word to guide you in knowing the truth. *H.W.M.*

TO MEMORIZE: For the word of the Lord is right and true. *Psalm 33:4* (NIV)

16 *September*

A SOMETIMES FRIEND

FROM THE BIBLE:

If we love our Christian brothers and sisters, it proves that we have passed from death to eternal life. But a person who has no love is still dead. Anyone who hates another Christian is really a murderer at heart. And you know that murderers don't have eternal life within them. We know what real love is because Christ gave up his life for us. And so we also ought to give up our lives for our Christian brothers and sisters. But if anyone has enough money to live well and sees a brother or sister in need and refuses to help—how can God's love be in that person?

Dear children, let us stop just saying we love each other; let us really show it by our actions.

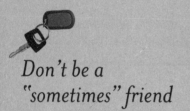

1 JOHN 3:14-18

Don't be a "sometimes" friend

DANNY HAD TRIED to be a good friend to Ho. When some kids called Ho "Slant-eyes," Danny defended him. When his friends failed to include Ho in their plans, Danny stood up for him. But now that Ho had more friends, he was ignoring Danny.

"I'm through helping him," Danny told his dad. "I'll give him a taste of his own medicine. I'm going to ignore him."

At that moment, the telephone rang, and Danny hurried to answer it. "Hello, Danny," came a familiar voice on the other end of the line. "This is Ho."

"Yeah, Ho," he said unenthusiastically. "What's up?" After listening a few minutes, Danny said, "I'll see. Can't promise. Bye."

Danny sighed. "Ho wants me to help him with a project. He only calls me when he wants something."

Danny's father was quiet. "I wonder if God feels that way," he said soberly. "He probably wants us to come and simply have a friendly talk with him now and then, but we only call on him when we need something."

Danny got the message. He wanted to ignore Ho's requests because Ho so often ignored him. But as he thought more, he was glad that God didn't act that way. Danny decided to be more faithful about talking to God. And if he wanted to be like Jesus, he guessed he'd better see what he could do to help Ho, too.

HOW ABOUT YOU? Do you have friends that seem to use you—that talk to you only when they want something? Do you ever treat others that way? Do you treat God that way? Don't be a "sometimes" friend. Don't use people to get things you want. Talk to God every day. Then, remembering how gracious God is, be patient with your friends, too. *R.I.J.*

TO MEMORIZE: Love must be sincere. Hate what is evil; cling to what is good. *Romans 12:9* (NIV)

EXPENSIVE CANDY

FROM THE BIBLE:

Yet true religion with contentment is great wealth. After all, we didn't bring anything with us when we came into the world, and we certainly cannot carry anything with us when we die. So if we have enough food and clothing, let us be content. But people who long to be rich fall into temptation and are trapped by many foolish and harmful desires that plunge them into ruin and destruction. For the love of money is at the root of all kinds of evil. And some people, craving money, have wandered from the faith and pierced themselves with many sorrows.

But you, Timothy, belong to God; so run from all these evil things, and follow what is right and good. Pursue a godly life, along with faith, love, perseverance, and gentleness.

1 TIMOTHY 6:6-11

"GIVE ME THE REST of your allowance," Jim told his little sister. "Then you can have the candy bar."

Danielle looked longingly at the candy and reluctantly gave Jim the rest of her allowance.

When Danielle heard the bell of the ice cream truck a few days later, she ran to ask her mother if she could buy some. "Sure," Mom said. "You get an allowance for things like that."

Danielle burst into tears. "But my allowance is gone." Danielle told her mother about the candy bar.

Mom called Jim into the room. "I don't like the way you treated your sister," she said. "You charged her far too much for the candy. God's Word has many warnings about greed. It says that the love of money is the root of all evil."

"But she didn't have to buy it," protested Jim.

"It was a greedy act just the same," insisted Mom. "God never wants us to abuse those who are younger, poorer, weaker, or those who don't have the advantages we do. He wants us to help them and watch out for them. Taking a fair profit is fine, but we must not love money more than people. Now, what could you do to make things right again?"

"I guess I could return Danielle's money, minus the price of the candy bar," admitted Jim.

Mom smiled at Jim. "Good for you."

HOW ABOUT YOU? Are you careful to be fair in your dealings with younger brothers and sisters, or with small neighborhood children? It's sometimes a great temptation to charge too much from those who don't know the value of money. God tells Christians to "flee" from the temptation to seek the riches of this world. He says to follow after things pleasing to the Lord instead. *C.E.Y.*

TO MEMORIZE: For the love of money is a root of all kinds of evil. *1 Timothy 6:10* (NIV)

Love others, not money

18 September

THE BIKE ACCIDENT

FROM THE BIBLE:

Not even a sparrow, worth only half a penny, can fall to the ground without your Father knowing it. And the very hairs on your head are all numbered. So don't be afraid; you are more valuable to him than a whole flock of sparrows.

MATTHEW 10:29-31

God cares for you

JUSTIN COULD hardly sit still as he and Mom arrived at the bike shop. He had been working hard and saving his money so he could purchase a new racing bike. Justin fell in love with a shiny red one on sale. Soon he was the proud owner of the new bicycle. What fun he was going to have! During devotions that night, he thanked God for his new bike.

The next day Justin was riding his bike down a steep hill. He started going faster and faster. Suddenly he hit a bump and lost control of the bike! Before he knew what had happened, Justin found himself lying on the pavement. He felt pain on his knee and looked down to see blood and dirt covering a jagged scrape. He stumbled to his feet and pushed his bike home. He was sniffling and fighting back tears as he limped through the door. "Mom," he groaned, "I'm hurt!"

Mom came quickly and gently began to wash Justin's knee. "Why did God let me fall?" he whimpered. "Doesn't he care if I get hurt?"

Mother smiled. "He cares for you even more than I do," she assured him. "Remember last spring when that baby bird fell out of the tree? God says that not one sparrow can fall to the ground without him knowing it. Yet you are more important to him than many sparrows!" Mom hugged Justin as he walked back outside, quite pleased with the huge bandage.

HOW ABOUT YOU? When you fall, or even get hurt in your heart, do you know God cares? Do you "run" straight to him in prayer like Justin ran to his mom? If you feel hurt or sad right now, pray and ask God to help you.

TO MEMORIZE: Are not two sparrows sold for a penny? Yet not one of them will fall to the ground apart from the will of your Father. *Matthew 10:29* (NIV)

19 September

NOT ENOUGH TIME

FROM THE BIBLE:

This is true, and everyone should accept it. We work hard and suffer much in order that people will believe the truth, for our hope is in the living God, who is the Savior of all people, and particularly of those who believe.

Teach these things and insist that everyone learn them. Don't let anyone think less of you because you are young. Be an example to all believers in what you teach, in the way you live, in your love, your faith, and your purity. Until I get there, focus on reading the Scriptures to the church, encouraging the believers, and teaching them.

1 TIMOTHY 4:9-13

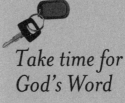

Take time for God's Word

TOBY'S MOTHER called outside, "Toby, have you finished your Sunday school lesson? If I remember correctly, you need to read several chapters this week."

"I haven't had time yet," said Toby as he shot baskets. That had been his answer each time Mother had reminded him of his lesson. Now it was Wednesday; there were only a few days left to do it.

That evening, Toby noticed Mom writing on some kind of chart. But when he asked what it was, she told him he'd find out later.

On Saturday night, Mom again asked Toby about his lesson. "Oh, I started it, but I only finished one of the chapters we're supposed to read. It's too long," he complained. "Mr. Powell will just have to understand how busy I am. I don't have time to read all of it."

Mother pulled out the chart. "I've noticed how busy you are, Toby," she said. "In fact, I've been keeping track. Since Wednesday, you have spent six hours watching TV, five hours playing ball, four hours listening to tapes or the radio, about three hours reading books and magazines, and a couple of hours just lounging around saying, 'I don't have anything to do.' " With a smile, she handed him the chart.

Toby blushed as he looked at it. "Wow!" he exclaimed, putting the sports magazine down. "I guess I can't say I don't have time to do my Sunday school lesson. I better go finish my reading right now!"

HOW ABOUT YOU? Do you sometimes claim that you don't have the time to read God's Word? You have the time to do whatever is important to you. Is the Bible important enough to make you willing to give up some of your leisure time in order to read it? It would certainly be worth it. *R.E.P.*

TO MEMORIZE: Focus on reading the Scriptures. *1 Timothy 4:13*

20 September

THE WRONG FINGER

FROM THE BIBLE:

After dark one evening, a Jewish religious leader named Nicodemus, a Pharisee, came to speak with Jesus. "Teacher," he said, "we all know that God has sent you to teach us. Your miraculous signs are proof enough that God is with you."

Jesus replied, "I assure you, unless you are born again, you can never see the Kingdom of God."

"What do you mean?" exclaimed Nicodemus. "How can an old man go back into his mother's womb and be born again?"

Jesus replied, "The truth is, no one can enter the Kingdom of God without being born of water and the Spirit. Humans can reproduce only human life, but the Holy Spirit gives new life from heaven. So don't be surprised at my statement that you must be born again."

JOHN 3:1-7

You must be born again

"SURE, I'M a Christian," Mark told his friend Brandon. "My parents go to church all the time. Dad's on the church board, and Mom teaches Sunday school. And last week they both gave testimonies about when they were saved."

Overhearing the conversation, Mark's mother decided to have a talk with her son. Later, Mark came in. "Mom, can I have a Band-Aid?"

Mother looked at the cut on Mark's finger. After getting the Band-Aid, she tore it open and carefully put it on her own finger. "There," she said. "That should take care of the problem."

Mark stared at his mother. "Mom! What are you doing? *I* need the Band-Aid."

"Oh?" Mother looked at him. "You mean the bandage on my finger doesn't help yours?"

"Of course not!" Mark couldn't understand his mother's behavior at all.

"Well, I don't know," she said. "A little while ago, I heard you claim that because Dad and I are Christians, you are too. We took the cure for sin—we accepted Jesus as Savior. If that makes you a Christian, too, then I think this Band-Aid on my finger should also take care of your cut."

Mark stared thoughtfully at his mother. "I guess you're right," he admitted. "I need to accept Jesus myself, don't I? Will you show me how to do that?"

"Yes." Mother smiled, putting a Band-Aid on Mark's finger. "Let's go talk about it."

HOW ABOUT YOU? Are your parents Christians? Do your grandparents know the Lord, too? Are your relatives saved? If you answered yes, that's wonderful. But here's the real question—have you accepted Jesus as your own personal Savior? If not, you are not a Christian. Even Nicodemus, a religious ruler, had to be born again. Won't you accept Jesus today? *H.W.M.*

TO MEMORIZE: For you have been born again, not of perishable seed, but of imperishable, through the living and enduring word of God. *1 Peter 1:23* (NIV)

21 September

TOO DIRTY FOR HEAVEN

FROM THE BIBLE:

And the city has no need of sun or moon, for the glory of God illuminates the city, and the Lamb is its light. The nations of the earth will walk in its light, and the rulers of the world will come and bring their glory to it. Its gates never close at the end of day because there is no night. And all the nations will bring their glory and honor into the city. Nothing evil will be allowed to enter—no one who practices shameful idolatry and dishonesty—but only those whose names are written in the Lamb's Book of Life.

REVELATION 21:23-27

Sin can't enter heaven

THE STEVENSONS were getting new carpeting and furniture delivered for their living room. Everyone was excited—even their dog, Buffy! He raced around the room, barking.

"Kyle," called Mother, "please take Buffy outdoors until the movers have finished."

Later that day when everything was done, Kyle came in to take a look. "Wow! Everything looks so clean and pretty now!"

Just then, Buffy ran into the room. "Oh, no!" exclaimed Mother. "Get that dog out of here right now!"

Kyle went over and picked up Buffy. "But, Mom, you've always let him come in here before," he said.

"That was when we had our worn-out furniture and that grimy old rug. I want our new things kept clean," she explained.

That night, Dad told about a man he had witnessed to during the day. "Jerry couldn't seem to understand that he was a sinner," said Dad. "He kept saying he was no worse than anyone else. He thought he was good enough to make it into heaven without Christ."

"He's like Buffy," observed Kyle. "Buffy thinks he's good enough to be in the living room because he was allowed in our old, worn-out one. But when he tried to go into our new, clean one, Mom kicked him out!"

"Right!" said his father. "We may be 'good enough' for this sinful old world, but God would never let us into his sparkling, clean heaven the way we are. Until we let Christ wash away our sin with his blood, we're just 'too dirty' to live in heaven."

HOW ABOUT YOU? Do you think you're "no worse than anyone else"? You may be pretty good by this world's standards, but God's standard is absolute holiness. You can only get into heaven if you let Christ wash all your sins away by his blood. Receive him today! *S.L.K.*

TO MEMORIZE: Your eyes are too pure to look on evil; you cannot tolerate wrong. *Habakkuk 1:13* (NIV)

22 September

SINCERELY WRONG

FROM THE BIBLE:

"I assure you, I am the gate for the sheep," Jesus said. "All others who came before me were thieves and robbers. But the true sheep did not listen to them. Yes, I am the gate. Those who come in through me will be saved. Wherever they go, they will find green pastures. The thief's purpose is to steal and kill and destroy. My purpose is to give life in all its fullness."
JOHN 10:7-10

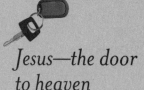

Jesus—the door to heaven

"HOW CAN YOU believe that there's only one way to heaven?" Connor asked Julio. "There are lots of good people following different ways to heaven."

Julio spoke firmly. "Jesus says he is the only door to heaven. We can only be saved through him."

Connor shook his head. "My dad says nobody has all the truth, and a person will go to heaven if he does what he sincerely believes is right."

"Those people may be sincere, but they're sincerely wrong," Julio answered. "Jesus is the only door."

The boys changed the subject, but Julio kept praying that he could lead Connor to Jesus. A few days later, Connor called Julio. "Want to go over to school with me?" he asked. "I left my trumpet there."

"Sure," agreed Julio, "but I doubt if you can get in. I'm sure it's locked up."

When the boys arrived at the school, they tried all the doors, but everything was locked. Just as they were leaving, a custodian saw them and let them in. They got the trumpet and headed for home.

"Hey, Connor," Julio said, "you sincerely thought there would be a door open, but you were sincerely wrong. In a way, the janitor was 'the door' for you to get into school. It was only when he unlocked the door that we could get in. Does this remind you of anything?"

Connor grinned. "I guess maybe you're right. I'll have to think about this. Jesus is the only door, huh?"

HOW ABOUT YOU? Do you sincerely believe you can get to heaven by being good? Do you think that anyone who earnestly does his best will be OK? Satan wants you to believe that, but Jesus says he is the only door. Trust him. *R.E.P.*

TO MEMORIZE: I am the gate. Those who come in through me will be saved. *John 10:9*

23 September

HIS LIFE FOR MINE

FROM THE BIBLE:

Now, no one is likely to die for a good person, though someone might be willing to die for a person who is especially good. But God showed his great love for us by sending Christ to die for us while we were still sinners. And since we have been made right in God's sight by the blood of Christ, he will certainly save us from God's judgment.
ROMANS 5:7-9

Jesus died for you

HUNTER LIKED Bible club, but he just couldn't understand why Jesus would allow himself to be crucified if he was really God.

One weekend, Mr. Taylor, the Bible club leader, took the boys camping. They visited a lookout tower deep in the woods. Mr. Davis, the forest ranger, told them about his work.

After the boys left the tower, Mr. Davis detected a gray cloud of smoke. He immediately reported to headquarters. Men, trucks, and equipment were sent to fight the blaze. Campers were evacuated, but no one could find Mr. Taylor and the boys. The fire was raging, so the sheriff told Mr. Davis he'd better leave.

"No," insisted Mr. Davis. "I have to find that group." He continued to search. Suddenly he saw Mr. Taylor and the boys! He quickly reported their exact location. Helicopters were sent, and they were saved!

After their rescue, the sheriff came in. "Boys," he said, "Mr. Davis got hurt in that fire. He stayed to save your lives. It was after I tried to talk Mr. Davis into leaving the tower that he spotted you. If he hadn't continued to search, you wouldn't be here now."

"You know, Hunter," said Mr. Taylor as they left, "this may help you understand how Jesus gave his life for us. He could have saved himself—but if he had, we could not have been saved from our sins. He was willing to die in our place, and he rose from the dead and is now in heaven. If you trust him as Savior, you will one day go to live with him forever."

HOW ABOUT YOU? Do you understand that you cannot save yourself? Have you asked Jesus to be your Savior? Won't you ask him today? *J.L.H.*

TO MEMORIZE: I lay down my life—only to take it up again. No one takes it from me, but I lay it down of my own accord. *John 10:17-18* (NIV)

24 September

THE SURPRISE PACKAGE

FROM THE BIBLE:

As Jesus continued on toward Jerusalem, he reached the border between Galilee and Samaria. As he entered a village there, ten lepers stood at a distance, crying out, "Jesus, Master, have mercy on us!"

He looked at them and said, "Go show yourselves to the priests." And as they went, their leprosy disappeared.

One of them, when he saw that he was healed, came back to Jesus, shouting, "Praise God, I'm healed!"

LUKE 17:11-15

Don't forget to say "thanks"

"THIS HAS BEEN one of the best birthdays I've ever had," said Jake as he looked at his gifts. There was a computer game, a magazine subscription, a sweater, a ten-dollar check, a new jacket, and a bike.

"Here's one more gift for you." Mom smiled as she handed him a small box.

"Another one?" Jake was surprised. "I thought I had opened them all." Quickly he ripped the paper off. "What is this? A box of stationery for a boy?"

"A box of thank-you notes, complete with stamps," said Mom. "Before you do another thing, sit down here and write thank-you notes to everyone who gave you a gift."

"Oh, Mom, I'll do it later," argued Jake. "I don't have time right now. I want to ride my bike and play with my computer game."

Mom shook her head. "Everyone who bought you a special gift spent time and money on you—time and money they could have used somewhere else. Certainly you have time to sit down and write a short note of thanks to each one."

Jake grumbled a bit, but he obeyed. Thirty minutes later, the notes were written, and Jake spent the rest of the evening enjoying his gifts.

At bedtime Dad remarked, "Every day the Lord gives us gifts, too, but so often we're in such a hurry to enjoy them that we neglect to tell him 'Thanks.' "

"Know what I'm going to start doing?" said Jake. "I'm going to start with 'thank-you prayers' before I ask the Lord for anything. And I'm going to start right now!"

HOW ABOUT YOU? Have you been putting off writing a thank-you note to someone? And what about the Lord? Do you owe him a "thank-you prayer"? Take time to offer your thanks now. You'll be glad you did. *L.M.W.*

TO MEMORIZE: It is good to give thanks to the Lord, to sing praises to the Most High. *Psalm 92:1*

25 September

JUNK FOODS

FROM THE BIBLE:

Now you can have sincere love for each other as brothers and sisters because you were cleansed from your sins when you accepted the truth of the Good News. So see to it that you really do love each other intensely with all your hearts.

For you have been born again. Your new life did not come from your earthly parents because the life they gave you will end in death. But this new life will last forever because it comes from the eternal, living word of God. . . .

And that word is the Good News that was preached to you.

So get rid of all malicious behavior and deceit. Don't just pretend to be good! Be done with hypocrisy and jealousy and backstabbing. You must crave pure spiritual milk so that you can grow into the fullness of your salvation. Cry out for this nourishment as a baby cries for milk, now that you have had a taste of the Lord's kindness.

1 PETER 1:22-23, 1:25–2:3

Improve your spiritual diet

"SOMEBODY MUST have decided we shouldn't eat junk food," grumbled Leslie when she came home from school one day. "They're taking the candy and pop machines out of the cafeteria and replacing them with machines that give fruit, raisins, milk, and juice."

"Good," approved Mom. "Those are better foods to eat. After all, food affects your health. Did you know that a Brazilian parrot changes color, depending on what kind of fish it eats?"

"If I eat candy, will I change color?" laughed Leslie. "Where do you learn such odd facts?"

"I learned that one in nurses' training. We were taught that we are what we eat." As Leslie turned on the TV, Mom added, "That applies to the mind, too."

"And you classify TV as junk food," Leslie finished.

"Suppose we didn't have television," suggested Mom. "What would you do instead?"

Leslie thought about it. "I don't know. Call a friend. Read a book. Maybe even do homework!" she said with a laugh.

"That would be considered good food, like apples, raisins, and juices," Mom said. "But you also need some meat or protein in your diet. What do you think that might be?"

"Bible reading," answered Leslie, as she turned off the TV. "And attending church and Sunday school."

"Good," agreed Mom. "Let's both work on improving our diets. You can start by eating an apple while you memorize your verse for Sunday school."

HOW ABOUT YOU? How is your diet? Are there some mental and spiritual junk foods you need to get rid of—things like books or TV programs that use bad language or have ungodly characters and dirty jokes? Are there healthy foods you need to add—like daily devotions and faithful attendance at church? Follow a spiritual diet that is pleasing to the Lord. *V.L.C.*

TO MEMORIZE: You must crave pure spiritual milk so that you can grow into the fullness of your salvation. *1 Peter 2:2*

26 September

THE DARK SMUDGE

FROM THE BIBLE:

Think clearly and exercise self-control. Look forward to the special blessings that will come to you at the return of Jesus Christ. Obey God because you are his children. Don't slip back into your old ways of doing evil; you didn't know any better then. But now you must be holy in everything you do, just as God—who chose you to be his children—is holy. For he himself has said, "You must be holy because I am holy."

And remember that the heavenly Father to whom you pray has no favorites when he judges. He will judge or reward you according to what you do. So you must live in reverent fear of him during your time as foreigners here on earth. . . .

Now you can have sincere love for each other as brothers and sisters because you were cleansed from your sins when you accepted the truth of the Good News. So see to it that you really do love each other intensely with all your hearts.

1 PETER 1:13-17, 22

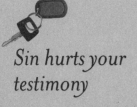

Sin hurts your testimony

"OK, SO I probably shouldn't have done it," admitted Jana. "But it's just one little thing!"

Mother sighed. "When you joined your friends in making fun of Jillian's stutter, you were not only hurting Jillian, you were grieving the Lord and hurting your testimony as well. You owe Jillian an apology."

Jana shrugged. "Why should anyone get so upset about one little incident? I said some nice things, too. Besides, Jillian's used to being teased."

The next Sunday, Jana decided to wear her favorite light blue dress to church. "You look very nice, dear," commented Mother as Jana entered the kitchen. "Here, have some waffles."

As Jana took the last delicious bite, her fork slipped, and some sticky syrup landed right in the middle of her lap. "Mother!" she wailed. "My dress! Now I'll have to go and change."

Mother surveyed the damage and shrugged. "Why get so upset about one little smudge?" she asked. "The rest of the dress looks very nice."

Jana stared. "But, Mother, the smudge is all that people will notice!"

Mother smiled. "You're right, of course," she agreed. "Now, I wonder if you can see that a smudge on your testimony is something like a smudge on your clean dress. It's the smudge that stands out, not the clean part."

Jana nodded thoughtfully. She would be sure to apologize to Jillian tonight. Little things did count!

HOW ABOUT YOU? Do you think it doesn't matter that you cheated just once? That you snubbed that unattractive person? That you went to a questionable activity? Remember, people are watching you. Even one sin can mar your testimony. Confess that sin to God. Determine with his help to live a holy life before him and others. *H.W.M.*

TO MEMORIZE: But just as he who called you is holy, so be holy in all you do; for it is written: "Be holy, because I am holy." *1 Peter 1:15* (NIV)

27 September

ALWAYS THERE

FROM THE BIBLE:

You chart the path ahead of me
and tell me where to stop
and rest.
Every moment you know
where I am.
You know what I am going
to say
even before I say it, Lord.
You both precede and follow me.
You place your hand of
blessing on my head.
Such knowledge is too wonderful
for me,
too great for me to know!
I can never escape from your
spirit!
I can never get away from
your presence!
If I go up to heaven, you
are there;
if I go down to the place of
the dead, you are there.
If I ride the wings of the
morning,
if I dwell by the farthest
oceans,
even there your hand will
guide me,
and your strength will
support me.

PSALM 139:3-10

"DON'T BE SCARED, Adam." Esther comforted her little brother. "Jesus will be with you when you're getting your teeth fixed."

Mom smiled. "That's right, Adam. Jesus is with you all the time."

When he came back out of the dentist's office, Adam was smiling. "It didn't hurt too bad," he said.

"See? I told you Jesus would be with you," said Esther as they left the office. "I get to sit in front with Mom," she added, running ahead to the car.

"No! I do!" protested Adam.

"I said so first," insisted Esther. She shoved Adam away, and he shoved back.

Mom pretended not to notice the children fighting. "God is with me today," she sang. "God is with me always. He's with me when I work, and he's with me when I play. He sees all I do." Adam and Esther looked uncertainly at each other.

"I know Jesus is with us when we're afraid," Esther said, "or when we need help with something. But I never thought about him being with us when we fight."

"He is, indeed," answered Mom. "He promised never to leave us. But we often forget that he sees everything we do."

"I'm sorry I was mean to you, Adam," said Esther. "You can sit in the front with Mom."

HOW ABOUT YOU? If you're a Christian, Jesus is always with you. That's a great comfort when you take a test or go to a new school. It's good to know he's with you when you're home alone or out in the dark. But don't forget, he's there through all the ordinary, routine things you do, too. Will he be pleased with what he sees you do today? Will he be pleased with what he hears? *H.W.M.*

TO MEMORIZE: The Lord your God will go ahead of you. He will neither fail you nor forsake you. *Deuteronomy 31:6*

God is always with you

28 September

SPECIAL IDENTITY
(PART 1)

FROM THE BIBLE:

He is the God who made the world and everything in it. Since he is Lord of heaven and earth, he doesn't live in man-made temples, and human hands can't serve his needs—for he has no needs. He himself gives life and breath to everything, and he satisfies every need there is. From one man he created all the nations throughout the whole earth. He decided beforehand which should rise and fall, and he determined their boundaries.

His purpose in all of this was that the nations should seek after God and perhaps feel their way toward him and find him—though he is not far from any one of us. For in him we live and move and exist. As one of your own poets says, "We are his offspring."

ACTS 17:24-28

Abortion is murder

CARLA DASHED into the house, waving a paper. "Hey, Mom, may we go to this?" she asked. The notice announced a free fingerprinting clinic at the mall for all children accompanied by a parent.

"Sure," said Mom. "No one else in all the world has fingerprints just like you, Carla. You're one of a kind."

Her older brother David read the notice. "When I did a report on abortion for health class, I found out that a person's fingerprint pattern appears on the fingers four or five months before he's even born. They stay the same throughout his lifetime."

"That shows how special a life is to God," said Mom. "Before we are born, God forms every little detail. It's sad that so many people regard the life of a preborn baby so lightly that they feel they have the right to end that life just because having a baby would be inconvenient."

Carla nodded. "Mrs. Weaver, my Sunday school teacher, is pregnant. Her doctors think there might be some problems with the baby, but she says God knows just what kind of baby she needs, and whatever he sends will be perfect for her."

"That's great," Mother exclaimed. "To take a life is never right, even if it's a life that is yet unborn and even if we fear it may have some defect. Life and death must be left in the hands of God."

HOW ABOUT YOU? Have you heard that the mother of an unborn child should be allowed to decide whether or not to have her baby? The decision should not be up to the mother. It should be up to God. Abortion—the killing of a preborn baby—is sin. It is murder. Christians should have no part of it. Rather, they should do all they can do to see that it is stopped. *J.L.H.*

TO MEMORIZE: He himself gives life and breath to everything. *Acts 17:25*

29 September

SPECIAL IDENTITY
(PART 2)

FROM THE BIBLE:

"I knew you before I formed you in your mother's womb. Before you were born I set you apart and appointed you as my spokesman to the world."

"O Sovereign Lord," I said, "I can't speak for you! I'm too young!"

"Don't say that," the Lord replied, "for you must go wherever I send you and say whatever I tell you. And don't be afraid of the people, for I will be with you and take care of you. I, the Lord, have spoken!"

Then the Lord touched my mouth and said, "See, I have put my words in your mouth! Today I appoint you to stand up against nations and kingdoms. You are to uproot some and tear them down, to destroy and overthrow them. You are to build others up and plant them."

JEREMIAH 1:5-10

God has a plan for you

CARLA AND HER mother headed for the fingerprinting clinic in a nearby mall. Just the day before, her Sunday school teacher had given birth to a baby girl. "Just think," squealed Carla, "Mrs. Weaver named her baby 'Carlotta'—almost the same as my name! I wonder what she'll be when she grows up."

"I don't know," Mother said, "but God does. He knows who we are before we are born. He has a special plan for our lives. Even before they were born, the Lord chose Jeremiah to be a prophet, Samson to be a Nazarite, and John the Baptist to be a forerunner of Christ."

"That's neat," said Carla. "Say, Mom, can we buy a gift for Mrs. Weaver and the baby?"

Mother agreed, so after the fingerprinting session, Carla and her mother shopped for a gift. They chose a plant and a pastel colored planter, shaped like a building block. Carla idly turned the planter over. "Mom, what is this?" she asked, pointing to a mark on the bottom of the planter.

Mother examined the planter. "That's the artist's initials," she said. "They identify the artist's work."

"Like my fingerprints identify me?" asked Carla.

"Something like that," agreed Mother. "God made you in his image, Carla, and gave you a special identity. He has a plan for your life. Obey him. Then you'll be a credit to his name."

"I will," Carla said. "I want my life to be beautiful and useful like this planter."

HOW ABOUT YOU? Did you know that you are a "designer's special"? God made you as you are for a particular purpose. He made you just right. He has a plan for your life. Be willing to accept whatever plans he has for you. You'll be glad you did. *J.L.H.*

TO MEMORIZE: I knew you before I formed you in your mother's womb. Before you were born I set you apart and appointed you as my spokesman to the world. *Jeremiah 1:5*

30 September

DON'T BE A BABY

FROM THE BIBLE:

You have been Christians a long time now, and you ought to be teaching others. Instead, you need someone to teach you again the basic things a beginner must learn about the Scriptures. You are like babies who drink only milk and cannot eat solid food. And a person who is living on milk isn't very far along in the Christian life and doesn't know much about doing what is right. Solid food is for those who are mature, who have trained themselves to recognize the difference between right and wrong and then do what is right.

HEBREWS 5:12-14

Learn a new verse

IT WAS DEVOTION time at the Ryan home. "Tonight," began Dad, "let's each quote a Bible verse. Choose one that has had special meaning to you recently."

Uh-oh, thought Andy. *I haven't learned any new verses in weeks.*

Andy listened to his big sister, Angela. "Psalm 119:97: 'Oh, how I love thy law! It is my meditation all the day,' " she quoted. "This verse reminds me to think about God's Word during the day."

"A good lesson for us all," said Dad. "How about you, Andy?"

"I like John 3:16," Andy replied. " 'For God so loved the world that he gave his only begotten Son, that whosoever believeth in him should not perish, but have everlasting life.' "

"You always say the same verse," fussed Angela, rolling her eyes. "Don't you ever learn any new ones?"

"It's an important verse," Mom assured him, "and I'm glad you like it. But it's also important to add new verses to our memory."

"Think of it this way," said Dad. "Mom gives Sarah baby food, right? But what if she gave all of us strained food?"

"Yuck!" Andy wrinkled his nose. "Baby food is for babies. We need solid food so we can grow."

"Right," said Dad. "John 3:16 is an important verse—just like baby food is important for Sarah. But as we grow in our Christian lives, we need to add solid foods to our spiritual diet so we won't be spiritual weaklings."

"In that case," said Andy, "please pass the Bible. I don't want to be a baby."

HOW ABOUT YOU? Have you learned any new verses lately? Are you adding new truths from the Bible to your spiritual life? It's important to remember verses we learned when we first became Christians, but we also should be learning new things so we can keep on growing. *D.L.R.*

TO MEMORIZE: Open my eyes to see the wonderful truths in your law. *Psalm 119:18*

IT DOES TAKE PRACTICE

FROM THE BIBLE:

*Great is the Lord! He is most
worthy of praise!
His greatness is beyond
discovery!
Let each generation tell its
children
of your mighty acts.
I will meditate on your majestic,
glorious splendor
and your wonderful miracles.
Your awe-inspiring deeds will be
on every tongue;
I will proclaim your greatness.
Everyone will share the story of
your wonderful goodness;
they will sing with joy of your
righteousness. . . .
The Lord is good to everyone.
He showers compassion on all
his creation.
All of your works will thank you,
Lord,
and your faithful followers
will bless you.
They will talk together about the
glory of your kingdom;
they will celebrate examples
of your power.
They will tell about your
mighty deeds
and about the majesty and
glory of your reign.*

PSALM 145:3-12

"I'M A FAILURE," Luis muttered as he walked home after school. "When Jeremy asked why I go to church, it was a perfect chance to tell him I go there to worship God and learn about his Son, Jesus. But I just changed the subject."

That evening Luis noticed his brother talking in front of his bedroom mirror. "What are you doing?" Luis asked.

Carlos turned around and laughed. "I'm practicing," he said. "Remember when I first started my speech class? I was scared silly to get up in front of the class. But I kind of like it now!"

"Aren't you scared anymore?" asked Luis.

Carlos nodded. "Yeah, but not quite as bad, thanks to my teacher."

"How did your teacher help you?"

"He said you have to practice to play a musical instrument well, and you also have to practice to become a good speaker," explained Carlos. "So I do, and it works."

Luis watched as Carlos turned back to his mirror and began his speech again. *Practice,* thought Luis as he went to his own room. *That's what I have to do too.*

When Carlos passed Luis's room a little later, Luis was in front of his mirror saying, "I'm a Christian, and you can be one too." He cleared his throat. "I'm a Christian," he repeated, "and you can be one too." He paused. "The Bible says . . ." Carlos smiled and walked on as Luis continued to practice witnessing.

HOW ABOUT YOU? Do you have trouble knowing how to talk about Jesus? Practice at home in front of a mirror. Then you may want to practice with a friend or a parent. Soon you'll find it natural to speak up for the Lord whenever you have a chance. You can be a witness for him. *H.W.M.*

TO MEMORIZE: Your awe-inspiring deeds will be on every tongue; I will proclaim your greatness. *Psalm 145:6*

Practice witnessing

2 October

THE GIFT OR THE GIVER?

FROM THE BIBLE:

But God shows his anger from heaven against all sinful, wicked people who push the truth away from themselves. For the truth about God is known to them instinctively. God has put this knowledge in their hearts. From the time the world was created, people have seen the earth and sky and all that God made. They can clearly see his invisible qualities—his eternal power and divine nature. So they have no excuse whatsoever for not knowing God.

Yes, they knew God, but they wouldn't worship him as God or even give him thanks. And they began to think up foolish ideas of what God was like. The result was that their minds became dark and confused. Claiming to be wise, they became utter fools instead. . . .

So God let them go ahead and do whatever shameful things their hearts desired. As a result, they did vile and degrading things with each other's bodies. Instead of believing what they knew was the truth about God, they deliberately chose to believe lies. So they worshiped the things God made but not the Creator himself.

ROMANS 1:18-22, 24-25

Love the giver, not the gift

DAN'S UNCLE JACK was driving through town on a business trip and had stopped in a brief visit. "It sure is good to see you all!" he exclaimed. "I only have an hour before I must drive on." He handed Dan a package. "Here's a little something for you."

"Thanks!" said Dan as he unwrapped a kit for building a ship inside a bottle. Soon he was busy sorting the pieces and putting the model together. Mom suggested that he put it aside until later. "OK," he agreed, but he was having so much fun, he kept right on working. Suddenly he heard Uncle Jack say, "Well, I'm sorry I have to leave so soon."

"Uncle Jack!" exclaimed Dan. "You're not leaving already, are you?"

Uncle Jack smiled. "I really must be going now."

After Uncle Jack's car pulled away, Mom turned to Dan and asked, "Why did you ignore your uncle?"

"Uh . . . well," said Dan, "I didn't mean to ignore him. It's just that I got so interested in that model, I sort of forgot he was here."

Dad said, "Your uncle looked disappointed when you didn't pay any attention to him."

"But, Dad," said Dan, "didn't he want me to enjoy the gift he gave me?"

"Sure," his father replied, "but you got so interested in the gift, you forgot about the giver."

"I guess you're right," Dan said. "I'll go write a note to Uncle Jack. I want him to know that I love him more than the gift he gave me."

HOW ABOUT YOU? God has given you many good things to enjoy. Do you sometimes pay more attention to the gifts than to the Giver? God's gifts should never take the place of God himself. It's the Giver who really counts! *S.L.K.*

TO MEMORIZE: Their trust should be in the living God, who richly gives us all we need for our enjoyment. *1 Timothy 6:17*

3 October

IT CAME UP SQUASH

FROM THE BIBLE:

Don't be misled. Remember that you can't ignore God and get away with it. You will always reap what you sow! Those who live only to satisfy their own sinful desires will harvest the consequences of decay and death. But those who live to please the Spirit will harvest everlasting life from the Spirit. So don't get tired of doing what is good. Don't get discouraged and give up, for we will reap a harvest of blessing at the appropriate time. Whenever we have the opportunity, we should do good to everyone, especially to our Christian brothers and sisters.

GALATIANS 6:7-10

"OH, THIS MEAL looks delicious," said Mason's dad as they began to eat. "Mason, please pass the watermelon."

Mason paused with his fork halfway to his mouth. "Watermelon?" He looked around.

"Right there in that bowl in front of you," said Dad.

Mason looked at the bowl heaped full of golden squash. Then he noticed the smile on his dad's face and he understood. "Oh, sure, Dad. Here's the watermelon." He laughed as he passed the squash.

"I don't get it," said Mason's sister, Melanie. "Why are you calling the squash *watermelon?*"

Mason explained. "Well, ah . . . I made a little mistake when we were planting the garden, and Dad won't let me forget it."

"Mason wanted to plant watermelon," said Dad, "and I told him he was using squash seeds. But he insisted they were watermelon seeds."

"A perfectly innocent mistake," murmured Mason.

"He said that when they grew, I'd see for myself," continued Dad, "and here's the finished product." Everyone chuckled good-naturedly.

"You always reap what you sow," said Mother. "That's true, both in a garden and in life. Even as Christians we need to be careful to sow the right kind of seeds."

"That's right," agreed Dad. "If we sow evil, we can expect to reap evil and sorrow. If we sow good, we can expect to reap happiness and blessings."

HOW ABOUT YOU? Are you sowing any evil seeds, such as lies, disrespect for authority, and unfaithfulness in church? Or are you sowing good seeds, such as obedience, cheerful giving, and reverence for God? The things you do now may seem small and unimportant, but little seeds grow. Make sure you sow things now that you'll want to reap later. *H.W.M.*

TO MEMORIZE: Don't be misled. Remember that you can't ignore God and get away with it. You will always reap what you sow! *Galatians 6:7*

You reap what you sow

4 October

THE TALKING TOOLS

FROM THE BIBLE:

Yes, the body has many different parts, not just one part. If the foot says, "I am not a part of the body because I am not a hand," that does not make it any less a part of the body. And if the ear says, "I am not part of the body because I am only an ear and not an eye," would that make it any less a part of the body? Suppose the whole body were an eye—then how would you hear? Or if your whole body were just one big ear, how could you smell anything?

But God made our bodies with many parts, and he has put each part just where he wants it. What a strange thing a body would be if it had only one part! Yes, there are many parts, but only one body. The eye can never say to the hand, "I don't need you." The head can't say to the feet, "I don't need you."

In fact, some of the parts that seem weakest and least important are really the most necessary.

1 CORINTHIANS 12:14-22

Be God's tools

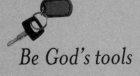

AS RYAN HELPED Uncle Ken replace his porch floor, he worked quietly with no smile.

"Your friend Jason sang a great solo with the junior choir," Uncle Ken said as he pulled nails. Ryan didn't answer. Uncle Ken looked at him curiously. "Have you two been playing tennis lately?"

"No!" snapped Ryan

"Have you been arguing with Jason?" Uncle Ken probed.

Ryan sighed heavily. "No," he said, "it's just that he does everything better than I do. I used to sing solos. Now Jason sings them. He's the star student in Sunday school, too. He brings more visitors, learns more Bible verses—and he even beats me at tennis."

"Ryan," said Uncle Ken, "what if the hammer got mad when we started using the tape measure? Or what if the saw said, 'I'm tired of cutting boards. If you don't let me pull nails, I won't work'?"

Ryan grinned. "That won't happen. Tools have to do what they're made to do."

Uncle Ken picked up the saw. "You're right," he agreed. "And, as Christians, we're like tools in God's hands. We must do what we are designed to do."

"But Jason does everything I do," Ryan said, "only better."

"How many hammers are in my toolbox, Ryan?"

"Two."

"And God doesn't have just one soloist or one witness or one worker," said Uncle Ken. "But when you're a tool, you don't tell the carpenter when you'll work or what you'll do. You simply lie in his hand and let him use you."

"You're right, Uncle Ken. From now on, I'll work or wait, whatever God says."

HOW ABOUT YOU? Do you tell God what you will do and what you won't do? Be a tool God can use—willing to do whatever he wants you to do. *B.J.W.*

TO MEMORIZE: All of you together are Christ's body, and each one of you is a separate and necessary part of it. *1 Corinthians 12:27*

THE UNIFORM WON'T HELP

FROM THE BIBLE:

He saved us, not because of the good things we did, but because of his mercy. He washed away our sins and gave us a new life through the Holy Spirit. He generously poured out the Spirit upon us because of what Jesus Christ our Savior did. He declared us not guilty because of his great kindness. And now we know that we will inherit eternal life.
TITUS 3:5-7

Salvation is not by works

"I SEE IT, but I don't believe it!" exclaimed Shelby. Her brother had just come into the room wearing a professional basketball uniform.

Andy laughed. "The Basket-Masters were at our high school assembly, and I won the door prize. I get to play with their team for a few minutes at their exhibition game tonight."

"This is really going to be good. The biggest basketball klutz in town playing with the most famous team in the world!" teased Shelby.

And it *was* good. During the short time Andy was on the floor, the Basket-Masters fed him the ball several times. Once he dropped it; once he passed it to a member of the wrong team; once he even took a shot at the wrong basket. He laughed along with everyone at his mistakes.

The next Sunday a friend brought Andy to Sunday school. "So glad you came," Mr. Markham, the teacher, said. "Do you have a church family?"

"Oh, sure," responded Andy. "I go to church, I pray before meals, and I try to help people. I'm a good Christian."

Mr. Markham smiled. "Say, I saw you play basketball the other night. That uniform looked great on you."

"Yeah, but I wasn't much of a basketball player."

"Sometimes people wear another 'uniform'—that of a Christian," said Mr. Markham. "They may look like Christians, but they're not unless they've accepted Christ as Savior."

Andy looked puzzled. "I thought I just had to live right. Explain that again."

HOW ABOUT YOU? Are you a Christian? Or are you just "wearing the uniform"—trying to live a good life? Wearing the uniform won't save you. You're saved by believing that Jesus is God's Son and that he died for your sins. Trust in what he has done for you rather than in what you do yourself. *H.W.M.*

TO MEMORIZE: He saved us, not because of the good things we did, but because of his mercy. *Titus 3:5*

6 October

AS I SEE IT

FROM THE BIBLE:

Do for others as you would like them to do for you.

Do you think you deserve credit merely for loving those who love you? Even the sinners do that! . . .

Love your enemies! Do good to them! Lend to them! And don't be concerned that they might not repay. Then your reward from heaven will be very great, and you will truly be acting as children of the Most High, for he is kind to the unthankful and to those who are wicked. You must be compassionate, just as your Father is compassionate.

Stop judging others, and you will not be judged. Stop criticizing others, or it will all come back on you. If you forgive others, you will be forgiven. If you give, you will receive. Your gift will return to you in full measure, pressed down, shaken together to make room for more, and running over. Whatever measure you use in giving—large or small—it will be used to measure what is given back to you.

LUKE 6:31-38

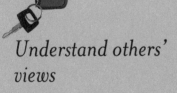

Understand others' views

"GUESS WHERE Joseph Gordon thinks our gym class should go for a field trip?" said Kevin. He was sitting on the steps with his friend Jay, watching the clouds float by. "To see a high school football game," continued Kevin, sounding disgusted.

"Oh, no!" groaned Jay. "I'd rather go to Sportland. I suppose he'll try to get everybody to vote for the football game. I can't stand that guy!"

"Me neither," agreed Kevin. He pointed up at one of the clouds. "Speaking of footballs, that cloud looks like a foot kicking a football."

Jay looked where Kevin was pointing. "I see a dog with a bone."

"How about that one?" Kevin pointed again. "That's a dragon."

"Naw, that's an alligator," said Jay with a grin. The boys spent the next few minutes pointing out pictures they saw in the clouds. Sometimes they agreed on what the clouds looked like; sometimes they didn't.

"You know," Kevin said, "it doesn't make us mad that we don't look at the clouds in the same way. Maybe we shouldn't be mad if people look at other things differently too."

Jay looked at his friend. "You mean Joseph, don't you?" he said. He sighed. "I guess there's no law that says he has to like the same things we like. But I'm still going to try to get kids to vote for Sportland, and may the best man win!"

HOW ABOUT YOU? People look at many things in different ways. You need to love people and accept them even if they don't see things exactly as you do. Just agree to disagree as long as their opinions are not in opposition to the Scriptures. (For example, the Bible teaches that things such as stealing, murder, and homosexuality are wrong. You do not have to accept lifestyles that conflict with what God teaches.) *H.W.M.*

TO MEMORIZE: Do for others as you would like them to do for you. *Luke 6:31*

DUMB DUCKS

FROM THE BIBLE:

Be strong with the Lord's mighty power. Put on all of God's armor so that you will be able to stand firm against all strategies and tricks of the Devil. For we are not fighting against people made of flesh and blood, but against the evil rulers and authorities of the unseen world, against those mighty powers of darkness who rule this world, and against wicked spirits in the heavenly realms.

Use every piece of God's armor to resist the enemy in the time of evil, so that after the battle you will still be standing firm. Stand your ground, putting on the sturdy belt of truth and the body armor of God's righteousness. For shoes, put on the peace that comes from the Good News, so that you will be fully prepared. In every battle you will need faith as your shield to stop the fiery arrows aimed at you by Satan. Put on salvation as your helmet, and take the sword of the Spirit, which is the word of God. Pray at all times and on every occasion in the power of the Holy Spirit.

EPHESIANS 6:10-18

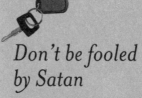

LUKE WATCHED as his big brother, Ryan, got ready to go duck hunting. "What are you going to do with those?" asked Luke, pointing to some painted wooden ducks.

"These are decoys," Ryan explained. "No duck will come near me if he sees me with a gun in my hands. So I hide, but I put these decoys in the lake. When the ducks flying overhead see them, they think to themselves, *If that's a good spot for our brothers to land, it must be a good place for us.* Then down they come."

"What dumb ducks!" said Luke.

That evening Luke and Ryan watched a football game on TV. During a commercial, Ryan opened a magazine. But he noticed his younger brother watching a liquor advertisement. "Don't be a dumb duck," said Ryan.

"What are you talking about?"

"Satan might be fooling you with the 'decoys' in that commercial," said Ryan. "The people in that ad look happy and healthy. You never see someone with a hangover or a smashed-up car in those ads. You only see the 'decoys.' "

After turning the channel, Luke pointed to an ad in his brother's magazine. "Don't be a dumb duck yourself. In a few years, the strong, healthy guy in that cigarette ad could be gasping in pain from lung cancer."

"You're right," Ryan said, turning the page. "Let's both be smart guys, not dumb ducks."

HOW ABOUT YOU? Does Satan fool you by making sin look attractive? A good report card may make cheating seem worthwhile. A candy bar may make stealing look attractive. Being accepted by the other kids may make it seem all right to laugh at a dirty joke. Don't be fooled by the decoys Satan shows you. *H.W.M.*

TO MEMORIZE: Put on all of God's armor so that you will be able to stand firm against all strategies and tricks of the Devil. *Ephesians 6:11*

Don't be fooled by Satan

8 October

PASSING THE TEST

FROM THE BIBLE:

Joseph returned to Egypt with his brothers and all who had accompanied him to his father's funeral. But now that their father was dead, Joseph's brothers became afraid. "Now Joseph will pay us back for all the evil we did to him," they said. So they sent this message to Joseph: "Before your father died, he instructed us to say to you: 'Forgive your brothers for the great evil they did to you.' So we, the servants of the God of your father, beg you to forgive us." When Joseph received the message, he broke down and wept. Then his brothers came and bowed low before him. "We are your slaves," they said.

But Joseph told them, "Don't be afraid of me. Am I God, to judge and punish you? As far as I am concerned, God turned into good what you meant for evil. He brought me to the high position I have today so I could save the lives of many people. No, don't be afraid. Indeed, I myself will take care of you and your families." And he spoke very kindly to them, reassuring them.

GENESIS 50:14-21

Be sweet when tested

"TESTS! TESTS! TESTS!" grumbled Brooke and Tucker to Gramps Wilson one day. "We hate tests!"

Gramps smiled. "I reckon we all do," he agreed, "but tests are a part of life. Everybody has 'em."

"You don't," protested the children. "You're out of school."

But before long Tucker and Brooke learned that not all tests are on paper, and not all lessons are learned from a book. The next time Gramps saw them, they looked unhappy. He asked what was wrong. "Our friend Eric is moving away," mumbled Tucker. "His folks are getting a divorce."

"Oh, Gramps, Eric doesn't understand why they're splitting up," cried Brooke. "He thinks his parents don't love him anymore."

"Oh, I'm sure they love him," Gramps said. "This is a hard test for your friend—and you, too, because you'll miss him."

"I hate tests!" declared Tucker.

As the children talked with Gramps, he reminded them of Joseph, who had been sold into Egypt by his brothers. Joseph faced many difficulties, but he didn't become bitter. He stayed kind and obedient to God and even forgave his brothers.

"That's what we're going to have to do," Brooke suddenly exclaimed. "We'll try to be patient and kind to Eric's parents. We'll encourage Eric to trust God through all of this."

Gramps nodded. "I'm sure the whole family is pretty unhappy," he said. "Try to help your friend not to be bitter or angry. And don't you be bitter or angry about his moving away. Ask the Lord to help you 'pass' this test."

HOW ABOUT YOU? Are you or a friend facing a difficult test? A divorce? Loss of a parent's job? Whatever it is, trust the Lord. Wait to see what he is working out for you. Meanwhile, be patient and kind. Help those around you pass their tests too. *B.J.W.*

TO MEMORIZE: When the way is rough, your patience has a chance to grow. *James 1:3* (TLB)

9 October

DIRTY HANDS

"YOU SURE TOLD old Frazier off," laughed Nate.

Derrick shrugged. "So he thinks I cheated on a test. Let him prove it!"

At the bus stop, Nate sighed. "I sure hate going home. My folks fight all the time."

"It was that way at our house, too, before we became Christians," Derrick said.

"What do you mean, '*before* we became Christians'?" Nate sneered. "I sure would have hated to know you before that happened."

Derrick's face turned red. "Why, you . . ."

"See what I mean?" Nate laughed. "You're ready to fight at the drop of a hat."

When Derrick got home, his mother said, "Aunt Velma invited us over for dinner."

"Oh, no! I can't stand to eat there! Her hands are always dirty."

"Relax," his mother said. "We can't go this time. Dad has to work late."

Later, as they sat on the porch, Derrick told his folks about Nate's problems. "I tried to tell him that Jesus could help his family, but he wasn't interested." Just then Nate came up the street on his bike.

"Derrick sure told old Frazier off today," Nate said. Word for word Nate repeated the incident. The silence following his story let Nate know that Derrick's role was not appreciated by his folks, so he soon left.

"No wonder Nate wasn't interested when you witnessed to him," Dad said. "You were offering Jesus, the 'Bread of Life,' with dirty hands."

Mom nodded. "No matter how good the food is that Aunt Velma prepares, her dirty hands make it unappealing. If we offer people the 'Bread of Life' with dirty hands, they won't accept him."

HOW ABOUT YOU? Have you ever had your friends reject your witness? Check up on yourself. Are you living a Christian life or just talking about it? Are your "hands clean"? *B.J.W.*

TO MEMORIZE: Wash your hands, you sinners, and let your hearts be filled with God alone. *James 4:8* (TLB)

FROM THE BIBLE:

He gives us more and more strength to stand against such evil desires. As the Scriptures say,

"God sets himself against the proud,

but he shows favor tp the humble."

So humble yourselves before God. Resist the Devil, and he will flee from you. Draw close to God, and God will draw close to you. Wash your hands, you sinners; purify your hearts, you hypocrites. Let there be tears for the wrong things you have done. Let there be sorrow and deep grief. Let there be sadness instead of laughter, and gloom instead of joy. When you bow down before the Lord and admit your dependence on him, he will lift you up and give you honor.

Don't speak evil against each other, my dear brothers and sisters. If you criticize each other and condemn each other, then you are criticizing and condemning God's law. But you are not a judge who can decide whether the law is right or wrong. Your job is to obey it.

JAMES 4:6-11

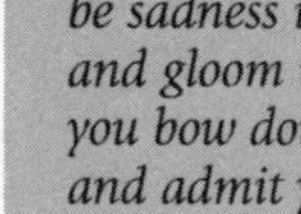

Live what you talk

10 October

DIFFERENT GIFTS

FROM THE BIBLE:

Now there are different kinds of spiritual gifts, but it is the same Holy Spirit who is the source of them all. There are different kinds of service in the church, but it is the same Lord we are serving. . . . A spiritual gift is given to each of us as a means of helping the entire church.

To one person the Spirit gives the ability to give wise advice; to another he gives the gift of special knowledge. The Spirit gives special faith to another, and to someone else he gives the power to heal the sick. He gives one person the power to perform miracles, and to another the ability to prophesy. He gives someone else the ability to know whether it is really the Spirit of God or another spirit that is speaking. Still another person is given the ability to speak in unknown languages, and another is given the ability to interpret what is being said. It is the one and only Holy Spirit who distributes these gifts. He alone decides which gift each person should have.

1 CORINTHIANS 12:4-11

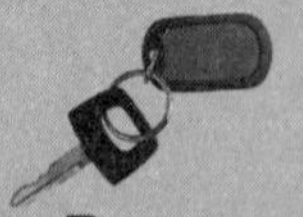

Be yourself

WHEN THE MARTIN boys came in from school, Mark bounded into the kitchen, and Matt went into his room. "I made all As on my report card," announced Mark proudly.

Mom hugged him. "Good for you! That makes me very happy. Where's Matt?"

Mark shrugged. "Gone to his room, I guess."

Mom went down the hall. "May I come in, Matt?"

"I guess so," came the muffled reply. "I suppose you want to see my report card." Without looking at Mom, Matt handed it to her.

"Hmmm . . . not bad," Mom said with a smile.

"And not too good either," Matt added angrily. "Mark got all As. I didn't even make the honor roll."

Mom sat down beside Matt. "I'm proud of both you and Mark. You're brothers, but you're very different, and that's good. Mark loves to read and study. You—"

"Are stupid," Matt interrupted.

"Matt, don't say that," Mom scolded. "You're smart in a different way than Mark. For instance, when his bike was broken, who fixed it?"

"I did, but there wasn't much wrong with it," Matt said with a shrug.

"You have mechanical abilities that Mark doesn't have. Last year we gave Mark a chess game, and we gave you a set of tools, remember? Did it make you mad because we gave you different birthday gifts?" Mom asked.

"Of course not," said Matt.

"God gives each Christian different gifts, too, as we read from 1 Corinthians this morning," Mom explained. "Don't think less of your abilities just because they're not like Mark's. Thank God for the talents you have, and use them."

HOW ABOUT YOU? Do you compare your abilities with those others have? God didn't give you the same gifts he gave others. Just be yourself. Use the talents God gave you, and they will grow. *B.J.W.*

TO MEMORIZE: Each one should use whatever gift he has received to serve others. *1 Peter 4:10* (NIV)

11 October

LUIS'S LESSON

FROM THE BIBLE:

Oh, how I love your law!
I think about it all day long.
Your commands make me wiser
than my enemies,
for your commands are my
constant guide.
Yes, I have more insight than my
teachers,
for I am always thinking of
your decrees.
I am even wiser than my elders,
for I have kept your
commandments.
I have refused to walk on any
path of evil,
that I may remain obedient to
your word.
I haven't turned away from
your laws,
for you have taught me well.
How sweet are your words to my
taste;
they are sweeter than honey.

PSALM 119:97-103

"Eat" the Bible

"SOMETIMES THE Bible uses funny language, Mom," said Luis one evening.

"Funny language?" Mom repeated. "In what way?"

"Well, our Sunday school lessons have been about the Bible. Last week we read some verses from Jeremiah 15," explained Luis. "There's a verse about 'eating' God's Word."

Mom chuckled. "When you were a baby, there was one time you literally tried to eat the Bible. You were sitting on my lap in church. When I looked down, there you were, chewing on my Bible."

They laughed together. "Well, I know I'm not supposed to really eat my Bible," Luis responded. "So what does it mean when it says that?"

Mom thought for a moment, then smiled. "Can you remember when you were smaller and baseball was all you ever wanted to play? You watched baseball on TV and always wanted me to buy cereals with pictures of baseball players. You collected all the baseball cards you could afford. Grandma used to say, 'That boy lives, eats, and sleeps baseball.' "

"Oh, I see," Luis answered. "So 'eating the Bible' means to let the Bible become really important in my life—even more important than food, I guess."

Just then Luis's older sister, Juanita, walked into the room with her nose buried in a book. "Juanita, I've just made oatmeal cookies. Do you want one?" Mom asked. But Juanita was so interested in her book that she didn't even hear.

"I'll take hers," Luis laughed. "She's 'eating' her book right now."

HOW ABOUT YOU? How important is the Bible to you? Do you ever "eat" it—that is, become thoroughly engrossed in it? Make time in your schedule to read the Bible. Find a quiet place and ask God to help you understand it. Doing this daily will help you develop a love for the Bible. *R.E.P.*

TO MEMORIZE: When your words came, I ate them; they were my joy and my heart's delight. *Jeremiah 15:16* (NIV)

12 October

FORGIVE ME! FORGIVE ME!

FROM THE BIBLE:

This is the message he has given us to announce to you: God is light and there is no darkness in him at all. So we are lying if we say we have fellowship with God but go on living in spiritual darkness. We are not living in the truth. But if we are living in the light of God's presence, just as Christ is, then we have fellowship with each other, and the blood of Jesus, his Son, cleanses us from every sin.

If we say we have no sin, we are only fooling ourselves and refusing to accept the truth. But if we confess our sins to him, he is faithful and just to forgive us and to cleanse us from every wrong.

1 JOHN 1:5-9

Accept God's forgiveness

"PLEASE FORGIVE ME. In Jesus' name. Amen." There! Darla felt better. This was the third time she had asked God to forgive her for lying because every now and then she still felt guilty. Now Mother smiled at her, tucked her into bed, and kissed her good night.

The next afternoon Mother suddenly exclaimed, "Oh, Darla, I was supposed to ask if you wanted to go shopping with Grandma today. I forgot, and now it's too late. I'm so sorry. Can you forgive me?"

Darla nodded. "Sure, Mom. Grandma and I can shop another day."

At the supper table Mother said, "Darla, I am sorry about the shopping trip. Forgive me."

"That's OK," Darla replied.

After supper as Darla loaded the dishwasher Mother said, "Honey, I feel bad that you missed shopping with Grandma. Will you please forgive me?"

"I *told* you—it's OK."

When Darla was ready for bed, Mother came into her room. "About the shopping trip, honey. I hope you'll forgive me."

"Mother! You've apologized for that same thing over and over! You act as if you don't believe me when I say I forgave you!"

Mother smiled. "Isn't that the way you've been treating God?" she asked. "You were sorry that you lied about where you had been the other day. So you confessed it to me and to God. You know I forgave you. The Bible says that God forgives you too. Yet you confess the same thing again and again. You act as if you don't believe him."

"You're right," admitted Darla. "I don't need to feel guilty anymore!"

HOW ABOUT YOU? Do you keep asking God's forgiveness over and over for the same sin? He forgave you the first time you sincerely asked him to. Believe his promise to forgive. *H.W.M.*

TO MEMORIZE: If we confess our sins to him, he is faithful and just to forgive us and to cleanse us from every wrong. *1 John 1:9*

13 October

COME TO ME!

FROM THE BIBLE:

Then Jesus prayed this prayer: "O Father, Lord of heaven and earth, thank you for hiding the truth from those who think themselves so wise and clever, and for revealing it to the childlike. Yes, Father, it pleased you to do it this way!

"My Father has given me authority over everything. No one really knows the Son except the Father, and no one really knows the Father except the Son and those to whom the Son chooses to reveal him."

Then Jesus said, "Come to me, all of you who are weary and carry heavy burdens, and I will give you rest. Take my yoke upon you. Let me teach you, because I am humble and gentle, and you will find rest for your souls. For my yoke fits perfectly, and the burden I give you is light."

MATTHEW 11:25-30

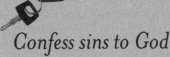

Confess sins to God

BROCK FELT guilty as he jumped into bed. Earlier at his friend's house he had watched a TV program that he was not allowed to see at home. Now Bible reading and praying didn't appeal to him, so he went to sleep instead.

After school the next day Brock idly bounced a ball in the family room even though he knew it was against the rules to play ball in the house. He tossed the ball again and was horrified to hear a loud crash. One of his father's glass paperweights lay shattered on the floor! "Oh, no!" Brock cried. He quickly swept up the pieces and threw them out.

At the supper table Dad asked, "How about a game of checkers tonight?"

"You won't want to play with me when you know what I did," said Brock. Then he told his dad what had happened.

"I'm disappointed that you disobeyed me," Dad said. "But I'm glad you told me about it. I want you to always feel free to come to me, no matter what you've done. We may need to have a serious talk about it, but I'll never turn you away."

"Thanks, Dad," said Brock softly.

"Our heavenly Father has set a good example for us. He won't turn us away either," Dad replied.

Brock thought about that and knew he had to confess some things to God. His guilt had caused him to avoid Dad's company—and God, too. He wanted to make things right. He had a great dad and an even greater God!

HOW ABOUT YOU? When you have done something wrong, do you sometimes avoid God? He wants you to confess your sin to him and spend time with him. *J.L.H.*

TO MEMORIZE: Let us come boldly to the throne of our gracious God. There we will receive his mercy, and we will find grace to help us when we need it. *Hebrews 4:16*

14 October

A CRAZY AFTERNOON

FROM THE BIBLE:

As for you, promote the kind of living that reflects right teaching. Teach the older men to exercise self-control, to be worthy of respect, and to live wisely. They must have strong faith and be filled with love and patience.

Similarly, teach the older women to live in a way that is appropriate for someone serving the Lord. They must not go around speaking evil of others and must not be heavy drinkers. Instead, they should teach others what is good. These older women must train the younger women to love their husbands and their children, to live wisely and be pure, to take care of their homes, to do good, and to be submissive to their husbands. Then they will not bring shame on the word of God.

In the same way, encourage the young men to live wisely in all they do. And you yourself must be an example to them by doing good deeds of every kind. Let everything you do reflect the integrity and seriousness of your teaching. Let your teaching be so correct that it can't be criticized.

TITUS 2:1-8

Love children

CASSANDRA WONDERED if the afternoon would ever end. She was baby-sitting the three Norris children while their mother ran some errands, and things weren't going well. So far Tina had unrolled an entire package of paper towels, Tracy had spilled a box of cereal, and Tyler kept crying for his mother.

"Can't you make us some popcorn?" Tracy whined.

Cassandra shook her head. "No, Tracy. Your mother said you could have some cereal and that was all."

"Please," Tracy begged. "I'm hungry."

"No, but I could read you a story," suggested Cassandra.

Surprisingly, Cassandra's suggestion worked. Tyler even stopped crying. By the time Cassandra finished reading, he was asleep on the couch. "Girls, let's see how quietly we can walk to the playroom," whispered Cassandra. "I'll help you with that big puzzle."

"Ooh, that will be fun!" Tracy whispered back.

When Mrs. Norris arrived home she said, "Looks as if everything is under control. Thanks a lot, Cassandra."

Later Cassandra told her mother about the afternoon. "Once we got busy doing something together, I even enjoyed it," she said.

"Great," approved Mother. "And did you know you got some good training?"

"Good training in what?" asked Cassandra.

"In Titus 2 the Lord gives a list of things young men and women are to learn. One of the things is to learn to love children."

"Wow," Cassandra said. "I didn't realize I was taking a course in loving children this afternoon."

HOW ABOUT YOU? Have you ever had an opportunity to entertain a young child for an hour or so? The Lord says that learning to love and care for children is something you should do. Be responsible and caring toward those whom you watch. *L.M.W.*

TO MEMORIZE: Older women must train the younger women to love their husbands and their children. *Titus 2:4*

THE BROKEN PROMISE

FROM THE BIBLE:

Since God chose you to be the holy people whom he loves, you must clothe yourselves with tenderhearted mercy, kindness, humility, gentleness, and patience. You must make allowance for each other's faults and forgive the person who offends you. Remember, the Lord forgave you, so you must forgive others. And the most important piece of clothing you must wear is love. Love is what binds us all together in perfect harmony. And let the peace that comes from Christ rule in your hearts. For as members of one body you are all called to live in peace. And always be thankful.

Let the words of Christ, in all their richness, live in your hearts and make you wise. Use his words to teach and counsel each other. Sing psalms and hymns and spiritual songs to God with thankful hearts. And whatever you do or say, let it be as a representative of the Lord Jesus, all the while giving thanks through him to God the Father.

COLOSSIANS 3:12-17

AMY WAS SO EXCITED she could hardly sit still. As soon as the car stopped, she jumped out and bounded up the walk. She glanced at her watch—exactly 9:25 A.M., the time she had told Larissa they'd pick her up for Sunday school. Just last evening Larissa had promised to be ready.

Amy rang the doorbell, but no answer. She rang again. Still no answer. Then Amy noticed that the Andersons' car was gone. She stalked back to the car and slammed the door. "She's not home. She didn't even bother to let me know she couldn't come, so we drove clear across town for her. That's rude," Amy stormed. "She broke her promise!"

"Perhaps they had an emergency," suggested her mother.

"She could have called," Amy insisted. To herself she added, *I'll not bother to invite her again.*

Amy was still angry when she entered her Sunday school classroom. "Good morning, Amy," Miss Mason greeted her. "I missed you yesterday."

Amy's mouth fell open. She had promised to help decorate their classroom, and she had forgotten. "Ooohh, I'm so sorry, Miss Mason," Amy gasped. "I forgot! We went to my grandparents' farm."

Miss Mason smiled gently. "That's all right, Amy. I forget things myself sometimes. Maybe you can help me next month."

Amy nodded. *And maybe Larissa can come to Sunday school next Sunday,* she thought.

HOW ABOUT YOU? Have you ever made a promise and then forgotten it? Has anyone broken a promise to you? Did it make you angry? God says if we want forgiveness, we must give it. *B.J.W.*

TO MEMORIZE: Be kind to each other, tenderhearted, forgiving one another, just as God through Christ has forgiven you. *Ephesians 4:32*

Forgive those who forget

16 October

UNDER THE SKIN

FROM THE BIBLE:

Try to live in peace with everyone, and seek to live a clean and holy life, for those who are not holy will not see the Lord. Look after each other so that none of you will miss out on the special favor of God. Watch out that no bitter root of unbelief rises up among you, for whenever it springs up, many are corrupted by its poison.
HEBREWS 12:14-15

Dig out bitterness

ERIN'S TEARS blurred the beauty of the roses she was clipping. Her friend Hannah had become best friends with Caitlin, the new girl in town. Now Erin was lonely. "So who cares?" she muttered angrily. "I'll find a new friend. I'll—ouch!" Looking at her thumb, Erin saw a drop of blood. She could feel the thorn under her skin.

"Erin!" her mother called. "Telephone!"

Erin picked up the roses and went into the house. "Hello. . . . Oh, hi, Hannah. . . . To your house? Who's there? . . . Caitlin? Well, I don't think so. I'm busy. Good-bye." Erin looked angry as she mocked her friend, "Just Caitlin and me."

"Are you going to Hannah's house?" Erin jumped at the sound of her mother's voice.

"No. Caitlin's over there. Hannah doesn't need me." Then she changed the subject. "Where do you want these roses?"

The next day Erin's thumb throbbed. "It's that thorn," she remembered. She showed it to her mother, who, after considerable digging and probing, pulled out a tiny sliver. "Reminds me of the way you feel about Caitlin," her mother said. "She's like a thorn in your flesh. She gets under your skin. And you know, honey, if you allow the bitterness to remain, the hurt will become worse. Why not dig it out and ask the Lord to give you love for Caitlin?"

As Erin went to her room, she rubbed her thumb. "Lord," she whispered, "I can't stand this dull throb in my heart any longer. Will you help me?"

HOW ABOUT YOU? Does someone get "under your skin"? Ask the Lord to show you how to dig out any resentment and bitterness you feel and to replace those feelings with love. *B.J.W.*

TO MEMORIZE: Stop being mean, bad-tempered and angry. Quarreling, harsh words, and dislike of others should have no place in your lives.
Ephesians 4:31 (TLB)

HURT ON THE INSIDE

FROM THE BIBLE:

Do not bring sorrow to God's Holy Spirit by the way you live. Remember, he is the one who has identified you as his own, guaranteeing that you will be saved on the day of redemption. . . .

Live a life filled with love for others, following the example of Christ, who loved you and gave himself as a sacrifice to take away your sins. And God was pleased, because that sacrifice was like sweet perfume to him.

EPHESIANS 4:30; 5:2

Be kind to others

"LOOK! HERE COMES that retarded girl on her three-wheeled bike," said Jason. "Let's pretend to run her down."

Jason and Barrett steered their bikes toward the girl. Fear spread across her face as they came closer. "Stop!" she shouted.

"Retard! Retard!" chanted Jason. Barrett joined in. Laughing loudly, they steered away before actually running into the frightened girl.

Just then Mrs. Brown, Jason's Sunday school teacher, came out of her house. Feeling guilty, Jason turned his head away. And before he realized what was happening, he had run into Barrett. Down they went, a tangle of boys and bikes! Jason felt a sharp pain where his arm was skinned, and Barrett was limping when he got up. Mrs. Brown invited them into her house to get cleaned up.

As Mrs. Brown got out the bandages she asked, "How would you have felt if I had pushed you over and laughed about it?"

The boys looked at her in wonder. "That would have been mean," Jason answered.

Mrs. Brown nodded. "Yet that's something like what you did to that little girl."

"We didn't hurt her," protested Barrett. "We just teased her a little."

"You didn't hurt her on the *outside,*" corrected Mrs. Brown. "But you hurt her on the *inside.* She feels hurt when people make fun of her." Mrs. Brown continued, "Jesus taught us to treat others with love."

Both of the boys looked ashamed. "We're sorry," they said.

"We'll remember that it hurts to be hurt," added Jason. "And we won't make fun of that girl again."

HOW ABOUT YOU? Do you sometimes tease kids who are different? Teasing can be very painful. Jesus was kind to everyone and wants us to be like him. Be a friend, not a tease or a bully. *C.E.Y.*

TO MEMORIZE: Live a life filled with love for others, following the example of Christ. *Ephesians 5:2*

18 October

A WILLING HEART

FROM THE BIBLE:

Take care! Don't do your good deeds publicly, to be admired, because then you will lose the reward from your Father in heaven. When you give a gift to someone in need, don't shout about it as the hypocrites do—blowing trumpets in the synagogues and streets to call attention to their acts of charity! I assure you, they have received all the reward they will ever get. But when you give to someone, don't tell your left hand what your right hand is doing. Give your gifts in secret, and your Father, who knows all secrets, will reward you.

MATTHEW 6:1-4

Give willingly

CORETTA SMILED as she shook the coins out of her bank. She counted two dollars and decided to give one dollar for the missionary offering at church. That would leave a dollar to spend on herself.

When she arrived at church the next morning, several kids were already waiting for the teacher. "Hi, Coretta!" Felicia greeted her. "Did you remember your offering?"

"Sure did," Coretta replied. "Did you?"

Felicia nodded. "My mom gave me five dollars to put in the offering plate!"

"My aunt gave me money for my birthday, and I'm going to give five too," said Malcolm proudly.

"How about you, Coretta?" asked Felicia.

The dollar she was going to give didn't sound like much anymore. "Uh—two dollars," Coretta mumbled. When the offering plate was passed, she dropped the money into it reluctantly.

Later Coretta looked glum as she rode home with her parents. Her mother was surprised at her mood. "You were so eager to get to church this morning. What happened?"

Coretta told about her Sunday school class. "I don't understand," she said. "I gave twice as much as I planned to give, so I should be twice as happy, right?"

"Not necessarily," Mom replied. "The dollar you were going to give was a love gift to God. You gave the extra dollar just to impress your friends."

Dad nodded. "It's always better not to discuss with friends the amount you plan to give. You should ask the Lord what he wants you to give. Then give the amount cheerfully."

HOW ABOUT YOU? Do you ever put money in your church offering simply because it's expected of you? Talk with God about what he wants you to give, and do it with a cheerful, willing heart. Your attitude means more to God than your money does! *S.L.K.*

TO MEMORIZE: God loves the person who gives cheerfully. *2 Corinthians 9:7*

19 October

FROM EARTH TO HEAVEN

FROM THE BIBLE:

For we know that when this earthly tent we live in is taken down—when we die and leave these bodies—we will have a home in heaven, an eternal body made for us by God himself and not by human hands. We grow weary in our present bodies, and we long for the day when we will put on our heavenly bodies like new clothing. For we will not be spirits without bodies, but we will put on new heavenly bodies. . . . We want to slip into our new bodies so that these dying bodies will be swallowed up by everlasting life. God himself has prepared us for this, and as a guarantee he has given us his Holy Spirit.

So we are always confident, even though we know that as long as we live in these bodies we are not at home with the Lord. That is why we live by believing and not by seeing. Yes, we are fully confident, and we would rather be away from these bodies, for then we will be at home with the Lord.

2 CORINTHIANS 5:1-8

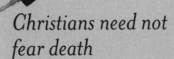

Christians need not fear death

JENNIFER UNDERSTOOD the reality of death. Her grandmother had died and gone to be with Jesus. But now Jennifer's friend Monica had a disease that was incurable. Unless God worked a miracle, Monica was going to die.

Monica was a Christian, and Jennifer knew that when Christians die they go to be with Jesus. Of course, Jennifer was sad when she thought about never being able to play with Monica again. But even that wasn't the thing that bothered her right now. She was just wondering what it would be like to die—how it would feel.

She talked to her mother about it. "Honey," her mother answered, "do you remember that as a little girl you were sometimes afraid in the night? You would crawl into bed with Daddy and me." Jennifer nodded. "Where did you find yourself in the morning?" Mom asked.

Jennifer thought about it. "Why, back in my own bed," she said.

"That's right." Mom smiled. "After you'd fall asleep, Daddy would pick you up and move you to your own bed." Mom paused. "I think that must be what death is like," she said at last. "We go to sleep here on earth and wake up in heaven."

As Jennifer thought about that explanation, she smiled. It was a beautiful thought. At the right time Monica would be taken to heaven to be with Jesus, her Lord, forever. When Jennifer thought of it that way, she felt happy for her friend.

HOW ABOUT YOU? Every Christian will someday be moved from earth to God's beautiful heaven. The most important thing is to be sure that you are a child of God. Then you can know that at just the right time God will take you to your new home in heaven. Won't that be wonderful? *R.I.J.*

TO MEMORIZE: We would rather be away from these bodies, for then we will be at home with the Lord. *2 Corinthians 5:8*

20 October

DON'T TOUCH

FROM THE BIBLE:

Don't you realize that your bodies are actually parts of Christ? Should a man take his body, which belongs to Christ, and join it to a prostitute? Never! And don't you know that if a man joins himself to a prostitute, he becomes one body with her? For the Scriptures say, "The two are united into one." But the person who is joined to the Lord becomes one spirit with him.

Run away from sexual sin! No other sin so clearly affects the body as this one does. For sexual immorality is a sin against your own body. Or don't you know that your body is the temple of the Holy Spirit, who lives in you and was given to you by God? You do not belong to yourself, for God bought you with a high price. So you must honor God with your body.

1 CORINTHIANS 6:15-20

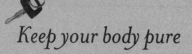

Keep your body pure

PRINCESS PURRED as four tiny kittens nestled beside her. As she gently licked their fur, they squirmed closer to her. Then Princess closed her eyes. She seemed to be daydreaming when Kimberly leaned over the kittens' box. Princess's eyes flew open, and she hissed and swatted the air. Kimberly jumped back.

Later when Kimberly checked on the kittens, they were gone! It took Kimberly a whole day to find them. Princess had moved the kittens to the linen closet. "Clever hiding place," Kimberly said as she reached for a kitten. Princess hissed and swatted at Kimberly just as she had before.

Then it happened again. Princess moved the kittens. "I can't understand her," Kimberly told her mother. "I only want to pet the kittens."

"Princess is being a good mother cat. She doesn't want to take the chance of someone hurting her kittens."

"I suppose so," said Kimberly reluctantly. "But I thought I could convince her it would be OK."

"Kimberly," Mother said, "Princess has a responsibility to protect her kittens. That's why she won't allow you to touch them. You know what this reminds me of, honey? God wants us to keep our bodies pure. Usually there is nothing wrong with a light touch or a gentle hug. But some parts of the body should be kept private. If anyone ever tries to touch your body in an improper way, you must say no. Do you understand what I'm saying?"

"Yes, Mother," Kimberly answered. "I'll do what you say. And I'll quit buggin' Princess, too."

HOW ABOUT YOU? If someone does something to your body that makes you feel uncomfortable or guilty, tell that person to stop. Talk to God about the problem. Then tell your mother or dad or some other trusted adult too. They will help you handle the situation. *J.L.H.*

TO MEMORIZE: God bought you with a high price. So you must honor God with your body.
1 Corinthians 6:20

WAITERS AND WAITRESSES

FROM THE BIBLE:

To you, O Lord, I lift up
my soul.
I trust in you, my God!
Do not let me be disgraced,
or let my enemies rejoice in
my defeat.
No one who trusts in you will
ever be disgraced,
but disgrace comes to those
who try to deceive others.
Show me the path where I
should walk, O Lord;
point out the right road for
me to follow.
Lead me by your truth and
teach me,
for you are the God who
saves me.
All day long I put my hope
in you.

PSALM 25:1-5

Serve the Lord

THE RESTAURANT hostess led the Blake family to a table and handed them menus. "Your waitress will be with you in a minute. Enjoy your meal," she said. Patrick didn't even open his menu. "I know what I want—a cheeseburger, french fries, and a large Coke," he said. "I wish the waitress would hurry. I'm hungry!"

Kayla watched a waitress take a tray of food to the next table. "I don't think I'd want to be a waitress. It looks like hard work."

"It is," agreed Mother. "A good waitress must be courteous, efficient, and have a good memory."

"And be fast," added Patrick. "I wish she would hurry. I don't like to wait, especially when I'm hungry."

Mr. Blake frowned. "Be patient, Patrick. She'll soon be here to wait on us."

" 'Wait patiently for the Lord,' " quoted Kayla. "That's what Psalm 27:14 says. If we need to wait for the Lord patiently, I guess we should wait for our waitress that way too!"

Dad smiled. "And while we're waiting—for our waitress and for the Lord—we can be the Lord's waiters and waitresses. We can serve him by doing the work he has given us to do until he comes back."

"Like praying, witnessing, and helping others," Mom explained.

"I still wish someone would wait on us," Patrick grumbled. "I feel like I've been waiting for hours. I'm—"

"May I help you?" interrupted a soft voice.

"You certainly may," Patrick said, grinning.

HOW ABOUT YOU? Are you waiting on the Lord, working for him while you wait for him to return to earth? The best way to wait for the Lord is to wait on others. Are you a good waiter or waitress? Make plans today to wait by serving. *B.J.W.*

TO MEMORIZE: Wait patiently for the Lord. Be brave and courageous. Yes, wait patiently for the Lord. *Psalm 27:14*

22 October

THE WORDS OF MY MOUTH

FROM THE BIBLE:

He has paid a full ransom for
his people.
He has guaranteed his
covenant with them forever.
What a holy, awe-inspiring
name he has! . . .
The high and lofty one who inhabits eternity, the Holy One, says this: "I live in that high and holy place with those whose spirits are contrite and humble. I refresh the humble and give new courage to those with repentant hearts." . . .
Pray like this: Our Father in heaven, may your name be honored.

PSALM 111:9; ISAIAH 57:15; MATTHEW 6:9

Don't use nicknames for God

WHEN MOM CALLED the family to the table, Caleb hurried in to take his place. "Golly, dinner smells good!" he exclaimed.

"Caleb!" exclaimed Mom. "Just yesterday we discussed the seriousness of taking God's name in vain, and already you're back to your old habits."

"I didn't use God's name, Mom," Caleb answered.

Dad spoke up. "I think dinner had better wait for a few minutes while you get the dictionary," he said. "Look up *golly* for us, Caleb."

Reluctantly, Caleb did so. "Here it is. It says, 'An exclamation of surprise, a euphemism for God.' What's a *euphemism?*" he asked.

Mom answered. "It's one word substituted for another. That means *golly* is just a substitute for *God.* The dictionary says the same thing for *gosh,* and you'll find that *gee* is a substitute for *Jesus.*"

"You mean kinda like a nickname?" Caleb asked.

"Yes," answered Dad. "But these are put-down names. God has many holy names, but no nicknames.

"You should also know," continued Dad, "that *heck* is another form of *hell* and *darn* is a substitute for *damn.*"

"I sure didn't know that," said Caleb. "I'll ask God to forgive me. But how can I stop saying those words? The kids at school say them all the time."

Dad said, "Every day you can pray like David did—that the words you say will be pleasing to God. We'll pray for you too. Now, is everybody hungry?"

HOW ABOUT YOU? You may not have been aware that some words are substitutes for God's name. Look up each of today's Scripture verses and be reminded that God's name is holy. Whenever it is used, whether in songs or conversations, it must be used in a reverent manner. *A.G.L.*

TO MEMORIZE: May the words of my mouth and the thoughts of my heart be pleasing to you, O Lord, my rock and my redeemer. *Psalm 19:14*

WORKING FOR PEACE

(PART 1)

FROM THE BIBLE:

Come, my children, and listen
to me,
and I will teach you to fear
the Lord.
Do any of you want to live
a life that is long and good?
Then watch your tongue!
Keep your lips from telling
lies!
Turn away from evil and do
good.
Work hard at living in peace
with others.
The eyes of the Lord watch over
those who do right;
his ears are open to their
cries for help.

PSALM 34:11-15

Don't gossip

JASMINE LIKED ANGELICA, who lived in a big house and had a "doctor dad." She also liked Carmen, who was smart and pretty, had no dad, and lived in an average house. But Angelica and Carmen didn't like each other, and often Jasmine felt caught in the middle, with both girls getting mad at her as well as at each other.

One day Jasmine discussed the problem with her father. "Hmmm," he murmured. "What do you do, Jasmine, when you hear one of the girls say something unkind about the other? Do you keep it to yourself? Or do you repeat to the girls the things they say about each other?"

Jasmine flushed. "Well, not too often," she stammered.

"Any repeating of such words is too often, Jasmine," Dad told her. "The Bible says, 'Quarrels disappear when gossip stops.' As a Christian you don't want to be stirring up quarrels between the girls. Now, if Angelica says good things about Carmen, or if Carmen says good things about Angelica, it might be a good idea to repeat *that.* If each one hears that the other has said something good about her, perhaps the girls will decide to like one another."

This was a new idea to Jasmine. "You mean I should start listening for compliments instead of criticism?" she asked.

Her dad smiled. "Could be. Pray about it and keep your eyes and ears open. And determine never to repeat any of the things that would cause anger or hurt."

HOW ABOUT YOU? Do you gossip, stirring up trouble by telling your friends and classmates the unkind things someone has said about them? Today's Scripture reading tells us to seek peace. One way to do this is to keep to yourself any unkind words you may hear someone say about another person. Refuse to be a person who gossips. *B.J.W.*

TO MEMORIZE: Quarrels disappear when gossip stops. *Proverbs 26:20*

24 October

WORKING FOR PEACE
(PART 2)

FROM THE BIBLE:

One day as the crowds were gathering, Jesus went up the mountainside with his disciples and sat down to teach them.

This is what he taught them:
"God blesses those who realize
their need for him,
for the Kingdom of Heaven is
given to them.
God blesses those who mourn,
for they will be comforted.
God blesses those who are gentle
and lowly,
for the whole earth will belong
to them.
God blesses those who are
hungry and thirsty for
justice,
for they will receive it in full.
God blesses those who are
merciful,
for they will be shown mercy.
God blesses those whose hearts
are pure,
for they will see God.
God blesses those who work
for peace,
for they will be called the
children of God.
God blesses those who are
persecuted because they
live for God,
for the Kingdom of Heaven
is theirs.

MATTHEW 5:1-10

Work for peace

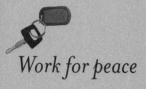

JASMINE HOPED to hear Carmen and Angelica tell her nice things about each other. Then she planned to tell each of them about it, hoping that the two girls would stop quarreling.

Here's what Jasmine heard Angelica say: "I hate school, but I suppose Carmen likes it since she's the smartest girl in class. It's disgusting. Oh, here comes Miss America! Her pretty hair makes mine look like a haystack. And did you know she made that cute skirt she had on yesterday? She makes me sick."

And Jasmine heard Carmen say, "The skirt I made isn't as pretty as Angelica's new skirt. Her clothes always look so cute on her. She's lucky her dad's a great doctor. And she lives in that fancy house."

She decided to share these compliments. "Do you know what Angelica said about you?" she asked Carmen. "She said you were the smartest girl in the class. And she thinks your hair is pretty. She likes your new skirt, too."

"Really?" Carmen was surprised. "Maybe I ought to invite her over."

Then Jasmine talked to Angelica. "Carmen said your clothes are beautiful and look cute on you. And she said she loves your house and thinks your dad is great."

"No kidding? Maybe that's because she doesn't have a dad. Say, I'm going to ask Mom if I can have you and Carmen over Friday night."

Jasmine's dad smiled while she told him what she'd done. "You've been a real peacemaker, Jasmine. That's a good description for a child of God."

HOW ABOUT YOU? Will you listen for good things about another person and pass along what you hear? See what a difference it will make. It will please your friends, God, and yourself. Find at least one compliment today to carry to someone else. *B.J.W.*

TO MEMORIZE: God blesses those who work for peace, for they will be called the children of God. *Matthew 5:9*

FEEDING THE FIRE

FROM THE BIBLE:

Here is a description of worthless and wicked people: They are constant liars, signaling their true intentions to their friends by making signs with their eyes and feet and fingers. Their perverted hearts plot evil. They stir up trouble constantly. But they will be destroyed suddenly, broken beyond all hope of healing.

There are six things the Lord hates—no, seven things he detests:
haughty eyes,
a lying tongue,
hands that kill the innocent,
a heart that plots evil,
feet that race to do wrong,
a false witness who pours out lies,
a person who sows discord among brothers.

PROVERBS 6:12-19

Don't talk about a friend's faults

APRIL WAS ON the phone when her mother came into the room. "You're stupid, Paige! You'd better study hard so you get a better grade on your next spelling test, OK? Talk to you later."

When April hung up the phone, Mom asked, "Why did you tell Paige that she's stupid?"

"Because she *is*," April replied.

Mom raised her eyebrows. "You and Paige have been fighting a lot lately. Do you think you just added fuel to the fire?"

"What do you mean?" asked April.

Mom pointed at the smoldering fire in the fireplace. "What would happen if I added a log to the fire?"

"The fire would get bigger," April replied.

"What if I didn't add any wood to it?" Mom asked.

"It would die out," April answered.

"Right!" said Mom. "It's like that between friends. A fight usually dies out if no one keeps it going. But if you keep telling Paige about her faults—" The ring of the telephone interrupted her.

"I'll get it. It's probably Paige again. She was going to call me back." April was glad to end the conversation.

At dinnertime April came to the table with red, puffy eyes. "What's the matter?" Dad asked.

"Paige asked someone else to go to the riding stables with her tomorrow." April choked back a sob. "She's mad at me for telling her that she's stupid."

"Is it time to put out the fire?" Mom asked gently.

"Yeah," said April. "I'll tell Paige I'm sorry. And I won't talk about her faults anymore."

HOW ABOUT YOU? Are you tempted to tell your friends all about their faults? Do what you can to help your friends, but don't focus on their faults. Show love to them and ask God how to encourage them to do better instead of putting them down. *B.J.W.*

TO MEMORIZE: Disregarding another person's faults preserves love; telling about them separates close friends. *Proverbs 17:9*

26 October

DEADLY ARROWS
(PART 1)

FROM THE BIBLE:

Yanking a dog's ears is as foolish as interfering in someone else's argument.

Just as damaging as a mad man shooting a lethal weapon is someone who lies to a friend and then says, "I was only joking."

Fire goes out for lack of fuel, and quarrels disappear when gossip stops.

A quarrelsome person starts fights as easily as hot embers light charcoal or fire lights wood.

What dainty morsels rumors are—but they sink deep into one's heart.

PROVERBS 26:17-22

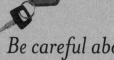

Be careful about teasing

"WHAT'S WRONG, Shawn?" Eric asked his friend as they walked home from school.

Shawn looked gloomy. "I don't want to tell—you'll laugh."

"Aw, come on. We're friends. Tell me what's bothering you," coaxed Eric.

"Well," said Shawn, "some of the guys learned my middle name is Thomas, which makes me *S.T.* Bernard. They all started calling me 'Saint Bernard' and barking at me."

"Don't let it bother you. They'll get over it," said Eric. As he thought about it, however, he couldn't resist a joke that came to mind. "Wait till I tell the guys that I 'walk the dog' home from school every day!" he teased.

Shawn looked at Eric in disbelief. "You said you wouldn't laugh, and I trusted you," he said, and he began running home as fast as he could.

"Hey, I was only kidding!" Eric called after him. But Shawn was gone.

Several days went by, but Shawn refused to talk to Eric or walk home with him. Eric felt Shawn was being stubborn. Then one morning Eric was reading Proverbs 26. He came to these verses: "Just as damaging as a mad man shooting a lethal weapon is someone who lies to a friend and then says, 'I was only joking.' "

Uh-oh, thought Eric. *I've got to ask Shawn to forgive me.* After a hasty breakfast, he grabbed his books.

"What's the big hurry?" asked his mother.

"I'll explain tonight," answered Eric. "Right now, I've got to see Shawn." And he ran all the way to Shawn's house.

HOW ABOUT YOU? Are you in the habit of teasing people in a way that hurts them? If you have hurt someone, you should ask for forgiveness. Learn to say things that help people rather than hurt them. *S.L.N.*

TO MEMORIZE: Just as damaging as a mad man shooting a lethal weapon is someone who lies to a friend and then says, "I was only joking."
Proverbs 26:18-19

27 October

DEADLY ARROWS
(PART 2)

FROM THE BIBLE:

If people persecute you because you are a Christian, don't curse them; pray that God will bless them. . . . Don't try to act important, but enjoy the company of ordinary people. And don't think you know it all!

Never pay back evil for evil to anyone. Do things in such a way that everyone can see you are honorable. Do your part to live in peace with everyone, as much as possible.

Dear friends, never avenge yourselves. Leave that to God. For it is written,

"I will take vengeance;
I will repay those who deserve it,"
says the Lord.

Instead, do what the Scriptures say:

"If your enemies are hungry, feed them.
If they are thirsty, give them something to drink,
and they will be ashamed of what they have done to you."

Don't let evil get the best of you, but conquer evil by doing good.

ROMANS 12:14-21

***I GUESS I WOULDN'T** like to be called Saint Bernard either,* Eric admitted to himself as he hurried to his friend's house to apologize for having teased him. He slowed down as he approached the Bernard home. On the lawn he saw a handmade sign that said, "Beware of dog"—and Shawn didn't even have a dog! *Uh-oh,* Eric thought. *I wonder who put that sign up. That's gonna make Shawn mad. Maybe I should forget about apologizing and go to school early.*

Just then the front door opened. "Hi, Eric," said Shawn.

"Hi," Eric replied, feeling a little off guard because Shawn was smiling and friendly. He decided to get the apology over with. "Look, Shawn," he said. "I want to apologize for teasing you the other day. I didn't mean to hurt your feelings, but I did and I was wrong."

"Oh, I forgive you," said Shawn. "I was silly to take the teasing so seriously. I talked to my dad about it last night, and he said I'd better get used to it. He told me the kids used to tease him about his big feet when he was a boy. Some of his friends still do. He said it really helps if a person can play along with the teasing." Shawn pointed across the lawn. "How do you like my sign?"

"Your sign?" asked Eric in surprise.

"Yep!" Shawn said, nodding. "I've decided to take Dad's advice and enjoy being Steven Thomas Bernard from now on."

HOW ABOUT YOU? Have you ever been teased? Maybe you've been teased for being a Christian. God says you are to bless people who persecute you. So don't let teasing upset you. That just makes people tease you more. You can be content being who you are—a child of God! *S.L.N.*

TO MEMORIZE: If people persecute you because you are a Christian, don't curse them; pray that God will bless them. *Romans 12:14*

Don't let teasing upset you

28 October

WHAT ARE YOU THINKING?

FROM THE BIBLE:

Now I, Paul, plead with you. I plead with the gentleness and kindness that Christ himself would use, even though some of you say I am bold in my letters but timid in person. I hope it won't be necessary, but when I come I may have to be very bold with those who think we act from purely human motives. We are human, but we don't wage war with human plans and methods. We use God's mighty weapons, not mere worldly weapons, to knock down the Devil's strongholds.

2 CORINTHIANS 10:1-4

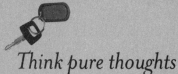

Think pure thoughts

CHAD WAS IN the locker room getting ready for gym when he overhead David tell a dirty joke. The other boys laughed, but Chad quickly left the room.

All day the story kept popping back into Chad's mind. He told God he was sorry he heard it, but still he seemed unable to forget it.

After several days he decided to talk to his father about it. Dad understood. "Satan wants to control your mind," he told Chad. "So he keeps bringing back the nasty things you see and hear. Now, you know the law of space, don't you?"

"Sure," answered Chad. "No two things can occupy the same space at the same time."

"Right." Dad smiled. "Take this book lying on the table, for example. Nothing else can occupy that space until the book is removed. It's the same way with your mind. Keep it filled with the Word of God and other good things. Then no filth can occupy the space that the good things take up."

"I read my Bible," said Chad. "But I still can't forget that joke."

"Well, now comes God's part," said Dad. "When you received Jesus as Savior, you also received the Holy Spirit. He gives you the power to overcome evil. Whenever this dirty story pops into your mind, ask the Holy Spirit to cleanse your mind, and he will. You'll think of that story less and less often until finally you'll forget it."

"Really, Dad?" exclaimed Chad. "I'm glad! I hope I never hear a dirty joke again."

HOW ABOUT YOU? Do you ever have trouble with your thoughts? Avoid situations in which you know you'll hear or read unwholesome things. Then fill your mind with good things. Finally, ask the Holy Spirit to cleanse your thoughts. He will give you victory over every bad thought. *A.G.L.*

TO MEMORIZE: God blesses those whose hearts are pure, for they will see God. *Matthew 5:8*

NO ANGRY ANSWER

FROM THE BIBLE:

A gentle answer turns away wrath, but harsh words stir up anger.

The wise person makes learning a joy; fools spout only foolishness.

The Lord is watching everywhere, keeping his eye on both the evil and the good.

Gentle words bring life and health; a deceitful tongue crushes the spirit.

PROVERBS 15:1-4

Don't react with anger

SINCE NICHOLAS became a Christian he had been trying to follow his Sunday school teacher's advice about having devotions each day. So far he hadn't missed many days. One day, after reading his Bible and devotional book, he took time to learn the suggested memory verse: "A gentle answer turns away wrath, but harsh words stir up anger." After praying, he hurried off to school.

The bell rang just as Nicholas reached his seat. While he opened his English book, Megan slipped him a note. It read, "I think you're cute. I love your dimples."

Nicholas blushed and quickly shoved the paper into his desk, but not quickly enough. Devon, who sat behind him, murmured, "Nicholas has a girlfriend," in a singing voice.

Nicholas turned angrily, but before he could say anything the teacher told him to turn around. *I'll tell Devon off in a note,* Nicholas said to himself. *He always picks on me, and I'm tired of it.* As Nicholas started writing, the verse he had memorized that morning came back to his mind. He crumpled the note and started doing his homework instead.

At lunch time Devon started teasing Nicholas again about having a girlfriend. "Oh, I don't think so," Nicholas said. He spoke in a quiet voice because he kept remembering the Bible verse he had learned.

While they ate, Devon continued to bring up the subject. But Nicholas just smiled and wouldn't show any anger. Finally Devon stopped teasing. He even invited Nicholas to join his team for a ball game. Nicholas agreed, and he silently thanked God for the day's memory verse.

HOW ABOUT YOU? How do you react when your family or friends tease you? Follow the advice from God's Word. You'll find that a quiet reaction, instead of anger, will make you and others happier.

TO MEMORIZE: A gentle answer turns away wrath, but harsh words stir up anger. *Proverbs 15:1*

30 October

A GOOD NAME

FROM THE BIBLE:

There was a believer in Joppa named Tabitha (which in Greek is Dorcas). She was always doing kind things for others and helping the poor. About this time she became ill and died. Her friends prepared her for burial and laid her in an upstairs room. But they had heard that Peter was nearby at Lydda, so they sent two men to beg him, "Please come as soon as possible!"

So Peter returned with them; and as soon as he arrived, they took him to the upstairs room. The room was filled with widows who were weeping and showing him the coats and other garments Dorcas had made for them.

ACTS 9:36-39

Desire a good name

"I HATE MY NAME, Grandpa," said Edna one day. "I wish I had a name that wasn't so old-fashioned, like Amanda or Jennifer or Alyssa."

Grandpa smiled. "I think Edna is a pretty name," he told her. "Your mom named you after her grandmother, who was my mother and the sweetest person you could ever meet—a lovely person to be named after."

"But what about the kids at school, like Jared McCormick and Trevor Bristol?" she complained. "They keep asking me how things were in the 'olden days.' I think I'll change my name someday. The Bible even says I should."

Grandpa looked surprised. "Where'd you get that idea?"

"The Bible says, 'A good name is more desirable than great riches.' "

"Oh, Edna, that verse isn't talking about changing your name!" Grandpa said. "It's talking about what people think of your character when they hear your name."

"They think of 'old lady,' " Edna said, pouting.

"Oh," laughed Grandpa, "I doubt that. I'll bet they think of what you are like as a person. Are you friendly, mean, kind, bitter?" Edna shrugged.

"What do you think of when you hear the name Jared McCormick?" asked Grandpa.

"I think of a boy who picks on girls and calls them names," Edna answered.

"Exactly!" Grandpa said. "Funny that you never said he was a boy with an up-to-date name. It was his personality you described. So even though you don't like your name, try to live so that when people think of Edna Grant, they will think happy thoughts. That's what 'a good name' in that Bible verse is all about."

HOW ABOUT YOU? What do people think of when they hear your name? Live your life so people will think of a godly person when they hear your name—one who loves the Lord and lives to please him. *S.L.N.*

TO MEMORIZE: A good name is more desirable than great riches. *Proverbs 22:1* (NIV)

BEHIND THE MASK

FROM THE BIBLE

This is what the Lord says:
"Cursed are those who put their trust in mere humans and turn their hearts away from the Lord. They are like stunted shrubs in the desert, with no hope for the future. They will live in the barren wilderness, on the salty flats where no one lives.

"But blessed are those who trust in the Lord and have made the Lord their hope and confidence. They are like trees planted along a riverbank, with roots that reach deep into the water. Such trees are not bothered by the heat or worried by long months of drought. Their leaves stay green, and they go right on producing delicious fruit.

"The human heart is most deceitful and desperately wicked. Who really knows how bad it is? But I know! I, the Lord, search all hearts and examine secret motives. I give all people their due rewards, according to what their actions deserve."

JEREMIAH 17:5-10

God sees your heart

"TRICK OR TREAT!" said kids all over the neighborhood. The Walters family chose not to celebrate Halloween because of its pagan roots. But they did use the opportunity to share the Good News with neighborhood kids.

Three-year-old Jamie hid behind his mother as she opened the door. When he saw a pirate and a tramp on the front porch, he ducked behind a chair. "Hi, Mrs. Walters," said the pirate.

"Come on, Jamie," Mom encouraged. "You know these kids."

Jamie peeked out. No—he certainly didn't know anyone who looked like that!

"Hey, Jamie! Remember me?" called the pirate. That voice sounded familiar, but Jamie still wasn't convinced. The pirate reached up and took off his mask, and the tramp did the same. Why, these were the two big boys who lived in the house next door! When Jamie saw that it was only children dressed up in costumes, he spent the rest of the afternoon helping Mom pass out candy and gospel tracts.

Finally, the last trick-or-treater had come and gone. "Well," said Mom, "everyone who stopped by got a piece of candy and a good gospel tract. I do hope the boys and girls will read them—and their parents, too!"

Just then Dad arrived home. "You know," he said to Mom, "all those costumes and masks remind me of many people who go around wearing a 'mask' every day. They try to look like something they're not. They smile, act pleasant, and do good deeds. They may go to church. To us they appear to be Christians—but underneath the masks, they have sinful hearts. They need Jesus."

HOW ABOUT YOU? Do you wear a mask to hide a sinful heart? Do you only pretend to be a Christian, or have you asked Jesus to wash away your sin? Remember, you may fool others, but you can't fool God. He sees your heart. *H.W.M.*

TO MEMORIZE: I, the Lord, search all hearts. *Jeremiah 17:10*

1 November

COUNT ON ME

FROM THE BIBLE:

And now, dear brothers and sisters, we give you this command with the authority of our Lord Jesus Christ: Stay away from any Christian who lives in idleness and doesn't follow the tradition of hard work we gave you. For you know that you ought to follow our example. We were never lazy when we were with you. We never accepted food from anyone without paying for it. We worked hard day and night so that we would not be a burden to any of you. . . . Even while we were with you, we gave you this rule: "Whoever does not work should not eat."

Yet we hear that some of you are living idle lives, refusing to work and wasting time meddling in other people's business. In the name of the Lord Jesus Christ, we appeal to such people—no, we command them: Settle down and get to work. Earn your own living. And I say to the rest of you, dear brothers and sisters, never get tired of doing good.

2 THESSALONIANS 3:6-13

Be helpful

EVERYONE WAS having a good time at the pizza party in the church basement. "We need help cleaning up," Mr. Trenton reminded the sixth-grade class toward the end of the evening.

The kids intended to help later, but right now they were having too much fun talking and goofing around. Heidi went into the kitchen to help Mrs. Trenton for a few minutes, but soon she was laughing and talking again. Then, one by one, the kids disappeared as their parents came for them.

At nine o'clock, Heidi's dad came to pick her up. He had agreed to drive several other children home too. "I feel like a bus driver," he told Heidi good-naturedly half an hour later. They had been all over town and were once again driving past the church on their way home. "The lights are still on," Dad said in surprise. "I wonder if something's wrong." He slowed down and turned in to the parking lot.

Heidi knew what was wrong as soon as she and her dad walked into the youth room. Mr. and Mrs. Trenton were still cleaning up the mess that the young people had made. How guilty Heidi felt as she and her dad both pitched in to help!

"I'm sorry," she apologized. "You two do so much for us, but we sure don't do much for you in return. You can count on me to help clean up next time. I promise!"

HOW ABOUT YOU? Do you enjoy parties at church? What do you do to help? Today's Scripture says that those who won't work shouldn't eat. That's true about parties as well as about daily life. Next time adults plan a special event for you, tell them "Thank you" and show them you mean it by doing what you can to help. That would please them—and God! *L.M.W.*

TO MEMORIZE: Dear brothers and sisters, never get tired of doing good. *2 Thessalonians 3:13*

NOTS AND KNOTS

FROM THE BIBLE:

Then God instructed the people as follows:

"I am the Lord your God, who rescued you from slavery in Egypt.

"Do not worship any other gods besides me.

"Do not make idols of any kind, whether in the shape of birds or animals or fish. You must never worship or bow down to them, for I, the Lord your God, am a jealous God who will not share your affection with any other god! I do not leave unpunished the sins of those who hate me, but I punish the children for the sins of their parents to the third and fourth generations. But I lavish my love on those who love me and obey my commands, even for a thousand generations.

"Do not misuse the name of the Lord your God. The Lord will not let you go unpunished if you misuse his name."

EXODUS 20:1-7

God says no for your good

"DON'T TALK TO me about religion, Cory," said Derek as the boys walked home from school. "You know how I feel about all those 'Thou shalt nots.' I like my freedom."

It's so frustrating, Cory thought as he walked up to his house. *Whenever I mention becoming a Christian or invite Derek to Sunday school, all he thinks of is what Christians can't do.*

The next Saturday Derek and his father invited Cory to go boating. The wind was blowing and the waves were choppy, but they had fun. When they came back to the dock, Derek showed Cory how to make a good knot with the rope to hold the boat to the dock. "But why tie it down?" asked Cory. "Why not give it freedom?"

"Are you kidding?" laughed Derek. "It would drift out into the lake and be lost in no time. Or it might hit another boat. But this little knot I made will protect the boat from harm."

"So," said Cory, "you have your knots and I have mine!"

"What's that supposed to mean?"

"Well, you say you don't want to become a Christian because there are too many 'thou shalt *nots.*' But God tells us not to do certain things—like lie or steal—to keep us from ruining our lives or hurting others. Just like that knot in the rope protects your boat."

Derek looked surprised. "That does make sense," he admitted.

"How about coming to church with me tomorrow?" Cory suggested.

Derek nodded his agreement.

HOW ABOUT YOU? Are you resentful because of the things God says not to do? He made you, and he knows what will help you and what will hurt you. When he tells you not to do something, it's to keep you from trouble. *S.L.N.*

TO MEMORIZE: Don't be impressed with your own wisdom. Instead, fear the Lord and turn your back on evil. *Proverbs 3:7*

3 November

ONLY A DREAM

FROM THE BIBLE:

My child, don't lose sight of good planning and insight. Hang on to them, for they fill you with life and bring you honor and respect. They keep you safe on your way and keep your feet from stumbling. You can lie down without fear and enjoy pleasant dreams. You need not be afraid of disaster or the destruction that comes upon the wicked, for the Lord is your security. He will keep your foot from being caught in a trap.
PROVERBS 3:21-26

Sleep in peace

SOMETHING WAS chasing Kendra, and she ran as fast as she could. Suddenly, she felt herself falling! Then she heard herself screaming as she fell! That woke her up. Yes, Kendra had been dreaming!

Her scream also woke her dad, who came into her room and asked, "What's the matter, honey?" With a shaking voice, Kendra told him about the dreadful "thing" that had chased her.

"Calm down, Kendra, it was just a dream," comforted Dad.

"I know, but it seemed so real. Where do dreams come from, anyway?" Kendra wanted to know.

"Well," replied Dad, "scientists say that dreams show some of our hidden fears. But what you think about before going to sleep also has a big effect on your dreams. That's why it's better to read a good book or some Bible verses before going to bed, rather than reading a scary story or watching a horror movie on TV."

Kendra had another question. "Does God talk to us through our dreams?"

"Well, in Bible times, God often talked to his people through dreams. But now we have the Bible to guide us," answered Dad. "Of course, God can put thoughts into our minds. But we're much better off trusting his written Word for direction in our lives than trusting some dream we've had."

Kendra nodded and yawned. "I think I can go back to sleep now. Maybe whatever was trying to catch me is chasing somebody else in a dream." She chuckled as she snuggled under the covers and closed her eyes.

HOW ABOUT YOU? Are you careful about what you put into your mind just before bedtime? Make a habit of reading a few verses from the Bible and praying just before going to sleep. And don't trust your dreams for direction in your life. It's much better to trust what the Bible says! *C.Vm*

TO MEMORIZE: You can lie down without fear and enjoy pleasant dreams. *Proverbs 3:24*

4 November

HELP NEEDED

FROM THE BIBLE:

How we thank God, who gives us victory over sin and death through Jesus Christ our Lord!

So, my dear brothers and sisters, be strong and steady, always enthusiastic about the Lord's work, for you know that nothing you do for the Lord is ever useless.

1 CORINTHIANS 15:57-58

Keep on witnessing

"I'LL NEVER invite Ricardo to Sunday school again!" Juan yelled as he slammed the door shut.

Mom wrinkled her brow. "Why not?" she asked.

"Because he laughed at me!" Juan choked down a sob.

His mother sighed. "Juan, don't feel angry at Ricardo. He doesn't realize—"

She was interrupted by a sharp yip followed by a howl of pain. "It's Mitzy," Juan cried as he shot out the back door. He found his puppy with a paw caught under the fence. Juan reached for the trapped paw.

Grrrr! growled Mitzy. Juan drew back in surprise.

Mom reached for the puppy's paw, and Mitzy snapped at her. "Hold her head, Juan, and talk to her gently. I'll see if I can help."

As Juan talked softly and patted the whining puppy, Mom freed the paw and examined it. "There's a little cut, but it'll be fine." Mom laughed as Mitzy tried to lick her. "Juan, what if we had walked off and left Mitzy when she growled at us?"

"She'd still be caught!" Juan exclaimed. "Mitzy needed our help, but she didn't realize we were trying to help her."

"Neither does Ricardo realize what he is doing when he laughs at you for inviting him to Sunday school," Mom said gently. "He does not realize he is caught in the trap of sin and needs your help."

"OK, I'll keep trying," he agreed. "Maybe one day, Ricardo will thank me too."

HOW ABOUT YOU? Are you tempted to give up praying for your friends, inviting them to Sunday school, or telling them about Jesus? Never give up on it. Even when they snap back at you, they need your help. Be faithful in your efforts to bring them to Christ. *B.J.W.*

TO MEMORIZE: Don't get tired of doing what is good. Don't get discouraged and give up, for we will reap a harvest of blessing at the appropriate time. *Galatians 6:9*

5 November

TWO LISTS

FROM THE BIBLE:

Praise the Lord!
Praise God in his heavenly
dwelling;
praise him in his mighty
heaven!
Praise him for his mighty works;
praise his unequaled
greatness!
Praise him with a blast of
the trumpet;
praise him with the lyre
and harp!
Praise him with the tambourine
and dancing;
praise him with stringed
instruments and flutes!
Praise him with a clash of
cymbals;
praise him with loud clanging
cymbals.
Let everything that lives sing
praises to the Lord!
Praise the Lord!

PSALM 150:1-6

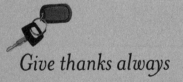

Give thanks always

PETER BEGAN working on a list of things for which he was thankful. Well, Peter could think of a lot of things he *wasn't* thankful about. For example, his mother had sent him to his room yesterday because he told a lie. So he began a second list—things he wasn't thankful for. On it he wrote the word *punishment.* On the first list he wrote the word *parents.* Yes, he was thankful for them. They took care of him every day.

Peter looked again at the words *punishment* and *parents.* Maybe he should be thankful that his parents cared enough to punish him when he did wrong things. He thought about it awhile and then finally crossed off *punishment.*

On the "thankful" list, Peter wrote the word *church.* That was definitely something to be thankful for. Then he thought of the verse he was to learn before Sunday morning. He hated to memorize. So he wrote *memorization* on the list of things for which he was not thankful.

Suddenly a Bible verse popped into Peter's mind. He found himself repeating it word for word. "Always give thanks for everything to God the Father in the name of our Lord Jesus Christ. Ephesians 5:20."

Well, that verse sure blew the idea of listing things for which he was not thankful. He crossed out the word *memorization.* Then he crossed out the words on the thankful list, too. In place of them he wrote in big letters: *EVERYTHING!*

HOW ABOUT YOU? Are there things you do not thank God for? Maybe you hate to study. Maybe your father lost his job. Or maybe something didn't happen when you wanted it to happen, and you grumbled about it. The Bible says to give thanks for all things. Can you do that? *R.I.J.*

TO MEMORIZE: Always give thanks for everything to God the Father in the name of our Lord Jesus Christ. *Ephesians 5:20*

6 November

THE OIL MAN

FROM THE BIBLE:

The Spirit of the Sovereign Lord is upon me, because the Lord has appointed me to bring good news to the poor. He has sent me to comfort the brokenhearted and to announce that captives will be released and prisoners will be freed. He has sent me to tell those who mourn that the time of the Lord's favor has come, and with it, the day of God's anger against their enemies. To all who mourn in Israel, he will give beauty for ashes, joy instead of mourning, praise instead of despair. For the Lord has planted them like strong and graceful oaks for his own glory. . . .

I am overwhelmed with joy in the Lord my God! For he has dressed me with the clothing of salvation and draped me in a robe of righteousness. I am like a bridegroom in his wedding suit or a bride with her jewels.

ISAIAH 61:1-3, 10

"DAD, MAY I use your can of oil?" Zachary's father looked up at his eager young son. "I want to 'unsqueak' the cupboard doors for Mom. She says the squeaky hinges are driving her wild."

Dad took the oil can from the workbench and handed it to Zachary. "Then by all means, take the squeak away!"

When Zachary returned the oil can, he said to his dad, "I oiled the hinges all over the house. And I told Mom that if she heard any squeaks now, it would be mice. She says that will really drive her wild!"

That afternoon Zachary went sledding with his friends. At dinner he shared the neighborhood news. "Todd and Jon are mad at each other," he said. "Did you know Mrs. Gentry broke her arm? And Mr. Snell sat by his window almost all afternoon watching us play in the snow."

"I guess the people in our neighborhood could use some oil," observed Dad. "The Bible speaks of the 'oil of joy.' Since, you're the new 'oil man,' Son, I think you should spread some of that joy around the neighborhood."

"Yeah?" Zachary looked thoughtful. "Maybe I can take a piece of pie to Mr. Snell. And I can offer to run errands for Mrs. Gentry. What can I do about Todd and Jon?"

"I don't know," said Mom. "But I'm sure you'll think of something."

HOW ABOUT YOU? Do you spread joy? God's Word says Jesus came to bring comfort and joy to people. So you should do those things also. Offer a smile to help someone feel better. Take time to chat with a lonely person. Lend a helping hand. Do it for Jesus. *H.W.M.*

TO MEMORIZE: You love what is right and hate what is wrong. Therefore God, your God, has anointed you, pouring out the oil of joy on you. *Hebrews 1:9*

Spread gladness

7 November

LET IT HEAL

FROM THE BIBLE:

Do not spread slanderous gossip among your people.

Do not try to get ahead at the cost of your neighbor's life, for I am the Lord.

Do not nurse hatred in your heart for any of your relatives.

Confront your neighbors directly so you will not be held guilty for their crimes.

Never seek revenge or bear a grudge against anyone, but love your neighbor as yourself. I am the Lord.

LEVITICUS 19:16-18

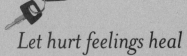

Let hurt feelings heal

"MY FINGER'S bleedin' again, Mama!" Jason cried.

Mother sighed and handed a paper towel to her four-year-old. Jason wrapped it around his finger and watched as the red stain grew. Just then the front door slammed. Stacy stomped into the room and threw her books on the table.

"Look, Stacy!" Jason held his finger in front of his big sister's face. "My finger's bleedin' again."

Stacy snorted. "Stop picking it!"

"How was school today?" Mother asked.

"Terrible!" complained Stacy. "Jodi thinks she can treat me like an old shoe. Last week she ignored me. This week she wants me to be her friend."

Mother frowned. "I thought Jodi apologized for not inviting you to her slumber party," she said.

"Oh, she did," Stacy said. "Since I had said that we were going to Grandma's, she thought I couldn't come. If she had asked, I would have told her Dad had changed our plans. But did she ask? Oh, no!"

"Now, Stacy," Mother said. "You need to stop picking the sore, or it will leave a scar that will mar your friendship forever."

Stacy stammered, "But I don't know what you . . ." She paused. "I do see what you mean, Mom," she finally admitted. "I've been acting just like Jason."

"You cut your finger, Stacy?" Jason asked.

Stacy grinned. "No, but my feelings were hurt."

Jason unwrapped the paper towel from his finger. "Look, Mama. It stopped bleedin.' Did your hurt feelings stop bleedin', Stacy?"

Stacy laughed. "Yes. Everything will be all right now."

HOW ABOUT YOU? Has someone wounded your feelings or hurt your pride? Are you picking the sore, refusing to forgive and forget? Promise yourself right now to stop thinking about your hurt and let it heal.
B.J.W.

TO MEMORIZE: Bear with each other and forgive whatever grievances you may have against one another. Forgive as the Lord forgave you.
Colossians 3:13 (NIV)

8 November

THE THERMOSTAT

FROM THE BIBLE:

And so, dear brothers and sisters, I plead with you to give your bodies to God. Let them be a living and holy sacrifice—the kind he will accept. When you think of what he has done for you, is this too much to ask? Don't copy the behavior and customs of this world, but let God transform you into a new person by changing the way you think. Then you will know what God wants you to do, and you will know how good and pleasing and perfect his will really is. . . .

Don't let evil get the best of you, but conquer evil by doing good.

ROMANS 12:1-2, 21

Be a good influence

"WE SURE had fun at school today," said David during dinner. "Everybody ran around and talked while Mrs. Edwards went to the office. She came back mad as a wet hen—said she could hear us way down the hall. Then she told us to sit with our heads on our desks while she went back to the office. When she left, everybody went wild again."

"Including you?" Mom asked.

David looked startled. "Well, yeah. Everybody did." He quickly changed the subject, hoping to avoid a lecture. "Can I turn the heat up? It's so chilly in here that my food is getting cold."

"When the sun goes down, it does get cold," agreed Mom. "Go ahead, turn up the thermostat."

After David returned to his seat Dad observed, "A thermostat is a great invention. It doesn't just read the temperature; it does something about it. It tells the furnace when to go on and off. Some people are like thermostats."

"They tell the furnace when to go on and off?" asked David.

Dad smiled. "No, but some people do something about what is going on around them," he said. "They don't just go along with the crowd."

David gulped. "You mean, if I had been quiet and stayed in my seat today, some of the other kids would have too?"

"Maybe," said Mom. "Try it next time. Meanwhile, I think you owe your teacher an apology, don't you?" Silently, David nodded.

HOW ABOUT YOU? Do you go along with the crowd? Do you think the fact that "everybody is doing it" makes it OK? If you're a Christian, you should be like a thermostat. Decide how God would want you to act. Then behave in that manner and influence your friends to follow your example. *H.W.M.*

TO MEMORIZE: Become blameless and pure, children of God without fault in a crooked and depraved generation in which you shine like stars. *Philippians 2:15* (NIV)

9 November

THE FRIENDLY SECRET

FROM THE BIBLE:

Is there any encouragement from belonging to Christ? Any comfort from his love? Any fellowship together in the Spirit? Are your hearts tender and sympathetic? Then make me truly happy by agreeing wholeheartedly with each other, loving one another, and working together with one heart and purpose.

Don't be selfish; don't live to make a good impression on others. Be humble, thinking of others as better than yourself. Don't think only about your own affairs, but be interested in others, too, and what they are doing.

PHILIPPIANS 2:1-4

Be friendly

ONCE UPON A time, there were three Baars: Mr. Baar, Mrs. Baar, and Merry Baar. One day while driving home from church, Mr. Baar growled, "I'm never going back there again. No one spoke to me."

Mrs. Baar nodded. "Not one person talked to me, either."

Merry bounced in the backseat and said, "Let's not go back there."

So they tried other churches, but no one paid much attention to them.

One day the pastor from the last church they visited came to their home. "We have so many nice people in our church," he said. "Did you meet any of them?"

Mr. Baar shook his head. "No one talked to me."

"No one welcomed me," added Mrs. Baar.

"Me, either," Merry said in her high voice. "We squeezed in the back row just before church started, and we ran out as soon as it ended."

"Ahhh." The pastor smiled. "Perhaps you'd like to try an experiment. Look for other people who seem lonely and talk with them. Would the three of you try that on Sunday?" All three Baars nodded.

The next Sunday they went to church a little earlier. They saw a family that didn't seem to know where to go. Quickly the Baars went to talk with the family. Then they all sat together during the church service.

"This is a friendly church," Mr. Baar said later, beaming at the pastor.

"You've learned the secret of finding a friendly church," the pastor said. "It's not waiting for someone to talk with you. It's finding someone to talk with."

All the Baars nodded happily.

HOW ABOUT YOU? Do you feel left out at church? It could be because you don't give others a chance to meet you. If you make an effort to say hi to others, you'll find that they usually respond to you. *C.E.Y.*

TO MEMORIZE: A real friend sticks closer than a brother. *Proverbs 18:24*

10 November

GOD'S MAGIC SLATE

FROM THE BIBLE:

Have mercy on me, O God,
because of your unfailing love.
Because of your great
compassion,
blot out the stain of my sins.
Wash me clean from my guilt.
Purify me from my sin.
For I recognize my shameful
deeds—
they haunt me day and night.
Against you, and you alone, have
I sinned;
I have done what is evil in
your sight.
You will be proved right in what
you say,
and your judgment against me
is just.
For I was born a sinner—
yes, from the moment my
mother conceived me.
But you desire honesty from the
heart,
so you can teach me to be wise
in my inmost being.
Purify me from my sins, and I
will be clean;
wash me, and I will be whiter
than snow.

PSALM 51:1-7

"SEE WHAT I bought, Mother," said Megan excitedly as she took a magic slate out of a sack. She began scribbling on it as they drove home. "Now look," she said as she lifted the top plastic sheet. "The writing is gone." As she talked, her brother, Andy, stared out the window. He wasn't hearing the conversation or seeing the scenery.

"Andy!" Mother raised her voice. "This is the third time I've called your name. Is something wrong?"

"No." Andy lapsed into silence again.

And now you've told another lie, his conscience said. *That makes two.*

Andy sighed deeply. *But it was such a little lie,* he argued with his conscience.

"I know something is bothering you, Andy," insisted Mother. "Do you want to talk about it?"

"I told Dad a lie yesterday," Andy blurted out.

Mother said softly, "He knows that, but he is waiting for you to admit it."

Megan, busy with her magic slate, chuckled as she said, "Oop! I put a long tail on a rabbit! Oh, well! I'll just erase it and start over." Again she lifted the top plastic sheet and, like magic, her picture disappeared.

Mother smiled and told Andy, "When you sin, it's like writing on a magic slate. If you don't do anything about it, the sin remains there. But if you're sorry and confess your sins to God, he will erase them. Tell both your dad and the Lord that you're sorry, and the slate will be clean."

Megan smoothed the plastic sheet on her slate. "This time I'm going to do it right," she announced.

"Me, too, Megan," echoed Andy. "Me, too."

HOW ABOUT YOU? Have you told a lie? Disobeyed? Been sassy? Cheated? Right now, confess to God whatever sin you are aware of and let him wipe the slate clean. *B.J.W.*

TO MEMORIZE: I live in that high and holy place with those whose spirits are contrite and humble. *Isaiah 57:15*

Confess your sin

11 November

A READING LESSON

FROM THE BIBLE:

Are we beginning again to tell you how good we are? Some people need to bring letters of recommendation with them or ask you to write letters of recommendation for them. But the only letter of recommendation we need is you yourselves! Your lives are a letter written in our hearts, and everyone can read it and recognize our good work among you. Clearly, you are a letter from Christ prepared by us. It is written not with pen and ink, but with the Spirit of the living God. It is carved not on stone, but on human hearts.

We are confident of all this because of our great trust in God through Christ. It is not that we think we can do anything of lasting value by ourselves. Our only power and success come from God. He is the one who has enabled us to represent his new covenant. This is a covenant, not of written laws, but of the Spirit. The old way ends in death; in the new way, the Holy Spirit gives life.

2 CORINTHIANS 3:1-6

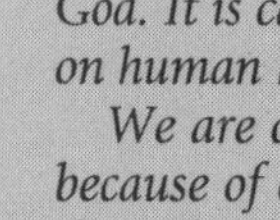

Live for Jesus

BETHANY STARED out the window at the rain. Her brother thumbed through a sports magazine. "What can we do, Mom?" asked Bethany.

Her mother smiled. "I thought you were learning your memory verse for Sunday school."

"I know it already," said Bethany. "It's 2 Corinthians 3:2, and it says, 'Your lives are a letter written in our hearts, and everyone can read it.' "

"Maybe you'd like to help me with this picture album," suggested Mom.

Bethany and Matthew joined Mom at the table and began looking at the pictures. "Oh, look!" squealed Bethany. "Here's a picture of Matthew when he was two. He looks so funny in those big sunglasses!"

Matthew grinned. "You think that's funny? Look at this family reunion picture. You're bald!"

Bethany laughed with Matthew. "There's Dad's aunt from Ohio," she said. "She looks mad."

"Yeah," said Matthew. "She was so grumpy that day." He picked up another picture. "Mom, isn't this man with the mustache your uncle? He scolded me for getting mad at the ball game. But when he struck out, he got so mad that he turned red as a beet. What a fake."

"I notice you're both 'reading' people," observed Mom.

"What do you mean?" asked Matthew.

"As you saw the people at the reunion, you 'read' one as 'grumpy' and another as 'fake.' "

"Oh, I get it!" exclaimed Bethany. "What we remember about other people is what we 'read' from their actions."

"And they remember us by 'reading' our actions too," added Matthew. "So we need to make sure they can see we're Christians by the way we live."

HOW ABOUT YOU? How are people "reading" you? Do you act grumpy or happy? Do your actions show obedience to authority, love for others, and honesty? Ask God to help you live for him. *G.W.*

TO MEMORIZE: Your lives are a letter written in our hearts, and everyone can read it. *2 Corinthians 3:2*

12 November

THROUGH IT ALL

FROM THE BIBLE:

But now, O Israel, the Lord who created you says: "Do not be afraid, for I have ransomed you. I have called you by name; you are mine. When you go through deep waters and great trouble, I will be with you. When you go through rivers of difficulty, you will not drown! When you walk through the fire of oppression, you will not be burned up; the flames will not consume you. For I am the Lord, your God, the Holy One of Israel, your Savior. I gave Egypt, Ethiopia, and Seba as a ransom for your freedom.

ISAIAH 43:1-3

God is with you

JOSHUA WAS STUNNED. He had just learned that Uncle Brian had cancer and even surgery might not help. "Are you going to die?" he whispered.

Joshua's uncle answered, "Only God knows. We need to trust God and submit to his will."

"But, Uncle Brian," Joshua protested, "I need you. Aunt Kathy needs you, and . . . it just seems all wrong."

"God never makes mistakes," said Uncle Brian. "I love you very much, and I love your Aunt Kathy. I know everyone in the family loves me too. But no matter how much we love one another, God loves us even more. And he will be with us through it all. All he asks us to do is pray to him and trust him."

Joshua walked away thinking about his uncle's words. Sure, he knew God never makes mistakes, but . . .

Suddenly Joshua stopped. What had Uncle Brian said? "God loves us and will be with us through it all." With determination in his heart, Joshua spoke silently to the Lord. *Thank you for being with Uncle Brian and Aunt Kathy and me and everyone else in the family. I know you can heal my uncle if that's what is best. I also know he will go to live with you if that's what you choose for him. Help me to trust you, no matter what.*

HOW ABOUT YOU? How do you react when really hard things come into your life? Perhaps a relative dies or leaves the family, a friend is hurt in an accident, or you get very sick. Do you get bitter and angry? Or do you remember that God has promised to be with you through it all? You're not alone! And remember that God never makes mistakes. *R.I.J.*

TO MEMORIZE: When you go through deep waters and great trouble, I will be with you. When you go through rivers of difficulty, you will not drown!
Isaiah 43:2

13 November

THE WAY YOU LOOK

FROM THE BIBLE:

"But the word of the Lord will last forever." And that word is the Good News that was preached to you.

So get rid of all malicious behavior and deceit. Don't just pretend to be good! Be done with hypocrisy and jealousy and backstabbing. You must crave pure spiritual milk so that you can grow into the fullness of your salvation. Cry out for this nourishment as a baby cries for milk, now that you have had a taste of the Lord's kindness.

Come to Christ, who is the living cornerstone of God's temple. He was rejected by the people, but he is precious to God who chose him.

And now God is building you, as living stones, into his spiritual temple. What's more, you are God's holy priests, who offer the spiritual sacrifices that please him because of Jesus Christ.

1 PETER 1:25–2:5

Listen in church

THE CHURCH SERVICE had just begun, and Christopher pulled out his Sunday school paper. Soon he was deep into an exciting story. When he finished reading, he sighed and looked up toward the pulpit. Pastor Baker was sitting on the platform, reading the local paper!

The pastor crumpled the paper loudly and stood up behind the pulpit. "Every Sunday I see boys and girls, and even a few adults, hide behind Sunday school papers as soon as the sermon begins. The way I looked to you just now is the way you look to me when I see you reading as I preach."

Pastor Baker left the platform and came down the aisle, stopping beside Christopher. Pointing his finger, the pastor shouted, "The way I looked to you is the way you look to me!"

Red-faced, Christopher squirmed in his seat. "I'm sorry!"

"Chris! Wake up!" Someone was nudging him. Quickly he sat up, surprised to find himself in his own bed. "It's time to get up. You must have been dreaming," Mother said.

Christopher jumped out of bed. As he got ready, he remembered something his dad had said about proper behavior in church. Dad had suggested that people would remember more of the sermon if they tried taking notes.

When they left for church that morning, Christopher had a small notepad and pencil with him. He reached for it when the sermon began.

HOW ABOUT YOU? Do you think sermons are hard to understand? Take a pad and pencil next Sunday. Write down the Bible text, the title of the sermon, and one or two important sentences from the sermon. Then look at your notes during the week. You'll be surprised how much you can learn from the preaching of God's Word. *J.A.G.*

TO MEMORIZE: "The word of the Lord will last forever." And that word is the Good News that was preached to you. *1 Peter 1:25*

14 November

STRAIGHT WALLS

FROM THE BIBLE:

Then he showed me another vision. I saw the Lord standing beside a wall that had been built using a plumb line. He was checking it with a plumb line to see if it was straight. And the Lord said to me, "Amos, what do you see?"

I answered, "A plumb line."

And the Lord replied, "I will test my people with this plumb line. I will no longer ignore all their sins." . . .

So think clearly and exercise self-control. Look forward to the special blessings that will come to you at the return of Jesus Christ. Obey God because you are his children. Don't slip back into your old ways of doing evil; you didn't know any better then. But now you must be holy in everything you do, just as God—who chose you to be his children—is holy. For he himself has said, "You must be holy because I am holy."

AMOS 7:7-8; 1 PETER 1:13-16

ANDREA COULD hardly wait till Grandpa finished building the playhouse he was making for her. She watched as he raised his arm to the top of one wall. He was holding a long cord with a weight attached at the bottom. "I know what that is," said Andrea.

Grandpa was surprised. "You do?"

Andrea nodded. "It's a plumb line," she said. "The weight at the end makes the string hang straight down. When you hold it along the wall, you can tell if the wall is straight."

"Well, I'm impressed!" exclaimed Grandpa. "Where did you learn about plumb lines?"

"In Sunday school," replied Andrea. "My teacher read how God showed Amos a plumb line. God said he would check his people against it. He would see if they measured up to what his laws said they should do. It would be like checking against a plumb line."

"It's not easy to measure up to God's standards," said Grandpa. "His standard for us is to be holy, just as he is holy. We can't do it without Jesus. I'm thankful that he came to be our Savior so we can trust him. With his help we can please God each day." He smiled at Andrea. "When your playhouse is finished, would you like a plumb line to hang on one of your walls as a reminder of God's standard for your behavior?"

Andrea nodded. "I'll decorate the weight on the end," she said eagerly. "Can I start now?"

HOW ABOUT YOU? Are you aware of God's standard for Christians? Maybe you think you're better than other kids in your class or not as good as your teachers and pastor. But God isn't comparing you to people. His standard is himself. Tell him you want Jesus' help to measure up and be the person he wants you to be. *H.W.M.*

TO MEMORIZE: He himself has said, "You must be holy because I am holy." *1 Peter 1:16*

Live by God's standards

15 November

STAYING CLEAN

FROM THE BIBLE:

Don't team up with those who are unbelievers. How can goodness be a partner with wickedness? How can light live with darkness? What harmony can there be between Christ and the Devil? How can a believer be a partner with an unbeliever? And what union can there be between God's temple and idols? For we are the temple of the living God. As God said:

"I will live in them
and walk among them.
I will be their God,
and they will be my people.
Therefore, come out from them
and separate yourselves from them, says the Lord.
Don't touch their filthy things,
and I will welcome you.
And I will be your Father,
and you will be my sons and daughters,
says the Lord Almighty."

Because we have these promises, dear friends, let us cleanse ourselves from everything that can defile our body or spirit. And let us work toward complete purity because we fear God.

2 CORINTHIANS 6:14–7:1

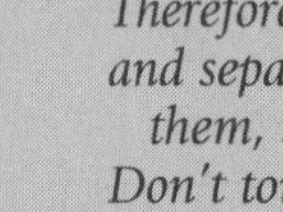

Keep your life clean

"I DON'T SEE how it will hurt me to go to one party!" Marla argued.

Her mother sighed. "Jessica and her friends go places Christians should not go," Mom explained. "They have bad habits, foul language—"

"But how can I win them to the Lord if I don't run around with them?" interrupted Marla.

"Being friendly is one thing, Marla. Running around as best friends is another." Just then the twins came in from playing outside. "Oh, no! Look at you!" Mom scolded them. "You're filthy again!"

"We played with Woof," Shawn said, grinning.

"Woof rolled over and over in the mud," Samantha explained.

Mom groaned. "Marla, you clean Samantha. I'll take Shawn."

Later at the dinner table, Marla asked Dad if she could go to the party at Jessica's house. Dad raised one eyebrow. "Is Jessica the girl with the loud mouth?"

Marla nodded. "Maybe I can win her to the Lord."

"Marla, when the twins went out to play, they were clean. Why didn't they get Woof clean?" Dad asked.

Marla shrugged. "I don't know."

"They didn't get him clean because dirt rubs off. Instead of getting their puppy clean, he got them dirty," Dad said. "We want you to win Jessica and her friends to the Lord, but you cannot do it by 'playing in the dirt' with them. Your life needs to be a clean, godly life."

"It's easy to get dirty, but it takes work to stay clean," Mom added. "Now, how about helping me get the dishes clean?"

HOW ABOUT YOU? Do you try to witness by going along with the crowd? That is not God's way. You witness best by showing how good it is to be a Christian. *B.J.W.*

TO MEMORIZE: Let us cleanse ourselves from everything that can defile our body or spirit. And let us work toward complete purity because we fear God. *2 Corinthians 7:1*

16 November

THE SAMPLE

FROM THE BIBLE:

For when we brought you the Good News, it was not only with words but also with power, for the Holy Spirit gave you full assurance that what we said was true. And you know that the way we lived among you was further proof of the truth of our message. So you received the message with joy from the Holy Spirit in spite of the severe suffering it brought you. In this way, you imitated both us and the Lord. As a result, you yourselves became an example to all the Christians in Greece. And now the word of the Lord is ringing out from you to people everywhere, even beyond Greece, for wherever we go we find people telling us about your faith in God. We don't need to tell them about it, for they themselves keep talking about the wonderful welcome you gave us and how you turned away from idols to serve the true and living God.

1 THESSALONIANS 1:5-9

"CAN I GO to the store with you, Mom?" asked Ethan. "You need me along to make sure you get the right cereal."

Mom laughed. "Come along," she agreed.

At the store they saw Ethan's friend Andrew. "Hey, Ethan," called Andrew, "my mom says I can go to Sunday school with you tomorrow."

"Oh, great!" exclaimed Ethan. "It starts at nine-thirty."

"I'll be there. Want to know why?" Without waiting for an answer, Andrew continued. "I know I've teased you about going to Sunday school. But lately I've been thinking about how you helped me with my paper route when I was sick, and you stood up for me when the guys gave me a rough time in gym class. Anyway, if it's Jesus who makes you a good friend, I want to know more about him. Well, I've gotta go. See ya."

As Ethan and his mother turned down another aisle, they saw a lady handing out sample ice-cream bars. "Yummy!" exclaimed Ethan, taking a bite. "Let's get some of these, Mom."

"OK. One box," agreed Mom.

"How can the store afford to give away so much ice cream?" asked Ethan.

Mom smiled. "The samples cause people to want the product, so the store will sell lots of ice cream bars today," she explained. "You know, Ethan, this reminds me of you."

"Me?" asked Ethan. "What do you mean?"

"Your life has given Andrew a sample taste of what it means to be a Christian," said Mom. "Now he wants more. You've been a good sample."

HOW ABOUT YOU? Do you know that you, too, can be a "sample" Christian? People need to see Jesus in you. Your words and actions should cause them to want to know him. Be the kind of person that Jesus wants you to be. *G.W.*

TO MEMORIZE: You yourself must be an example to them by doing good deeds of every kind. *Titus 2:7*

Let Jesus be seen in you

17 *November*

A ZOO FULL OF PEOPLE

FROM THE BIBLE:

Evil words destroy one's friends; wise discernment rescues the godly.

The whole city celebrates when the godly succeed; they shout for joy when the godless die.

Upright citizens bless a city and make it prosper, but the talk of the wicked tears it apart.

It is foolish to belittle a neighbor; a person with good sense remains silent.

A gossip goes around revealing secrets, but those who are trustworthy can keep a confidence.

PROVERBS 11:9-13

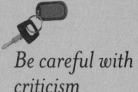

Be careful with criticism

MICHAEL AND EMILY were visiting the city zoo with their mother. "Look at the fat panda bear!" exclaimed Emily. "Look at him waddle. Doesn't he remind you of someone?"

"Yeah—old Mrs. Tompkins." Michael laughed. "And see those funny geese? Look how they strut around with their noses in the air. They remind me of Sarah Hayes."

Then they stopped to look at a wide-eyed owl. "Oh, and here's my teacher, Miss Williams," he said. "You know how she looks with those thick glasses."

"Here's an animal that reminds me of someone," Mom said.

Emily read the sign. "A vulture?" she asked. "Who does that remind you of, Mom?"

"Well, a vulture doesn't attack strong, healthy animals. He only lands on sick or injured ones," explained Mom. "He reminds me of people who like to point out the faults and weaknesses of others."

"I . . . I think I know who you mean," Emily stammered. "You're talking about us, aren't you?"

"Yes," Mom said. "The two of you *are* critical of others. That makes you blind to their strengths—and also to your own faults."

"But it's not always wrong to tease people, is it?" asked Michael.

"Not always." Mom smiled. "It's OK to tease if it's done in the right spirit and you're not hurting someone's feelings. But if there's any doubt, don't do it."

"Those doves over there remind me of you, Mom," Emily said. "They're so gentle, they wouldn't hurt a fly. We'll try to be more like them and you, Mom."

HOW ABOUT YOU? Do you enjoy teasing others? Make sure that you're not hurting someone's feelings by pointing out weaknesses. *S.L.K.*

TO MEMORIZE: Your own soul is nourished when you are kind, but you destroy yourself when you are cruel. *Proverbs 11:17*

18 November

THE PAPER ROUTE

FROM THE BIBLE:

Then the Lord rose up as though waking from sleep,
like a mighty man aroused from a drunken stupor.
He routed his enemies
and sent them to eternal shame.
But he rejected Joseph's descendants;
he did not choose the tribe of Ephraim.
He chose instead the tribe of Judah,
Mount Zion, which he loved.
There he built his towering sanctuary,
as solid and enduring as the earth itself.
He chose his servant David,
calling him from the sheep pens.
He took David from tending the ewes and lambs
and made him the shepherd of Jacob's descendants—
God's own people, Israel.
He cared for them with a true heart
and led them with skillful hands.

PSALM 78:65-72

LUCAS TOSSED his newspaper bag down on the kitchen floor. "I feel like quitting this paper route, Dad," he complained. "It's such a hassle to get up so early in the morning to deliver papers. Besides, I've earned enough to buy the tennis shoes I wanted."

"You've only had the route for a couple of months, Lucas," said Dad. "When your mother and I gave you permission to take this job, we all agreed you would keep it for a year."

"But I didn't know it would be so hard," protested Lucas as he slumped onto a kitchen chair. "Besides, what good will it really do me?"

"That's hard to say," said Mother as she joined Dad and Lucas at the table. "God uses many different experiences in our lives to develop qualities in us that he can use."

"That's right," agreed Dad. "I'm sure that you remember the Bible story about a shepherd boy who became a king. Psalm 78 says that God took David from being a shepherd of sheep and placed him as a shepherd of his people. When he became the king of Israel, he was able to use the principles of leadership and trust in God that he had learned as a shepherd."

"Yeah, but what can I learn from having a paper route?" asked Lucas.

"Responsibility, for one thing," offered Mother. "God wants us to learn to finish what we start."

"You'll learn lots of other things, too," said Dad, smiling. "Just wait and see."

HOW ABOUT YOU? Do you feel like quitting when things get too hard? Maybe you can't see any reason to learn math or to keep your bedroom clean. Even a job that doesn't seem to matter is part of God's plan for making you what he wants you to be. Keep at it! *D.L.R.*

TO MEMORIZE: My dear brothers and sisters, be strong and steady, always enthusiastic about the Lord's work. *1 Corinthians 15:58*

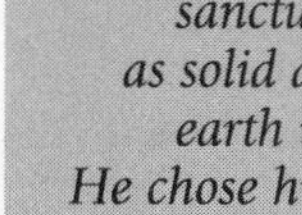

Don't be a quitter

19 November

BRACES

FROM THE BIBLE:

My children, listen to me. Listen to your father's instruction. Pay attention and grow wise, for I am giving you good guidance. Don't turn away from my teaching. For I, too, was once my father's son, tenderly loved by my mother as an only child.

My father told me, "Take my words to heart. Follow my instructions and you will live. Learn to be wise, and develop good judgment. Don't forget or turn away from my words." . . .

Pay attention, my child, to what I say. Listen carefully. Don't lose sight of my words. Let them penetrate deep within your heart.
PROVERBS 4:1-5, 20-21

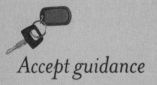

Accept guidance

DANIEL PLOPPED down on the bed. He had been sent to his room without dessert! "So I forgot to take out the trash! So I was 15 minutes late for lunch!" he mumbled. "Someone is always telling me to do this or not to do that."

Later Dad came into Daniel's room. "Son, will you help me plant a peach tree?"

"I guess so," Daniel replied slowly.

After they dug a hole and planted the tree, Dad used stakes and twine to make several braces for it. "This will help it grow straight and tall," he explained.

Then Dad asked, "How are you getting along with the braces on your teeth?"

Daniel shrugged. "All right."

"They may be a bit uncomfortable now, but it will be worth it when your teeth are straight," Dad assured him.

Daniel observed, "We put braces on our trees and braces on our teeth. A girl in my class even has a brace on her back."

Dad nodded. "God has given us braces for our lives, too," he said. "He wants us to grow spiritually straight and strong. Right now, Daniel, your mother and I have set rules for you that are like braces. Sometimes you pull against them, but someday you'll appreciate having had them."

Daniel wondered, "When will you take the braces off the peach tree?"

"When it's strong enough to stand straight and tall by itself," Dad said. Then he smiled and added, "We'll remove your 'braces,' too, as soon as you show that you can stand straight without help."

HOW ABOUT YOU? Do you feel like your life is controlled by others? Do you long for the day you can set your own rules? Stop pulling at the braces. Thank God for them because they will help you cope with the problems of life. *B.J.W.*

TO MEMORIZE: May our sons flourish in their youth like well-nurtured plants. May our daughters be like graceful pillars. *Psalm 144:12*

20 November

STAR OR SUN?

FROM THE BIBLE:

After they arrived at Capernaum, Jesus and his disciples settled in the house where they would be staying. Jesus asked them, "What were you discussing out on the road?" But they didn't answer, because they had been arguing about which of them was the greatest. He sat down and called the twelve disciples over to him. Then he said, "Anyone who wants to be the first must take last place and be the servant of everyone else."

MARK 9:33-35

Praise Christ, not men

AS REVIVAL MEETINGS were being held at Vanessa's church, many people asked Jesus to be their Savior. This bothered Vanessa. Her dad was pastor of the church, but for some time nobody had become a new Christian. Then an evangelist named Ben Henderson came, and lots of people accepted Jesus.

Vanessa's father said to her after the meeting one evening, "Why are you so quiet, honey? Don't you like the meetings?"

"You're just as good as that evangelist, Dad!" Vanessa responded. "Now lots of people are getting right with God, and he's getting the credit. It's not fair."

Dad was quiet for a moment, then asked her to go with him outdoors. "Which star is the brightest?" he asked.

Vanessa looked up. "That one up there is," she decided. "Or . . . no, that one way over there. Or is it . . . ?"

Dad smiled. "When the sun comes up tomorrow, which star will be the brightest?"

"Well, I don't know," she began. Then she thought of something. "The sun is a star, and it's the brightest of all! You can't see other stars when the sun is shining."

"Exactly," said Dad, "and it's that way in the ministry, too. It doesn't make any difference which preacher is best. When Jesus, God's Son, is preached, he is the brightest of all."

HOW ABOUT YOU? Do you think pastors or missionaries who lead many people to the Lord are better than those who help only a few people? Do you think it's unfair when one person witnesses to someone and another person leads him or her to Jesus? We should not worry about who will be greatest in God's kingdom. Jesus will be the greatest of all! *R.E.P.*

TO MEMORIZE: The ones who do the planting or watering aren't important, but God is important because he is the one who makes the seed grow. *1 Corinthians 3:7*

21 November

BOTH SAD AND GLAD

FROM THE BIBLE:

The law of the Lord is perfect,
reviving the soul.
The decrees of the Lord are
trustworthy,
making wise the simple.
The commandments of the
Lord are right,
bringing joy to the heart.
The commands of the Lord
are clear,
giving insight to life.
Reverence for the Lord is pure,
lasting forever.
The laws of the Lord are true;
each one is fair.
They are more desirable
than gold,
even the finest gold.
They are sweeter than honey,
even honey dripping from
the comb.
They are a warning to those who
hear them;
there is great reward for those
who obey them.

PSALM 19:7-11

Memorize God's Word

DURING FAMILY devotions, Dad smiled at Nicole. "I believe it's your turn to say today's Bible verse first."

"The laws of the Lord . . . are more desirable than gold, even the finest gold. They are sweeter than honey," Nicole quoted. "It's found in Psalm 19, verse ten."

"Very good," declared Dad. "Now, it's your turn, Aaron."

"The laws of the Lord are . . . uhhh . . . more desirable . . . uhhh," Aaron stammered. "I don't know it! I don't know why we have to memorize Bible verses anyway!"

"Aaron! You are talking about the Word of God!" said Mother.

"I didn't want to memorize the Word of God for a while either," Dad said. "But I'm older and wiser now. Let me tell you a parable I read the other day."

A young man was walking down a country road. He met a strange-looking old man who said, "Pick up some of the stones beside the road and put them in your pocket. Tomorrow you will be both glad and sad." Curious as to how that could be, the young man picked up a few stones and put them in his pocket. Then he said good-bye to the old man. The next day the young man discovered the stones had turned to precious jewels—diamonds, rubies, and emeralds. So the young man was glad for the jewels but sad he had not picked up more stones.

Mother nodded. "I like that parable. Learning Bible verses may seem like carrying stones now, Aaron. But every verse you learn will one day become a precious jewel to you. You will only be sorry you did not learn more."

HOW ABOUT YOU? Do you memorize Bible verses? If not, start today to collect "jewels" from God's Word. *B.J.W.*

TO MEMORIZE: [The laws of the Lord] are more desirable than gold, even the finest gold. They are sweeter than honey. *Psalm 19:10*

22 November

THANKS FOR FOOD STAMPS

FROM THE BIBLE:

Shout with joy to the Lord,
O earth!
Worship the Lord with
gladness.
Come before him, singing
with joy.
Acknowledge that the Lord is
God!
He made us, and we are his.
We are his people, the sheep
of his pasture.
Enter his gates with
thanksgiving;
go into his courts with praise.
Give thanks to him and bless
his name.
For the Lord is good.
His unfailing love continues
forever,
and his faithfulness continues
to each generation.

PSALM 100:1-5

Be thankful

"ALICIA, WOULD YOU go to the grocery store for me?" Mom asked. "We need bread and milk." Mom handed Alicia a book of food stamps. "And don't forget to—" A look of disgust mingled with anger covered Alicia's face. "What's the matter?"

"I'm not going to buy anything with these stupid food stamps!" Tears rolled down Alicia's cheeks. "I hate them!"

Mom sighed. "But, honey, you should be thankful we have food stamps. We'll use them only until I can get a job."

"But it's so humiliating!" Alicia wailed. "Oh, why did Daddy have to get hurt in that accident?"

Mom put her arm around Alicia. "This hasn't been easy for any of us, but we can learn from this experience."

"Learn what?" Alicia asked.

"Well, I've been humbled by all that has happened. I didn't realize I was so proud. I've also learned to be more compassionate," said Mom. "When we had plenty, I often thought that those who had less were lazy."

"They probably say that about us now," Alicia sobbed.

Mom sighed. "Perhaps a few people do, but most of them understand and care," she said.

Later, Alicia burst into the kitchen, her eyes shining. "Guess what, Mom! As I was paying for the groceries, Mr. Bryant asked if you needed a job. He needs a checker and wants you to call right away."

As Mom picked up the phone, she said to herself, *God will supply all of our needs. Thank you, Lord!*

HOW ABOUT YOU? Are you ever ashamed that your family has less than others? Can you express thankfulness to God for what you do have? When you thank him, your blessings will start to multiply. Try it today. *B.J.W.*

TO MEMORIZE: [Paul wrote,] "This same God who takes care of me will supply all your needs from his glorious riches, which have been given to us in Christ Jesus." *Philippians 4:19*

23 November

TWO THANKSGIVINGS

FROM THE BIBLE:

I will praise the Lord at all
times.
I will constantly speak his
praises.
I will boast only in the Lord;
let all who are discouraged
take heart.
Come, let us tell of the Lord's
greatness;
let us exalt his name together.
I prayed to the Lord, and he
answered me,
freeing me from all my fears.
Those who look to him for help
will be radiant with joy;
no shadow of shame will
darken their faces.
I cried out to the Lord in my
suffering, and he heard me.
He set me free from all my
fears.
For the angel of the Lord guards
all who fear him,
and he rescues them.
Taste and see that the Lord is
good.
Oh, the joys of those who
trust in him!

PSALM 34:1-8

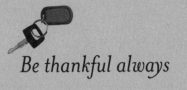

Be thankful always

THANKSGIVING was a joyful time for the Donnelly family. Grandpa and Grandma always came over, and after dinner Grandpa would tell stories. He cleared his throat. "Let me tell you about the first two Thanksgivings."

"Two?" said Andrew and Cory.

"Yes, the first two." Grandpa nodded. "At the first Thanksgiving there was plenty of food due to good weather and a big harvest. The Pilgrims and Indians thanked God for their good year. I read that one Indian, named Quadequina, brought deerskin bags full of popping corn, and it filled several bushel baskets when popped."

"Was that the first time the Pilgrims ate popcorn?" Andrew asked.

"I would think so," chuckled Grandpa. "Their eyes must have really opened wide when those white kernels jumped out of the hot pan." The children laughed.

Grandpa shifted in his chair. "The second Thanksgiving was different. Many people had died during the year, and others still faced possible starvation because of poor crops. But the Pilgrims set aside a time for Thanksgiving anyway!"

"They were probably thankful just to be alive," suggested Andrew.

"Perhaps," agreed Grandpa. "And they knew that even though life had changed for them, God had not! He still loved them and cared for them." Grandpa paused and looked at the boys. "When we face difficult times, it's important to recognize that God won't leave us."

"And we can still have Thanksgiving," declared Cory.

HOW ABOUT YOU? If you've had a good year, thank God for that. If it has been a hard year, thank God anyway. Thank him for his love, his gift of salvation, the roof over your head, the air you breathe, and the land you live in. Look around you, and you'll find many more things for which to thank God. *J.A.G.*

TO MEMORIZE: I will praise the Lord at all times. I will constantly speak his praises. *Psalm 34:1*

24 November

IN GOD'S SIGHT

FROM THE BIBLE:

Praise the Lord, I tell myself;
with my whole heart, I will
praise his holy name.
Praise the Lord, I tell myself,
and never forget the good
things he does for me.
He forgives all my sins
and heals all my diseases.
He ransoms me from death
and surrounds me with love
and tender mercies.
He fills my life with good things.
My youth is renewed like the
eagle's!
The Lord gives righteousness
and justice to all who are
treated unfairly.
He revealed his character to
Moses
and his deeds to the people of
Israel.
The Lord is merciful and
gracious;
he is slow to get angry and full
of unfailing love.

PSALM 103:1-8

Count your blessings

SIERRA SQUEALED with joy as her dad pulled up to the ice-cream shop. "Oh, goody! I want a big hot fudge sundae with nuts."

Mother shook her head. "It's too near dinner. A single-dip cone will be enough."

Sierra's mouth tightened. "I don't see why—"

"What flavor do you want?" interrupted Dad, opening his door.

"I guess chocolate almond," Sierra replied gruffly. "I don't see how it would hurt me to have a hot fudge—"

"Sierra, how do you suppose God feels right now?" asked Mother. "Only three hours ago you had a delicious lunch. Yet you're pouting because you get only one dip of ice cream—"

"Oh, Mom," interrupted Sierra. "I hope you aren't going to start talking about starving kids in some foreign county!"

Mother ignored her. "At the same time God sees you, he also sees another ten-year-old looking through a garbage can for a bite to eat."

"But I can't do anything about that."

"Remember how you threw a fit last Sunday because Amy had a new sweater and you didn't?" Mother asked. "God saw you standing in front of your closet full of sweaters. At the same time he saw another girl putting on an old sweater, but she was smiling as she got ready for church."

"Awww, Mom, you're just imagining that," protested Sierra.

"No, I am not. It happens every day somewhere," Mother replied.

Sierra looked out the window. She didn't like the picture her mother was painting. She started thinking about things she could do to change the picture.

HOW ABOUT YOU? How does God see you at this Thanksgiving time? Are you "spoiled" or thankful? This would be a good time to count your blessings. *B.J.W.*

TO MEMORIZE: Praise the Lord, O my soul, and forget not all his benefits. *Psalm 103:2* (NIV)

25 November

BAD ADVICE

FROM THE BIBLE:

Let me hear of your unfailing
love to me in the morning,
for I am trusting you.
Show me where to walk,
for I have come to you in
prayer.
Save me from my enemies, Lord;
I run to you to hide me.
Teach me to do your will,
for you are my God.
May your gracious Spirit lead me
forward
on a firm footing.
PSALM 143:8-10

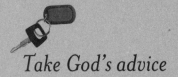

Take God's advice

LYNN HAD A decision to make. Should she go on her class hayride, or should she go to the church party being held the same night? She had prayed about it and knew that some of the kids going on the hayride were pretty wild, but she still wanted to go! *I know,* she thought. *I'll ask Jennifer what she thinks.*

"I think you should go on the hayride," advised her friend Jennifer. "The kids might think you're a snob if you don't show up." Lynn was easily convinced. She would go to the school hayride.

The hayride was rowdy from the start. Some of the kids carried things too far, roughly pushing each other off the wagon as it moved slowly down the dark country road. Lynn fell with a thump to the road. In spite of her bruised knee, she had to jump up quickly and run to catch up and climb back on the wagon. She was surprised that the parents who were along to supervise didn't try to calm things down. Fun was fun, but this was just too rough!

Later Lynn lay in bed, feeling her throbbing knee and thinking about how she could have been hurt even worse. *Oh, why did I take Jennifer's advice,* she thought, *when I knew all the time what God wanted me to do!* Before going to sleep she silently asked God to help her follow his direction in the future.

HOW ABOUT YOU? Has there ever been a time when you knew what *God* wanted you to do, but you waited for someone to advise you to do what *you* wanted to do? When you know God's will, do it. Then you can put your name in the place of Ezra's in today's memory verse. *P.R.*

TO MEMORIZE: Ezra had prepared his heart to seek the law of the Lord, and to do it. *Ezra 7:10* (NKJV)

26 November

WHO NEEDS BROTHERS?

FROM THE BIBLE:

Then his brothers came and bowed low before him. "We are your slaves," they said.

But Joseph told them, "Don't be afraid of me. Am I God, to judge and punish you? As far as I am concerned, God turned into good what you meant for evil. He brought me to the high position I have today so I could save the lives of many people. No, don't be afraid. Indeed, I myself will take care of you and your families." And he spoke very kindly to them, reassuring them.

GENESIS 50:18-21

AS DAD BEGAN to read the Bible one morning, Kendra felt a sharp poke under the table. Glaring at her brother, she whispered, "Knock it off, Kyle."

"A friend is always loyal," Dad read from the book of Proverbs, "and a brother is born to help in time of need."

Kendra frowned. "Brothers are good for nothing. They don't know what you need and they don't care," she said.

"Hold it!" responded Dad. "What about the time you fell down the stairs, Kendra, and your brother felt so bad he cried harder than you?"

"And when you dropped your notebook yesterday," Mother reminded Kendra, "who ran after the papers that went blowing away?"

"Yeah!" Kyle piped up, poking his sister again. "I ran halfway down the street after 'em!"

"And you, young man," Dad continued, "who helped you finish shoveling the snow so you could go to the zoo with your friends?"

"Uh, Kendra," mumbled Kyle. Then he quickly added, "But that verse isn't talking about sisters."

"Oh, yes, it is," said Dad. "The phrase 'a brother is born to help' means that God gave us brothers *and* sisters, not to bring us trouble, but to be there when trouble comes. You should ask God to help you begin solving your differences without fights. If you thank the Lord for one another, he will help you appreciate each other in spite of your differences."

HOW ABOUT YOU? Have you learned to appreciate the brothers or sisters God has given you? Today's Scripture gives the example of Joseph's love for his brothers, even after they had mistreated him. Love your brothers and sisters, and thank God for the ways they help you. Then be a good brother or sister to them—help them when they need you. *S.L.N.*

TO MEMORIZE: A friend is always loyal, and a brother is born to help in time of need.
Proverbs 17:17

Appreciate brothers and sisters

27 November

THE BUMPY ROAD

FROM THE BIBLE:

And a main road will go through that once deserted land. It will be named the Highway of Holiness. Evil-hearted people will never travel on it. It will be only for those who walk in God's ways; fools will never walk there. Lions will not lurk along its course, and there will be no other dangers. Only the redeemed will follow it. Those who have been ransomed by the Lord will return to Jerusalem, singing songs of everlasting joy. Sorrow and mourning will disappear, and they will be overcome with joy and gladness.
ISAIAH 35:8-10

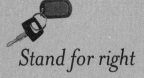

Stand for right

NOEL SHUT the front door behind him, but he could not shut out the taunts ringing in his head. He walked slowly down the hall to the room where he heard the whir of his mother's sewing machine. "Did you have a good day, Noel?" asked Mom. Tears filled Noel's eyes, and he shook his head. Mom pointed to a chair beside the sewing machine. "Sit down and tell me about it."

Noel sat down. "At lunch Matt told a dirty joke, so I got up and left."

"Good for you," Mom said.

Noel snorted. "Oh, yeah, good for me! Good old Holy Noel! That's what they called me the rest of the day!"

"Doing the right thing is not always easy," Mom started taking pins out of a piece of material.

Noel sniffed as he changed the subject. "What are you making?"

"A corduroy jacket for Kim," his mother replied.

"Corduroy sure is bumpy," Noel said, feeling the material.

"Just like the corduroy roads they used to make by laying logs side by side," said Mom. "Imagine riding in a wagon or stagecoach down a corduroy road. *Bump-bump, bumpity-bump.*" Mom paused. "I guess you hit a corduroy stretch today, Noel. But you made it across."

Noel stood up and grinned. "There are worse things to be called than 'Holy Noel'! I think I'll go ride my bike. There's one stretch of Oak Street that's almost as bumpy as a corduroy road. It's fun to ride on it."

HOW ABOUT YOU? Have you run into some rough roads lately? Maybe you had to go down a different road from your friends. Maybe you had to say no or take a stand against some things they were doing. Living a Christian life is not always easy, but it is always best. *B.J.W.*

TO MEMORIZE: A main road will go through that once deserted land. It will be named the Highway of Holiness. *Isaiah 35:8*

28 *November*

SWAYING CASTLE

FROM THE BIBLE:

An honest witness tells the truth; a false witness tells lies.

Some people make cutting remarks, but the words of the wise bring healing.

Truth stands the test of time; lies are soon exposed.

Deceit fills hearts that are plotting evil; joy fills hearts that are planning peace!

No real harm befalls the godly, but the wicked have their fill of trouble.

The Lord hates those who don't keep their word, but he delights in those who do.

PROVERBS 12:17-22

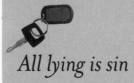

All lying is sin

"THERE!" PETER exclaimed as he finished pounding a nail. "This is the best tree house in town! I can't wait to sleep here. The way this tree sways, we'll be rocked to sleep in seconds!"

Michael nodded. "Let's ask if we can sleep out here tonight."

"I know my dad won't let me," said Peter. "He wants to check it out first to be sure it's safe."

"Hey! I know!" Michael exclaimed. "Let's each ask our folks for permission to spend the night with each other. They'll think we're at each other's houses."

Peter agreed to try it.

The plan worked, but in the middle of the night they were awakened by thunder! "Hey! I'm getting wet!" yelled Peter. "It's pouring, and the roof is leaking. Come on! Let's get over to my house."

The storm had awakened Peter's parents, too, and they were surprised when the boys stumbled into the kitchen. "Where have you been? Why were you out in this storm?" Peter's dad asked.

"We . . . ah . . . we were sleeping in the tree house, Dad," answered Peter.

"The tree house? You asked if you could stay at Michael's house overnight."

"Not really," replied Peter. "I just asked if I could spend the night with Michael."

"I see," said Dad. "But since you deceived us, you were really lying. Can you both see that?"

"Yes," admitted the boys together, and both apologized.

"I'm thankful God protected you tonight," said Dad, "but I'm afraid the tree house will be off-limits for a while."

HOW ABOUT YOU? Are you guilty of giving false impressions or of telling "fibs" or "tiny lies"? God hates every form of lying and deception. He is pleased only when our intentions as well as our words are pure. *A.G.L.*

TO MEMORIZE: The Lord hates those who don't keep their word, but he delights in those who do. *Proverbs 12:22*

29 November

JUST A BABY

FROM THE BIBLE:

Dear friends, even though we are talking like this, we really don't believe that it applies to you. We are confident that you are meant for better things, things that come with salvation. For God is not unfair. He will not forget how hard you have worked for him and how you have shown your love to him by caring for other Christians, as you still do. Our great desire is that you will keep right on loving others as long as life lasts, in order to make certain that what you hope for will come true. Then you will not become spiritually dull and indifferent. Instead, you will follow the example of those who are going to inherit God's promises because of their faith and patience.
HEBREWS 6:9-12

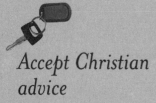

Accept Christian advice

JENNA'S LITTLE brother spied a glittering piece of broken glass on the ground. He picked it up and was about to put it into his mouth when Jenna stopped him. Immediately, young Justin let out a loud scream that brought Mother out to see what was happening. "I just took this piece of glass away from him," Jenna explained.

Mother picked up the little boy. "I'm glad you were watching him," she said to Jenna. "You probably saved him from being cut very badly."

Jenna shrugged her shoulders. "Yeah, but Justin sure didn't appreciate it."

"That's because he's just a baby," Mother explained.

Later Jenna talked to her mother about a friend. "Kerry is mad at me," she said. "Her mom won't let her watch some of the TV shows they used to watch before they were Christians. I agreed with her mom, so now Kerry's mad at me, too."

"That's too bad," sympathized Mother. "Try to be patient with her. Sometimes baby Christians react exactly as Justin did when you took the broken glass away. They don't understand when someone who has been a Christian for a longer time tries to protect them from dangerous things."

When Jenna thought about it, she knew she was sometimes like that, too. She didn't want others, especially her parents, to tell her how to live as a Christian. Now she was determined to be more patient with Kerry and to listen to the advice of other Christians herself.

HOW ABOUT YOU? Do you accept the advice and help that is offered to you by your parents? Your pastor? Your Sunday school teacher? They are all more experienced in life and know more than you do about the dangers and tricks of Satan. Be open to their guidance. *R.I.J.*

TO MEMORIZE: Follow the example of those who are going to inherit God's promises because of their faith and patience. *Hebrews 6:12*

30 November

LEFTOVERS

FROM THE BIBLE:

The Lord Almighty says to the priests: "A son honors his father, and a servant respects his master. I am your father and master, but where are the honor and respect I deserve? You have despised my name!

"But you ask, 'How have we ever despised your name?'

"You have despised my name by offering defiled sacrifices on my altar.

"Then you ask, 'How have we defiled the sacrifices?'

"You defile them by saying the altar of the Lord deserves no respect. When you give blind animals as sacrifices, isn't that wrong? And isn't it wrong to offer animals that are crippled and diseased? Try giving gifts like that to your governor, and see how pleased he is!" says the Lord Almighty. . . .

"I wish that someone among you would shut the Temple doors so that these worthless sacrifices could not be offered! I am not at all pleased with you," says the Lord Almighty, "and I will not accept your offerings."

MALACHI 1:6-10

"NOT LEFTOVERS tonight," grumbled Kendall as he slid into his chair. "Ugh!"

Mom frowned, and Dad spoke sternly. "That's enough, Kendall! Now let's give thanks."

Kendall and Madeline picked at their food until Mom asked, "Who wants peach cobbler?"

"I do," the children replied in unison. Madeline mumbled to Kendall, "At least there's one leftover thing that's good."

As Mom dished out the cobbler she said, "We'll have family devotions after we finish dessert."

"I don't have time this evening," Madeline said quickly. "I have a pile of homework."

"And I have to do some research on the Morgan case," Dad said. "Maybe we should skip devotions tonight."

"Yeah," agreed both of the children.

"We skipped devotions last night and the night before," Mom reminded them. "We've been giving God our leftover time—that is, when we've had any time left over."

Dad raised his eyebrows. "I hadn't thought of that," he admitted. "You're right. We are guilty—especially me, and I'm sorry."

"I wonder if God likes leftovers any better than we do," said Kendall.

"Probably not," replied Mom. "In fact, I'm sure he doesn't. In Old Testament times he often told his people, the Israelites, how much he disliked getting leftover offerings from them."

Dad stood up. "Looks like we need to rearrange our schedule starting right now. Get your Bibles. Family devotions will begin in the living room in five minutes."

HOW ABOUT YOU? Do you read your Bible and pray only when you have time? Are you giving God your leftovers? He wants the first part of your time and talents, as well as your money. Make up your mind right now to start putting God first in all things. *B.J.W.*

TO MEMORIZE: Honor the Lord by giving him the first part of all your income. *Proverbs 3:9* (TLB)

Put God first

1 December

THE TRICKSTER

FROM THE BIBLE:

About three o'clock in the morning Jesus came to them, walking on the water. When the disciples saw him, they screamed in terror, thinking he was a ghost. But Jesus spoke to them at once. "It's all right," he said. "I am here! Don't be afraid."

Then Peter called to him, "Lord, if it's really you, tell me to come to you by walking on water."

"All right, come," Jesus said.

So Peter went over the side of the boat and walked on the water toward Jesus. But when he looked around at the high waves, he was terrified and began to sink. "Save me, Lord!" he shouted.

Instantly Jesus reached out his hand and grabbed him. "You don't have much faith," Jesus said. "Why did you doubt me?" And when they climbed back into the boat, the wind stopped.

Then the disciples worshiped him. "You really are the Son of God!" they exclaimed.

MATTHEW 14:25-33

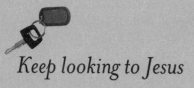

Keep looking to Jesus

"I CAN'T FIGURE out how magicians do those things," said David as he and Phil waited outside the library to see the magic show.

"David," Phil whispered. "I think I've got it figured out. Let's do the opposite of what he says! If he says to watch his hands, look at what he's holding."

Sure enough, the boys were able to see one or two small movements, which gave them clues as to how the tricks were done. But although they tried hard, they couldn't catch on to much of what he was doing. "I still think half the trick is getting the audience to look where you tell them to," said Phil as the boys walked home. "When he holds up his hands and says, 'Look here,' it's hard not to do that."

That weekend the boys told their story to their Sunday school teacher. "That's interesting," said Mr. Pierce. "Do you remember the story of Peter walking on the water?"

"Yes," David answered. "When he stopped looking at Jesus and looked at the water, he started to sink."

"That's right," said Mr. Pierce. "Satan is a great trickster, you know. He loves to get our attention on anything except Jesus. If he can do that, he's happy. Don't be fooled by his methods."

HOW ABOUT YOU? Do you worry so much about things going on in the world—wars, drugs, diseases—that you forget about Jesus himself? Do you get so busy with schoolwork, a paper route, or even church activities that you don't have time to spend with the Lord? Remember, Satan likes you to stay so busy—even with good activities—that you neglect to think about Jesus. Keep your eyes on Jesus. Read God's Word, pray, and think often about your Lord. *C.R.*

TO MEMORIZE: Keeping our eyes on Jesus, on whom our faith depends from start to finish. *Hebrews 12:2*

SOUR LEMONS

FROM THE BIBLE:

Not that I was ever in need, for I have learned how to get along happily whether I have much or little. I know how to live on almost nothing or with everything. I have learned the secret of living in every situation, whether it is with a full stomach or empty, with plenty or little. For I can do everything with the help of Christ who gives me the strength I need.

PHILIPPIANS 4:11-13

Look for what's good

AS MOM put warm, buttery popcorn into bowls, Peter scowled at his sister. "Hey, Mandy! Get out of my chair!"

"You always get to sit by the window," replied Mandy. "I want to sit here for a change."

"It's my place," said Peter angrily. "Dad! Make Mandy get out of my chair!"

"Don't you kids ever stop fighting?" asked Dad. "Just sit over there, Peter, so we can enjoy our snack."

As they ate popcorn and sipped glasses of lemonade, Dad said, "It seems to me you were fighting over chairs last night, too. Only then, wasn't it Peter who wanted to sit in the chair Mandy usually had?" Mandy just shrugged, and Peter nodded sheepishly.

Mom smiled. "I think it's time you children learn to take a sour lemon and make lemonade."

"What do you mean?" asked Mandy.

Dad laughed. "That's an old saying," he explained. "This good lemonade we're enjoying started out as sour lemons. Mom didn't moan about how sour they were. She made something good out of them. And instead of complaining about what happens in your life, you should make the best of every situation. Like the apostle Paul said, we should be content in whatever situation we find ourselves."

"Or in whatever 'chair' we're in," laughed Peter. "I guess I don't mind sitting over here by the fireplace. It's nice and warm."

"I like it too," agreed Mandy. "It really doesn't matter that much, does it, Peter?"

"I'm glad that's settled." Mom smiled. "Now how about some more lemonade?"

HOW ABOUT YOU? Do you complain when you don't get what you want? The next time things don't go the way you want them to, stop and look for something good in the situation. Or do what you can to improve it. Give up your "sour" attitude and enjoy the lemonade! *S.L.K.*

TO MEMORIZE: True religion with contentment is great wealth. *1 Timothy 6:6*

3 December

OK, SO I GOOFED

FROM THE BIBLE:

Oh, what joy for those
whose rebellion is forgiven,
whose sin is put out of sight!
Yes, what joy for those
whose record the Lord has
cleared of sin,
whose lives are lived in
complete honesty!
When I refused to confess
my sin,
I was weak and miserable,
and I groaned all day long.
Day and night your hand of
discipline was heavy on me.
My strength evaporated like
water in the summer heat.
Finally, I confessed all my sins
to you
and stopped trying to hide
them.
I said to myself, "I will confess
my rebellion to the Lord."
And you forgave me! All my
guilt is gone.

PSALM 32:1-5

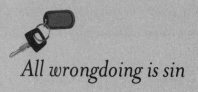

All wrongdoing is sin

DOUGLAS JONES did not like to admit that he was a sinner. Whenever he did something wrong, he would shrug his shoulders and say, "OK, so I goofed." One day after he had taken a toy car from another boy's desk, he was ordered to report to the principal's office. When he got there, he saw his mother.

Douglas squirmed as the school principal entered the room. After explaining to Douglas's mother what had happened, Mr. Seivert looked at Douglas.

"I didn't mean to do anything wrong," Douglas said. "I just goofed again."

Mrs. Jones turned to face the principal. "May I talk with Douglas alone?"

Mr. Sievert nodded and left the room.

"Douglas," Mother said, "did you steal that toy car?"

"I borrowed it, sort of," mumbled the boy. "I goofed."

"Taking what doesn't belong to you is stealing. It's not just a goof. God wants to forgive you. But first you have to admit that you did more than goof or make a mistake."

Douglas looked down as he told his mother, "I thought it wouldn't sound as bad if I said I goofed. But I did steal, and that's a sin."

"Thank you for admitting that, Douglas," said Mother. "Now, what else must you do to make things right?"

"I want to ask Jesus to forgive me."

After Douglas told Jesus he was sorry, he and his mother talked again to the principal. Then Douglas went to tell the other boy that he was sorry.

HOW ABOUT YOU? Do you try to cover your sinful actions? You can't cover up sins by calling them "goofs." You do wrong things because you are a sinner. It's only when you admit this and confess your sin to God that you have forgiveness. *R.I.J.*

TO MEMORIZE: I confessed all my sins to you and stopped trying to hide them. *Psalm 32:5*

THE CIRCLE

FROM THE BIBLE:

Lord, through all the generations
you have been our home!
Before the mountains were created,
before you made the earth and the world,
you are God, without beginning or end.
You turn people back to dust, saying,
"Return to dust!"
For you, a thousand years are as yesterday!
They are like a few hours!
PSALM 90:1-4

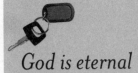

God is eternal

SEVEN-YEAR-OLD Becky was always full of questions. One day she asked her mother, "Who made God?"

"No one did," Mom answered.

"Then where did God come from?" asked Becky.

"God always has been," said Mom. "As you grow older, you'll understand it better, but even then it will be hard. You see, our minds are not as great as God's mind, and there are some things we won't really understand until we get to heaven someday. For now, we just have to accept the fact that God has always existed."

"But he had to come from somewhere," insisted Becky.

Mom took off her wedding ring and handed it to Becky. "I want you to tell me where this ring starts and where it stops," she said.

Becky looked at the perfect circle. "But it doesn't start or stop," she replied. "It's just a circle that doesn't have a beginning or an end."

"And that's like God, honey. God is eternal. He never had a beginning, and he has no ending." Mom put her ring on her finger as she continued. "You see, we think about minutes and days and weeks and years. But with God, there is no such thing as time. He is always the same—yesterday, today, and forever."

"Wow, that's really something to think about," Becky said.

Mom set a plate of peanut-butter crackers and a glass of milk on the table. "I think it's time you rested your brain and had a little snack," she said with a smile.

HOW ABOUT YOU? Aren't you glad God is so great that no human mind can fully understand him? That's one of the things that makes him God! Don't try too hard to understand how he could have no beginning. Accept the fact, and thank him for being so great and wonderful—and for loving you! *C.Vm*

TO MEMORIZE: You are God, without beginning or end. *Psalm 90:2*

5 December

THE WHOLE PARADE

FROM THE BIBLE:

And do not forget the things I have done throughout history. For I am God—I alone! I am God, and there is no one else like me. Only I can tell you what is going to happen even before it happens. Everything I plan will come to pass, for I do whatever I wish. I will call a swift bird of prey from the east—a leader from a distant land who will come and do my bidding. I have said I would do it, and I will.

ISAIAH 46:9-11

God's ways are right

"WHY, GOD?" Jolene's heart cried out. She had just learned that her baby brother, Jeremy, was deaf.

"Don't blame God, Jolene," Mother said gently. "We need to trust him even when we can't understand."

But Jolene wanted to understand. They were Christians. Wasn't God supposed to take care of them?

"Jolene, are you ready to go to the parade?" Mother asked one day. She held out her arms to the baby. "Come to Mother, Jeremy," she said.

"I don't see why you talk to him, Mother. He can't hear you!" Jolene said harshly.

Mother sighed. "It's important for him to see our lips move and feel the vibration of our words. Now let's go and have a good time."

People were standing three deep in front of Jolene's family. She got down and peered through the legs in front of her. "It would be so much better if I could see it all together instead of one row at a time," she wailed. Dad handed Jeremy to Mother, and with a swoop Jolene was on her father's shoulders. She clapped her hands. "Now I can see the whole parade," she said.

When they were driving home, Dad said, "Life is a lot like a parade. And we're like children in a crowd. We can only see one day at a time. But God sees the whole parade—the past and the future as well as the present. We wonder why Jeremy is deaf, but that's because we only see the present. God sees the whole picture."

Jolene squeezed her brother's hand. "I'll try to remember that, Dad," she promised.

HOW ABOUT YOU? Are you questioning God about something? God's ways are far above ours, and his ways are right. Trust him. You can say, "I don't understand, but I believe." *B.J.W.*

TO MEMORIZE: Trust in the Lord with all your heart; do not depend on your own understanding. *Proverbs 3:5*

6 December

THE BOOSTER BROTHER

FROM THE BIBLE:

Two people can accomplish more than twice as much as one; they get a better return for their labor. If one person falls, the other can reach out and help. But people who are alone when they fall are in real trouble. And on a cold night, two under the same blanket can gain warmth from each other. But how can one be warm alone? A person standing alone can be attacked and defeated, but two can stand back-to-back and conquer. Three are even better, for a triple-braided cord is not easily broken.

ECCLESIASTES 4:9-12

Help someone

"HELP ME put on my gloves," Daniel said as he tried to match fingers and glove openings.

Kent groaned. "You're in first grade. You should be able to help yourself. Who puts your gloves on you after school?"

"My teacher helps me." Daniel held his hand up to his big brother. "Will you pull me on my sled after school?"

Kent sighed. "Oh, all right."

"Are you boys ready for school?" Dad asked as he pulled on his coat. He led the way outside and across the snow-packed yard.

As they started to get in the car, Mr. Gleason from next door came toward them. "I hate to bother you, John, but my car won't start. Could you give me a boost?"

"Sure," Dad replied. He backed the car out of the drive and pulled in beside Mr. Gleason's. The boys watched as the men raised the hoods of the cars and attached jumper cables to the batteries. Then Mr. Gleason got in his car and started it.

When they were on their way to school, Daniel asked, "Why did you stretch those lines from our car to Mr. Gleason's?"

"We jumped some power from our battery to his. We gave him a boost," Dad explained.

Kent turned to Dad. "I think I'll run over and shovel Gramps' sidewalk after school."

"You gonna give Gramps a boost?" Daniel asked. "Like you gave me a boost with my gloves? And like you're going to give me a boost on the sled?"

Kent laughed. "Just call me the booster brother," he said.

HOW ABOUT YOU? Have you given anyone a boost lately? Can you think of someone who needs your help? Run an errand. Write a note. Say some kind words. Listen to someone who is lonely. Give someone a boost today. You'll be glad you did. *B.J.W.*

TO MEMORIZE: They encourage one another with the words, "Be strong!" *Isaiah 41:6*

7 December

NO THANKS

FROM THE BIBLE:

Therefore, since we have been made right in God's sight by faith, we have peace with God because of what Jesus Christ our Lord has done for us. Because of our faith, Christ has brought us into this place of highest privilege where we now stand, and we confidently and joyfully look forward to sharing God's glory.

We can rejoice, too, when we run into problems and trials, for we know that they are good for us—they help us learn to endure. And endurance develops strength of character in us, and character strengthens our confident expectation of salvation. And this expectation will not disappoint us. For we know how dearly God loves us, because he has given us the Holy Spirit to fill our hearts with his love.

ROMANS 5:1-5

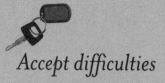

Accept difficulties

"I DON'T WANT to see Dr. Cook," sobbed Kerri, coughing. "He might want to give me a shot."

"Only if it's needed," said Mother.

"I'll be right with you," said the office nurse. "Your mom can come too."

After the doctor examined Kerri, her worst fears came true. "She has a bad infection," said Dr. Cook. "She needs a shot of penicillin." In spite of Kerri's wails, the doctor gave her the shot. He also handed Mother a prescription for tablets that Kerri had to take.

Mother listened as Kerri prayed by her bed that evening. "Dear Lord, thank you for Mommy and Daddy," she prayed. "Please bless them. Thank you for the nurse who was so nice to me. Bless her. Thank you for the pills that will help me get better. Please bless all my friends. In Jesus' name. Amen."

As Mother tucked the covers around Kerri she said, "I didn't hear you thank the Lord for Dr. Cook."

"I'm mad at him," said Kerri with a scowl.

Mother sat down on the bed. "You know he gave you the shot to help make you well again. Do you think he enjoyed making you feel afraid?"

"No." Kerri shook her head.

"So, was he being mean?" persisted Mother.

Kerri said, "No. I . . . I'm sorry I got mad. I want to ask God to bless him, too." She climbed out of bed and got back on her knees.

HOW ABOUT YOU? When God lets something happen that you don't want or like, do you get angry at him? Maybe a friend moves away, you get a terrible stomachache, or you don't have enough money for something special. Ask God to help you learn from those experiences. Thank him for hard things and even be joyful when those things happen. *H.W.M.*

TO MEMORIZE: Dear brothers and sisters, whenever trouble comes your way, let it be an opportunity for joy. *James 1:2*

WHY SO SNAPPY?

FROM THE BIBLE:

Finally, all of you should be of one mind, full of sympathy toward each other, loving one another with tender hearts and humble minds. Don't repay evil for evil. Don't retaliate when people say unkind things about you. Instead, pay them back with a blessing. That is what God wants you to do, and he will bless you for it. For the Scriptures say,

"If you want a happy life and good days,
keep your tongue from speaking evil,
and keep your lips from telling lies.
Turn away from evil and do good.
Work hard at living in peace with others."

1 PETER 3:8-11

ERIN SLAMMED the door behind her. "Oh, that Trina is so hateful!"

Mom looked surprised. "I thought Trina was your best friend," she said.

"She used to be," choked Erin, "but lately nothing I do pleases her."

"That's too bad," Mom sympathized, "but try to be patient with her. Maybe she doesn't feel well."

"I know," Erin sighed. "But if she doesn't stop snapping at me . . ." The squeal of tires and the loud yipping of a dog sent Erin and her mother running outside. "Oh, Mom! It's Rowdy." Erin ran to the curb, where a man was bending over the puppy.

"I'm so sorry," he told them. "The dog ran out right in front of me."

Mom knelt beside the whimpering puppy. As she started to touch him, Rowdy snapped at her. "It's OK, Rowdy," she said. Once more she reached for him, and again Rowdy snapped. "Erin, can you hold his jaws shut?" asked Mom. "I want to see how badly he's hurt before we move him."

Several hours later they returned from the vet with a stiff and sore puppy. Erin's father had arrived home from work by then. "Rowdy is awfully snappy," said Erin.

"That's because he's hurting," Dad told her, opening the newspaper. "Say, do you know the names of Trina's parents? Aren't they Phillip and Lisa?"

"Yes," Erin replied. "Why?"

"Because Lisa Clark is filing for divorce from Phillip Clark," replied Dad.

"Oh, no!" Erin took a deep breath. "No wonder Trina has been so snappy. She's hurting! I better be careful not to snap back at her."

HOW ABOUT YOU? When someone snaps at you, do you snap back? Before you do that, ask yourself, *Is he hurting?* If so, he needs your love and kindness. He needs your patience and your prayers. *B.J.W.*

TO MEMORIZE: Do not repay evil with evil or insult with insult, but with blessing. *1 Peter 3:9* (NIV)

Help those who hurt

9 December

THE ANTIQUE DISH

FROM THE BIBLE:

Now you can have sincere love for each other as brothers and sisters because you were cleansed from your sins when you accepted the truth of the Good News. So see to it that you really do love each other intensely with all your hearts.

For you have been born again. Your new life did not come from your earthly parents because the life they gave you will end in death. But this new life will last forever because it comes from the eternal, living word of God. As the prophet says,

"People are like grass that dies
away;
their beauty fades as quickly
as the beauty of wildflowers.
The grass withers,
and the flowers fall away.
But the word of the Lord will
last forever."

And that word is the Good News that was preached to you.

1 PETER 1:22-25

God's word is forever

"HERE WE ARE," said Mother as she pulled the car into a parking space. Jamie loved to go antique shopping with her mother. She liked to look at the colorful, hand-painted dishes and the sparkling cut-glass bowls and vases.

"Look at this beautiful cheese dish!" Mother exclaimed. "It's not expensive, and wouldn't it be pretty on the shelf in the dining room?"

"Oh, Mother, could we get it?" Jamie asked eagerly. Mother agreed.

When Mother showed the dish to Dad that night, Jamie asked, "Do we have to put it on the shelf? Can't we keep it out and use it?"

Mother shook her head. "No, I don't think so," she said. "This dish is very old, and someday it will be valuable. We might chip it if we use it, but it will last a long time if we put it where we can just enjoy looking at it."

"I have a riddle for you," said Dad. "What is very old, can be used all we want right now, and still will last forever?"

Jamie thought about it. "I can't think of anything that will last forever if it's used," she said. "Give me a clue."

Dad opened his Bible to 1 Peter. "The Word of the Lord will last forever," he read. He smiled and added, "God wants us to use our Bibles over and over, again and again."

"Oh, I didn't think of that!" exclaimed Jamie. "That's a good thing to remember."

HOW ABOUT YOU? Do you read God's Word every day, or is your Bible like the antique dish—sitting on a shelf not being used? The copy you're using may wear out, but God's message will always remain. Learn to live for him by reading his Word each day. Unlike an antique dish, you'll never wear out God's Word. *D.K.*

TO MEMORIZE: [Jesus said,] "Heaven and earth will disappear, but my words will remain forever." *Mark 13:31*

THERE WAS a dull thud, and the Taylor's house trembled slightly. Not far away, construction workers were using dynamite to make a tunnel through a mountain. "I wish those men were done exploding that stuff!" exclaimed Jessica. She covered her ears with her hands. "It makes me afraid."

"It *is* noisy, isn't it?" agreed Dad.

"And it crumbles things apart," Jessica added. "It won't crumble us apart, will it, Daddy?" She scooted over on the sofa, close to her father.

"No, honey," Dad said. "It can't hurt us as long as we stay away from it."

Reassured, Jessica went out to play. Soon she came back inside with a scowl on her face. "I'll never speak to Rodney again," she fumed. "He said I looked like a monkey. I hate him!" Her words were punctuated by the boom of another explosion.

Dad looked up. "You know, Jessica, anger can be like dynamite," he said. "It's loud, it's explosive, and it can hurt people."

Jessica thought about that. "Can it crumble us apart?"

"In a way," answered Dad. "I guess we could say that it crumbles our control. Anger is very powerful. If we lose control, it hurts us as well as the person with whom we are angry."

"So we should stay away from it, just like we have to stay away from the dynamite?" asked Jessica.

Dad nodded. "That's right. We need to let the Lord, not anger, control our actions."

As another explosion rumbled in the distance, Jessica said, "I think I'll go talk with Rodney for a while."

HOW ABOUT YOU? Does anger explode in you? Do you realize the damage it can do, both to you and to others? Next time you feel ready to explode, ask God to help you gain control over the situation. Ask him to control your life and actions. *V.L.R.*

TO MEMORIZE: Stop your anger! Turn from your rage! *Psalm 37:8*

DANGER: ANGER

FROM THE BIBLE:

The wise are cautious and avoid danger; fools plunge ahead with great confidence.
Those who are short-tempered do foolish things, and schemers are hated. . . .
People with good sense restrain their anger; they earn esteem by overlooking wrongs.
The king's anger is like a lion's roar, but his favor is like dew on the grass.

PROVERBS 14:16-17; 19:11-12

Control your temper

11 December

NOT MAKE-BELIEVE

FROM THE BIBLE:

You are a pleasure-crazy kingdom, living at ease and feeling secure, bragging as if you were the greatest in the world! You say, "I'm self-sufficient and not accountable to anyone! I will never be a widow or lose my children." Well, those two things will come upon you in a moment: widowhood and the loss of your children. Yes, these calamities will come upon you, despite all your witchcraft and magic.

You felt secure in all your wickedness. "No one sees me," you said. . . . So disaster will overtake you suddenly. . . .

Call out the demon hordes you have worshiped all these years. Ask them to help you strike terror into the hearts of people once again. You have more than enough advisers, astrologers, and stargazers. Let them stand up and save you from what the future holds. But they are as useless as dried grass burning in a fire. They cannot even save themselves! You will get no help from them at all. Their hearth is not a place to sit for warmth.

ISAIAH 47:8-14

Don't play Satan's games

JOSE AND ANTHONY grabbed their cereal bowls as they raced into the family room to watch Saturday morning cartoons. They were happy when Dad brought in his toast and joined them. "What are we watching, guys?" Dad asked.

"*Masters of the Sky*," said Jose. "The masters cast evil spells on the invaders of the sky kingdom."

Dad frowned as he listened to the boys describe the special powers that each cartoon character had. "This doesn't sound like something we should be watching, boys."

"Aw, Dad, it's only make-believe," pleaded Jose. "The other cartoons are for babies and scaredy-cats."

"The toy stores have games and dolls taken right from this cartoon," added Anthony. "How can something that's just fun be bad?"

"It sounds to me like Satan is up to his old tricks," responded Dad. "He's making people think that magic and evil spells are only make-believe, and that playing around with evil can't hurt them. But Christians have been warned to be on the lookout for his tricks."

Anthony sighed. "The guys at school think it's a really exciting program, but I guess we should turn it off."

Jose nodded as he got up to flip off the TV.

"Why don't we go over to the YMCA and shoot some baskets?" suggested Dad. "I think it will be a lot more fun than watching cartoons."

HOW ABOUT YOU? Have you ever noticed evil magic in the TV shows you watch or in the games you play? Have you read your horoscope just for the fun of it and then found yourself believing that it might be true? Satan wants to blend evil with what seems good. Be on the lookout for him! Don't be deceived by his games. *D.L.R.*

TO MEMORIZE: Satan himself masquerades as an angel of light. It is not surprising, then, if his servants masquerade as servants of righteousness. Their end will be what their actions deserve. *2 Corinthians 11:14-15* (NIV)

12 December

SPECIAL PLACE

SARA WAVED as her older sister, Linnea, walked to the car with her fiance, Jason. "Where are you going for lunch today?" she asked.

"To that little restaurant called Your Special Spot," Jason replied with a grin. "Only we call it 'Our Special Spot' now."

"How come you always go there?" Sara asked.

"We don't always," said Linnea. "But it is our favorite place. It's cozy and quiet—a good place to talk."

"It's where we went on our first date," added Jason, giving Linnea a squeeze. "And it's where we were when I asked your sister to marry me."

Sara went into the house after they left. "Linnea and Jason sure spend a lot of time together," she said to herself. "I guess that's because they love each other."

As Sara thought about it, she remembered how Pastor Grant always said, "If you love the Lord, you should spend time each day with him." Sara was trying to do that. Sometimes it was hard, though, because she shared a room with her younger sister. *I know!* Sara thought. *I need a special place for talking to the Lord just like Linnea and Jason have a special place to talk to each other.*

Sara asked her mother what to do. Mother said, "I think we could fix up a private corner for you in the attic."

"Can we go take a look?" Sara asked eagerly. Mother agreed, and they headed for the stairs.

HOW ABOUT YOU? If possible, find a special spot to meet with the Lord each day. If you have your own room, that may be the best place for you. But maybe you'll need to use a corner in the basement, the attic, or a storage room. Be sure to read your Bible and talk to God there each day. *H.W.M.*

TO MEMORIZE: I bow before your holy Temple as I worship. I will give thanks to your name.
Psalm 138:2

FROM THE BIBLE:

I give you thanks, O Lord, with
all my heart;
I will sing your praises before
the gods.
I bow before your holy Temple as
I worship.
I will give thanks to your name
for your unfailing love and
faithfulness,
because your promises are backed
by all the honor of your name.
When I pray, you answer me;
you encourage me by giving
me the strength I need.
Every king in all the earth will
give you thanks, O Lord,
for all of them will hear your
words.
Yes, they will sing about the
Lord's ways,
for the glory of the Lord is
very great.
Though the Lord is great, he
cares for the humble,
but he keeps his distance
from the proud.
Though I am surrounded
by troubles,
you will preserve me against
the anger of my enemies.
You will clench your fist against
my angry enemies!
Your power will save me.

PSALM 138:1-7

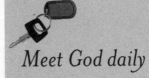

Meet God daily

13 December

THE BEST FOR FATHER

FROM THE BIBLE:

Yours, O Lord, is the greatness, the power, the glory, the victory, and the majesty. Everything in the heavens and on earth is yours, O Lord, and this is your kingdom. We adore you as the one who is over all things. Riches and honor come from you alone, for you rule over everything. Power and might are in your hand, and it is at your discretion that people are made great and given strength.

O our God, we thank you and praise your glorious name! But who am I, and who are my people, that we could give anything to you? Everything we have has come from you, and we give you only what you have already given us! We are here for only a moment. . . . Our days on earth are like a shadow, gone so soon without a trace.

O Lord our God, even these materials that we have gathered to build a Temple to honor your holy name come from you! It all belongs to you!

1 CHRONICLES 29:11-16

Give God what is his

MOTHER LOOKED at her watch. "Let's meet here at the Christmas tree in the mall in two hours," she said.

"OK," said Kara's big sister, Angela. "Come on, Kara. We've got lots of gifts to buy." She studied the Christmas list. "We should buy something nice for Dad first," she suggested.

Before long, both girls had several packages. They were at the stationery store when they met Kara's Sunday school teacher and her daughter, June. "From the evidence, I think you girls are Christmas shopping," said Mrs. Kimball with a smile.

"You sure have a lot of packages," June added. "How did you earn enough money to buy all those presents?"

"We didn't earn all of the money," Angela said. "Dad gives us extra money to buy Christmas gifts."

"Oh," June said. "Then you're buying your dad a gift with his own money."

"Yep," giggled Kara. "That's why we give him the best present of all. He deserves it, right?"

"You're absolutely right," Mrs. Kimball agreed. "You know, God is our heavenly Father, and he gives us a lot of things. He gives us our life, strength, time, and talents. We should never complain about giving those things back to him. We're only giving him what belongs to him in the first place."

"That's true," Angela said, glancing at her watch. "Oh, we better go or we won't get our shopping done."

"OK," said Mrs. Kimball. "Happy shopping!"

HOW ABOUT YOU? Do you ever complain about the time it takes to go to church? Do you wish you didn't have to put a tenth of your allowance in the offering? Think about it. All the blessings you have were given to you by God, your heavenly Father. Why shouldn't you give him back the best you have to offer? *J.L.H.*

TO MEMORIZE: Everything we have has come from you, and we give you only what you have already given us! *1 Chronicles 29:14*

14 December

ONIONS AND APPLESAUCE

FROM THE BIBLE:

Since you have been raised to new life with Christ, set your sights on the realities of heaven, where Christ sits at God's right hand in the place of honor and power. . . . For you died when Christ died, and your real life is hidden with Christ in God. And when Christ, who is your real life, is revealed to the whole world, you will share in all his glory.

So put to death the sinful, earthly things lurking within you. Have nothing to do with sexual sin, impurity, lust, and shameful desires. Don't be greedy for the good things of this life, for that is idolatry. God's terrible anger will come upon those who do such things. . . . Now is the time to get rid of anger, rage, malicious behavior, slander, and dirty language. Don't lie to each other, for you have stripped off your old evil nature and all its wicked deeds. In its place you have clothed yourselves with a brand-new nature that is continually being renewed as you learn more and more about Christ, who created this new nature within you.

COLOSSIANS 3:1-10

"JENNY WANTS me to come over this evening. May I go?" asked Amy as she and her mother prepared dinner. "There's a movie we want to watch on TV. I wouldn't be late."

"Amy . . . ," Mom hesitated. "I know you've watched movies at Jenny's house that are not suitable for a Christian."

"Oh, Mom! If there are bad parts, I'll ignore them," argued Amy. "No movie can hurt me."

"Yes, it can," insisted Mom, "because it might put sinful thoughts into your mind. If you and Jenny want to spend the evening together, see if she can come over here."

Amy didn't argue anymore, but she pouted as she helped her mother prepare the food. "Which dish do you want me to put the applesauce in?" she mumbled.

"Take that yellow bowl from the sink," Mom replied. "It had some chopped onions in it. But we'll just ignore the onions. The applesauce will be fine in that bowl."

"But, Mom," protested Amy. "We can't put clean food that we're going to eat into a dirty bowl. The applesauce will taste like onions!"

"You're right." Mom nodded. "And Amy, our minds are more important than our mouths. Just as the onions give a bad taste to the applesauce, the sinful and dirty things we see and hear give a bad flavor to our thoughts."

HOW ABOUT YOU? Are you careful about what you see and hear? God wants your mind clean so he can speak to you through his Word. Get rid of books or magazines that would displease him. Shut off TV programs that dirty your thoughts. Ask the Lord to help you keep pure thoughts. *D.K.*

TO MEMORIZE: You have clothed yourselves with a brand-new nature that is continually being renewed as you learn more and more about Christ, who created this new nature within you. *Colossians 3:10*

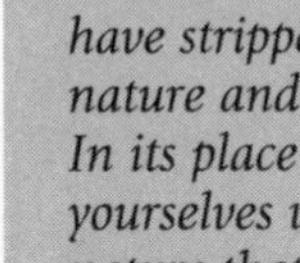

Keep a clean mind

15 December

SAY IT WITH MUSIC

FROM THE BIBLE:

Dear friend, don't let this bad example influence you. Follow only what is good. Remember that those who do good prove that they are God's children, and those who do evil prove that they do not know God.

3 JOHN 1:11

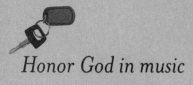

Honor God in music

WHEN ALYSSA'S MOTHER had an emergency operation, Alyssa felt—of all things—relief! Now her parents wouldn't be able to attend the school's pop band concert. Alyssa loved to play in the pop band, but she knew her folks wouldn't like the type of music they played.

After the concert, Alyssa was surprised to find her father waiting for her. "Is Mom OK? Did you hear us play?"

Dad nodded. "Your mother is fine. She insisted that I come to hear you," he said. "Alyssa, music is a powerful thing. For example, a mother sings a lullaby to quiet and soothe her baby. Now, a march wouldn't do that, would it?"

"I guess not," said Alyssa. "It would keep him awake."

"My grandfather told me that when he was young they had parades where they played marches and patriotic songs," continued Dad. "Young men joined the army in large numbers. A lullaby wouldn't have affected those young men that way, would it?"

Alyssa laughed. "Not very likely," she said.

Dad went on. "Music is often used to influence people. In the same way, our Christian songs move us by their words and music. God uses music to draw us to him, but Satan uses music to draw us away from God. Be sure that you're not working with Satan in your music."

Though Dad hadn't actually mentioned the band, Alyssa knew she had been drawn away from God by her involvement in it. And she felt a responsibility to those who might be influenced by her music. She knew she had to quit.

HOW ABOUT YOU? Have you been careful in your selection of music to play or listen to? Don't underestimate the powerful effect music has on you. How is the music you hear affecting you? How is your music affecting others? *A.G.L.*

TO MEMORIZE: Sing about the glory of his name! *Psalm 66:2*

16 December

THE PLIMSOLL MARK

FROM THE BIBLE:

Because God's children are human beings—made of flesh and blood—Jesus also became flesh and blood by being born in human form. For only as a human being could he die, and only by dying could he break the power of the Devil, who had the power of death. Only in this way could he deliver those who have lived all their lives as slaves to the fear of dying.

We all know that Jesus came to help the descendants of Abraham, not to help the angels. Therefore, it was necessary for Jesus to be in every respect like us, his brothers and sisters, so that he could be our merciful and faithful High Priest before God. He then could offer a sacrifice that would take away the sins of the people. Since he himself has gone through suffering and temptation, he is able to help us when we are being tempted.

HEBREWS 2:14-18

God helps you

GRANDPA BAKER loved making ship models out of pine and balsa wood. The finished models were works of art. When each of his grandchildren turned twelve, Grandpa would make a ship for that grandchild. This year Grandpa was making Eric's ship.

During Eric's birthday party, he received many nice gifts. But everyone knew that Grandpa Baker's gift would be the highlight. Carefully, Eric removed the wrapping paper from the box and lifted out the ship. "Wow, this is neat, Grandpa!" He gave his grandfather a hug, then turned to study the ship. "Grandpa, what's this line on the side of the ship?"

"That's called a Plimsoll mark, Eric," answered Grandpa. "Years ago, companies would often overload their ships. As a result, the ships would sink easily and lives would be lost. A man named Samuel Plimsoll worked to reform the shipping laws, and a new law was established. It required a mark to be made on each ship. If the water level was above that line, the ship was overloaded and some of the cargo had to be removed. The mark is now known as the Plimsoll mark."

"Hmmm, I never knew that," said Eric.

"I think Christians have a Plimsoll mark, too," Grandpa continued. "God knows just where it is. He understands how much we can handle, and he promises that we'll not be overloaded with greater problems than we can handle with his help!"

As Eric picked up his ship, he knew it would always remind him of Grandpa—and also of God's promise to help him through any difficulty!

HOW ABOUT YOU? Do you have such a big problem that it seems there is no solution? Talk to God about it. He will be with you through every problem and will help you. He promised. *L.M.W.*

TO MEMORIZE: Since [Jesus] himself has gone through suffering and temptation, he is able to help us when we are being tempted. *Hebrews 2:18*

17 December

DROP THE OARS

FROM THE BIBLE:

Then Jesus told this story to some who had great self-confidence and scorned everyone else: "Two men went to the Temple to pray. One was a Pharisee, and the other was a dishonest tax collector. The proud Pharisee stood by himself and prayed this prayer: 'I thank you, God, that I am not a sinner like everyone else, especially like that tax collector over there! For I never cheat, I don't sin, I don't commit adultery, I fast twice a week, and I give you a tenth of my income.'

"But the tax collector stood at a distance and dared not even lift his eyes to heaven as he prayed. Instead, he beat his chest in sorrow, saying, 'O God, be merciful to me, for I am a sinner.' I tell you, this sinner, not the Pharisee, returned home justified before God. For the proud will be humbled, but the humble will be honored."

LUKE 18:9-14

Simply trust Jesus

"MARK CAN'T COME over this afternoon," said Jon. "He has to go door-to-door with his mom and give out church literature."

"Is that right?" Mom was interested. "Are Mark and his family Christians?"

Jon shook his head. "I don't think so. They talk about Jesus, but they don't believe he's God. That doesn't make sense. They think they have to do good things to be saved—like this visitation program. And they think that if they miss church, they won't get to heaven. I don't think Mark knows that Jesus came to save him."

Dad spoke up. "Sounds to me like he needs to drop the oars and catch hold of the rope," he said.

"Drop what oars?" asked Jon.

"There's a river with a waterfall near the town where I grew up," explained Dad. "Just above the falls the water is wild and dangerous. It's unsafe for boating. I remember a man in a rowboat getting caught in the swift current. It was pulling him closer and closer to the falls. A crowd gathered on the bank, and people called to him to row harder. He tried, but we saw he wasn't going to make it. Someone threw a rope to him. Then the cry was, 'Drop your oars! Grab the rope!' He did, and some men pulled him to shore." Dad paused. "Like the man in the boat, Mark needs to stop working to save himself. The only way he can be saved is to stop struggling and trust Jesus."

HOW ABOUT YOU? Are you struggling to save yourself? Do you hope that going to church, praying, giving, or living a "good" life will save you from your sins and earn a place for you in heaven? These are things you should do, but you will be saved only when you trust Christ. Do that today. *H.W.M.*

TO MEMORIZE: God, be merciful to me, for I am a sinner. *Luke 18:13*

18 December

AN UNJOYFUL NOISE

FROM THE BIBLE:

It is good to give thanks
to the Lord,
to sing praises to the
Most High.
It is good to proclaim your unfailing
love in the morning,
your faithfulness in the evening,
PSALM 92:1-2

Serve joyfully

ANGIE PLAYED the flute, and her brother, Luis, played the clarinet. Since they both did well on their instruments, they were frequently asked to provide special music for church services. One day when they were rehearsing, they couldn't agree on what song to play. "Let's play page 105," Luis suggested.

"Yuck!" Angie exclaimed. "I hate that song!"

"It's a neat song," insisted Luis.

"I always knew you had bad taste," Angie retorted.

"Look who's talking!" he said angrily. "Last time you decided we should play that chorus we learned at camp, and it sounded horrible!"

"Did not!"

"Did too!"

"Well, anyhow," said Angie, "Let's play 'Praise to God.' " Luis snorted, but they played through the hymn.

"Boring," Luis told his sister when they finished.

"Just forget it then!" Angie snapped.

"It sounds like war in here!" said Mother as she walked into the room. "Why do you two bother to play at all?"

Luis was puzzled. "Because we were asked to play."

"It's . . . it's our ministry," said Angie. "We hope others will learn about the Lord through our music."

"That sounds good," said Mother. "And I like the words to the song 'Praise to God.' But I didn't hear any praises when you were deciding what number to play."

After Mother left the room, Luis and Angie looked at each other. "Mom's right," Angie said. "Let's pray about our music. Then let's start again."

HOW ABOUT YOU? What is your attitude when you're asked to do something in your church? Do you think of every possible excuse to keep from joining the children's choir? Do you slide down in your seat when your Sunday school teacher asks for someone to pray? The Bible says we are to joyfully serve the Lord. Check your attitude and make sure it's a joyful one! *L.M.W.*

TO MEMORIZE: Shout with joy to the Lord, O earth! *Psalm 100:1*

19 December

SPIRITUAL EXERCISE

FROM THE BIBLE:

Sing a new song to the Lord,
for he has done wonderful deeds.
He has won a mighty victory
by his power and holiness. . . .
He has remembered his promise
to love and be faithful to Israel.
The whole earth has seen the salvation of our God.
Shout to the Lord, all the earth;
break out in praise and sing for joy!
Sing your praise to the Lord with the harp,
with the harp and melodious song,
with trumpets and the sound of the ram's horn.
Make a joyful symphony before the Lord, the King!
Let the sea and everything in it shout his praise!
Let the earth and all living things join in.
Let the rivers clap their hands in glee!
Let the hills sing out their songs of joy before the Lord.
For the Lord is coming to judge the earth.
He will judge the world with justice,
and the nations with fairness.

PSALM 98:1-9

It helps to sing

"TIS SO SWEET to trust in Jesus; just to take him at his Word." The words to the song floated up the stairs. Danielle yawned and peeked at the sunlight playing on her bed. "Just to rest upon his promise," the quavering voice rang out over banging pots and pans. Danielle grinned. Grandma always sang in the morning. In fact, she always sang. Then Danielle frowned. How could Grandma sing this morning? After yesterday? A sob caught in Danielle's throat. "Jesus, Jesus, how I trust him." Grandma's song continued as Danielle got dressed.

At the breakfast table Danielle asked, "Grandma, how can you sing this morning?"

Grandma smiled. "Honey, a long time ago I learned to sing when I was sad and when I was glad. Your grandfather loved to hear me sing."

"But Grandpa died," Danielle blurted out. "We had his funeral yesterday."

"I know," Grandma answered gently. "I also know he wouldn't want me to stop singing now."

Danielle's mother nodded. "And neither do I," she said. She looked at Danielle. "Singing is good for you. I read an article that said it clears your lungs and helps your circulation. The article said singing sometimes prevents headaches by speeding blood to the brain. It even helps your digestive system and prevents ulcers."

"Besides all that, it will ease your heartaches," Grandma added knowingly.

Dad joined the conversation. "Singing is spiritual exercise. We walk to keep our body in shape. We sing for spiritual fitness."

Later as Danielle sat on her grandfather's tractor in the field, she sang, "When we all get to heaven, what a day of rejoicing that will be. . . ." And she realized Grandma was right. Singing did help.

HOW ABOUT YOU? Are you sad, worried, afraid, or discontented? Sing! Exercise your spirit. Sing unto the Lord, and you will feel better. *B.J.W.*

TO MEMORIZE: Sing a new song to the Lord, for he has done wonderful deeds. *Psalm 98:1*

20 December

THE RIGHT TIME

FROM THE BIBLE:

And the Lord God said, "It is not good for the man to be alone. I will make a companion who will help him." So the Lord God formed from the soil every kind of animal and bird. He brought them to Adam to see what he would call them, and Adam chose a name for each one. He gave names to all the livestock, birds, and wild animals. But still there was no companion suitable for him. So the Lord God caused Adam to fall into a deep sleep. He took one of Adam's ribs and closed up the place from which he had taken it. Then the Lord God made a woman from the rib and brought her to Adam.

"At last!" Adam exclaimed. "She is part of my own flesh and bone! She will be called 'woman,' because she was taken out of a man." This explains why a man leaves his father and mother and is joined to his wife, and the two are united into one. Now, although Adam and his wife were both naked, neither of them felt any shame.

GENESIS 2:18-25

Keep your body pure

ASHLEY LOOKED UP as her mother came into the room. "Want to go shopping with me?" Mom asked.

Ashley shook her head. "I need to wrap gifts."

After Mom left, Ashley looked in Lisette's room for the box of bows. There she saw a package with her name on it. She thought, *I'll take a peek, and no one will know.* Carefully she untied the ribbon and picked at the tape. A small box slid out, and inside it she found a beautiful necklace. Ashley quickly rewrapped the gift.

Soon it was Christmas. When Ashley opened her package from Lisette, she tried to act surprised, but it was hard. Having opened it ahead of time spoiled the fun of getting it now. She felt guilty, and she knew Lisette expected her to be more excited.

When the phone rang, Ashley answered it. But when she returned, she was upset. "What's wrong?" asked Mom.

"Kelly called," answered Ashley. "She says her big sister won't be returning to school after Christmas. She's pregnant."

Mom sighed. "You know, Ashley, intimacy between a man and a woman is a wonderful gift, but God knew what he was doing when he planned it for marriage. Taking that gift ahead of time causes much unhappiness."

Ashley thought about the Christmas gift she had opened ahead of time, and she thought about her friend's sister who hadn't waited until marriage to enjoy the gift of intimacy. Ashley didn't want to make that mistake. She wanted to follow God's plan.

HOW ABOUT YOU? Television programs, books, and even friends often imply that if you feel like having an intimate relationship with the opposite sex, it's OK. That's wrong! God's Word says to wait until marriage or you'll spoil the beauty of it. Wait! *J.L.H.*

TO MEMORIZE: Run from anything that stimulates youthful lust . . . and enjoy the companionship of those who call on the Lord with pure hearts.
2 Timothy 2:22

21 December

ORDINARY BUT PRETTY

FROM THE BIBLE:

[God] has given each one of us a special gift according to the generosity of Christ. That is why the Scriptures say,

"When he ascended to the heights,
he led a crowd of captives
and gave gifts to his people."

Notice that it says "he ascended." This means that Christ first came down to the lowly world in which we live. The same one who came down is the one who ascended higher than all the heavens, so that his rule might fill the entire universe.

He is the one who gave these gifts to the church: the apostles, the prophets, the evangelists, and the pastors and teachers. Their responsibility is to equip God's people to do his work and build up the church, the body of Christ.

EPHESIANS 4:7-12

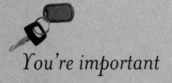

You're important

"I STILL WISH I could sing or act in the Christmas play," Samantha sighed. "I'd like to be important—to really be needed instead of just ironing dumb old costumes."

"You *are* important and needed," replied Mother. "But you seem determined not to believe that. Well, I'd better get supper ready."

"I'll set the table," Samantha offered. "Mom, can we use the pretty crystal goblets tonight?"

"Sure," said Mother. "But take this casserole to old Mrs. Jenkins first. Visit with her for a while too. Tell you what. I'll set the table tonight. Just be back by 5:30 for supper."

When Angela returned home, the family was just sitting down to eat. She sat down and was surprised to see two crystal goblets at each place but no plates.

After Dad thanked the Lord for the food, Mother handed a casserole dish to Angela. "Help yourself," Mother said.

Angela held the casserole. "Where are the plates?" she asked.

"Oh," said Mother. "The goblets are so pretty, I thought we'd just use them."

"But they aren't for food," protested Angela.

"So you admit that we need different utensils or containers for different jobs?" said Mother. "That's what I was trying to tell you earlier. In God's kingdom people are like utensils—like goblets and dishes. God needs some people who can sing, others who can preach, and still others who can visit lonely folks. Some jobs may seem 'prettier' than others, but each one is important."

Angela laughed. "I get the point," she said. "And right now, ordinary plates sound mighty 'pretty' to me."

HOW ABOUT YOU? Do you feel that the things you're asked to do for the Lord are really unimportant? That's not true. There is no such thing as an unimportant task when it's done for the Lord. *H.W.M.*

TO MEMORIZE: If you keep yourself pure, you will be a utensil God can use for his purpose.
2 Timothy 2:21

MADE TO BE USED

FROM THE BIBLE:

The Kingdom of Heaven can be illustrated by the story of a man going on a trip. He called together his servants and gave them money to invest for him while he was gone. He gave five bags of gold to one, two bags of gold to another, and one bag of gold to the last—dividing it in proportion to their abilities—and then left on his trip. The servant who received the five bags of gold began immediately to invest the money and soon doubled it. . . .

After a long time their master returned from his trip and called them to give an account of how they had used his money. The servant to whom he had entrusted the five bags of gold said, "Sir, you gave me five bags of gold to invest, and I have doubled the amount." The master was full of praise. "Well done, my good and faithful servant. You have been faithful in handling this small amount, so now I will give you many more responsibilities. Let's celebrate together!"

MATTHEW 25:14-23

Use your talents

AMBER HURRIED to answer the phone. It was the music director from church, and he wanted her to sing a solo at the Christmas program. "I . . . I couldn't," Amber stammered.

"You have a very pretty voice," said Mr. Bell. "We could use you."

"But what if I made a mistake or my voice cracked? I don't want to make a fool of myself," Amber sputtered. "I'll sing when I'm older."

"I hope you'll change your mind," said Mr. Bell. "I hope you'll decide not to put your voice on a shelf for now." Amber was puzzled by that remark and asked her mother about it after she hung up. Mom said they could talk about it later.

Amber went back to her knitting, putting the finishing touches on the scarf she was making for her grandmother. Mom came over and admired it. "It's lovely," said Mom. "I suppose Grandma will keep it on a closet shelf so it will stay nice."

Amber was shocked. "I made it for her to use, not to put away out of sight!"

"I see." Mom nodded. "You'd be hurt if she didn't use it, wouldn't you?"

"Yeah, I guess I would," admitted Amber. "But why wouldn't she use it?"

"I'm sure she will use it," said Mom. "But, Amber, this conversation reminds me of your conversation with Mr. Bell. God gave you a special talent to use, not to save."

"I never thought of that," Amber said slowly. "I think I'll call Mr. Bell. Maybe it's not too late to accept doing the solo."

HOW ABOUT YOU? Do you refuse to use your talents from fear of failure? Or because you're too busy? Or because you just don't feel like doing anything? God wants to use you. Don't disappoint him! *J.L.H.*

TO MEMORIZE: Our people should not have unproductive lives. They must learn to do good by helping others who have urgent needs. *Titus 3:14*

23 December

IT TAKES PRACTICE

FROM THE BIBLE:

Your decrees are wonderful.
No wonder I obey them!
As your words are taught, they give light;
even the simple can understand them.
I open my mouth, panting expectantly,
longing for your commands.
Come and show me your mercy,
as you do for all who love your name.
Guide my steps by your word,
so I will not be overcome by any evil.
Rescue me from the oppression of evil people;
then I can obey your commandments.
Look down on me with love;
teach me all your principles.
Rivers of tears gush from my eyes
because people disobey your law.

PSALM 119:129-136

Read the Bible regularly

JACOB GROANED as he picked himself up from the snow. He had saved his money and begged to go skiing with his big brother, Jared.

"Sure, you can come, but I'm warning you—it isn't as easy as it looks," his brother had said with a smile. Jacob found that out in a hurry.

"I'm gonna quit," Jacob said with a frown after falling for the umpteenth time.

"Tell you what," Jared said. "Your lift ticket includes some lessons for beginners. They're about ready to start the class. Why don't you join them?"

The ski instructor explained some of the basic moves. Then came the "bunny slope." The instructor held a long pole in front of Jacob so the young skier could hold on until he felt a bit steadier. "Hey, this is fun," Jacob yelled as Jared watched from the sidelines. "I think I'm ready for the big hill." Just then he lost his balance and fell sideways into the snow. "Oh well, give me a few more lessons," Jacob said with a grimace.

On the way home Jared gave his little brother a pat on the back. "Learning to ski well is like learning to understand the Bible better," Jared said. "Didn't you tell me the other day that you weren't getting much out of reading the Bible?"

Jacob nodded.

"Well, practice helps," said Jared. "The more you ski, the better you'll be. And the more you read your Bible, the more you'll understand it."

HOW ABOUT YOU? Have you gotten discouraged in your Bible reading? Don't start out on the "biggest hills." Read the Gospels and the Epistles before you tackle the books of prophecy. Spend time with a few verses every day and you'll find that the more you read, the better you'll understand. *C.Vm*

TO MEMORIZE: As your words are taught, they give light; even the simple can understand them. *Psalm 119:130*

THE REAL GIFT

FROM THE BIBLE:

Now this is how Jesus the Messiah was born. His mother, Mary, was engaged to be married to Joseph. But while she was still a virgin, she became pregnant by the Holy Spirit. Joseph, her fiancé, being a just man, decided to break the engagement quietly, so as not to disgrace her publicly.

As he considered this, he fell asleep, and an angel of the Lord appeared to him in a dream. "Joseph, son of David," the angel said, "do not be afraid to go ahead with your marriage to Mary. For the child within her has been conceived by the Holy Spirit. And she will have a son, and you are to name him Jesus, for he will save his people from their sins." All of this happened to fulfill the Lord's message through his prophet:

"Look! The virgin will conceive a child!
She will give birth to a son,
and he will be called Immanuel
(meaning, God is with us)."

MATTHEW 1:18-23

Honor the real gift

ON CHRISTMAS EVE, Mom held little Anna in her lap as Grandpa read from the Bible about the birth of Jesus. Tasha's mind wandered as Grandpa read about angels, shepherds, and wise men. This would be little Anna's first Christmas, and Tasha could hardly wait to see her excitement as she opened her presents. She just knew the baby doll she and Travis had bought would make Anna happy!

When Grandpa finished reading, Dad prayed, thanking God for the Savior who came to give them eternal life. Then Tasha and Travis passed out the presents. "Open your gifts, Anna," said Travis.

Anna didn't seem to know what to do. She just looked at the bright wrappings. "Here, open them like this," said Tasha as she pulled off the bow. Anna grabbed the ribbon and put it in her mouth.

Travis and Tasha began removing the wrapping paper.

Tasha put the baby doll in Anna's lap. "Pretty baby," said Tasha.

Anna flung the doll aside and reached for the wrapping paper. She laughed as she crinkled the paper in her fingers and draped the ribbons over her head.

"What a disappointment!" Travis exclaimed. "We give her a neat gift, and she ignores it."

"The bright trimmings have distracted her," said Mother.

"I wonder if God doesn't feel just as disappointed in us at Christmas time," commented Grandpa.

"Why?" Travis asked in surprise.

"God sent Jesus to save us from our sins," Grandpa said. "He's the real gift of Christmas, but many people ignore him. They get distracted by the trimmings of Christmas, like presents, lights, and gifts. Then they ignore the Savior."

HOW ABOUT YOU? What does Christmas mean to you? Do you worship Christ at Christmas time, or do you get caught up in the "trimmings"? Christ is the perfect gift. He gives meaning to life. *J.L.H.*

TO MEMORIZE: Thank God for his Son—a gift too wonderful for words! *2 Corinthians 9:15*

25 December

SAME OLD STORY

FROM THE BIBLE:

And while they were there, the time came for her baby to be born. She gave birth to her first child, a son. She wrapped him snugly in strips of cloth and laid him in a manger, because there was no room for them in the village inn.

That night some shepherds were in the fields outside the village, guarding their flocks of sheep. Suddenly, an angel of the Lord appeared among them, and the radiance of the Lord's glory surrounded them. They were terribly frightened, but the angel reassured them. "Don't be afraid!" he said. "I bring you good news of great joy for everyone! The Savior—yes, the Messiah, the Lord—has been born tonight in Bethlehem, the city of David! And this is how you will recognize him: You will find a baby lying in a manger, wrapped snugly in strips of cloth!"

LUKE 2:6-12

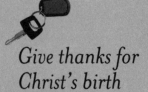

Give thanks for Christ's birth

"TODAY," Mrs. Peters told her Sunday school class, "we're going to review the record of Christ's birth, so please turn to the second chapter of Luke."

Manuel opened his Bible, but he tuned out the teacher's voice. During the last week he'd heard the Christmas story in Awana Club and he'd seen it acted out on television. So Manuel thought about the new bike he'd been given at Christmas instead.

When class was over, Manuel walked to the main auditorium with Kyle, who had been coming to church for only a few months. "Wow! That was a good story!" exclaimed Kyle.

Manuel looked at him in surprise. "I've heard it hundreds of times!"

"Well, I've heard it too," said Kyle. "But this is the first Christmas I've been a Christian, so it's the first year I've really understood what it meant. Just think, Manuel! Jesus came to earth for you and me! God must love us a lot to send his only Son to earth to die!"

Manuel sat down in a pew and thought about Kyle's words. Yes, he understood what God had done. He knew the story almost by heart, but he had stopped getting excited about it. Now Manuel opened his Bible to the second chapter of Luke again. He was going to read it while he waited for the church service to begin.

HOW ABOUT YOU? Do you get an "I've heard it all before" attitude when you listen to the Christmas story? Do you take Christ's birth for granted because you've heard about it so many times? The Bethlehem story should still be exciting each time you hear it. If Christ had not come, you would not have a Savior. Read the Scripture again. Really think about the wonderful thing that happened so long ago. Thank God for it. *L.M.W.*

TO MEMORIZE: For he, the Mighty One, is holy, and he has done great things for me. *Luke 1:49*

26 December

UNEXPECTED ANSWER

FROM THE BIBLE:

In Caesarea there lived a Roman army officer named Cornelius, who was a captain of the Italian Regiment. He was a devout man who feared the God of Israel, as did his entire household. He gave generously to charity and was a man who regularly prayed to God. . . .

Cornelius [said], "Four days ago I was praying in my house at three o'clock in the afternoon. Suddenly, a man in dazzling clothes was standing in front of me. He told me, 'Cornelius, your prayers have been heard, and your gifts to the poor have been noticed by God! Now send some men to Joppa and summon Simon Peter. He is staying in the home of Simon, a leatherworker who lives near the shore.' So I sent for you at once, and it was good of you to come. Now here we are, waiting before God to hear the message the Lord has given you."

ACTS 10:1-2, 30-33

Pray, then work

CHRISTMAS was over. Alan looked at the opened presents under the tree. Most of the gifts were very practical because Dad had been out of work for a while.

"God answered my prayers," commented Dad. "My best Christmas present is that he has provided a new job for me!"

Grandma noticed Alan's frown as he went into the family room. "Can I help with a problem, Alan?" she asked.

"God may have answered Dad's prayers," snorted Alan, "but he sure didn't answer mine! I prayed and prayed for a new sled, but all I got was stuff like socks and sweaters. I'm not prayin' anymore!"

Grandma asked, "Could it be that you missed God's answer?"

Alan sat up straight. "Is there another present under the tree?"

"That's not what I mean," she said. "What would you think if your dad turned down his job offer and then declared that he wasn't going to pray anymore because God wasn't providing for his family?"

Alan looked disgusted. "That would be silly."

"Yes," agreed Grandma, "yet your mother told me that Mrs. Brown wanted you to shovel her walks. It seems you were too busy to earn the money for a sled, and now you're blaming God. Isn't that silly?"

Alan stared at Grandma. "God did answer, didn't he?" he said finally. "I'd better see if Mrs. Brown still needs help. Maybe I can still earn my sled—by next winter!"

HOW ABOUT YOU? Do you pray for things and then refuse to work and earn them? Today's Scripture shows how God sometimes answers prayer by providing a task to be done. Cornelius didn't just pray; he sent men to Peter. When you pray, you need to be ready to work. *H.W.M.*

TO MEMORIZE: [An angel told Cornelius,] "Your prayers have been heard, and your gifts to the poor have been noticed by God! Now send some men to Joppa and summon Simon Peter." *Acts 10:31-32*

27 December

BORN AGAIN AND HUMAN

FROM THE BIBLE:

With the Lord's authority let me say this: Live no longer as the ungodly do, for they are hopelessly confused. Their closed minds are full of darkness; they are far away from the life of God because they have shut their minds and hardened their hearts against him. They don't care anymore about right and wrong, and they have given themselves over to immoral ways. Their lives are filled with all kinds of impurity and greed.

But that isn't what you were taught when you learned about Christ. Since you have heard all about him and have learned the truth that is in Jesus, throw off your old evil nature and your former way of life, which is rotten through and through, full of lust and deception. Instead, there must be a spiritual renewal of your thoughts and attitudes. You must display a new nature because you are a new person, created in God's likeness—righteous, holy, and true.

EPHESIANS 4:17-24

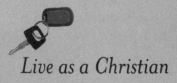

Live as a Christian

"WELL, I SUPPOSE I shouldn't have gotten mad when Kim fell and scratched my bike," admitted David as he and Mom drove home from town. "But I think God understands. He knows I'm only human."

"It seems to me you use those words as an excuse too often," observed Mom. "You said them when you forgot to do your chores and when you lied about your grade in math and when you—"

"Well, it's true," defended Dave. "I *am* human."

"But as a Christian, you have God's Word, which teaches you a better way," said Mom, pulling in to the driveway.

When David and his mother entered the kitchen, they saw the table cluttered with lunch dishes. Kim was sitting in front of the television. "Didn't you do anything all afternoon?" demanded Mom. "I asked you to clean up the house."

Kim shrugged. "I will after this show."

"I want you to clear the table and wash the dishes right now," said Mom.

"What a lazy bum," scolded David. "And after all Mom does for you!"

"Look who's talking," muttered Kim as she stood up. "Besides, I'm only human, you know."

David was startled, and Mom looked straight at him as she said, "I expect you to obey me, Kim, just as God expects obedience from his children. He tells us in his Word what he wants of us. And after all he's done for us, nothing he asks of us is too much."

HOW ABOUT YOU? Do you sometimes make excuses for your sinful behavior? If you're a Christian, you're no longer only human—you're a born-again human. God expects you to be honest, helpful, cheerful, kind, and humble. He expects you to study his Word and obey his commands. Ask him to help you do this. *H.W.M.*

TO MEMORIZE: You must display a new nature because you are a new person, created in God's likeness—righteous, holy, and true. *Ephesians 4:24*

28 December

AFTER-CHRISTMAS COOKIES

FROM THE BIBLE:

The people who walk in darkness will see a great light—a light that will shine on all who live in the land where death casts its shadow.

For a child is born to us, a son is given to us. And the government will rest on his shoulders. These will be his royal titles: Wonderful Counselor, Mighty God, Everlasting Father, Prince of Peace. His ever expanding, peaceful government will never end. He will rule forever with fairness and justice from the throne of his ancestor David. The passionate commitment of the Lord Almighty will guarantee this!

ISAIAH 9:2, 6-7

Make Jesus known

"WHAT CAN I DO?" whined Jessica a few days after Christmas.

"How about playing with your new doll or one of your games?" Mom suggested.

"I already did all that," Jessica complained.

Mom sighed. "Come and help me bake cookies."

"Mom," pouted Jessica, "Christmas is over. Why are we still making cookies?"

"Because we're going to give them away." Mother smiled. "Remember the letdown feeling you just had, wishing for something to do? Other people may have a letdown feeling, too—especially shut-ins and folks in nursing homes. They had lots of attention before Christmas—carolers, programs, and gifts. Now they may feel lonely. Wouldn't you like to cheer them up?"

"Yes," said Jessica. "I'll arrange a box of cookies for them. It'll be like an after-Christmas present."

That evening Jessica told her dad about the people at the nursing home. "They were so glad to see us!" she exclaimed. "An old man asked me why we were bothering with them after Christmas. I told him that Jesus loves him *after* Christmas too. He said he guessed he should know more about that. Then Mother shared the gospel with him, and he was saved! We're going to go see him again—all the other people too!"

"That's wonderful!" Dad exclaimed. He reached for the Bible and turned to Luke 2:15-20. "You remind me of the shepherds. After seeing baby Jesus, they told others about him. Let's read it together."

HOW ABOUT YOU? Christmas is exciting, isn't it? But that excitement should go on after Christmas as well. Can you think of a way to share Jesus' love with a friend? Can you do something nice for an older person? If you have "seen Jesus"—if you are saved—make it known to others through your words and actions. *H.W.M.*

TO MEMORIZE: Then the shepherds told everyone what had happened and what the angel had said to them about this child. *Luke 2:17*

29 December

COMING RIGHT UP

FROM THE BIBLE:

Teach me, O Lord,
to follow every one of your principles.
Give me understanding and I will obey your law;
I will put it into practice with all my heart.
Make me walk along the path of your commands,
for that is where my happiness is found.
Give me an eagerness for your decrees;
do not inflict me with love for money!
Turn my eyes from worthless things,
and give me life through your word.
Reassure me of your promise,
which is for those who honor you.
Help me abandon my shameful ways;
your laws are all I want in life.
I long to obey your commandments!
Renew my life with your goodness.
Lord, give to me your unfailing love,
the salvation that you promised me.
Then I will have an answer for those who taunt me,
for I trust in your word.

PSALM 119:33-42

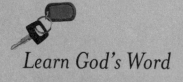

Learn God's Word

AS BRITTANY was getting ready for Sunday school, she remembered to work on her memory verse. She read it from her Bible, repeated it to herself several times, and then hurried down to breakfast. But when it was her turn to say it in class, she could only remember a few words. "This happens all the time," she mumbled to herself. "Why is it so hard to learn my memory verse?"

That afternoon Brittany heard her little brother, Anthony, singing in the family room. She found him playing with toys and loudly singing "Jesus Loves Me." Brittany smiled. "You know all the words, don't you?" she said.

Anthony beamed. "The words just come right up."

Later, Brittany told her mother what Anthony had said. Mother said, "The words come back to Anthony's mind so easily because he's heard and sung them so often."

I wish my memory verse would "come right up" when I need it, Brittany thought as she headed for her room. She looked at the Bible and her Sunday school book. *I guess I've been trying to learn my memory verse the wrong way. I'm going to try a new plan this week.*

Early on Monday morning Brittany began studying her memory verse, and she repeated it several times each day during the week. She thought about the words she was saying, and she prayed that God would help her understand them. When it was her turn to recite on Sunday morning, the words "came right up"! Her new plan had worked.

HOW ABOUT YOU? Do you find it difficult to memorize your Sunday school memory verse? Begin studying it on Monday. Each day repeat it several times, think about it, and pray that the Lord will help you understand and memorize it. He will be glad to help you. *J.A.G.*

TO MEMORIZE: I have hidden your word in my heart, that I might not sin against you. *Psalm 119:11*

30 December

THE KEY

FROM THE BIBLE:

But when you pray, go away by yourself, shut the door behind you, and pray to your Father secretly. Then your Father, who knows all secrets, will reward you.

When you pray, don't babble on and on as people of other religions do. They think their prayers are answered only by repeating their words again and again. Don't be like them, because your Father knows exactly what you need even before you ask him! Pray like this:

Our Father in heaven,
may your name be honored.
May your Kingdom come soon.
May your will be done here on earth,
just as it is in heaven.
Give us our food for today,
and forgive us our sins,
just as we have forgiven those who have sinned against us.
And don't let us yield to temptation,
but deliver us from the evil one.

MATTHEW 6:6-13

Prayer is a key to God

JOSH STRUGGLED into his pajamas, raced to Elizabeth's room, skidded on the rug next to the bed, and dropped to his knees next to his little sister. Elizabeth rolled her eyes and giggled. Josh was always late for bedtime prayers!

Elizabeth squeezed her eyes tightly shut and folded her hands on the bed. Josh also folded his hands and tried to keep his eyes shut. Mom was right beside them. "Dear Lord," she prayed, "please keep my children safe tonight. Help us appreciate things we have and not worry over what we don't have. Thank you, Lord, for our health, our happiness, and our home. Help us to be kind to others." Twice Mom had to pause and wait patiently as Josh picked something off the floor and got back into position. Then he prayed and Elizabeth did too.

"Thank you for hearing our prayers and being with us always," Mom added in closing. "In Jesus' name. Amen."

Elizabeth hopped into bed as Josh fumbled around with something. "Josh, what do you have there?" asked Mom.

Josh held out a small metal key. "Just this key to my bike lock," he said. "I forgot to put it away after I locked my bike up tonight."

Mom smiled as she took the key. "Did you know that prayer is a key too? It opens us up to the Lord. When we pray, we're in the presence of our great God. So it's important to pay attention."

"Where's my key?" asked Elizabeth, not understanding.

Mom smiled. "Your key is your prayer to God. You can't see it, but it's very real."

HOW ABOUT YOU? Do you use your key and talk to God? As you start a new year, make it your habit to open and close each day with a prayer. *V.L.R.*

TO MEMORIZE: Morning, noon, and night I plead aloud in my distress, and the Lord hears my voice. *Psalm 55:17*

31 December

THROW OUT THE JUNK

FROM THE BIBLE:

We have stopped evaluating others by what the world thinks about them. Once I mistakenly thought of Christ that way, as though he were merely a human being. How differently I think about him now! What this means is that those who become Christians become new persons. They are not the same anymore, for the old life is gone. A new life has begun!

All this newness of life is from God, who brought us back to himself through what Christ did. And God has given us the task of reconciling people to him. For God was in Christ, reconciling the world to himself, no longer counting people's sins against them. This is the wonderful message he has given us to tell others. We are Christ's ambassadors, and God is using us to speak to you. We urge you, as though Christ himself were here pleading with you, "Be reconciled to God!" For God made Christ, who never sinned, to be the offering for our sin, so that we could be made right with God through Christ.

2 CORINTHIANS 5:16-21

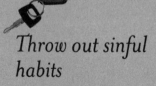

Throw out sinful habits

"JUST THINK, Dad—we get to stay up till one o'clock!" Mario exclaimed as he told his dad about the New Year's Eve party his Sunday school class would be having.

"Sounds great," Dad said. "Have I ever told you about a New Year's Eve celebration we had when I was a boy in Italy?"

"Did you have a parade?" Mario asked.

"Yes, and fireworks, too," Dad said. "Then, as midnight approached, people gathered up all the things they wanted to get rid of. There was a New Year's Eve custom of 'throwing out the old to make way for the new,' so they simply tossed it all out the windows."

"I hope nobody was standing below those windows," laughed Mario.

Dad smiled. "We can learn a lesson from that custom," he said thoughtfully. "The Bible says that when we become Christians, 'the old life is gone. A new life has begun!' But we sometimes try to begin a new life of Christian habits—prayer, attending church, witnessing—without making sure that our old life of sinful habits is gone. God cannot help us to grow until we get rid of the 'old junk.' "

Mario looked thoughtful. "One thing I need to 'throw out' is my sin of laziness."

Dad smiled. "Let's both make a list of 'junk' we need to get rid of."

HOW ABOUT YOU? Do you sometimes wonder why it's so hard to form good habits or to grow as a Christian? Perhaps there's some "junk" in your life that needs to be thrown out. It might be a CD collection, cigarettes, or drugs. Or maybe it's a sin like anger or envy. If you get rid of it, God will give you something new and much better! *S.L.K.*

TO MEMORIZE: Those who become Christians become new persons. They are not the same anymore, for the old life is gone. A new life has begun! *2 Corinthians 5:17*

INDEX OF TOPICS

Abortion
September 28

Accepting Christ as Savior
January 8; February 11, 12, 14; March 6, 19; May 3, 4, 6, 18; June 19, 20; July 5, 17, 19, 20; September 20, 21; December 17

Advertising
March 16

Anger
December 10

Astrology
August 3

Authority
April 3; June 21; August 30; September 14; November 19, 29

Babies
March 15

Beauty
August 25

Bible reading and study
January 1, 6; February 4, 10; March 10; April 15; May 2, 15; June 1, 14, 29; July 2, 14; August 17; September 15, 19, 30; October 11; November 21, 30; December 9, 23, 29

Brothers and sisters
November 26

Children
October 14

Church, behaving in
January 12, 13; July 1; November 13

Communion, Holy
May 28

Content, being
January 18, 20; February 18; July 18; September 7, 29; October 10; December 2

Creation
May 26

Criticism, accepting
August 2

Death, fear of
October 19

Death of a loved one
February 3, 28; April 13, 27

Dentist, going to the
September 27

Distractions from Jesus
December 1, 24

Dreams
November 3

Evolution
August 18

Example, setting an
March 31

Faith in what is not seen
March 24

Fellowship, Worship
February 8; March 2, 12; April 14; July 6; September 10; November 9

Finishing what we start
January 27

Forgiveness
January 3; March 23; August 21; October 16; November 7

Friends
January 2; April 6; May 19; June 28; July 12, 27; September 16; October 29; November 4

Gifts of the Spirit
April 16, 17, 18, 19, 20, 21, 22, 23, 24

God's greatness
December 4

Handicapped people
February 23

Healing people who hurt
April 5

Holy Spirit
April 30

Homework
September 9

Hymns
July 29; December 19

Income, loss of family
November 22

Joy, Gladness
March 9; September 11; November 6

Jumping to conclusions
February 9

Lying
November 28

Manners
March 1

Military, Patriotism
May 27; July 4

Missions
January 11; March 7

Money, Possessions
June 4, 5; August 13; September 2, 17; October 2

Movies
December 14

Moving
August 15

Neighbor, love of
June 26

New school
January 10

Obeying God
February 16; March 4; April 28; August 31; October 4; November 2, 25

Occult
September 18; December 11

Offerings
October 18

Older adults
May 17

Parents, loving and respecting
February 17; May 10, 11, 14; June 10, 16, 17; August 6; September 5

Pastors
November 20

Patience in trouble, Trusting God
January 24; February 5, 21; March 3, 18; April 2; May 29; August 4, 5, 12, 19, 23; September 12; October 8; November 5; December 5, 7, 16

Peacemaking
October 24, 25

Prayer
January 30; February 13; April 7; May 9; June 3, 13, 27; August 20; September 12, 24; December 26, 30

Prejudice, Judging, Criticism
January 25, 26; February 15, 22, 26; March 13, 30; April 12; May 31; August 8, 9; September 4, 13; October 6, 17, 26, 27; November 14, 17; December 8

Promises, keeping
January 14; August 24; October 15

Rock music
January 29; June 6; December 15

Salvation, the gift of
February 27; March 8, 20; May 1; June 15, 18; September 22, 23; October 5

Second Coming of Jesus
June 25; August 29; October 21

Servant, being a
January 15, 28, 31; February 29; March 21; April 8, 10; May 23, 25, 30; June 22, 23; July 8, 15, 21, 24, 25, 26; September 1; November 1, 18; December 6, 8, 21, 22

Sexuality
February 2; December 20

Sickness
April 27; November 12

Sin in our lives
January 9, 23; February 1; March 28, 29; April 29; May 5, 13; July 30; August 7, 26, 27; September 3; October 3, 7, 9, 12, 13, 28; November 10; December 3, 27, 31

Smoking
August 28

Speech
May 21; June 2, 8; July 13, 31; October 22, 23

Spiritual growth
January 17, 22; February 19, 20, 24; March 5, 22; April 25; May 7; June 9; July 28; August 1; September 9, 25; December 12

Stepmothers
May 12

Suicide
August 11

Taxes
February 6

Television viewing
January 4; February 25

Temptations, Worldliness
January 5, 7, 16, 19, 21; February 7; March 11; April 26; May 16, 20, 21, 24; June 11, 12; July 7, 9; August 14; September 6, 26; October 20; November 8, 15, 27

Thanking God
November 23, 24; December 13, 25

The Trinity
March 25, 26, 27

Witnessing
March 14, 17; April 1, 4, 9, 11; May 8, 22; June 7, 24, 30; July 3, 11, 16, 19, 22, 23; August 10, 16, 22; October 1, 30, 31; November 11, 16; December 28

INDEX OF SCRIPTURE IN DAILY READINGS

Genesis 1:20-28 *August 18*
Genesis 1:26-28 *February 2*
Genesis 2:18-25 *December 20*
Genesis 37:19-27 *January 20*
Genesis 50:14-21 *October 8*
Genesis 50:18-21 *November 26*
Exodus 4:10-12 *March 21*
Exodus 20:1-7 *November 2*
Exodus 33:17-23 *March 24*
Leviticus 6:1-6 *January 3*
Leviticus 19:16-18 *February 9, November 7*
Deuteronomy 18:9-13 *August 3*
Deuteronomy 23:21-23 *August 24*
Deuteronomy 33:24-27 *May 29*
Joshua 24:14-19, 21-22 *May 30*
Ruth 1:8-18 *August 15*
1 Samuel 16:14-23 *July 29*
1 Samuel 19:1-6 *May 19*
2 Samuel 9:3, 5-7, 11 *May 31*
1 Chronicles 28:9, 20 *January 15*
1 Chronicles 29:11-16 *December 13*
Nehemiah 4:7-9 *January 30*
Psalm 1 *August 1*
Psalm 16:8-11 *April 10*
Psalm 19:7-11 *January 6, June 1, November 21*
Psalm 25:1-5 *October 21*
Psalm 32:1-5 *April 29, August 26, December 3*
Psalm 33:1-4 *January 29*
Psalm 33:12-13, 15-20 *July 4*
Psalm 34:1-8 *November 23*
Psalm 34:11-15 *October 23*
Psalm 34:11-17 *May 11*
Psalm 48:9-14 *March 3*
Psalm 51:1-7 *November 10*
Psalm 51:1-7, 10-12 *February 1*
Psalm 55:1-2 *February 13*
Psalm 66:16-20 *January 9*
Psalm 78:1-6 *September 5*
Psalm 78:65-72 *November 18*
Psalm 86:1-7 *April 7*
Psalm 90:1-4 *December 4*
Psalm 90:9-15 *August 16*
Psalm 91 *August 4*
Psalm 91:4, 9-10 *January 10*
Psalm 92 *December 18*
Psalm 96:8-13 *March 2*
Psalm 98 *December 19*
Psalm 99:1-7 *July 30*
Psalm 100 *June 6, November 22*
Psalm 101:1-6 *March 1*
Psalm 103:1-5 *June 5*
Psalm 103:1-8 *November 24*
Psalm 111:9 *October 22*
Psalm 119:1-7 *February 25*
Psalm 119:1-8 *March 12*
Psalm 119:9-16 *May 2, July 14*
Psalm 119:33-42 *January 13, December 29*
Psalm 119:89-96 *July 2*
Psalm 119:97-103 *October 11*
Psalm 119:97-104 *March 10, June 29*
Psalm 119:105-112 *January 1*
Psalm 119:129-136 *September 15, December 23*
Psalm 121 *May 13, August 5*
Psalm 127:3-5 *March 15*
Psalm 133 *May 12*
Psalm 138:1-7 *December 12*
Psalm 139:1-6 *March 18*
Psalm 139:1-10 *August 19*
Psalm 139:3-10 *September 27*
Psalm 139:7-12 *June 8*
Psalm 139:13-16 *February 23*
Psalm 139:13-18 *August 6*
Psalm 143:8-10 *November 25*
Psalm 145:3-12 *October 1*
Psalm 150 *November 5*
Proverbs 1:1-8 *August 17*
Proverbs 3:21-26 *November 3*
Proverbs 4:1-5, 20-21 *November 19*
Proverbs 4:1-10 *June 10*
Proverbs 4:12-23 *June 7*
Proverbs 4:14-19 *March 11*
Proverbs 4:14-23 *February 7*
Proverbs 6:12-19 *October 25*
Proverbs 10:18-21, 31-32 *July 13*
Proverbs 11:9-13 *November 17*
Proverbs 12:17-22 *November 28*
Proverbs 14:16-17 *December 10*
Proverbs 15:1-4 *October 29*
Proverbs 16:7, 20-24 *September 13*
Proverbs 18:6-8, 21, 24 *June 2*

Proverbs 19:11-12	*December 10*
Proverbs 26:17-22	*October 26*
Proverbs 27:1-2	*August 22*
Proverbs 28:13-14	*September 3*
Proverbs 31:30-31	*August 25*
Ecclesiastes 3:1-8	*March 22, August 21*
Ecclesiastes 4:9-12	*December 6*
Ecclesiastes 5:1-7	*January 12*
Isaiah 9:2, 6-7	*December 28*
Isaiah 35:8-10	*November 27*
Isaiah 43:1-3	*August 23, November 12*
Isaiah 46:9-11	*February 5, December 5*
Isaiah 47:8-14	*December 11*
Isaiah 53:3-6	*May 3*
Isaiah 55:1-3, 10-11	*May 15*
Isaiah 55:8-13	*February 3*
Isaiah 57:15	*October 22*
Isaiah 61:1-3, 10	*November 6*
Jeremiah 1:1-2, 4-9	*June 22*
Jeremiah 1:5-10	*September 29*
Jeremiah 17:5-10	*October 31*
Jeremiah 18:1-6	*February 12*
Lamentations 3:22-26	*July 12*
Ezekiel 3:17-19	*July 11*
Daniel 1:1, 3-6, 8	*January 7*
Daniel 4:17	*May 18*
Amos 7:7-8	*November 14*
Malachi 1:6-10	*November 30*
Matthew 1:18-23	*December 24*
Matthew 4:17-22	*July 3*
Matthew 5:1-10	*October 24*
Matthew 5:13-16	*April 9, June 30*
Matthew 5:21-24	*June 28*
Matthew 5:23-24	*January 2*
Matthew 5:38-42	*July 15*
Matthew 6:1-4	*July 24, October 18*
Matthew 6:1-6	*March 4*
Matthew 6:5-8	*June 3*
Matthew 6:6-13	*December 30*
Matthew 6:9	*October 22*
Matthew 7:1-5	*August 9*
Matthew 7:1-5, 12	*February 26*
Matthew 7:7-11	*February 16*
Matthew 7:13-14, 21-23	*February 11*
Matthew 10:29-31	*September 18*
Matthew 11:25-30	*October 13*
Matthew 12:34-37	*July 31*
Matthew 14:25-33	*December 1*
Matthew 17:24-27	*February 6*
Matthew 20:25-28	*January 31*
Matthew 21:12-15	*April 21*
Matthew 21:28-32	*January 14*
Matthew 21:33-40	*August 30*
Matthew 22:34-40	*June 26*
Matthew 25:14-15, 19-21	*April 22, July 8*
Matthew 25:14-23	*December 22*
Matthew 25:34-40	*April 20*
Mark 9:33-35	*November 20*
Luke 2:6-12	*December 25*
Luke 6:31-38	*October 6*
Luke 6:36-38	*April 12*
Luke 8:5-8, 11-15	*March 14*
Luke 9:23-26	*May 22, June 24*
Luke 10:30-37	*July 10*
Luke 11:5-8	*May 9*
Luke 14:18-24	*April 11*
Luke 16:10-12	*May 23*
Luke 17:11-15	*September 24*
Luke 18:9-14	*December 17*
Luke 21:1-4	*June 23*
John 1:1-12	*March 25*
John 1:5-10	*June 9*
John 3:1-7	*June 18, September 20*
John 3:14-18	*July 19*
John 6:53-58	*January 19*
John 8:30-36	*May 24*
John 10:1-11	*July 17*
John 10:7-10	*September 22*
John 10:27-30	*March 20*
John 14:23-25	*June 20*
John 15:1-5	*July 25*
John 15:1-8	*September 7*
John 16:12-13	*March 26*
John 17:14-19	*July 7*
Acts 1:6-8	*July 23*
Acts 9:36-39	*October 30*
Acts 10:1-2, 30-33	*December 26*
Acts 10:25-28	*January 25*
Acts 13:6-11	*April 4*
Acts 16:22-28	*September 8*
Acts 17:24-28	*September 28*
Romans 1:18-22, 24-25	*October 2*
Romans 4:4-8	*February 27*
Romans 5:1-5	*December 7*
Romans 5:3-5	*April 19*
Romans 5:7-9	*September 23*
Romans 6:20-23	*June 12*
Romans 8:2-7	*January 28*
Romans 8:26-28	*June 27*
Romans 8:26-31	*January 24*
Romans 8:31-39	*July 20*
Romans 10:8-13	*March 6*
Romans 10:13-15	*March 19*
Romans 12:1-2, 21	*November 8*

Romans 12:3-8	*April 5*
Romans 12:5-10	*May 25*
Romans 12:9-16	*March 29*
Romans 12:14-21	*October 27*
Romans 12:17-21	*March 23*
Romans 13:1-5	*April 3*
Romans 13:1-6	*May 27, September 14*
Romans 13:7-8	*June 4*
Romans 13:11-14	*April 26*
Romans 14:8-13	*September 4*
Romans 14:10-13	*January 26, August 7*
Romans 15:1-7	*January 22*
1 Corinthians 2:7-12	*April 15*
1 Corinthians 3:1-5	*January 17*
1 Corinthians 3:5-11	*March 17*
1 Corinthians 3:9-15	*August 31*
1 Corinthians 3:11-15	*August 13, September 9*
1 Corinthians 3:16-21	*August 28*
1 Corinthians 6:15-20	*October 20*
1 Corinthians 6:19-20	*March 16*
1 Corinthians 9:19-23	*March 7*
1 Corinthians 9:25-27	*April 24*
1 Corinthians 10:12-13	*January 5*
1 Corinthians 11:23-26	*May 28*
1 Corinthians 12:4-11	*October 10*
1 Corinthians 12:14-22	*October 4*
1 Corinthians 12:18-26	*July 26*
1 Corinthians 12:20-27	*April 14*
1 Corinthians 13:4-8, 11-13	*April 16*
1 Corinthians 13:9-13	*March 27*
1 Corinthians 15:57-58	*November 4*
2 Corinthians 1:3-7	*April 27*
2 Corinthians 2:9-11, 14-15	*March 28*
2 Corinthians 3:1-6	*November 11*
2 Corinthians 5:1, 6-8	*February 28*
2 Corinthians 5:1-2	*April 13*
2 Corinthians 5:1-7	*April 30*
2 Corinthians 5:1-8	*October 19*
2 Corinthians 5:16-21	*December 31*
2 Corinthians 6:14–7:1	*November 15*
2 Corinthians 10:1-4	*October 28*
2 Corinthians 10:17-18	*August 22*
Galatians 3:26-29	*September 10*
Galatians 6:1-6	*April 25*
Galatians 6:7-10	*October 3*
Ephesians 1:3-8	*January 16*
Ephesians 2:1, 4-10	*March 8*
Ephesians 2:4-10	*July 21*
Ephesians 4:7-12	*December 21*
Ephesians 4:17-24	*December 27*
Ephesians 4:30	*October 17*
Ephesians 5:1-2, 8-13	*April 1*
Ephesians 5:2	*October 17*
Ephesians 5:25-27	*July 6*
Ephesians 6:10-18	*October 7*
Ephesians 6:18-20	*July 22*
Philippians 1:3-6, 9-11	*February 19*
Philippians 1:3-7	*January 11*
Philippians 1:9-11	*May 8*
Philippians 2:1-4	*November 9*
Philippians 2:14-18	*February 21*
Philippians 2:5-11	*September 1*
Philippians 2:14-16	*July 16*
Philippians 2:14-18	*September 11*
Philippians 3:5-10	*May 4*
Philippians 4:4	*April 17*
Philippians 4:4-7	*September 12*
Philippians 4:4-9	*March 9*
Philippians 4:5	*April 24*
Philippians 4:6-7, 11-13	*January 18*
Philippians 4:6-9	*April 18*
Philippians 4:11-13	*December 2*
Colossians 1:9-14	*May 7*
Colossians 3:1-4	*September 6*
Colossians 3:1-10	*December 14*
Colossians 3:8-16	*June 14*
Colossians 3:12-17	*May 20, August 10, October 15*
Colossians 3:15	*April 18*
Colossians 3:20-25	*May 14*
1 Thessalonians 1:5-9	*November 16*
1 Thessalonians 4:9-12	*February 29*
1 Thessalonians 5:14-23	*April 6, August 14*
2 Thessalonians 3:6-13	*November 1*
1 Timothy 4:9-13	*September 19*
1 Timothy 4:11-16	*March 31, July 28*
1 Timothy 5:1-4	*February 17*
1 Timothy 6:6-8	*July 18*
1 Timothy 6:6-10	*September 2*
1 Timothy 6:6-11	*September 17*
1 Timothy 6:6-12	*February 18*
2 Timothy 2:3-4	*May 16*
2 Timothy 2:19-22	*February 20, June 11*
2 Timothy 2:24	*April 23*
2 Timothy 3:14-17	*February 10*
2 Timothy 4:6-8	*May 17*
2 Timothy 4:7-8	*January 27*
Titus 2:1-8	*October 14*
Titus 3:1-8	*May 1*
Titus 3:3-7	*June 15*
Titus 3:5-7	*October 5*
Hebrews 2:1-4	*July 1*

Hebrews 2:14-18	*December 16*
Hebrews 3:7-10, 12-13	*January 8*
Hebrews 5:12-14	*March 5, September 30*
Hebrews 6:9-12	*November 29*
Hebrews 9:11-14	*August 27*
Hebrews 10:19-25	*February 8*
Hebrews 11:3	*May 26*
Hebrews 12:1-2	*May 16*
Hebrews 12:1-4	*April 2*
Hebrews 12:5-11	*June 16*
Hebrews 12:14-15	*October 16*
Hebrews 13:20-22, 25	*July 27*
James 1:22-25	*January 23, April 28*
James 2:1-4, 9-10	*February 15*
James 2:5-9	*March 13*
James 2:14-18	*August 20*
James 3:1-8	*May 21*
James 4:4-10	*January 21*
James 4:6-11	*October 9*
James 4:7-12	*August 8*
1 Peter 1:3-7	*August 12*
1 Peter 1:6-9	*April 17*
1 Peter 1:13-16	*November 14*
1 Peter 1:13-17, 22	*September 26*
1 Peter 1:18-21	*May 5, July 5*
1 Peter 1:22-25	*December 9*
1 Peter 1:22–2:3	*September 25*
1 Peter 1:25–2:5	*November 13*
1 Peter 2:1-3	*September 25*
1 Peter 2:1-5	*February 24*
1 Peter 2:13-17	*June 21*
1 Peter 2:18-23	*May 10*
1 Peter 3:3-4	*August 25*
1 Peter 3:8-11	*December 8*
1 Peter 4:7-11	*April 8*
1 Peter 5:5-7	*June 17*
1 Peter 5:6-11	*July 9*
2 Peter 1:4-9	*March 30*
2 Peter 1:5-10	*August 2*
2 Peter 3:3-9	*June 25, August 29*
1 John 1:5-9	*October 12*
1 John 2:15-17	*January 4*
1 John 3:14-18	*September 16*
1 John 4:1-4	*February 4*
1 John 4:7-10	*February 14*
1 John 4:20-21	*February 22*
1 John 5:9-15	*June 13*
1 John 5:10-13	*June 19*
3 John 1:11	*December 15*
Revelation 20:11-15	*May 6, August 11*
Revelation 21:23-27	*September 21*

INDEX OF SCRIPTURE MEMORY VERSES

Genesis 1:1	*May 26*
Exodus 4:11	*February 23*
Leviticus 5:16	*January 3*
Deuteronomy 5:16	*September 5*
Deuteronomy 28:9	*February 25*
Deuteronomy 33:27	*May 29*
Joshua 24:15	*May 30*
1 Samuel 16:7	*February 26*
1 Kings 8:39	*May 31*
1 Chronicles 29:14	*December 13*
Ezra 7:10	*November 25*
Job 23:10	*March 18*
Psalm 1:2	*May 2*
Psalm 16:8	*April 10*
Psalm 19:8	*June 1*
Psalm 19:10	*November 21*
Psalm 19:14	*October 22*
Psalm 23:1	*July 17*
Psalm 23:3	*July 18*
Psalm 27:1	*January 10*
Psalm 27:14	*October 21*
Psalm 32:5	*December 3*
Psalm 33:4	*September 15*
Psalm 33:12	*July 4*
Psalm 34:1	*November 23*
Psalm 34:11	*May 11*
Psalm 37:8	*December 10*
Psalm 39:1	*June 2*
Psalm 51:2	*January 23*
Psalm 51:10	*February 1*
Psalm 55:17	*December 30*
Psalm 66:2	*December 15*
Psalm 66:18	*January 9*
Psalm 68:19	*June 5*
Psalm 89:14	*July 30*
Psalm 90:2	*December 4*
Psalm 92:1	*September 24*
Psalm 92:5	*April 15*
Psalm 96:1	*July 29*
Psalm 98:1	*December 19*
Psalm 100:1	*December 18*
Psalm 100:2	*January 15*
Psalm 100:4	*March 2*
Psalm 101:2	*March 1*
Psalm 101:3	*January 4*
Psalm 103:2	*November 24*
Psalm 118:8	*August 3*
Psalm 118:24	*March 9*
Psalm 119:11	*December 29*
Psalm 119:14	*July 14*
Psalm 119:16	*July 2*
Psalm 119:18	*September 30*
Psalm 119:97	*June 29*
Psalm 119:103	*March 10*
Psalm 119:105	*January 1*
Psalm 119:117	*August 4*
Psalm 119:130	*December 23*
Psalm 121:2	*May 13*
Psalm 121:5	*August 5*
Psalm 126:6	*March 14*
Psalm 127:3	*March 15*
Psalm 133:1	*May 12*
Psalm 138:2	*December 12*
Psalm 139:7	*August 19*
Psalm 139:14	*February 2*
Psalm 139:16	*August 6*
Psalm 144:12	*November 19*
Psalm 145:6	*October 1*
Proverbs 3:5	*December 5*
Proverbs 3:7	*November 2*
Proverbs 3:9	*November 30*
Proverbs 3:12	*June 16*
Proverbs 3:24	*November 3*
Proverbs 11:17	*November 17*
Proverbs 12:15	*August 2*
Proverbs 12:22	*November 28*
Proverbs 13:20	*March 11*
Proverbs 15:1	*October 29*
Proverbs 15:13	*June 7*
Proverbs 16:7	*September 13*
Proverbs 17:9	*October 25*
Proverbs 17:17	*April 6, November 26*
Proverbs 18:24	*November 9*
Proverbs 22:1	*October 30*
Proverbs 23:5	*September 2*
Proverbs 23:12	*August 17*
Proverbs 25:25	*January 11*
Proverbs 26:18-19	*October 26*
Proverbs 26:20	*October 23*
Proverbs 28:1	*August 27*
Proverbs 28:13	*August 26*
Proverbs 28:14	*September 3*

Proverbs 31:30	*August 25*
Ecclesiastes 5:1	*January 12*
Ecclesiastes 5:3	*July 13*
Ecclesiastes 5:4	*August 24*
Isaiah 26:3	*August 23*
Isaiah 35:8	*November 27*
Isaiah 41:6	*December 6*
Isaiah 42:8	*August 22*
Isaiah 43:2	*November 12*
Isaiah 43:25	*August 21*
Isaiah 46:10	*February 5*
Isaiah 53:5	*May 3*
Isaiah 55:9	*February 3*
Isaiah 57:15	*November 10*
Isaiah 64:6	*June 15*
Jeremiah 1:5	*September 29*
Jeremiah 15:16	*October 11*
Jeremiah 17:10	*October 31*
Jeremiah 23:24	*June 8*
Jeremiah 27:5	*August 18*
Jeremiah 29:11	*August 12*
Jeremiah 31:3	*March 3*
Jeremiah 33:3	*April 7*
Lamentations 3:23	*July 12*
Ezekiel 3:17	*July 11*
Daniel 1:8	*January 7*
Habakkuk 1:13	*September 21*
Matthew 4:19	*July 3*
Matthew 5:6	*May 15*
Matthew 5:8	*October 28*
Matthew 5:9	*October 24*
Matthew 5:14	*June 30*
Matthew 5:16	*April 1*
Matthew 5:41	*July 15*
Matthew 6:1	*March 4*
Matthew 6:4	*July 24*
Matthew 6:7	*June 3*
Matthew 7:2	*August 9*
Matthew 10:29	*September 18*
Matthew 12:36	*July 31*
Matthew 19:19	*July 10*
Matthew 20:26	*January 31*
Matthew 22:39	*June 26*
Matthew 24:14	*July 23*
Matthew 24:44	*June 25*
Matthew 26:41	*January 30*
Mark 1:17	*April 11*
Mark 4:24	*January 29*
Mark 8:38	*June 24*
Mark 13:31	*December 9*
Mark 16:15	*April 4*
Luke 1:49	*December 25*
Luke 2:17	*December 28*
Luke 2:52	*March 22*
Luke 6:31	*October 6*
Luke 9:23	*May 22*
Luke 12:7	*March 13*
Luke 16:10	*May 23*
Luke 18:13	*December 17*
Luke 21:15	*March 21*
Luke 21:19	*February 21*
John 1:18	*March 24*
John 3:3	*June 18*
John 3:18	*July 19*
John 6:57	*January 19*
John 8:32	*May 28*
John 8:36	*May 24*
John 10:9	*September 22*
John 10:17-18	*September 23*
John 10:29	*March 20*
John 10:30	*March 25*
John 13:34	*March 30*
John 13:35	*February 22*
John 15:4	*September 7*
John 15:5	*July 25*
John 15:8	*July 16*
John 15:19	*July 7*
Acts 10:31-32	*December 26*
Acts 10:34	*January 26*
Acts 16:25	*September 8*
Acts 17:11	*February 4*
Acts 17:25	*September 28*
Acts 17:26	*January 25*
Romans 4:5	*February 11*
Romans 5:8	*February 14*
Romans 6:23	*February 27*
Romans 8:4	*January 28*
Romans 8:26	*June 27*
Romans 8:28	*January 24*
Romans 8:32	*July 20*
Romans 10:13	*March 6*
Romans 10:15	*March 19*
Romans 12:1	*July 21*
Romans 12:6	*May 25*
Romans 12:9	*September 16*
Romans 12:10	*February 17*
Romans 12:12	*July 27*
Romans 12:14	*October 27*
Romans 12:21	*March 23*
Romans 13:1	*April 3*
Romans 13:6	*February 6*
Romans 13:7	*May 27*
Romans 13:8	*June 4*
Romans 13:11	*April 26*

Romans 14:10	*August 7*
Romans 14:12	*September 9*
Romans 14:13	*September 4*
Romans 15:1	*January 22*
Romans 15:2	*April 25*
Romans 16:19	*March 12*
1 Corinthians 3:7	*November 20*
1 Corinthians 3:9	*March 17*
1 Corinthians 3:14	*August 31*
1 Corinthians 4:2	*July 8*
1 Corinthians 6:19	*August 28*
1 Corinthians 6:20	*March 16, October 20*
1 Corinthians 9:22	*March 7*
1 Corinthians 10:13	*January 5*
1 Corinthians 10:31	*May 20*
1 Corinthians 12:26	*July 26*
1 Corinthians 12:27	*April 14, October 4*
1 Corinthians 13:4	*January 20*
1 Corinthians 13:12	*March 27*
1 Corinthians 15:58	*November 18*
1 Corinthians 16:14	*June 23*
2 Corinthians 1:4	*April 27*
2 Corinthians 1:22	*April 30*
2 Corinthians 2:7	*January 2*
2 Corinthians 2:9, 11	*March 28*
2 Corinthians 3:2	*November 11*
2 Corinthians 5:8	*October 19*
2 Corinthians 5:17	*December 31*
2 Corinthians 5:20	*July 22*
2 Corinthians 6:2	*January 8*
2 Corinthians 7:1	*November 15*
2 Corinthians 9:7	*October 18*
2 Corinthians 9:15	*December 24*
2 Corinthians 10:5	*July 1*
2 Corinthians 11:14-15	*December 11*
2 Corinthians 12:9	*June 22*
Galatians 3:26	*September 10*
Galatians 5:22	*April 16-24*
Galatians 6:2	*May 19*
Galatians 6:7	*October 3*
Galatians 6:9	*November 4*
Galatians 6:10	*August 20*
Ephesians 1:13	*February 20*
Ephesians 2:8-9	*March 8*
Ephesians 4:2	*June 28*
Ephesians 4:24	*December 27*
Ephesians 4:29	*May 21*
Ephesians 4:31	*October 16*
Ephesians 4:32	*October 15*
Ephesians 5:2	*October 17*
Ephesians 5:8	*June 9*
Ephesians 5:15-16	*August 16*
Ephesians 5:19	*June 6*
Ephesians 5:20	*November 5*
Ephesians 5:25	*July 6*
Ephesians 6:1	*May 14*
Ephesians 6:2	*June 10*
Ephesians 6:11	*October 7*
Philippians 1:6	*February 19*
Philippians 1:21	*February 28*
Philippians 2:15	*November 8*
Philippians 3:9	*May 4*
Philippians 4:4	*September 11*
Philippians 4:6	*September 12*
Philippians 4:8	*June 11*
Philippians 4:11	*August 15*
Philippians 4:13	*April 2*
Philippians 4:19	*November 22*
Colossians 1:9	*July 28*
Colossians 2:7	*August 1*
Colossians 3:2	*September 6*
Colossians 3:10	*February 12, December 14*
Colossians 3:13	*November 7*
Colossians 3:16	*June 14*
Colossians 4:5	*August 10*
Colossians 4:6	*April 9*
1 Thessalonians 2:4	*August 30*
1 Thessalonians 4:11	*February 29*
1 Thessalonians 4:13	*April 13*
1 Thessalonians 5:18	*February 18*
1 Thessalonians 5:21-22	*August 14*
2 Thessalonians 3:13	*November 1*
1 Timothy 4:12	*March 31*
1 Timothy 4:13	*September 19*
1 Timothy 5:22	*February 7*
1 Timothy 6:6	*December 2*
1 Timothy 6:7	*August 13*
1 Timothy 6:10	*September 17*
1 Timothy 6:17	*October 2*
2 Timothy 2:15	*January 13*
2 Timothy 2:21	*December 21*
2 Timothy 2:22	*December 20*
2 Timothy 3:16	*February 10*
2 Timothy 4:7	*January 27*
2 Timothy 4:7-8	*May 17*
Titus 2:4	*October 14*
Titus 2:7	*November 16*
Titus 3:5	*October 5*
Titus 3:8	*May 1*
Titus 3:14	*December 22*
Hebrews 1:9	*November 6*
Hebrews 2:3	*May 18*
Hebrews 2:18	*December 16*
Hebrews 4:16	*October 13*

Hebrews 5:14	*March 5*
Hebrews 6:12	*November 29*
Hebrews 10:25	*February 8*
Hebrews 12:1	*May 16*
Hebrews 12:2	*December 1*
Hebrews 12:11	*June 17*
Hebrews 13:5	*January 18*
Hebrews 13:17	*June 21*
James 1:2	*December 7*
James 1:3	*October 8*
James 1:15	*June 12*
James 1:17	*February 16*
James 1:19	*February 9*
James 1:21	*January 6*
James 1:22	*April 28*
James 2:9	*February 15*
James 4:3	*June 13*
James 4:4	*January 21*
James 4:8	*October 9*
James 4:10	*September 1*
James 4:11	*April 12*
James 4:12	*August 8*
James 4:17	*March 29*
James 5:16	*May 9*
1 Peter 1:15	*September 26*
1 Peter 1:16	*November 14*
1 Peter 1:20	*July 5*
1 Peter 1:23	*September 20*
1 Peter 1:25	*November 13*
1 Peter 2:2	*January 17, September 25*
1 Peter 2:9	*January 16*
1 Peter 2:13	*September 14*
1 Peter 3:8	*April 5*
1 Peter 3:9	*December 8*
1 Peter 4:9	*April 8*
1 Peter 4:10	*October 10*
1 Peter 5:7	*February 13*
1 Peter 5:8-9	*July 9*
2 Peter 3:9	*August 29*
2 Peter 3:18	*February 24*
1 John 1:9	*October 12*
1 John 2:1	*April 29*
1 John 3:18	*May 8*
1 John 4:13	*March 26*
1 John 5:12	*June 20*
1 John 5:13	*June 19*
3 John 1:5	*January 14*
Jude 1:24-25	*May 7*
Revelation 1:5-6	*May 5*
Revelation 20:15	*May 6*
Revelation 21:4	*August 11*

For Men

The One Year® Devotions for Men on the Go

The One Year® Devotions for Men

For Couples

The One Year® Devotions for Couples

For Families

The One Year® Family Devotions

For Teens

The One Year® Devos for Teens

The One Year® Devos for Sports Fans

For Bible Study

The One Year® Life Lessons from the Bible

The One Year® Praying through the Bible

The One Year® Through the Bible

For Personal Growth

The One Year® Devotions for People of Purpose

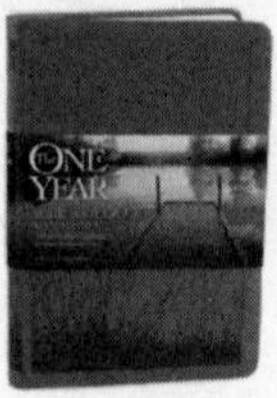

The One Year® Walk with God Devotional

The One Year® At His Feet Devotional

The One Year® Great Songs of Faith

The One Year® On This Day

The One Year® Life Verse Devotional

It's convenient and easy to grow with God the One Year way.

CP0145